THE FEMALE FACE OF SHAME

THE **FEMALE FACE** OF **SHAME**

EDITED BY
ERICA L. JOHNSON
AND
PATRICIA MORAN

Indiana University Press

Bloomington and Indianapolis

This book is a publication of

Indiana University Press
Office of Scholarly Publishing
Herman B Wells Library 350
1320 East 10th Street
Bloomington, Indiana 47405 USA

iupress.indiana.edu

Telephone orders   800-842-6796
Fax orders   812-855-7931

∞ The paper used in this publication meets the minimum
requirements of the American National Standard for Information
Sciences—Permanence of Paper for Printed Library Materials,
ANSI Z39.48–1992.

Manufactured in the United States of America

Library of Congress Cataloging-in-Publication Data

The female face of shame / edited by Erica L. Johnson and Patricia
Moran.
    pages cm
 Includes bibliographical references and index.
 ISBN 978-0-253-00863-3 (pbk. : alk. paper) — ISBN 978-0-253-
00855-8 (cloth : alk. paper) — ISBN 978-0-253-00873-2 (e-book)
1. Women in literature. 2. Shame in literature. 3. Human body
in literature. I. Johnson, Erica L., [date]- editor of compilation.
II. Moran, Patricia (Patricia L.) editor of compilation.
 PN56.5.W64F456 2013
 809'.93352042—dc23

        2013003157

1 2 3 4 5   18 17 16 15 14 13

"What does it feel like?" he asked—and his mothers, seeing his bewilderment, essayed explanations. "Your face gets hot," said Bunny-the-youngest, "but your heart starts shivering."

"It makes women feel like to cry and die," said Chhunni-ma, "but men, it makes them go wild."

—*Shame*, Salman Rushdie

Contents

Part 3. Nations of Shame

Acknowledgments

I HAVE BEEN BLESSED with many good friends who have given generously of their time and support during the writing and editing of this book. Sandra King has proved a friend indeed: there to help with dogs, textiles, and the search for Sheelas; my life in Ireland would not have been the same without her. I also thank her husband, Bobby, for aiding and abetting us and for outings to Linnane's. David Coughlan was my first friend at the University of Limerick and remains one of the best ever: thanks for all your support. Sinead McDermott and Yianna Liatsos have been exemplary colleagues, making my first years in Ireland and the University of Limerick enjoyable as well as productive. Breeda Kennedy has been that transformative student who has become a treasured friend: thanks for all your help. Suzette Henke and Mark Hussey have been helpful and supportive throughout. The friends in California who were there all along include Andrea Cohen, Joanne Feit Diehl, Cindy Debrunner, Gayle Danelius, and Jack LaPointe; I make special mention here of Maj-Britt Mobrand, who has taught me so much more than weaving. Judy Law deserves mention for her professionalism and for giving meaning to the phrase "grace under pressure." Cindy Crampsey and Frann Michel have stood by me for decades: thanks for your unwavering support and for believing I could pull off what seemed impossible. It has been a privilege to work with my co-editor, Erica, whose intelligence, insight, and empathy have been much needed and much appreciated; this book would not exist without her. Finally, I thank my son, Patrick Higgins, whose courage, cheer, and optimism provide color to life's daily gray: you have been an inspiration all along.

Patricia Moran

* * *

MANY PEOPLE HAVE given me their ears and support during the process of writing and editing this volume. First, I thank my co-editor, Patricia Moran, for showing me how important it is to understand the workings of shame, for her friendship, and for being as fearless as she is. Thanks to Liz Constable for her inspiration, support, and exquisite work on the topic of shame. Thanks to Natalie Edwards, Christopher Hogarth, and Johanna Rossi Wagner for providing not only moral support but venues, in the forms of conference panels and book chapters, through which I explored the topic of shame. I am grateful to New York University for its Faculty Resource Network and the tremendous access it granted me to important resources as I wrote and edited. At

Wagner, I thank my splendid department of Anne Schotter, Ann Hurley, Peter Sharpe, Susan Bernardo, Steve Thomas, and Eloise Brezault as well as my dear colleague Patricia Moynagh, whose insight, good cheer, and friendship are integral to everything I do there. Thanks to Wendy Nielsen for always listening and for her wisdom and unconditional support. Thanks to my parents, Lew and Enid Cocke, for sharing with me a love of books and curiosity about the world. Thanks to my sister Meagan Schipanski for always, always being on the other end of the phone when I call and for talking through anything and everything with me. And, as always, thanks to my amazing husband and son, Patrick and Max Johnson: this, as everything I do, is dedicated to you.

Erica L. Johnson

THE FEMALE FACE OF SHAME

Introduction

MAXINE HONG KINGSTON opens her now classic *The Woman Warrior: Memoirs of a Girlhood among Ghosts* with the harrowing account of how her aunt, her father's sister, committed suicide after suffering the villagers' punishing assault upon her family home on the night she gave birth to an illegitimate child. Related to Kingston by her mother, the story functions as a disciplinary, cautionary tale: "Don't let your father know that I told you," Brave Orchid warns Kingston. "He denies her. Now that you have started to menstruate, what happened to her could happen to you. Don't humiliate us. You wouldn't like to be forgotten as if you had never been born. The villagers are watchful" (Kingston, 5). Not content with her mother's bare-bones factual account and cognizant of her own need to find personal meaning in the story—"Unless I see her life branching into mine, she gives me no ancestral help," Kingston comments (8)—Kingston fleshes out her mother's skeletal narrative, speculating about the motives and desires that might have impelled her aunt to transgress "boundaries not delineated in space" (8), thereby incurring the wrath of the villagers for daring to imagine her life as separate from that of the community: "The frightened villagers, who depended on one another to maintain the real, went to my aunt to show her a personal, physical representation of the break she had made in the 'roundness.' Misallying couples snapped off the future, which was to be embodied in true offspring. The villagers punished her for acting as if she could have a private life, secret and apart from them" (12–13). Nor is the villagers' punishment her aunt's only trial: while the family actively encourages wanderlust in men, they "expected her alone to keep the traditional ways, which her brothers, now among the barbarians, could fumble without detection. The heavy, deep-rooted women were to maintain the past against the flood, safe for returning" (8). Hence in choosing forbidden desire, Kingston's aunt "gave up family" (8). In memorializing her aunt Kingston not only repairs the broken ancestral branch between herself and her "forerunner," she breaks the family taboo on naming her aunt and thus defies her family's even more draconian punishment of sentencing the aunt to an eternity of exile: "The real punishment was not the raid swiftly inflicted by the villagers, but the family's deliberately forgetting her. Her betrayal so maddened them, they saw to it that she would suffer forever, even after death" (16). The opening line of Kingston's memoir underscores the author's common cause with her aunt, Kingston's similar transgression of boundaries not delineated in space, for Kingston's telling about her aunt violates her mother's cautionary injunction that Kingston "must not tell anyone what I am about to tell you" (3).

Kingston's account of the No Name Woman is an apt introduction to *The Female Face of Shame,* for it illustrates the densely intertwined dimensions of the shame affect, its operation at the intrapsychic and intersubjective level, on the one hand, and the cultural and social level, on the other. Liz Constable speaks of these intertwined dimensions as the "relational grammar" of shame, a grammar that necessitates holding both dimensions in an "unsettled and unsettling tension" (Introduction, 9). "No Name Woman" exemplifies this tension, moving fluidly from the intersubjective realm of mother-daughter interaction to the cultural and social contexts of Chinese mores and family expectations, all held in the intrapsychic register of Kingston's personal reclamation of her aunt as a forerunner whose life branches into Kingston's own. Above all, "No Name Woman" functions as a specifically *female* and gendered account of shame, wherein female sexuality figures as the site and source of shaming: No Name Woman's body betrays her shameful illicit sexuality, which in turn shames and humiliates her family. Even in death No Name Woman exists as an exemplary lesson on how the daughter can shame her family: Brave Orchid tells this story to Kingston when the latter begins to menstruate, underlining for Kingston the special and potentially shameful burdens imposed by femininity and female embodiment. Embedded in personal, familial, and cultural contexts, "No Name Woman" articulates the overarching ways shame constitutes an integral element of femininity.

While *The Female Face of Shame* focuses on the link between shame and femininity, it is important to note that shame has long been viewed as a primary human affect in, for example, Charles Darwin's identification of blushing as "the most peculiar and most human of all expressions." Blushing is, of course, one of the most visible markers of a range of emotions—embarrassment, humiliation, the sense of being caught out and exposed, of being caught *short*—that all derive from the experience of feeling shamed. Moreover, blushing registers one's perception of oneself *through another,* and it is thus a marker of self-consciousness and of consciousness itself. Yet even as shame serves as a marker of humanity in Darwin's view, it is, more accurately, a marker of female humanity. As Kingston illustrates, the mere advent of menstruation ushers a girl into the status of potential shame: she bears within her body the seeds of sexual shame in such a way that this *feeling* about herself detaches from any act she may or may not commit, for shameful acts can merely confirm this dreadful self-knowledge. In contrast to guilt, which is evoked by an action or behavior about which one feels badly and for which one might hope to make amends, shame resides so deeply within one's sense of being that it cannot be absolved. Gershen Kaufman and Lev Raphael capture this phenomenon in their analysis of the continuum between gay pride and gay shame, when they point out that gays and lesbians "become people haunted by shame, not because of particular actions but, more profoundly, because of who they *are*" (7). And sexuality, whether gay or straight, is hardly the only liability of the female body; as Simone de Beauvoir suggests, the very ability to give birth—whether to a socially legitimate or a shameful child—makes the female body an uncanny threshold between life and death that provokes discomforting feelings of mortality. Menstruation and birth are also productive functions—productive of uncontained flows and contaminating tissues—and they therefore register the female body as an uncontrolled site of excess and bared secrets, as Elizabeth Grosz has shown in *Volatile Bodies*. The body itself is therefore a starting point in understanding why the primal affect of shame has been assigned to femininity, and the chapters in this book begin with the question of the body in order to seek an answer to the long-proven yet heretofore baffling finding by researchers that women are more shame-prone than men.

Answering this question has proven to be a difficult task, in part because the shame affect is so complex in its make-up, and in part because shame is not only an individual, embodied experience but one rooted in familial and cultural contexts. The shame affect may be hardwired into human physiology, as Silvan Tomkins argues in *Affect, Imagery, Consciousness*, but it arises in both intrapsychic and interpersonal contexts, and those in turn differ from family to family and culture to culture. What is clear, though, is that the link between femininity and shame holds across a wide variety of cultural contexts. Given the prevalence of this experience among women worldwide, the topic deserves much more attention than it has been given in literary, feminist, and cultural studies, particularly in light of the recent "affective turn" these fields have taken. Through a comparative study of twentieth-century texts, this book shows how shame structures relationships and shapes women's identities across the three major aspects of subject formation around which the chapters are organized: the individual, the familial, and the cultural or national. In so doing, this volume fills an important scholarly gap, for persistent evidence of female shame has largely gone unnoticed and unanalyzed because it has been subsumed by discussions of oppressive ideologies such as sexism, homophobia, racism, and colonialism. Yet as this volume demonstrates, those oppressive ideologies damage, cripple, and distort female subjects precisely because they function as *shaming* ideologies.

At the same time, shame is a non-dialectical flow between and within individuals. It can bind or divide; it can distort reality or serve as a moral compass. Significantly, shame can function as a tool of critique, for does the critic not shame the perpetrators of patriarchy, homophobia, and colonialism in his/her parsing of such ideologies? This introduction will provide an overview of shame studies and set forth the uses of shame as a topic of study and tool of analysis.

Shame: A Primary Affect

Before outlining the specific ways in which theorization of shame intersects with gender and sexuality, it is necessary to trace the lines of development which inform that intersection. Recent interest in affect theory can be traced back to seminal works on the topic of shame by Helen Block Lewis, Leon Wurmser, and Andrew P. Morrison, and by the revival and extension of the affect theorist Silvan Tomkins in the work of Donald L. Nathanson, Gershen Kaufman, and others, including Eve Kosofsky Sedgwick and Adam Frank, whose *Shame and Its Sisters: A Silvan Tomkins Reader* (1995) notably sparked interest in literary criticism. Scholars agree that the shame affect notably evokes a "doubleness of experience," involving not just an intrapsychic apprehension of the self as diminished, but an intersubjective apprehension of the self *as diminished in the eyes of another.* An early pioneer in shame studies, Helen Block Lewis, writes of this doubled apprehension thus:

> Because the self is the focus of awareness in shame, "identity" imagery is usually evoked. At the same time that this identity imagery is registering as one's own experiences, there is also vivid imagery of the self in the other's eyes. This creates a "doubleness of experience," which is characteristic of shame. Shame is the vicarious experience of the other's negative evaluation. In order for shame to occur, there must be a relationship between the self and the other in which the self cares about the other's evaluation. Fascination with the other and sensitivity to the other's treatment of the self render the self more vulnerable in shame. ("Shame and the Narcissistic Personality," 107–108)

So profound is this experience of doubleness that an actual other need not even be present to cause this sense of being judged by another. As Benjamin Kilborne writes, "Since shame is at bottom shame about the self, felt in interaction with an other, I am ashamed as I imagine I appear to you . . . shame deals not only with appearances (i.e., how I appear to you), but also with *imagined* appearances (i.e., how I *imagine* I appear to you), shame allows me to realize that I am that object that another is looking at and judging" ("The Disappearing Who," 38). In a similar vein the feminist philosopher Sandra Lee Bartky describes shame as "the distressed apprehension of the self as inadequate or diminished: it requires if not an actual audience before whom my deficiencies are paraded, then an internalized audience with the capacity to judge me . . . shame requires the recognition that I *am*, in some important sense, as I am seen to be" (86). These descriptions of shame all bring out the mechanism of shame's origin in the regard of another, and its subsequent installation in the core of the shamed person, who then apprehends him/herself as flawed, dirty, weak, inadequate—in short, the shamed person turns contempt on the self (Wurmser, "Shame," 67).

Idiomatic expressions of the shame affect underscore its deadliness and its reach into the deepest layer of the psyche. Lewis calls the consequences of shame "malignant": "The metaphors for shame—'I could have died on the spot'; 'I wanted to sink through the floor' or 'crawl into a hole'—reflect our everyday understanding of shame's momentary lethal impact on the self" (Lewis, Introduction, 1). For lesbians, this gesture toward self-erasure and invisibility is the premise for the gay pride expression "coming out," for "to proclaim oneself openly as gay is, above all else, to come out of shame—profoundly, to break the silence. This is why the term 'coming out' is a shame metaphor" (Kaufman and Raphael, 11). Andrew P. Morrison notes that one term for shame, "mortification," gestures toward this lethal quality, in the word's invocation of death: to feel mortified is to feel self-destructive to the point of being suicidal (Morrison, "Eye Turned Inward," 287). Again, the peculiar doubleness of the shame affect heightens its lethal erasure of the self. There is literally no place to hide from the contempt leveled at the self either by others or by oneself, with the result that one is left with the rawness of such contempt. As Silvan Tomkins writes:

> [S]hame is the affect of indignity, of defeat, of transgression, and of alienation. Though terror speaks to life and death and distress makes of the world a vale of tears, yet shame strikes deepest into the heart of man. Shame is felt as an inner torment, a sickness of the soul. It does not matter whether the humiliated one has been shamed by derisive laughter or whether he mocks himself. In either event he feels himself naked, defeated, alienated, lacking in dignity or worth. (Tomkins, "Shame," 133)

Tomkins explains why shame is experienced more closely than other affects, more *as* self, in his observation that it is registered on the face and involves in particular emotional constellations linked to the perceptual register, to seeing and being seen. In answer to his own question of why shame is so close to the experienced self, Tomkins answers that "[i]t is because the self lives in the face, and within the face the self burns brightest in the eyes. Shame turns the attention of the self and others away from other objects to this most visible residence of self, increases its visibility, and thereby generates the torment of self consciousness" (136).

Helen Block Lewis extends this observation to the rest of the body, noting that shame involves physical, bodily reactions that are automatic and that underscore the self's helpless captivity to the shame affect, explaining that, in contrast to the experience of guilt, shame is vested in a "bodily awareness" (blushing, sweating, a pounding heart) that accompanies and augments the "imaging of the self from the other's point of view" ("Shame and the Narcissistic Personality," 108). Feeling shame can lead to *more* shame, as the shamed person reacts helplessly to the feeling of being exposed and vulnerable. Knowing that one is blushing can increase the affect and so one blushes more furiously. The cycle of feeling ashamed of being ashamed works crucially through the body, for the visual manifestations of shame make it impossible to hide or conceal this visibly shamed self. In fact, Otto Fenichel equates "I feel ashamed" with "I do not want to be seen" (in Wurmser, "Shame," 67). Therefore, persons who feel ashamed hide themselves or at least avert their faces. However, they also close their eyes and refuse to look. This is a kind of magical gesture, arising from the belief that anyone who does not look cannot be looked at. Like Tomkins, Wurmser identifies the perceptual register as the locus of shame: "[T]he eye is the organ of shame par excellence," he writes ("Shame," 67).

Because the doubled experience of shame involves both the self and an (imagined or real) other, theorists often stress either the intrapsychic/intersubjective pole or the cultural/social pole in writing of the shame affect. The shame affect invites, for example, a sustained inquiry into the intrapsychic/intersubjective dimension, which in turn shapes and is shaped by the cultural and social dimensions. For a number of shame theorists, shame "protects against violations of the inner boundaries of the self and of sensitive areas of human life that should not be subjected to exposure" (Adamson and Clark, 17). Such boundaries protect or contaminate self *and* other, a process that demonstrates the deterritorialized properties of shame as a flow connecting individuals: as Wurmser observes, "If one also crosses another's inner limits, one violates his privacy, and he feels shame. The transgressor himself may now feel both guilt—for the transgression of the first boundary, for having inflicted hurt—and shame, owing to identification with the exposed object. Violation of privacy tends to evoke shame in both subject and object" ("Shame," 62). Severe shaming—as in the context of traumatic events such as the Holocaust or the American institution of slavery—can easily spread beyond the individual to infect entire communities and histories. Hence individual shaming carries profound societal and cultural resonances. But where does it begin?

For theorists such as Tomkins, Wurmser, and Morrison, shame begins in the earliest stages of development. Tomkins, the originator of affect theory, posits the existence of nine affects, mechanisms with which human beings are hardwired to experience emotion. Shame-humiliation is one of the four innate negative affects, functioning as part of the ambivalent desire to look, to explore something with pleasure and curiosity, "an auxiliary to the affect interest-excitement and enjoyment-joy" (Nathanson, "Timetable for Shame," 20). In Tomkins's formulation, shame performs the critical function of modulating "interest"; he "places shame, in fact, at one end of the affect polarity *shame-interest,* suggesting that the pulsations of cathexis around shame, of all things, are what either enable or disenable so basic a function as the ability to be interested in the world" (Sedgwick and Frank, Introduction, 5). Building on Tomkins's identification of shame as a vital affect, Wurmser explores further the ways in which severe shaming damages one's desire to explore and to take interest in the world. Wurmser writes that feelings of weakness, defectiveness, and dirtiness make one feel not only unlovable, but that one is undeserving of love and unworthy of a place in society ("Shame," 78). Cases of severe or chronic shaming eventually shape the perceptual register in such a way that one is not only subject to others' shaming perceptions of oneself, but the shamed person feels his/her own perceptions to be flawed and dirty (78), a scenario that blocks engagement with the world altogether. The result is what Wurmser calls "depersonalization," a state of profound passivity, in which one feels unreal and all feelings toward the world—whether characterized by a sense of desperation or a yearning to be loved—are repressed (80).

Wurmser, like Andrew P. Morrison, draws on the work of the psychoanalyst Heinz Kohut in developing his formulations of the intersubjective origins of shame. In his later work, Kohut turned to the exploration of narcissistic disorders of the self in order to trace the different paths taken toward healthy self-esteem, on the one hand, and pathological narcissism, on the other. Healthy development involves three types of what Kohut labeled "selfobjects," the first (typically the mother) of whom can shape the child's very sense of perception and who can support the child's budding sense of self with joy and approval. The second selfobject can function as an object "of calmness, infallibility, and omnipotence" with whom the child can experience a sense of merger, and the third selfobject provokes in the child a sense of likeness. In particular, Kohut stresses the need for "empathic response" from the child's selfobjects. As Stephen Mitchell observes, development for Kohut shifted to issues of "creativity, feelings of internal coherence and viability, and functional harmony . . . the capacity to feel one's life experience as energized, creative, and personally meaningful" (Mitchell, 164). Failures in empathic responsiveness result in narcissistic disorders and faults in the self, which Kohut believes can be repaired through the empathic responsiveness of the analyst. As we shall see in our section "Families of Shame," Morrison's analysis of shame as the by-product of the failure of support and empathy from a mirroring other forms at least one strand of the mother-daughter relationship, for mothers are nearly universally cast in the role of selfobject. This has repercussions when the mother attempts to inure her daughter to a female's diminished expectations in the cultural and social realms, thereby casting the child's desires as narcissistic, unattainable delusions of grandeur that the child grows to feel shame in failing to reach.

Gershen Kaufman has also written extensively about how early affective bonds can shape the experience of shame. Very early preverbal shame experiences, he observes, derive from the breaking of the "interpersonal bridge" between parent and child, through the parent's refusal to touch the child or through measures which effectively tell the child s/he is rejected and repulsive to the parent. Further, Kaufman explores the many shaming messages parents routinely impart to their children in their efforts to control the child or to break his/her will. Such messages may be unintentional and appear benign, but their chronic usage will result in a shame-prone personality:

> *Shame on you* is a direct and familiar scene. *You're embarrassing me* burdens the child with the parent's shame; the face of the child now merges with the face of the parent. The two become one and the child becomes but an extension of the self of the parent. *I'm disappointed in you* is another scene that creates a global accusation. More direct shaming strategies include open *disparagement* or belittling, direct *transfers of blame* for mishaps, *contempt,* and total *humiliation* and defeat (as in physical beatings). *Performance expectations* comprise a further source of shame. (*Shame,* 54)

Such parental messages illustrate vividly the intertwined dimensions of the shame experience, for parents—often with the best of intentions and by necessity acting as mediators between their children and their culture—may well be transmitting cultural and social expectations to their children in their use of shame as a potential inhibitor of behavior. Maxine Hong Kingston's mother, for example, relays the shame-laden story of the No Name Woman as such an inhibitor.

We have noted that the intrapsychic/intersubjective register of the shame affect shapes and is shaped by cultural and social mores that define what is felt to be shameful and that use shame as a tool of demarcation for inclusion/exclusion in a social group. Gershen Kaufman calls shame a "multidimensional, multi-layered experience" that is not only an individual phenomenon but "equally a *family* phenomenon and a *cultural* phenomenon. It is reproduced within families, and each culture has its own distinct sources as well as targets of shame" (*Shame*, 191; italics in original). As Constable observes:

> Shame . . . does double duty for individuals and groups by *uniting* and *differentiating* simultaneously. It produces both the feeling of shared regard between and amongst subjects ("We *all* recognize this as shameful") and yet, in that same experience of affective belonging, shame just as powerfully marks out the behaviours or desires which earn exclusion from such regard and recognition ("You must be shameless!" or "Shame on you!"). (Introduction, 3; italics in original)

In a passage that anticipates this volume's third section, "Nations of Shame," Constable notes in particular the use of shame as a powerful cultural and social force capable of mobilizing entire groups or states:

> [T]remendous rhetorical power . . . lies in the marshalling and instrumentalizing of shame: in totalizing and totalitarian denials of state recognition to a particular group; in the recent appeals to the supplemental 'community strengthening' potential of scenes of public humiliation deemed capable of remedying the failures of legal sanctions here in the U.S.; or in the spate of public apologies by Heads of State and High Court rulings, apologies that seek to arouse feelings of collective shame for past denials of recognition . . . by mobilizing national shame in the face of a shameful past. (Introduction, 3)

Constable gestures here to the shame experience as one inherently concerned with the boundary between self (selves) and other (others). The sociologist Thomas Scheff has written extensively about how shame functions as an essential component of communal life, emphasizing the poles of affective interest/enjoyment on the one hand and shame, on the other, as key regulators of social interaction (Adamson and Clark, Introduction, 3). Once again Kingston's story of the No Name Woman springs to mind as an example of how the group may act to enforce the boundaries of acceptable and unacceptable behavior by enforcing the boundaries between inclusion in or exclusion from the group: the villagers, the larger social group, punish the aunt by enacting her "break" in the roundness of village life, while the smaller social group, the family, punishes her with eternal exile and exclusion from family memory. "No Name Woman" demonstrates vividly the powerful threat that the loss of affective bonds and attachments entails: it is, in fact, the core of the lesson that Kingston's mother impresses upon her: "Don't humiliate us. You wouldn't like to be forgotten as if you had never been born. The villagers are watchful" (Kingston, 5).

Shame theorists concerned with the social and cultural dimensions of the shame affect point to the tremendous power that unacknowledged shame can generate among a people or nation. Scheff, for example, has written at length about how unacknowledged shame in Germany eventually resulted in Hitler's rise to power: "both Hitler and his public were in a state of chronic emotional arousal, a chain reaction of shame and anger, giving rise to humiliated fury . . . to a cycle generating rage and destructive aggression since the shame component was not adequately acknowledged" (Scheff, *Bloody Revenge*, 31). In a similar vein Morrison has pointed to talk-show culture as evidence of a shame culture in contemporary American society, in its airings of personal humiliations and failings for public *consumption* (Morrison, *Culture of Shame*, 196).

Yet many writers on shame also emphasize the *positive* uses of shame at individual, familial, and cultural levels. Carl Schneider, far from discerning a culture of shame in the United States, argues in support of a "mature sense of shame" in the face of what he sees as a large-scale desire to socially eradicate shame. Schneider calls for a more complex and nuanced understanding of the ways shame functions as a form of respect for privacy and agency that is essential to a healthy sense of self and healthy relationships. Shame alerts us to the need for privacy, for covering that which should not be exposed:

> I propose that there are times and places in all phases of human life where covering is appropriate—indeed, needed—not because something is amiss, awry, or wrong, but because it *is* appropriate, that is, "fitting, proper." Human beings are, in Bachelard's lovely phrase, "half-open beings," always partly exposed, partly covered. Human experience, always vulnerable to violation, needs protection. Thus an element of reticence is always present and always appropriate to human relationships, including one's relation to oneself. To ignore or deny this is to be shameless. (Schneider, "Mature Sense of Shame," 200)

Similarly, Elsbeth Probyn argues in *Blush: Faces of Shame* that being attuned to one's sense of shame is not only of great social value, but of personal value as well in that feelings of shame guide one toward truths about oneself and toward moral behavior. Who would want to live in a shameless society? And, on a personal level, doesn't the inability to feel shame signify a failure in one's regard for others? A number of theorists have in fact identified shame as an essential component of moral emotion (e.g., Boonin; Manion; Nussbaum; Rawls; Taylor; Thrane). And shame can well be a motivating factor as individuals or groups actively *counter* shame. In her assessment of the role shame can or should play in feminist thought, Jill Locke urges positive, active modes for counteracting shame's disabling grip in her view that shame is not a useful endpoint even when it is mobilized for positive goals. In other words, while national shaming over historical injustice, for example, may be apt, it is not enough to shame the shamer. Instead, Locke suggests that the positive moves facilitated by shame lie beyond this inversion of shame and in actions taken toward a more democratic and egalitarian society less susceptible to the shaming relations of the past. While such social movements will not eradicate bigotry, ignorance, and shaming, "alternative places and worlds—'houses where freedom can dwell'—may lessen shame's grip" (Locke, 159). Adamson and Clark, in tracing the link between shame and creativity, suggest that creative efforts may work to surmount "shame in its destructive aspect": "If severe feelings of shame compel us to hide and conceal inner reality from others and from ourselves, it is often countered in the writer by a creative ideal, a defiant and even ruthless decision not to turn away or to lie, a courageous and almost *shameless* will to see and to know that which internal and external sanctions conspire to keep us from looking at and exploring" (Adamson and Clark, 29). The fact of non-representation, of silence, functions as oppression (Kaufman and Raphael, 10). Thus, *representing* women's shame is an inherently proactive endeavor even if the content of such representations reveals how women have been condemned to a shame status.

Shame: A Primary Female Affect

We now return to the question that opens this introduction and that forms the central concern of this volume: Why does research consistently find that women are more shame-prone than men? Freud's assertion that shame is a feminine characteristic with its origins in "genital deficiency" points the way to one central component of shame-proneness in women: the fact that the female body bears extraordinary cultural weight in defining legitimate, appropriate, and socially approved or sanctioned ways of being in the world. Indeed, "our existence can only take place in an embodied self" (Gilbert, 27), and the body therefore functions as a primary site of perception and identity—one that is linked with shame in that it must be covered or hidden. In *Embodied Shame*, J. Brooks Bouson helpfully summarizes the insights of Lewis and Morrison: "Because of the Freudian view that attachment is regressive and that women are shame-prone as a result of their need to conceal their 'genital deficiency,' there is an implicit hierarchy in classical psychoanalytic discourse, which views shame as preoedipal and guilt as oedipal"; shame is seen as "the developmentally more primitive affect" (5). Historically, women have been defined as corporeal in a way that men are not, and the female body is thus a critical locus for discourses and representations that link femininity with shame.

A glance around the world reveals that women's bodies are clothed and covered in much more intricate and culturally freighted modes than are the bodies of men. The female body is experienced as much as a liability as it is a source of pleasure, as Gilbert notes in his point that "[c]ontrol of female sexuality (and the female body) has been institutionalized in social and religious forms for hundreds of years and more . . . often involving the shaming/stigmatising of female sexuality and appearance" (35).

Studies of female embodiment confirm and extend Gilbert's assessment. Numerous feminist theorists have shown the ways in which female embodiment heightens women's ambivalent and often shame-saturated relationship to their physicality. To begin with, women occupy the subordinate and denigrated pole of the binary division mind/body; being "cast in the role of the body" in effect means that women experience their bodies "as animal, as appetite, as deceiver, as prison of the soul" (Bordo, 3, 5;

see also Spelman). Furthermore, female bodies are particularly discomfiting because Western philosophical and religious traditions have long defined them as "unpredictable, leaky, and disruptive": "As the devalued processes of reproduction make clear, the body has a propensity to leak, to overflow the proper distinctions between self and other, to contaminate and engulf" (Price and Shildrick, 2–3). Similarly, Elizabeth Grosz terms women's bodies "volatile": "Can it be that in the West, in our time, the female body has been constructed not only as a lack or absence but . . . as a leaking, uncontrollable, seeping liquid; as formless flow; as viscosity, entrapping, secreting . . . a formlessness that engulfs all form, a disorder that threatens all order?" Grosz asks (*Volatile Bodies*, 203). Indeed, Julia Kristeva has argued that the female body is for everyone the first experience of abjection, the horrific, repudiated, overwhelming sensation of embodiment: when the infant learns to demarcate itself from the mother, "what [has] been the mother will turn into an abject" (*Powers of Abjection*, 13). Abjection occurs when the boundaries that define "the clean and proper body" fail. But because abjection has its primal and primary source in the relationship to the female body, abjection will always recall its female origins, so that critics may make the seemingly universal observation that shame is "experienced at the threshold of the self and not-self, of object and abject" (Pajaczkowska and Ward, 3), yet what is at play in this narrative of infant development is the transformation of the *mother's* body into other and abject. Kristeva argues that in cultures that develop rigid gender distinctions and that subordinate women to men, women will seem irrational, uncontrollable, needing restraint and confinement—restraint and confinement often targeting the female body and its primal status as abject.

When female bodies differ from a cultural feminine norm—as is the case with disabled women, visibly ill women, or women whose bodies seem aberrant or grotesque—Bordo's identification of women as the debased "body" component of the mind/body split becomes even more fraught with the potential for shaming. Rosemarie Garland Thomson observes that "[m]any parallels exist between the social meanings attributed to female bodies and those assigned to disabled bodies" (*Extraordinary Bodies*, 19):

> [M]ale, white, or able-bodied superiority appears natural, undisputed, and unremarked, seemingly eclipsed by female, black, or disabled difference . . . without the monstrous body to demarcate the borders of the generic, without the female body to distinguish the shame of the male, and without the pathological to give form to the normal, the taxonomies of bodily value that underlie political, social, and economic arrangements would collapse. (20)

Yet so pervasive is the association of femaleness with disability that disabled women suffer multiple erasures as female subjects. Thomson notes that disabled women "often encounter 'asexual objectification,' the assumption that sexuality is inappropriate in disabled people" (25). The disabled female body may be dismissed as unfit, unbeautiful, aberrant; always that body is subject to the stares of others, which "sculpt the subject into a grotesque spectacle" (26). Mary K. DeShazer's study of women's cancer writings similarly shows how women suffering from breast, uterine, and ovarian cancer struggle with their "medicalized, leaky, amputated, prosthetic, (not) dying" bodies (13); like disabled women, visibly ill women must cope with a double disenfranchisement in terms of physicality, for, just as the female body is often equated with disability, so too is the female body often equated with illness. In fact, any female body that differs from the cultural norms governing femininity risks being viewed and treated as deviant and aberrant. Thomson remarks that the "aberrant figure of woman has been identified variously as . . . black, fat, lesbian, sexually voracious, disabled, or ugly . . . this figure's deviance and subsequent devaluation are always attributed to some visible characteristic that operates as an emblem of her difference, just as beauty has always been located in the body of the feminine woman" (28). Bouson contributes a critical point to this discussion in her caution that "a collective form of denial exists among critics who in effect have turned what is often described as the unruly, transgressive female body into an abstraction: a cultural text that can be 'fixed' within the fixated gaze of the critical establishment" (13), while the real experiences of shamed women continue. One of this book's contributors, Eliza Chandler, makes an important link between the theoretical and the personal in taking up the subject of how shame is deeply embodied.

Moreover, Chandler makes the same point about disability pride that the editors of a volume on gay shame do about gay pride when they say that "gay pride has never been able to separate itself entirely from shame, or to transcend shame. Gay pride does not even make sense without some reference to the shame of being gay, and its very successes (to say nothing of its failures) testify to the intensity of its ongoing struggle with shame" (Halperin and Traub, 4). Chandler's argument that disability pride necessarily hinges on a strategy of shame management confirms this notion that the "aberrant figure" (in this case, male or female) claims agency through an emergence from shame. The significant overlap between analyses of disability, sexuality, and gender shame stems from the extent to which each of these elements of identity are embodied.

The female body, then, is one powerful strand in understanding the gendered construction of shame. Yet another strand is a consistent finding that women are more "field dependent" than men, a finding first advanced by Helen Block Lewis and since confirmed by a number of other researchers. Field dependence—"a cognitive style that catches the self in relation not only to its physical surround but in relation to others" (Lewis, "Shame and the Narcissistic Personality," 103)—means that women "organize their personal sense of self around feelings of shame . . . around a sense of disappointment in failing to meet some proposed ideal, especially in the eyes of others" (Manion, 24). Lewis contends that two major elements form the basis of women's more intensified states of shame: women are defined more by their ability to maintain interpersonal relations than are men, an ability which in turn makes them more vulnerable to social pressures to conform to traditional feminine norms.

Hence unacceptable expressions of rage and hostility may be turned against the self: Lewis's research confirms the link between field dependence, humiliated rage, and depression in women. Significantly, Lewis locates one such experience of humiliated rage in sexual and physical abuse: "Humiliated fury has very little place to go except back down on the self . . . to become a component of one's humiliation" (Lewis, 100). While researchers such as Aart Broek and Nancy Van Deusen have argued that shame sparks violence—such as sexual and physical abuse—this finding applies primarily to men, as Van Deusen notes. Lewis's point is that for women, shame tends to provoke feelings of violence primarily toward the self. Finally, in contrast to guilt, which Lewis finds accessible to verbalization, shame is silent, image-dependent, and bodily based. Shame thus remains less accessible to consciousness, even as it continues to exert its debilitating effects on the female sense of self.

For these reasons, intimate relationships prove fertile ground for female experiences of shame. Women's descriptions of shaming often feature family members—parents; lovers and partners; close circles of friends. Transmission of cultural norms implicitly and explicitly targets the girl as a possible conduit of shame *for the family*, as in Brave Orchid's warning to Kingston, "Don't humiliate us." In twinning her daughter's transition to puberty with a shame state, the mother passes on what the chapters in this volume reveal to be a cross-cultural practice of saddling the female body with the weight of collective honor, be it familial or national. Broadly defined as an injunction against the female body's implicit shamefulness, the value of cultural honor undermines female subjectivity even as it invests women with the responsibility of embodying the highest of shared values.

Insofar as the axis of shame and honor can and does place women in important social roles, the tension surrounding the female body paradoxically establishes a baseline of shame that undermines the potentially positive function of shame that we visited earlier. Jennifer Manion cautions against the wholesale adoption of shame as a moral emotion, given the specifically damaging nature of female shame. Pointing to the body of work that has built upon Lewis's formulations—work that reveals that women feel responsibility for the maintenance of interpersonal bonds, that women's self-sacrifice and socialization in repressing anger both result in increased rates of depression for women, and that women tend to turn their anger on themselves with self-punitive judgments—Manion asks us to reconsider the potential for women to experience "good" shame, arguing that shame is such a deeply gendered affect that its moral applications differ between men and women. Pajaczkowska and Ward point to a gendered differentiation in the very etymology of shame, which they trace back to the Indo-European *skam* or *isikam*, the first of which is active and unambiguous, usually associated with uninflected "bad" states. The second is the allied concept relating to modesty and humility, as virtues deriving from the raw experience of shame in the former sense. The "raw" meaning of shame is attributed to masculinity and agency whereas the version of shame that has become acculturated is attributed to femininity and passivity (9).

These attempts to sort out the gendered workings of shame are taken up by critics attentive to the workings of shame in specific texts and contexts, for as Adamson and

Clark note, creative texts that engage with shame not only recognize its origins and contexts but help us to work through its damaging and toxic psychic traces. It is to those texts that we now turn our attention.

Representing Women's Shame

The Female Face of Shame is organized into three basic areas of subject formation: "Bodies of Shame," "Families of Shame," and "Nations of Shame." This tripartite structure allows us to include a wide range of work on our topic while offering cohesive analyses of how shame shapes subjectivity, intersubjective relations, and discourses of identity in the twentieth century. The chapters in "Bodies of Shame" explore the intimate, embodied experience of shame in a variety of contemporary contexts. The first chapter, Jocelyn Eighan's "The Other Woman: Xenophobia and Shame," sets up a crucial premise by which shame operates: the self/other binary. Indeed, one of the most compelling dimensions of shame is that it works not as a structured hierarchy, but as a shifting relational axis between subjects. Therefore, even while one person may shame another, the flow of shaming is reversible given its relational grammar. Eighan brings this out in her analysis of Judith Merril's stories, in which female or feminine bodies are characterized as monstrous, alien, and most importantly, *foreign*. By showing how female forms are shamed, and how male subjects shame them, Eighan reveals how female bodies are circumscribed by shame, and she goes on to employ shame as an important means by which to critique xenophobia.

The following three chapters examine texts that incorporate shame into the representation of female sexuality, thus locating shame within the female body. Nicole Fayard makes the important link between shame and trauma in her analysis of Samira Bellil's memoir about being raped multiple times in the French *banlieues* (economically and ethnically marginalized suburban housing projects). Balancing a description of Bellil's internalization of the harm done to her as self-harm and as a source of silence, with her subsequent role as a now-celebrated witness able to testify to her own trauma, Fayard looks at how the self-representation of shame works as a therapeutic act—a point that the next author, Suzette Henke, advances in her influential theory of "scriptoanalysis" in her book, *Shattered Subjects*. Henke's contribution to *The Female Face of Shame* focuses on the extent to which shame is embedded in the female body in the site of the "weeping womb" in Angela Carter's *The Bloody Chamber*. Whereas Bellil depicts her already violated body, Carter's stories revolve around virginal bodies presented as always already *rapeable*. Carter's girls and women bear within them a potential chamber of shame which they variously defend or surrender to the violent forces at work in the fairy tale archetypes she revises.

Natalie Edwards brings in another author indispensable to the study of shame: the French writer Annie Ernaux. Ernaux's writing presents a sustained study of the ways in which shame informs female identity, and Edwards's piece focuses on how Ernaux, along with Christine Angot, embeds the shamed female body in emancipatory writing while at the same time confronting the reader with material designed to shock and thus interrogate the attachment of shame to particular iterations of female sexuality and desire.

Then, having demonstrated the ways in which shame is instilled in the female body, this part closes with a very important piece about how disabled women's bodies are regarded as sites of shame. Speaking from her experience of cerebral palsy, Eliza Chandler reflects on how her participation in the "disability pride" movement plays out as an ongoing dialogue between pride and shame. She in fact defines disability pride as a "turning away from shame," and goes on to suggest that because the body is the target of public shame, the narrative of disability pride may most accurately be described as "wavering and windy prides that are not constrained to a structure of departure and arrival." Chandler recognizes shame as something that cannot be purged by the celebratory but inaccurate narrative that one can arrive at a real experience of pride in the public sphere. Chandler's rethinking of the relationship between pride and shame in disability experience reminds us that because shame is an affect, it is one of the most powerful and persistent experiences of our embodied selves; it cannot be rationalized or theorized away but rather works to reveal painful truths about human experience.

Because shame is the product of intersubjective relations, part 2, "Families of Shame," elaborates on how individual women are made to experience shame in one of the most intimate relational sites: the family. Moreover, the families presented in these chapters are articulated by race and class differences, and therefore these analyses of family dynamics include important considerations of the ways in which difference is all too often mediated by shame, even among those who are otherwise so deeply connected.

The first chapter, Erica L. Johnson's analysis of colonial shame and postcolonial shaming in Michelle Cliff's autobiographical novel, *Abeng,* pays close attention to socially orchestrated differences within the family unit. Cliff's account of growing up in a Jamaican family starkly divided by race and class is shot through with "the colonized child's" (Cliff's) queasy sense that someone is always being humiliated—and that "someone" is often herself or, more aptly, parts of her divided self. The fact that shaming exchanges take place within the ostensibly united and loving unit of the family blocks young Clare Savage from seeing them as such; however, these family dynamics drive her to consult global and historical injustices such as the Holocaust in order to understand her deep-seated sense that shame lies hidden within her own home. Similarly, the next chapter, by Frann Michel, takes up the shaming ideologies of colonialism and racism in Octavia Butler's *Survivor.* In keeping with the previous chapter, Michel examines how women face the question of assimilation or resistance to such forces when they are introduced through the idiom of the family.

Continuing the theme of intergenerational shaming, Sinead McDermott analyzes two daughters' responses to the legacy of their mother's transgressive sexual liaison in Michele Roberts's *Daughters of the House*. McDermott's chapter brings out the responses caused by feelings of shame: in one daughter's case, self-mortification, and in the other's, anger. Extending the discussion of shame's role in driving women's actions as well as identities, McDermott complicates narratives of shame as a damaging affect to suggest that "women's shame and anger may ultimately have a politically and socially transformative function" (McDermott) if and when it morphs into fury. Given the highly gendered link between shame and violence (the notion that men commit violence against others in order to alleviate feelings of shame whereas women turn their feelings of shame inward), this reading of women's divergent responses to shame expands upon the volume's core question of how shame and gender intersect.

Patricia Moran's contribution details the dynamics of familial shaming in the spousal relationship. Taking as her subject the autobiographical trilogy of Norwegian modernist Cora Sandel, Moran identifies the author's struggle to become an artist as a (thwarted) struggle to overcome shame. Although Sandel's avatar, Alberta, succeeds in becoming a writer, she does so at tremendous personal cost, due to the baseline of shame that her mother instills in her as a child and that her husband reinforces during her adulthood. As is the case with the earlier chapters in "Families of Shame," social divisions bleed into family dynamics, and Alberta has first to grasp the nature of class and gender oppression in order to recognize her husband's humiliating treatment of her.

Laura Martocci broaches a question that comes up in Moran's and Johnson's chapters as well: How does one represent one's own shame? This cluster of three autobiographical representations of shame culminates in Martocci's sociological reading of a notoriously shame-fraught autobiographical novel: Margaret Atwood's *Cat's Eye*. Martocci's expertise is in bullying, and she shows how shame extends from the private sphere of the family into public intersubjective relations. This reading of Elaine's radical vulnerability to other girls' bullying and her lack of a safe space at home makes an important link between how families and friendships take over one's sense of being on an emotional level unavailable to the intellect but evident through the emotional mimesis of literature.

Finally, we close part 2 with a more abstract analysis of interpersonal relations in Tamar Heller's application of Simone Weil's important notion of "affliction" to Jean Rhys's searing portrait of shame in *Good Morning, Midnight*. While the shame of Rhys's protagonist in fact stems from her family's rejection of her ("Why don't you make a hole in the Seine," they ask her), Rhys presents a powerful portrait of the workings of intersubjectivity. Heller teases out the most essential affective conduits between self and other in her analysis of the novel's terrifying ending.

Of the many responses we received to our call for papers, the greatest number dealt with national shame, and hence we conclude the volume with "Nations of Shame." The chapters included here cover rich comparative ground from India and Pakistan to Mauritius, Algeria, and China. Given the twentieth-century focus of the volume, and the fact that nationalism is a defining phenomenon in this period so marked by decolonization and national conflicts, the nation is a critical register of collective identity. Thus, *The Female Face of Shame* moves from the personal to the familial to the national in a comprehensive survey of modern and contemporary representations of how shame inflects women's identities.

Peiling Zhao presents a particularly original and important analysis of how China's national identity has been forged as a masculine identity, with the corollary that femininity is synonymous with shame. Zhao identifies national campaigns to efface femininity from the 1950s through the 1980s in such cultural phenomena as a government-sponsored hair-cutting movement and the widespread adaptation of masculine dress for all. Moreover, she attributes these campaigns to deconstruct femininity to China's repudiation of Western shaming. This chapter thus addresses a critical global conversation about shame that stems from Ruth Benedict's notorious 1946 ethnography, *The Chrysanthemum and the Sword,* in which she characterizes Asian cultures as "shame cultures" in contrast to what she sees as the morally superior "guilt cultures" of the West. Zhao's fascinating presentation of the erasure of femininity in the People's Republic of China's early decades as a state reveals women and femininity to have been at the heart of both national identity and East-West tensions. Zhao then makes the fascinating move of reversing the flow of shame surrounding femininity to recast female bodies as sites of national pride, thus leveraging the axis of shame and pride that Chandler identifies in the preceding section.

Whereas Zhao depicts the forging of national identity, Namrata Mitra addresses examples of national disintegration, in the case of the partition of India and Pakistan. Women's bodies became targets of violence through which warring factions expressed their contempt for one another. In the case of partition, mass rape and mutilation were committed to shame the other side, and against this backdrop "the intent to humiliate the other community was carried out by uncovering women's bodies in the public sphere" (Mitra) on either side of the new border. Mitra looks at partition novels from India and from Pakistan in her study of "the nationalistic investment in gendered bodies and the forced silencing of shamed bodies thereafter" (Mitra).

The final two chapters of the book explore the theme of women's resistance to shame. Having demonstrated the myriad ways in which femininity and women's identities are subjected to feelings of shame in daily life, family life, and national discourse, the volume focuses as well on the dialogic nature of resistance that the final chapters, by Karen Lindo and Anna Rocca, emphasize. Lindo's "Interrogating the Place of *Lajja* (Shame) in Contemporary Mauritius" identifies the complicity of religious and national identity in "the domestication of the female body through shame" (Lindo), and acclaimed Mauritian author Ananda Devi's unburdening of the Indo-Mauritian body of such nationalist or religious duty. Rocca's analysis of Algerian writer Assia Djebar takes up Lindo's notion that the female body is given the charge of "organizing a coherent and systematic means of having bodies signify specific cultural values" (Lindo) in the case of a national identity emerging from generations of colonization. In a context of postcolonial nationalism, she argues, "Algerian women carry deeply the consequences of this adversity in that they are isolated in their shame and alienated from themselves" (Rocca). In her autobiography, then, Djebar witnesses and denounces the impossibility of belonging to a national symbolic order that shames women, but she fights her own self-effacement and strives for cognitive freedom through her undoing of shame and her ability to reconfigure her homeland by emotionally reconnecting with herself.

Living through Shame

On January 31, 1984, fifteen-year-old Irish teenager Ann Lovett left her school after morning classes, ostensibly to eat lunch at her family home, as was her custom. Instead of heading home, however, Ann went to a grotto dedicated to the Virgin Mary in an isolated part of town, on a hill next to the graveyard. There she was discovered hours later by some boys headed home from school. Only semiconscious, Ann was fatally weakened by exposure and bleeding. Next to her was her stillborn baby boy. Ann died several hours later.

Ann's death became a national scandal, coming as it did only four months after a divisive national referendum on abortion that ended with a two-thirds majority enshrining the right to life of the unborn in the Irish constitution. Discussed widely in the media and in government meetings, Ann's case is a glaring example of how the female body is the sounding board for national and cultural identity issues—and of the shifting signification of the shame that is so often attached to this body. While some may have seen her death as punishment for shameful sexual behavior, Ann's tragedy also sparked a counter-shaming event in the forum of Gay Byrne's popular and highly influential Irish radio program. Shortly after Ann's death, Byrne dedicated his show to her and to the many other women who had revealed through letters to him that they, too, had given birth in secret. For fifty minutes, their letters were read out with no commentary or interpretation. This public exposure of a painful secret that had been muffled by national shame worked not only to reveal but to alter women's shame by representing it, just as the texts considered in this volume identify and challenge women's shame through representation.

Even after twenty-six years, however, the mystery surrounding Ann's lonely plight remains. Did the teenager confide in no one? How was it that her family, friends, and teachers did not realize she was pregnant? Who was the baby's father? No one will ever know the answers to these questions. The people of the town who still remember Ann remain angry and defensive about their perceived indifference and heartlessness; her mother, an ardent practicing Catholic who gave birth to nine children, has never spoken publicly about her daughter's death.

Like the story of No Name Woman with which this introduction opens, the story of Ann Lovett haunts us not because it is unique—it is not—but because she took her story with her to her grave, leaving us with one salient fact: *shame kills*. Ann's choice of the grotto dedicated to the Virgin Mary—grottos common all over Ireland—underscores this fact, for Ann lay close to a kneeling figure of Mary Magdalene, a woman shunned because of her sexual sins. Caught and tangled in her woman's body, surrounded by familial and cultural interdictions about femininity voiced everywhere in the months leading up to her labor, Ann died alone wrapped in a shroud of shame and silence.

The silence surrounding the issue of women's shame is one of the most damaging mechanisms by which female subjectivity is subverted. Kaufman and Raphael affirm this in their observation that "shame can be so deeply buried, so rooted in our being, that we are blind to its presence in our lives. Internalized shame can completely capture us, yet we can still believe we have no shame" (11). This is a crucial point, and one that applies not only to the important scholarship these authors have done on gay shame but to the workings of any shaming ideology. It is our hope that by bringing gendered shame out into the open, by representing it, this volume will help to counteract shame's mortifying influence in women's lives.

PART 1

BODIES OF SHAME

1 The Other Woman

Xenophobia and Shame

Jocelyn Eighan

In the 1950s and 1960s, when science fiction predominantly consisted of works by male writers, Judith Merril emerged onto the science fiction scene with her ground-breaking texts which challenged the genre's pervasive focus on masculine concerns.[1] While the texts written by her male contemporaries often featured women as minor characters, many of Merril's stories distinctly centered on female characters and broached topics of motherhood, sexuality, and gender relations.[2] Interestingly, notions of gender inequality permeate Merril's plotlines; as the female characters grow increasingly isolated from their male counterparts, they become the dangerous and feared alien outsiders. What is at work, then, is an intricate interplay between fear (of the other) and shame as the male characters interact with the "alien" women. Indeed, as Andrew P. Morrison notes in *The Culture of Shame*, "We seem to need visible 'monstrosities' to depict our own disavowed self-images. Our feelings of defectiveness and imperfection find an outlet in the real-life 'freak,' who becomes the receptacle for our deepest fears" (27)—a notion particularly accurate, not only when applied to shame, but also when understood within the context of xenophobia. In this chapter, I explore representations of women *as* shame in a selection of Judith Merril's short stories and note the ways in which the female characters become alien "others" while scrutinized under the xenophobic male gaze. Focusing specifically on Merril's "That Only a Mother," "Whoever You Are," and "The Lady Was a Tramp," I argue that the female or feminine characters—by virtue of their alien/foreign otherness—embody stigma and shame. Paradoxically, however, the shame represented by these "alien" women mirrors the actual stigmatized feelings of the male characters. In light of this phenomenon, I investigate the specific textual moments in which the male characters utilize guises or "veils" to protect themselves from shame—notably through shame-rage, shame-pride, and narcissism.

As a literary phenomenon, the "alien" is difficult to define, and it is beyond the scope of this chapter to fully analyze the numerous renderings of the alien offered by critics and theorists; from bug-eyed monsters (BEMs) to humanoid aliens and BAMs, or beautiful alien monster-women,[3] the criterion of "otherness," however, remains universally accepted within these varied categorizations. It is precisely this sense of otherness—the stigma *attached to* this otherness, and its accompanying shame—that incites fear within those who deem themselves "normal." In traditional science fiction which posits the "man as human" and the "woman as other," the woman-as-alien motif works to solidify the masculine notion of the logical/rational versus the (feminine) emotional/irrational. As Patricia Monk notes in *Alien Theory,* the "woman as Other" functions as part of an androcentric encoding in which the human (understood as *man*) is identified "positively," while the "alien is defined with extreme negativity (the woman/alien is monstrous—a source of contamination and destruction)" (67). In light of this argument, the female alien (symbolically attached to irrationality/emotion) is threatening in her ability to contaminate masculine "reason" with her emotion—a fundamentally stigmatic trait. The female/feminized aliens in Merril's stories, however, are unique precisely because of their stigma and its power to unveil the more unconventional and unsettling notions of reason.

As one of the leading feminist science fiction writers, Merril is celebrated for her unique thematic contributions to the genre—notably female issues of love, motherhood, pregnancy, emotion (Pohl-Weary, 2). The significance of Merril's work rests in its ability to implement these themes in ways that challenge gender-role behavior. Merril consciously acknowledges the subversion of gender stereotypes as a major impetus for her work: "How much of what we consider 'feminine' or 'masculine' behavior is cultural, how much biological? One of the [science fiction] games is psycho-drama-on-paper. Set up an environment-shift or a role-switch, and see what happens" (Pohl-Weary, 156). In her own fiction, Merril uses the trope of the alien to confront widely held views of the irrational/emotional female other. From the hairless, sensual, "loving" beings to the mutated, monstrous humanoid child, Merril's aliens are remarkable in their unsettling, yet provocative representations of feminine embodiment.

Henrietta, the monstrous child that appears in Merril's "That Only a Mother" (1948), exemplifies the stigmatized alien other both in terms of gender and bodily difference. As a result of her exposure to bomb radiation while in the womb, Henrietta is born without limbs—a horrifying discovery for her father, Hank, who must carry the burden of his own shame over having produced a *defective* girl child. The first portion of the narrative is largely presented through a series of letters and telegrams between Henrietta's mother, Margaret, and Hank, who is away at war. In these exchanges, the dichotomy between emotion and reason is ever-present; even structurally, Margaret's letters are lengthy—detailing her anxiety over their daughter's impending birth in the wake of atomic weapons and radiation—while Hank's replies seem calculated, relatively disinterested, and brief. Through Margaret's letters, readers learn that atomic radiation has led to the development of mutations in newborns. Alarmingly, many of the mutated infants become victims of infanticide, and as Margaret tells Hank in a grim moment of foreshadowing, "It's the fathers who do it. Lucky thing you're not around, in case—" (Merril, "Mother," in *Homecalling*, 13). As the narrative follows Margaret through her pregnancy and into motherhood, readers bear witness to her distorted love. Indeed, Margaret's mother-love plays a large part in her refusal to acknowledge her daughter's physical abnormalities. Rather, she deems Henrietta a seven-month-old "prodigy," and notes Henrietta's exceptional ability to sing and "speak perfectly clear" (13).

When Hank returns home, the narrative shifts to reflect his point of view, and Henrietta's exceptional abilities are suddenly refocused to reflect gross deformities. Whereas Margaret likens Henrietta to a "snow-white potato sack with [a] beautiful, beautiful flower-face blooming on top" (15) and boasts her ability to "crawl," Hank gropes for her arm in a fit of terror only to discover "a moving knob of flesh at the shoulder" (19). His disgust is clearly palpable as he watches his deformed daughter crawl on her belly; he "sternly" says, "The way you wriggle . . . anyone might think you are a worm, using your tummy to crawl on, instead of your hands and feet" (19). In this moment of verbal condemnation, Henrietta's extraordinary talent is reconfigured into a grotesque display of her alienness. More specifically, Hank's accusations—that Henrietta crawls the *wrong* way, like a "worm"—draws attention to the act of crawling not as a developmental milestone, but rather as shameful movement indicative of dirtiness and defectiveness.

Like Henrietta's limbless body, which fundamentally becomes the source of Hank's shame, the stigmatized "disabled" body represents a threat to social order. In *Civilization and Its Discontents*, Freud specifies that "dirtiness of any kind" is "incompatible with civilization," and the "demand for cleanliness" extends beyond "civilized society" to encompass the human body (46–47). Similar ideas are echoed in the work of the anthropologist Mary Douglas, whose classification of dirt as "matter out of place" (44) perfectly aligns with the stigmatized body—an idea Rosemarie Garland Thomson explores extensively in *Extraordinary Bodies: Figuring Physical Disability in American Culture and Literature*. Drawing on Douglas's concepts of dirt, Thomson additionally contends, "Dirt is an anomaly, a discordant element rejected from the schema that individuals and societies use in order to construct a stable, recognizable, and predictable world" (33). Thus, the disabled body, like dirt, is "in some sense 'matter out of place' in terms of the interpretive frameworks and physical expectations our culture shares"; it is regarded as a "pollution or taboo or contagion"—something that needs to be eliminated in order to preserve a "normal" society (33–34).[4]

Keeping in line with Erving Goffman's notion that "we believe the person with a stigma is not quite human" (*Stigma*, 5), and Mary Douglas's observation that one must "avoid anomalous things" (49), there exists an underlying danger in the "normal's" association with the nonhuman/other—namely, the potential for sharing in the stigmatized other's shame. Goffman's idea of the "courtesy stigma," which he defines as the "tendency for a stigma to spread from the stigmatized individual to his close connections" (*Stigma*, 30), speaks to this phenomenon. In *Shame: The Exposed Self*, Michael Lewis builds on Goffman's theory, maintaining that courtesy stigmas are "contagious" in the way they act "like an infectious disease," not only affecting the stigmatized victim, "but all those who are associated with him or her" (201). Parents of stigmatized children are especially affected by their child's shame, first in expressing complete shock and disbelief at the child's imperfect health.[5] While Margaret seems overcome with disbelief, and in her sheer denial refuses to see her daughter's imperfections, Hank—viewing Henrietta as a malformed extension of himself—enters into a state of rage. Readers can speculate that Hank's rage perhaps stems from guilt over his involvement with atomic weapon research; as the narrative forebodingly implies, these mutations could have been prevented, making Hank fundamentally responsible for Henrietta's deformed body.

Since Hank shares in Henrietta's stigma and cannot overcome its accompanying shame, the only manner in which he can stifle his shame is by killing it, essentially by murdering its source. Using anger as an "emotional substitute" for his shame, Hank acts out his feelings of shame through aggression—a primary characteristic of shame-rage, in which one is so overcome by shame that one carries out one's feelings in the form of rage and violence.[6] Hank's shame-rage manifests itself in the narrative's final chilling scene:

> With infinite care he opened the knot at the bottom of the nightgown . . . His left hand felt along the soft knitted fabric of the gown, up toward the diaper that folded, flat and smooth across the bottom end of his child. No wrinkles. No kicking. *No . . .*
> "Maggie." He tried to pull his hands from the neat fold in the diaper, from the wriggling body. . . . His head was spinning, but he had to know before he let it go.
> "Maggie, why . . . didn't you . . . tell me?"
> "Tell you what, darling?"
> . . . *She didn't know.* His hands, beyond control, ran up and down the soft-skinned baby body, the sinuous limbless body. *Oh God, dear God*—his—head shook and his muscles contracted in a bitter spasm of hysteria. His fingers tightened on his child— *Oh God, she didn't know. . . .* (19)

Arguably, Hank's act of violence functions as a mode of concealment from shame. By murdering Henrietta, he "eliminates" the source of his shame—the stigmatized, alien other—"as dirt is thrown away" (Wurmser, *Mask*, 80). As this passage also demonstrates, the line between reason and emotion becomes so obscured that readers are left to question rationality entirely. Indeed, the story's irony emerges in this final moment of brutality, where the masculine "reason" traditionally idealized in science fiction transforms into an *irrational*, disruptive (and destructive) force. Hank's "spasms" recall feminine "hysteria" while the brutal image of his "fingers tightening" around his alien daughter underscores the "murderousness of rationality."[7] Taken a step further, Hank's act of murder offers another interpretive possibility; not only does his literal destruction of Henrietta function symbolically as an attempt to obliterate the horror and shame of the female otherness Henrietta embodies, but it also serves as a means through which Hank eradicates the shameful feminine other that stems from (within) him.

Like Henrietta in "That Only a Mother," the feminized aliens in Merril's "Whoever You Are" (1952) expose the "murderousness of rationality" by bringing emotion to the forefront of the plot. Thematically, the story tackles similar issues of unconditional love and motherly acceptance to those found in "That Only a Mother," while simultaneously exploring male preoccupation with the different (female) body. Even more telling is the story's title, which readers learn is derived from an anecdote of an orphan girl who tosses a note over the orphanage wall; the note reads "Whoever you are, I love you" (Merril, "Whoever," in *Homecalling*, 137). The narrative depicts a space crew on Scanliter Six who monitor alien ships by trapping them in a Web that surrounds the solar system. A group of unauthorized aliens has made an attempt to pass through the Web, endangering five billion (male) Solar citizens protected within the Web's "womb-enclosure" (126). The crewmen suspend the intruding ship, which allows them full access for exploration—an assignment officer Joe Fromm enthusiastically accepts. While aboard the alien ship, Fromm must record his observations, specifically noting the physical anomalies of the intruders in an effort to establish and reaffirm their "otherness."

Upon discovering the aliens, Fromm refers to each individual alien as "he," yet his depiction suggests otherwise: "*It's not a man; it's* . . . definitely humanoid . . . face is different, something funny about the mouth, sort of pursed-up-looking . . . [the aliens are] not very hairy" (129; italics in original). The images of the "pursed-up" lips and hairless bodies certainly portray strong evidence of femininity, though Fromm—daunted by the aliens' strong human likeness—never confirms their genders. In comparison to their grotesquely large bodies, the aliens' feminine features further disrupt expectations associated with a "normal body." In *Staring: How We Look*, Rosemarie Thomson suggests that such an "interruption of expectations, of the visual status quo, attracts interest but can also lead to disgust" (37). Because extraordinary bodies "fascinate," they also "demand that we 'sneak a second look'" (W. Miller qtd. in Thomson, *Staring*, 37). But the lingering gaze also has the power to provoke shame, making the starer "vulnerable for indulging in such profligate and inappropriate looking" (43).[8] Indeed, improper staring has the power to provoke embarrassment within the vulnerable starer, for unrestrained looking connotes a failure to control impulses.

This phenomenon surfaces in the pivotal moment of Fromm's investigation. He considers "[taking] the robe off one of the creatures first, [to] make sure of their anatomy," yet grows oddly reluctant: "They were too human . . . it seemed as if it wasn't *fair* somehow to go poking around under their clothes" (130). As a form of "less intense shame" (Lewis, *Shame*, 82), Fromm's embarrassment is motivated not only by the possibility of *exposing* the aliens' sex (via the most intimate, "shameful" part of the body), but more specifically by the fear of "being caught" as The Exposer who simultaneously *reveals* and *stares*. If the "eye is the organ of shame par excellence" (Wurmser, "Shame," 67), then this scenario produces additional possibilities: by looking at the alien, Fromm casts the shameful gaze that marks the alien as other, yet there also exists the potential risk of his own exposure—that he, too, will be discovered and subsequently marked by his peers, thus judged for exhibiting "intractable curiosity."[9] Fromm's hasty exit is proof of his overwhelming embarrassment: "*Hell! Let Bolster do it!* [Fromm] left the ship" (Merril, "Whoever," 130). By passing the responsibility (the literal "dirty work") to the other officer, Fromm resists the full-scale shame associated with staring, which—like "watching" or voyeurism—constitutes a "dangerous activity" that "may be punished" (Wurmser, *Mask*, 28).

It is important to note that Fromm's embarrassment also stems from the failure to meet the standards placed upon him by the other crewmen. In this pivotal narrative moment, the "label of incompetence" hovers over Fromm as he is unable to decide specifically *how* to separate the aliens from the humans. Indeed, the traditional dichotomy between the human and the other, a "we" versus "them," is further complicated by the possibility of a female alien—a being which, by virtue of its human likeness, is familiar yet definitively other in its feminine, alien characteristics. Perhaps the most defining aspect of the aliens' otherness, however, is their embodiment of "feminine" emotions.

In *Rationalizing Genius,* John Huntington maintains that "women do not figure prominently" within the science fiction genre, and "the emotions they represent tend to be avoided" (111); however, when women move from the margins of the narrative to the center (as in Merril's works), these emotions operate at the narrative's core to illustrate a reality that exists beyond "reason." In a masculine environment where rationality reigns supreme, love operates as a discordant element that breeds suspicion. The narrative, itself, claims to be a "love story," though not in the traditional sense; rather it tells of "the greatest need and greatest fear men know" (Merril, "Whoever," 123). While aboard the alien ship, Bolster discovers a mysterious letter from George Gentile which reveals that their captain has committed suicide. Since there is "nobody to order [them] home" (132), Gentile and three other officers have chosen to stay behind on the alien planet, sending aliens back as their replacements. Most importantly, however, Gentile's letter details the aliens' overwhelming kindness and acceptance; he proclaims that they "just seem to love everybody, humans as well as their own kind" (132). It is precisely this "love"—this "irresistible psychological weapon," a defining aspect of the aliens' femininity—which fuels the growing paranoia among the crew members on Scanliter Six.

Their suspicion is further reinforced after Fromm and the other officers discover the deceased captain's log. From the log, the Scanliter officers learn that two of the captain's crewmen have succumbed to the aliens' hypnotism:

> [The aliens] have greeted us warmly, and have done nothing to indicate any hostility or to harm us in any way—nothing but walk off with two of my crew in an apparently friendly fashion . . . If I believed for a moment that Gentile and Tsin were

responsible for their own actions, I should not hesitate to [leave them behind]. But their behavior is so entirely "out of character" that I can see no explanation except that they are acting under some form of hypnotic control. (137–138)

The shame that surrounds Gentile and Tsin materializes as they fall victim not only to foreign beings, but to a foreign emotion (the ultimate "weapon" of manipulation). Their shame functions as a contagion that threatens to contaminate the men on Scanliter Six. In this sense, Gentile and Tsin's shame is particularly dangerous, for their *weakness* defies the very rationality on which the men pride themselves. A "trigger for shame," weakness is "the subjective sense of powerlessness . . . of inability to stand on one's own two feet" (Morrison, *Culture,* 49). More importantly, weakness—like love— "relates to shame through the experience of need," for "being 'needy'" (or the idea of "need itself") is "seen as a sign of weakness and shameful dependency" (49). What Gentile and Tsin's bizarre behavior indicates, then, is the overwhelming power of love over rationality, and the fact that these "reasonable" men were unable to overcome a "feeling" suggests the probability that other men could fall under the spell of love.

Xenophobia, shame, and love culminate in the narrative during a final meeting between the Scanliter officers. As the men agonize over how to protect themselves against the aliens' power, the Psychofficer brings these crucial issues to light:

I think the human race is too damn scared and too damn hungry to be able to face this thing. Hungry for security, for reassurance, for comfort—for love. And scared! Scared of anything different, anything Outside, anything one degree more intense than the rules allow. (Merril, "Whoever," 141)

Implicit in love is the additional threat of vulnerability, and as the crewmen's apprehension demonstrates, defiance of "the rules" in favor of "anything Outside" (the aliens and their love) leads to vulnerability, weakness, and shame. In terms of shame content, the theorist Léon Wurmser claims in addition that love—by virtue of being "equated with weakness, subjugation by and submission to another's power"—is "derided as unmanly" (*Mask,* 175).[10] As the Psychofficer alludes to "Man"-kind during his revelation, he verbally exposes the shameful truth: "We want love. We need love. Every poor blessed damned soul among us. And we need it so much, it can be used as a weapon against us!" (Merril, "Whoever," 141). Lucy Ardin—the PR Deputy and the only female aboard the ship—counters, "I'm not scared of it. Maybe you need love that bad, Psychofficer, but I don't" (142). Interestingly, Lucy is the only human not afraid of the alien "others," whereas the male crew members exhibit strong mistrust. For the Scanliter men, however, their pride is at stake.

In "The Shame/Pride Axis," Donald Nathanson explores the concept of shame and pride in relation to inferiority versus superiority. While efficacy produces pride, its opposite—failure—induces shame. Nathanson asserts, "Destruction by a rival produces shame reflecting a heightened sense of a defective self, a decrease in self image and self-esteem . . . [I]f I have been defeated by another person, I have been ranked among humans and therefore experience shame" (194). Because the alien is "more commonly a focus of hatred" (Huntington, 111), and a source of fear, the idea of a loving foreign being is incomprehensible and only further complicates the crewmen's expectations. Arguably, the "destruction" by the female rivals in "Whoever You Are" occurs through the obliteration of normative (masculine) reactions toward the alien other (as Gentile and Tsin effectively illustrate).

To protect themselves from the aliens, or from the shame of *falling in love with the other*, the Scanliter men must protect their pride by proving their mastery; yet the only way they can achieve domination over the aliens is, ironically, through violence. As Fromm continues his investigation of the rival ship, the destructive alien forces are at work, threatening to pull him over to the "other" side. One of the aliens awakens and begins to communicate with him telepathically. Fromm reports back to the other officers: "He wants me to . . . to *love* him . . . he loves me . . . he loves all men" (Merril, "Whoever," 145). Here, the contagious nature of stigma re-emerges as Fromm's rationality is destroyed; in his association with and acceptance of the aliens, he becomes stigmatized and must be killed to prevent the spread of shame. In a final attempt to secure their pride, the Scanliter officers resolve to detonate the rival ship and murder Fromm in the process. But the shame spurred by the aliens' femininity is too infectious, and as Fromm recalls the story of the orphan girl in his final moments—"I understand now, it's the way human beings love when they're kids, like the note the girl wrote: Whoever you are . . ."—the Psychofficer reacts with "tears of frustration" (145). The Commander is stoic, his face "stern and set," until he sees the Psychofficer's tears "rolling unashamed down [his] face," and in this key moment, the "single flash" (145) from the Commander's eyes reveals his fear. While the Commander's panic perhaps stems from the recognition that the aliens' love has contaminated his crew, his observation of the Psychofficer's "unashamed" tears calls attention to an additional dilemma: the fear of shame that previously worked to reinforce the officers' rationality vanishes while under the aliens' "love" spell. The result—an affiliation with the female other, and the subsequent *inability* to be affected by shame—is even more terrifying, and before Fromm can utter his last words, ". . . I love you" (145), the Commander orders the destruction of the alien ship. Reminiscent of Hank's act of murder in "That Only a Mother," the Commander's order works as a frantic attempt to maintain the divide between reason and emotion, a divide that, ironically, can only be sustained by the fear of shame affiliated with female otherness and the men's simultaneous awareness and rejection of this shame.

As a story that convolutes the generic metaphor of the hostile, emotionless alien, "Whoever You Are" is profound in its unique rendering of xenophobia and in its ability to disrupt narrative expectations.[11] A similar manifestation of the nontraditional female alien surfaces in "The Lady Was a Tramp" (1956). Anita Ford, the only woman aboard a merchant spaceship called *The Lady Jane,* exemplifies the alien other who must be "conquered" by the men on the ship. Although, in this sense, the narrative presents the traditional binary opposition between the "alien" and humans, which "reinforce[s] relations of dominance and subordination" (Wolmark, 31), the story explores the paradoxical desire for and rejection of the other.

The narrative follows Terry Carnahan, a former naval officer, during his assignment as an IBMan aboard *The Lady Jane*. At first ambivalent about the "tramp assignment" (Merril, "Lady," in *Homecalling*, 480) Terry begins to shift his focus to the bizarre dynamics between Anita and the other men. While Anita works as the medic, implications arise that she is also the crew's whore and, like the ship itself, she is referred to as "the tramp." Tensions rise as the competition among the men increases, and Terry's initial ambivalence toward the ship (and Anita) transforms into a full-fledged longing to conquer "her."

In an interesting rhetorical maneuver, the narrative voice overlaps descriptions of *The Lady Jane* to match Anita, so that by the story's end the two have merged so closely together that it is difficult to decipher which is the real "tramp." For Terry especially, *The Lady Jane* and Anita are so linked in his mind that he has difficulty differentiating between them. When Chan asks Terry how he likes "the old bitch," adding that "she may not look like much, but she's a hell of a mess of boat for five men to run" (484), Terry must remind himself that Chan is referring to the ship and not to Anita. Added to these depictions are the complicated notions of attraction and repulsion toward the lone, other woman—the "alien life form" (487) surrounded by five men.[12] Like the "scratched and dented" yet alluring *Lady Jane*, Anita—the "terrible wonderful blonde" (480)—taunts Terry, and he is plagued by his overwhelming desire to capture her. In his competition with the other men especially, Terry finds the prospect of the tramp assignment more appealing, and the once "potbellied, dumpy, unbeautiful" tramp he first observed—"squat[ing] without impatience inside the steel framework of supports, while her tanks were flushed and her tubes reamed clean" (475)—begins to show signs of beauty, but only for those who know "where to look" (486).

The story is fundamentally about a battle over otherness. Each of the men desires the other, and wants to be uniquely loved by her—for by conquering the other, one *wins*, moving up the ranks in a system of comparison. Yet, the converse side suggests that there is shame inherent in being the other, for being the other additionally implies exclusion and unlovability. This scenario poses a paradox: How can one simultaneously desire and reject otherness? In the particular example of the men aboard *The Lady Jane*, there is a narcissistic drive—a "yearning for absolute uniqueness and sole importance" (Morrison, *Shame*, 49)—that operates as a defense against shame, so while the men compete for the (chance of becoming uniquely) other, they also work against the threat of being marginalized as the scorned and ridiculed (outside) other.

Added to this avoidance of shame are the enactments of sexual scripts within the story, in which the men sexually "use" Anita to demonstrate their competence. In *Shame and Pride: Affect, Sex, and the Birth of the Self*, Donald Nathanson remarks that "sexual competence can either make us forget about other areas of inadequacy or at least make them seem less important for the moment" (358). Individuals who use sexual scripts as defenses against shame have usually "been so injured in the area of self-esteem that they see their conduct only as a victory over the shame of seeming undesirable" (358). In the "world of machismo" aboard *The Lady Jane,* the men have sex with Anita for the sole purpose of promoting their own "competence and personal pride" (358) and avoiding the shame of unlovability. The "hedonistic" environment of the ship—the crewmen are frequently drunk and naked—additionally serves to down-play "chronic shame and distress" (358).[13]

The stakes are high for Terry. Even if the "battered old hulk" is "all he [can] have" (Merril, "Lady," 489), he will still manage to keep his pride intact. Moreover, by pre-vailing over the other men, he will shed his original status as the "outside" (incom-petent) officer. First, Terry must demonstrate his competence by flying the *Lady* over the moon, but his seemingly proud moment is ruined five hours later, when one of the other men offers to take control of the ship. Anita extends her hand to help Terry out of the pilot's seat, and in a fit of rage, he calls her a "whore" and orders, "Get away, bitch!" (490). In Nathanson's "Shame/Pride Axis," curse words are part of the language of shame; such derogatory language is often indicative of low self-esteem and reveals feel-ings of weakness in moments of embarrassment (198). In this moment of narcissistic defeat, Terry's shame is brought to fruition, for he has been scorned and ridiculed by his crewmates—labeled *incompetent.*

To protect himself from further defeat and shameful rejection, Terry "claims" Anita:

> *Bitch!* he thought. *Tramp! You don't want me!*
> He let her lead him out of the room, down the ladder, through yellow-green, to the door where the light would be flashing red outside.
> And there he stopped. There was something important to ask her; when he found out what it was, he started to smile. *Which one do you want?*
> Which one? How could she possibly tell?
> As well ask, *Which one needs her?*
> He laughed and stepped forward . . . and the tramp was his. (Merril, "Lady," 491)

This final moment, permeated in shame language, is illustrative of the classic narcis-sistic defense against shame. Indeed, by claiming Anita, Terry regains his sense of uniqueness and "sole importance to someone else, a 'significant other'" (Morrison, *Shame,* 49). But his veil of shame wears thin, and the stigma of shameful dependency (*neediness*) unmistakably reveals itself.

The alien, in its various complicated forms, works to expose human fears about anything foreign, different, or outside. More importantly, as the different manifesta-tions of the female/feminized aliens demonstrate, our fear of the other not only stems from the fear of difference, but from the fear of *sameness*—the frightening possibility that the aliens embody the very human emotions we ourselves are too ashamed to reveal. Like the freak who serves as the "scorned misfit of our imagination" and has the compelling ability to "generate feelings of shame" within us (Morrison, *Culture*, 27), the alien speaks to our fears of stigma and shame. Yet, like the male characters in Merril's stories, our common response to the threat of shame is the desire for concealment. As readers placed at the center of the shame dramas in Merril's stories, we are encouraged to explore the complex dichotomies between hu(man) and other, reason and emotion, love and shame.

Notes

1. In *Feminism and Science Fiction*, Sarah LeFanu defines masculine concerns as those which center on themes of "space exploration and the development of technology"—"masculine . . . because access to these areas was effectively denied to women in the real world" (3). For further discussion, see Sarah LeFanu's introduction in *Feminism and Science Fiction* (Bloomington: Indiana University Press, 1989), 1–9.

2. See also Emily Pohl-Weary's "Judith Merril's Legacy" in Judith Merril, *Homecalling and Other Stories*, 7–9.

3. See Jane Donawerth, "Beautiful Alien Monster-Women," in *Frankenstein's Daughters: Women Writing Science Fiction*.

4. Thomson expands on this notion, claiming that the "modern eugenics movement, which arose from the mid-nineteenth-century scientific community, and its current counterpart, reproductive technology designed to predict and eliminate 'defective fetuses,' reveal a determination to eradicate disabled people" (*Extraordinary Bodies*, 34).

5. This stage is followed by one of anger and rage, then one of sadness, until parents finally enter the "coping" phase.

6. See Lewis's discussion of anger, rage, and shame in *Shame: The Exposed Self*, 152–153.

7. See John Huntington, "Reason and Love," in *Rationalizing Genius*.

8. See also Thomson, *Staring*, 43–44, for a discussion on Jean-Paul Sartre and inappropriate staring.

9. See also Thomson, *Staring*, 63–76, for a discussion on the cultural contradictions of staring.

10. See Wurmser's discussion of unconscious shame contents in *Mask of Shame*, 174–176.

11. See also Jenny Wolmark's "Unpredictable Aliens" in *Aliens and Others: Science Fiction, Feminism and Postmodernism*.

12. The narrative equates Anita with the alien life-forms Terry and Chan observe while in the ship's bio lab.

13. For further discussion, see Nathanson on hedonism in relation to shame avoidance in *Shame and Pride*, 313.

2 Rape, Trauma, and Shame in Samira Bellil's *Dans l'enfer des tournantes*

Nicole Fayard

Samira Bellil is known in France as the "courageous writer who forced France to confront the outrage of gang rape" (George, 29) with her best-selling autobiographical narrative *Dans l'enfer des tournantes* (*In Gang-Rape Hell*) (2002). *Dans l'enfer* narrates Bellil's experience of gender violence while she was growing up in the Paris *banlieue* in the late 1980s. She was first gang-raped at age fourteen when her boyfriend Jaïd handed her to the rest of his gang. Gang leader K. raped her again a month later; aged seventeen, she was gang-raped for the second time in Algeria. Bellil describes the shame and isolation that befall the rape victim, together with her experience of depression and substance abuse, followed by her recovery through therapy. On the one hand, the book works as a personal narrative written from the perspective of a young French woman of Algerian origin living in the marginalized space of the French *banlieue*.[1] On the other hand, *Dans l'enfer*'s declared aim to break the law of silence (305) is intended as a broader denunciation of the gender and sexual violence that, Bellil says, is endemic in some French *banlieues*. The text therefore also performs a social function whose aim may be to renegotiate the rape victim's perception of her self by testifying about her experience of abuse and shame.

In her acknowledgments Bellil refers to the people who contributed to her "rebirth" by helping her reconstruct her inner self. Phrases such as "merci [pour] m'avoir aidée à devenir une vraie personne" (thank you for helping me become a real person) and "son regard sur moi" (her unbiased opinion of me) (7) evoke sensitivity of the self to the value judgments of others as well as a logic of alienation. The suggestion is that inner conflict has been resolved thanks to recognition by significant others. Bellil's acknowledgments speak of support and love "quand j'en avais tant besoin" (when I needed it badly) (8), and thus introduce a circle of recognition that negates its counterpart, rejection and humiliation. The main focus of the narrative is on the rejection which threatens the subject's identity: on the next page the text is headed by the definition of the term "reputation" according to the *banlieue* "dictionary": "statut attribué à une personne par une bouche à oreille fulgurant, cette image indissociable de l'être qui, dans tous les cas, brise des vies; que tu sois un bandit, un bouffon ou une 'taspé des caves'" (status that someone acquires by word of mouth and at lightning speed. The label sticks and, in all cases, destroys lives, whether you are a crook, a clown, or a "slag" men rape in the basement of buildings) (9).

Bellil's association of shame with public loss of honor exemplifies Helen Merrell Lynd's claim in her pioneering study of shame that "shame is defined as a wound to one's self-esteem, a painful feeling or sense of degradation excited by the consciousness of having done something unworthy of one's previous idea of one's own excellence" (23–24). Shame arises from "a feeling of inferiority" (22), the painful consciousness of having "violated a prescribed code" (23). This includes private and public transgressions which expose the self to the contempt of respected others, and cause huge narcissistic injuries. In the narrative, shame arises out of the violation of gender codes which make women the guardian of rules of honor in the French *banlieue,* and the text demonstrates in apt ways that the trauma of rape cannot be separated from the experience of fear, blame, and shame which annihilates the victim's self. *Dans l'enfer* also problematizes this central theme insofar as it argues that the trauma of rape and shame also has to be envisaged from the perspective of an individual's sense of place in a given society. The value of the text is therefore to set the shame of rape in the specific context of the drama of inequality of women living in the *banlieue* and, following Helen Lynd, provide clues "for a person to find identifications with social groups in ways that mean not a losing but a finding of the self" (Lynd, 211).

In this chapter, I consider the narrative by deploying both a gender-based analysis together with a psychoanalytical approach to draw out ways in which shame as an emotion is linked to various inequalities of power (Lewis, "Role of Shame," 29). I consider in a second section the isolation and identity crisis that are triggered by the trauma of rape and the ensuing shame. Finally, I move on to a discussion of Bellil's representation of recovery through testifying and the creative act of writing. The text is a narrative of reparation, but also one of emancipation which enables the narrator to transcend shame and provide a social commentary. However, I also question the therapeutic virtue of such testimonies insofar as they are inseparable from the construction of rape through the experience of suffering and shame.

The Drama of Inequality

One major theme in Bellil's book is that recognition and intersubjective connection are central to the shame affect because shame involves the desire for approval by another (Lacan, 181) and is a reaction to loss of face when this relationship breaks down. Shame arises from the objectification of the subject (Sartre, 320). This entails that shame is disempowering and may explain why, as the clinician Helen Block Lewis has argued, it is the trauma of the disempowered. Lewis has demonstrated the links between shame and the subjection of women ("Introduction," 4), declaring that "women's greater sociability and lesser aggression, taken together with their second-class status in the world of power, increase their tendency to the experience of shame" ("Role of Shame," 29). She argues that women are socialized to look to others for self-validation, which makes them particularly vulnerable to shame and depression following the breakdown of a relationship or when they are devalorized. Bartky broadens Lewis's definition by pointing out that the personal inadequacy that is implied in shame connects with all logics of unequal social relations (84). Shame arises both from abuse (physical and emotional) and from rejection by judging, dominant others. Shame also strengthens the perceived authority of the shamers. Furthermore, Thomas Scheff has pointed out the role of shame in policing social interactions and its importance in community relations (*Microsociology*, 15). The framing of shame through its reliance on a network of dependence and domination is helpful because it enables the reader not to read the shame that arises from rape as "simply" a moral or psychological reaction to sexual abuse. Instead, I propose that we look at shame in *Dans l'enfer* as arising from a logic of unequal social and sexual relations.

In this respect, I would argue that shame in the text simultaneously ensues from the manifold subordination endured by women who grow up in the French *banlieues*. This agenda brings together the personal and the social dimensions of Bellil's text: according to Elizabeth Fallaize, contemporary Francophone women's writing, "with its sense that the personal is political and its desire to address areas of women's experience previously ignored or fantasized in literature, was always likely to deal with autobiographical issues" (23). Despite being written with the help of an editor, *Dans l'enfer* fits neatly within this definition: it was marketed as an autobiographical testimony and corresponds to Philippe Lejeune's classic definition of autobiography (14). The interrogation of memory, agency and identity in the text, which is written in the first person, seems to place it into the category of life writing. The narrator, "Sam," is nominally identified with the author as "Samira" at the end of the book. In accordance with Fallaize's statement, this highly personal account puts forward a strong political agenda as Bellil focuses on the tensions to which young women of minority ethnic descent are confronted through family traditions and, more recently, in the marginalized spaces of the French *banlieues,* which are constructed as loci of male domination. She claims that women are expected to conform to a number of cultural and social scripts and that their autonomy and sexuality are policed and controlled: freedom of choice is limited in relation to marriage and divorce, education and career, movements, clothing, and friendships. In recent years, as Bellil illustrates, young women have suffered new pressures from their male peers, who, as Alec Hargreaves declares, "have sought to compensate for the social exclusion suffered in the face of majority ethnic racism by violent assertions of power over minority ethnic women," with the violence ranging from "intimidation and force designed to police the virginity of sisters, cousins and neighbors" to gang rape (46).

As in many male-dominated societies, strict codes of honor in the *banlieue* divide women into two arbitrary groups: the virgin and the whore. The female who departs from the prescribed honor scripts is seen as out of place (Hargreaves, 55). The narrator transgresses traditional roles by drinking, wearing makeup, smoking, and having sex with her boyfriend, and she holds a discourse of equality between men and women from the outset. Thus the text introduces in its early sections the theme of alienation: Sam is portrayed as emotionally isolated in her strict and stifling family environment, and she has difficulties reconciling the values of her Maghrebi heritage with the French values with which she identifies. Her isolation partly originates from a family secret, as her father did time in prison when she was a child and she was fostered in Flanders, a temporary spatial and linguistic shift which comes to symbolize her estrangement. This is a shaping aspect of the narrative as this hidden past and the wounds brought about by the father's incarceration become a vehicle for the tensions between her parents' values and her "rêves de liberté" (dreams of freedom) (Bellil, 24). These tensions are visited on the child, who becomes the scapegoat for parental mortification.

Bellil's depiction of inadequate parenting provides two examples of conflict from which the self is likely to derive shame. Firstly, according to Wurmser, shame ensues from a "primary conflict" which is dual in nature: the self feels overpowered by the object it wants to control; the self also wants to be loved by the other, but encounters indifference (*Mask of Shame,* 158–159). In Sam's case, as her twin demands for love and power (to be strong in the face of her father's hostility) are defeated, she develops a sense of her unlovability which triggers shame-anxiety. Secondly, Sam breaches the family code of honor by going out as well as by being raped; contradictory loyalties have therefore become diametrically divergent for her and her parents, and, as Wurmser puts it, "contradictory views of what is honourable and shameful emerge" (34). Her father's condemnation of her behavior causes massive narcissistic injuries and shame ensues.

According to Silvan Tomkins, to live with shame is to feel alienated and defeated; it is felt as "an inner torment, a sickness of the soul. [The humiliated one feels] naked, defeated, alienated, lacking in dignity and worth" (*Affect, Imagery, Consciousness,* 2:118). Bellil's work illustrates pertinently the ways in which the shamed subject internalizes the negative judgment of others, which can initiate a devastating assault on self-esteem. Bellil describes this breaking up of the self as her parents' cold hostility causes Sam to feel "rejetée. Inutile. Sale. Coupable. Je me fais toute petite, je fais le moins de bruit possible" (rejected. Useless. Dirty. Guilty. I shrink, I am as quiet as possible) (80).

The self can protect itself by using defense strategies such as fight or flight reactions. Lewis defines the former as "humiliated fury" used to deflect further scorn or ridicule from shaming others by "turning the tables." Flight reaction is less aggressive: "'One could crawl through a hole.' Or 'sink through the floor' or 'die' with shame" ("Role of Shame," 41–42). Sam withdraws from parental scorn and reterritorializes[2] herself in other environments, including the liminal space of the street. She also displaces herself within the male-dominated gangs of the *banlieue,* which become an idealized source of recognition.

Problematically, in gang culture the value hierarchy based on the honor and shame polarity is reproduced (Wurmser, *Mask of Shame,* 34); supporting Hargreaves's views, the text makes the point that one of the punishments visited on the female who breaches the codes of honor, especially when she is perceived to be sexually autonomous, is rape: "les filles . . . étaient la proie des bandes et subissaient leur violence dans la honte et le secret. L'habitude était de 'serrer des meufs' ou de les 'faire tourner'" (the gangs . . . preyed on the girls, who suffered their violence in shame and secrecy. It was common practice to rape the girls or pass them around like parcels among the gang) (53). Of all types of rape, gang rape has an enormous symbolic impact, now as in the past. Currently the media are particularly responsible for spreading the myth that gang rape occurs mainly in the *banlieue* (Mucchielli). However, gang rapes are not a new social phenomenon. They occur in all social milieus and are not infrequent: about 10 percent of all convicted rapes are gang rapes. Bellil's portrayal of gang rape makes it clear that gang rape is above all about male domination, not about deprivation or ethnicity. Sam's rapes are orchestrated according to power and honor-shame structures that intersect with the values of territory, hierarchy, and solidarity between men characteristic of gang culture (Hamel, 91). Sam's first gang rape is sanctioned by both boyfriend Jaïd and gang leader K. The youths construct their sexuality on models of unequal sexual encounters in which violence is the norm and women are viewed as objects and scapegoats for the men's own sense of sexual shame. The rapists blame Sam for their own impotence: "'Tu m'fais pas bander, sale pute!' me dit-il, et il me force à y remédier" ("You're not making me stiff, dirty slag!" he says, and forces me to remedy the problem) (Bellil, 34). In the youths' interaction with women, rape is therefore a way for the dominant to mark out their territories and assert their domination over those perceived as weaker, leading the rapist to believe in the normalization of gang rape (Hamel, 85–92).

The narrative consequently presents Sam as the ultimate victim. She becomes her family's scapegoat as her mortified parents rid themselves of their own shame at her expense. Her sense of inferiority experienced out of the trauma of parental rejection exacerbates her vulnerability as a female in the *banlieue.* The environment in which she withdraws is structured according to an honor-shame polarity that perpetuates gender domination and sexual violence. The consequence of the continuing pattern of abuse and alienation for the victim is the destruction of her sense of self.

Trauma and Shame

Within the wider debates on trauma and sexual violence, the experience of extreme physical or mental abuse is characterized by a wound which returns to haunt the survivor years later. This is why there is a paradoxical relationship between survival and destructiveness in trauma survivors (Caruth, 58) which comes to the fore in *Dans l'enfer* and connects with the networks of power and domination that trigger shame. The greatest challenge for Bellil's narrator is that the trauma of rape has left injuries to her sense of self which have shattered her identity. The wound of trauma and the dishonor of rape are reinforced by the anxiety triggered by the fear of exposure and the shaming procedures (contempt and rejection) that might follow. According to Lynd, "experiences of shame appear to embody the root meaning of the word—to uncover, to expose, to wound. They are experiences of exposure, exposure of peculiarly sensitive, intimate, vulnerable aspects of the self" (21–34). Behind shame stands the frightening experience of the isolation triggered by the break of trust: "the experience of shame is itself isolating, alienating, incommunicable" (67). Following Lynd and Julia Kristeva, who states that shame erases the power of the signifier, Bellil's writing of rape is structured around the motif of breakdown in communication. The act of rape itself cannot be communicated or written onto the page. It can only be expressed in "faire des trucs" (doing things) (Bellil, 34) as the victim cannot convey what was done to her: "[J]e n'ai pas les mots. . . . [R]ien ne sort de ma bouche" (I don't have the words. . . . Nothing comes out of my mouth) (162). Trauma and shame both cause the self to hide. The narrator withdraws by repudiating her violated body and leaving it behind, describing herself as estranged from herself: "Je m'enferme dans un trou noir, un grand vide . . . Mon corps ne m'appartient plus, peut-être est-il mort?" (I retreat into a black hole, a void . . . My body no longer belongs to me, maybe it is dead?) (35). The description of the rape victim as estranged from the world and the self brings together the alienation and fragmentation of the self that are germane to both the experience of trauma and shame-anxiety. Following her first rape, the narrator states: "[J]e suis là, la bouche cousue par la peur, la honte et la culpabilité. Je ne dirai rien" (I sit here, mute with fear, shame and guilt. I don't tell anyone) (43). Rape silences the self because it exposes the victim to censure from others.

If to feel shame is to feel seen and exposed, then shame acts as a powerful mechanism of social and internal sanction insofar as it causes the self to internalize injunctions about specific behaviors by identification with the shamer whose value judgments it cares about (Kaufman, *Psychology of Shame,* 195). For Helen Block Lewis, this leads to a "doubleness of experience"; as the self is concerned about being rejected (because rejection causes shame), the ego is divided between an observer and an observed self—a shamer and a shamed self ("Shame and the Narcissistic Personality," 107). Bellil shows the extent to which shame "can be an instrument of oppression and conformity . . . as the community identifies and persecutes its scapegoats" (Hirsh, 84). The text exposes the conflict experienced by the self as the narrator is constantly shifting from the shame of exposure to self-blame. This is represented through the dividing of Sam's self between observed and observer of her own behavior. The observer of Sam's behavior can be likened to the omnipresent gaze of social sanction: "Dans les yeux des gens je lis à livre ouvert . . . C'est de ma faute" (People's eyes are like an open book in which I read

. . . It's my fault) (Bellil, 134). Following exposure the victim becomes an object of deep interest, "un animal traqué" (a hounded animal) (142), which causes her to supervise her own behavior as she internalizes the values of her shamers: "Comment aurais-je pu ressentir pour moi un peu de positif alors que mes parents me renvoyaient une image si noire, si sale? J'avais totalement fait mienne l'image qu'ils avaient de moi" (How could I have felt anything remotely positive about myself when my parents saw me as so debased, so dirty? I completely made my own the image they had of me) (100). Her divided self—before and following the rapes—explains why the victim colludes with her aggressors as she puts herself at risk of further assaults.

The second step in the shaming script is to shun the scapegoat. The narrative closely associates the shame of rape with a discourse of discipline and punishment for the victim (rather than for the rapists). Wurmser notes that contempt shown by others degrades the subject, "equating him particularly with a debased, dirty thing—a derided and low animal" (*Mask of Shame*, 81). The shamed subject is "discarded from the communality of civilized society" (82), and Bellil describes the cycle of rejection and its consequences, which include the transfer of blame to the victim. Sam's complaints of rape are met with incredulity; following her official complaint, she is ostracized and exiled by her community, including former female allies, who blame her: "[S]i je n'ai rien dit, c'est que j'étais consentante" (In their eyes, if I didn't say anything, it's because I wanted it) (43). Bellil also argues that the gaze cast by the legal system on complainants acts as a powerful shaming agent. For example, Sam's (female) lawyer challenges her, surprised she was out late at night at the age of fourteen. Sam's third rape (and the second gang rape), in Algeria, is normalized by the local police because she had already lost her virginity. In the shaming gaze of the phallocentric structure which mirrors the rapists' sexist reference system, the raped body becomes an object of abjection and the victim is envisaged as a potential temptress or an object of contempt. The text shows how shame acts as a social regulator, which reinforces the authority of the shamers. In the case of rape, one of its roles is to serve as a warning to other women in the community.

This also participates in the common strategy whereby the raped woman who denounces her aggressors is accused of threatening the cohesion of the community and of victimizing the men from the *banlieues*. In her analysis of gang rape Sam explains: "[L]es violeurs se considèrent comme des victimes, ils sont les 'à plaindre' . . . parce qu'ils ont été 'donnés'" (The rapists see themselves as victims, they are the "heroes" that should arouse compassion . . . because they have been "grassed on") (56). Meanwhile the suffering of the victim can be dismissed, and the logic of domination that makes rape permissible is preserved. Shame is shown to be fundamentally objectifying and disempowering for the rape victim: when the woman's voice is silenced, generally her consent to sex is implicitly assumed, and the female is posited as a natural victim. *Dans l'enfer* therefore demonstrates that the incommunicability of shame extends to rape as the survivor's own status as the victim of a serious crime is negated in subtle ways. Sam reports her first two rapes to the police only following the entreaty of friends who have also been raped by K. Her initial silence is consistent with the behavior of the majority of rape victims in France, where only 12 percent of adult female victims report rape to the police (Bauer, 5).[3] In Sam's case the revelation of rape and of her relationship with Jaïd bring a particular form of dishonor, pointedly signified by the angry silence of the father: "Chez les musulmans, ne plus être vierge pour une jeune fille est un sacrilège et je sais que mon père pourrait me tuer pour cela" (It is a sacrilegious act for a Muslim girl to have lost her virginity. I know my father could kill me for this) (Bellil, 69). The trope of shame thus constructs rape as the ultimate form of violence against the female subject of minority ethnic descent.

In Sam's case shame is internalized. The narrative depicts the emotions and defenses that characterize the shame that accompanies exposure of the rape trauma: the self-blame, the self-loathing and self-disgust, the desire to hide, as well as humiliated rage. To deal with her shame, Sam feels the need to empty the body her rapists forcibly have penetrated: "Je voudrais les vomir et me vomir moi-même" (I would like to vomit them and vomit myself as well) (34), she says of her rapists. Shame and rage are embodied by the narrator, leading to a range of conditions (epilepsy, phlebitis, a broken ankle, vomiting, and diarrhea), self-harming, and a suicide attempt. Sickness and attempted suicide are also withdrawal strategies as the victim attempts to defend herself against shame and regain some control. Her rage turns against the self and causes fight and flight reactions (see the earlier discussion). First, in a classic attack scenario, Sam erects a wall of control around herself by showing aggression toward others, partying hard, drinking and taking drugs in order to silence her pain. Fight is also shown to combine with flight as Sam avoids one source of suffering by running away from home, first taking up with her new boyfriend, and then settling temporarily in shelters. Sam's desire for parental recognition causes her to keep coming back home and being confronted with further incomprehension: "Mon père m'ignore . . . Je rode comme un fantôme, personne ne me voit. On me laisse me décomposer comme une merde" (My father ignores me . . . I roam about like a ghost, no one seems to see me. They let me break down like a piece of shit) (168), leading to her depression.

Why, then, does Sam keep returning home? The conflict between Sam's need for recognition by significant others and her fear of their shaming gaze may go some way toward explaining this behavior. Tomkins contends that one draws upon familiar memories to respond to difficult, intolerable emotions, causing one to repeat familiar scenarios, however negative (*Affect, Imagery, Consciousness,* 96). He cites the triangular scene as an example because "the male child who loves his mother excessively can neither totally possess her (given an unwanted rival) nor totally renounce her. He is often destined, however, to keep trying and, characteristically, to keep failing" (96). When Tomkins's theory is applied to Sam's situation, she seems locked into a masochistic cycle of repetition: her compulsion to elicit forms of recognition her parents are unable to provide partly explains why she is drawn back home where rape cannot be spoken and shame poses a threat to her identity. Paradoxically, healing comes from the violated body of the survivor herself as the narrator's sick body acts as the language of trauma.

Transcending the Incommunicability of Shame

In the context of victims of the Holocaust, psychiatrist Dori Laub argues that victims of trauma need to tell their stories in order to survive (78). Finding a listener—a witness where there was not one before—enables them to be recognized as subjects (85, 82). This is why testifying in *Dans l'enfer* becomes an instrument of liberation and recognition, as well as a critical activity. The embodiment of trauma is first of all what leads the narrator in *Dans l'enfer* to transcend shame as, paradoxically, the sick body provides a language which attempts to communicate the break-up of the self: "[M]es crises [d'épilepsie] deviennent un nouveau mode d'expression . . . La pression de mes émotions bloquées se libère et tout le monde s'occupe enfin de moi" (My epileptic fits become a new mode of expression . . . My emotions are released and everyone is looking after me at last) (119). The language of the sick body, however, is not devoid of problems. Sam recounts how the diagnosis of illness strikes relief in her parents: "Mon père me parle enfin! . . . Il peut plus facilement venir vers une 'folle' que vers une 'violée'" (My father is talking to me at last! . . . He finds it easier to approach a woman who is mad than one who's been raped) (171). The attempt to turn her complaint into a problem that can be treated corroborates Arthur Frank's belief that "society prefers medical diagnoses that admit treatment, not social diagnoses that require massive change in the premises of what that social body includes as part of itself" (113). Bellil shows that when the problem is turned into a medical one, the larger, social problem of society's attitude to rape goes unnoticed, thus further naturalizing rape and the shame of rape.

I would argue, however, that the introduction of the language of sickness to discuss the raped female body is helpful, as it enables Bellil's testimony to place the body of the rape survivor at the very center of the debate. In this section, I will argue that by talking back, the wounded body provides the narrator with forms of recognition which had been removed by normalized responses to rape and shame. It is this recognition which, paradoxically, enables Sam to repair her shattered identity and enables Bellil to contest social norms by bringing the issue of gang rape into the public arena.

There are two significant ways in which Bellil engages with social norms. First, *Dans l'enfer* transcends the incommunicability of shame by identifying the intervention of language (bodily and verbal) as the source of survival of the self. This is achieved in three stages as the narrator breaks the veil of silence through psychotherapy, by testifying (and being heard) in a final court case, and, in particular, via the writing of her life story. Putting shame into words enables Bellil to name shame and engage with the origins of the shame scripts. This is of central importance because, for the subject, being able to name the problem makes it exist. For Kaufman, the aim of psychotherapy is to help the subject "[re-own] disowned parts of the self" (*Psychology of Shame*, 211). For Sam, psychotherapy leads first of all to the reclaiming of her dislocated body: "[D]ès les premières consultations, mon corps a répondu. Il s'est d'abord vidé complètement par des vomissements et des selles intenses" (From the very first sessions my body responded. First of all it completely emptied itself via intense vomiting and bowel movements) (Bellil, 266). The materiality of the body re-invests the excluded, abjected body with meanings of its own. Kaufman's analysis is thus further upheld as the narrator's recovery is experienced as a purging and a cleansing of the body in a process of rejection of the critical injunctions and the reclaiming of the body leads to the reclaiming of the self. Psychotherapy in Bellil is described as a life-giving experience: "[J]e me sens vivante . . . [C]'est mon moi intérieur qui se reconstruit pas à pas" (I feel alive . . . My inner self is rebuilding itself step by step) (260).

Second, Sam's acquisition of a new language of self-respect (Kaufman, *Psychology of Shame*, 263) is facilitated by the writing of her book. Life writing provides opportunities for the creation of new, self-affirming identity scripts. Bellil's narrator claims that "c'est de ma propre vérité qu'il s'agit dans ce livre" (what's written in the book is my own truth) (300). This truth is described as arising out of the desire to communicate to her entourage the role they have played in her suffering (300). The writing of the survivor's "truth," then, is a therapeutic exercise designed to release the shamed self from the influence of the community of shamers. Wurmser has also stated that creative acts can help rid individuals of shame as they provide opportunities for recognition (*Mask of Shame*, 293). In the final pages of the text Bellil's narrator corroborates this claim by stating: "Grâce au livre, je pense avoir retrouvé une dignité . . . Je n'ai plus à utiliser ma carte d'identité de victime, j'existe maintenant autrement. Je suis Samira" (Thanks to the book, I think I have regained my dignity . . . I no longer have to define myself as a victim, I have come into my own. I am Samira) (304). By rejecting the othering at work in the shaming processes, writing enables the narrator to emerge both as a subject and as a survivor of rape rather than an objectified victim. This also involves creating a new identity for herself as the author of the testimony as she also renegotiates family and community relations: "Peut-être [mes parents] me tourneront-ils le dos à tout jamais. Je suis prête à en prendre le risque" (Maybe [my parents] will turn their back on me forever. I am ready to take this risk) (300). Testifying thus involves a fundamentally critical activity (Felman, 206) with personal as well as, potentially, social consequences.

By redefining the victim's voice, *Dans l'enfer* embraces a wider social debate about gang rape in the French *banlieue*. In so doing the text also puts the ethnic-minority female subject as protagonist at the core of feminist reflection on sexual violence in contemporary France. The narrative of reparation serves as a narrative of emancipation and, as such, is representative of a growing corpus of works by women authors of immigrant descent who, since the 1980s, have given a voice to women living in France's *banlieues* and the descendants of immigrants, through autobiographies situating ethnic-minority women in narratives of victimhood. Since the year 2000 these accounts have raised awareness about the deteriorating conditions of women in the *banlieues,* with a particular focus on sexual violence and so-called "honor crimes" against women.[4] Although the idea of a woman "speaking out" is not new, *Dans l'enfer,* a commercial success, had a considerable impact because Bellil was said to be the first victim of gang rape to write under her own name (Hargreaves, 49) and because her text came to be regarded as "un révélateur des violences exercées contre les filles dans les cités" (revealing the violence done to women in the *banlieues*) ("Samira Bellil"). It thus became, as Alec Hargreaves observes, "emblematic of a more general 'social phenomenon'" (49).[5] Another reason is Bellil's active involvement, following publication of her book, in the *Marche des femmes des quartiers pour l'égalité et contre le ghetto* (a demonstration linking twenty-three towns against the abuse of women in the French *banlieues*), which took place in the spring of 2003, and with Ni Putes ni Soumises (NPNS),[6] a victim support group which at the time received a significant amount of media attention for defending the rights of women of minority ethnic descent in the *banlieues.* The strength of the text therefore lies in this political engagement though personal testimony, primarily because writing provides the narrator with the witnesses and recognition that shame had removed.

The narrator states that she decided to publish a book out of a desire to "atteindre la société dans son ensemble, briser cette loi du silence qui nous fait tant souffrir et avec laquelle nous avons accepté de vivre depuis trop longtemps" (reach the whole of society, break the law of silence which hurts us so much and which we have accepted for too long) (305). This statement exemplifies one way in which the narrative acts as an instrument of contestation of normalized attitudes about gang rape in the *banlieues* and rape in general, as well as engaging with the ways trauma and shame affect rape victims. Moreover, Helen Lynd has argued that the sharing of the experience of shame might provide ways of bringing the disempowered together: "What is directed against a group as a label of shame can be converted into a mark of honor, and the group itself gains in strength" (66). By addressing her book "à mes frangines de galère pour qu'elles sachent qu'on peut s'en sortir" (to my sisters in hell to let you know you can get out of it) (7), Bellil implies that it is intended to function as a narrative of empowerment for a community of fellow sufferers in similar marginal positions. The publication of her experiences works as a means of overturning her "reputation" and dishonor by playing out the mechanisms of violence against women. This critical activity is extended to descriptions of the narrator's involvement in political activism and her militant discourse about women's rights to suggest the recognition of women supporting other women and of potential alliances on the basis of shared sexual abuse. The appeal to an imagined sisterhood in the quotation above signals both political (feminist?) engagement and solidarity. An afterword recalls Ni Putes ni Soumises's manifesto, ultimately transforming the text into a powerful political document. The book ends with what is almost a call to arms, enjoining women to be "[t]outes prêtes et décidées à essayer d'arrêter la gangrène de souffrance qui ronge nos banlieues et nous enferme dans un ghetto mental" (ready and determined to try and stop the canker of suffering which wears down our *banlieues* and traps us into a mental ghetto) (307).

Consequently, in the text, revealing one's experiences of total subjugation and enjoining other women to testify against gang rape, including the shaming structures that cause them to be silenced, may help form a community of fellow sufferers who also refuse to be blamed for the violence they endure, hence making real change possible.

* * *

Writing, then, is empowering and an act of rebellion. It is conducive to a freeing of the self (Bellil, 301–302), a catalyst to the breaking of the barriers of shame and alienation: "C'est seulement à ce prix que je pouvais retrouver ma dignité" (It was at this price only that I could regain my dignity) (301).

Self-affirmation through writing is not without risks. The public exposure of the self through testimony inevitably (re)introduces the other into the text and leaves the subject open to vulnerability. This is indirectly acknowledged through various anecdotes and appeals to reader empathy with strategies of suspense and interpellation. More disturbingly, the text has also been attacked for disempowering women. Alec Hargreaves has argued against the possibility of women authors of Maghrebi descent in France, including Bellil, speaking outside of hegemonic representations and dynamics of subordination. I agree with Hargreaves that a huge industry is being built around such testimonies. This, he claims, leads to the subordination of the author's voice to commercial and ideological interests, in part because some of the texts are co-authored by hegemonic intermediaries (42). Another consequence is that this position may cause the texts to circulate dominant discourses in French culture that give a stereotyped or negative image of Maghrebi culture. In particular, the positions developed in narratives of emancipation such as Bellil's have been criticized for either stigmatizing women who fail to conform to the feminist ideal they promote (A. Kemp), or for victimizing young men of minority ethnic descent in the *banlieues* (Mucchielli). However, when one accuses women who speak about their abuse of stigmatizing men, one risks fudging the issues and condoning the hierarchies of violence. All that remains is the logic of shame and blame, which is akin to colluding with the perpetrators of gang rape who put pressure on their victims not to report the crime (Hamel; Bellil).

A number of narratives of victimhood make sexual violence and domination a core consideration. This locates them within a Foucauldian tradition of confession about sexuality (Foucault, *Histoire de la Sexualité*) with the aim of giving a public dimension to practices nowadays viewed as intolerable. This works in two ways for the women who situate their experiences in the public sphere. On the one hand, it can be argued that the texts' claim to authenticity and their declared intention to speak for all women may sit uncomfortably with post-colonial authors who are often reluctant to be seen as spokespersons for an entire community. This includes the support of activist support groups such as Ni Putes ni Soumises which made female victims, including Bellil, into figureheads for their movement and iconic symbols of empowerment.[7] There is a risk that presenting female victims as representative of other dominated women might essentialize and objectify them (Lazreg, 89). On the other hand, the discourse of victimization and the blame-shame paradigm inherent in the texts also risks rewriting ethnic-minority Frenchwomen as perpetual victims. The back cover of *Dans l'enfer* presents the author as "une rescapée" (a survivor) but also as a "victime" (victim) and "détruite" (broken up), and it highlights "la torture que subissent ces filles" (the torture suffered by these young women). Bellil is made into an exemplar for her "'frangines' victimes" (sisters in victimhood), a Madonna-like role which traps the rape survivor into the very image of pain and sacrifice from which Sam, in *Dans l'enfer*, is shown to have escaped by rewriting her identity scripts.

Bellil's testimony therefore reveals its complex nature. Despite the critical function of the testimony, there may be times when it will be difficult for ethnic-minority Frenchwomen to speak for themselves without their voices being re-appropriated by dominant discourses. However, the discourse of emancipation is first and foremost premised on women gaining agency by transcending their silencing. Sam could not be clearer when she exclaims: "Puisqu'on n'a jamais voulu m'écouter, on va me lire" (Since no one wanted to listen to me, they will read me) (299). I have also argued that writing is an innovative way for the victim to transcend the incommunicability of shame and convey her suffering. The all-important purpose of life writing for Samira is to "laisser une trace" (leave a trace behind) (280)—whatever the mode of writing—in order to reflect a lived reality in the fight against contemporary sexual violence. Irrespective of promotional strategies, therefore, inscribing rape into discourse still permits the critique of ideology. As Sunder Rajan (78) argues, "for women to 'speak' rape is itself a measure of liberation, a shift from serving as the object of voyeuristic discourse to the occupation of a subject-position as 'master' of narrative." With *Dans l'enfer des tournantes*, Samira Bellil testifies to her ability to overcome shame and trauma and is able to voice her new self.

Notes

1. The *banlieues* have traditionally been seen as areas of riots where male youths originating from multi-ethnic impoverished communities face problems of integration, exclusion, and racism (Jazouli, 1992). There is no suitable English alternative to the French term. For instance, "inner-city neighborhoods" does not apply to the multi-ethnic and multicultural "sink estates" found in the French "suburbs."

2. I am borrowing the concept of reterritorialization from Deleuze and Guattari (195–198). The concept of deterritorialization evokes another form of estrangement and violation from the subject's trusted environment.

3. This is based on a survey of victims aged 18–60 conducted for the years 2005 and 2006.

4. See for instance Leïla, *Mariée de force* (Paris: Oh! Editions, 2004) and Jamila Aït-Abbas, *La Fatiha: Née en France, mariée de force en Algérie* (Paris: Michel Lafon, 2003). Fadela Amara's *Ni Putes ni Soumises* provides an analysis of this degradation.

5. Publication of *Dans l'enfer* coincided with the murder of Sohane Benziane, who was burned alive in Vitry-sur-Seine in October 2002 for refusing the advances of her suitor. Sohane's murder was a trigger for the *Marche des femmes* in 2003.

6. This involvement is described in Bellil's afterword to the 2003 edition of the book, which is the edition used in this chapter. See Fayard and Rocheron on NPNS's campaigns.

7. Bellil was one of NPNS's Mariannes. NPNS's campaign *"Mariannes d'aujourd'hui: Hommage des femmes des cités à la République"* involved suspending the photographs of thirteen young women from the *banlieues* wearing the Phrygian cap, symbol of the Republic, across the front of the French National Assembly.

3 A Bloody Shame

Angela Carter's Shameless Postmodern Fairy Tales

Suzette A. Henke

IN HER SHORT story collection *The Bloody Chamber*, Angela Carter has re-appropriated the fairy-tale genre in the interests of feminist fantasy. Once an elusive emanation of oral and literary tradition, the so-called "bedtime story" was confiscated by male authors like Charles Perrault (whose work Carter translated in 1977) and the brothers Grimm, all of whom had the lessons of moral education on their aesthetic agendas. A compendium of cautionary tales about shame and retribution, these male-inscribed parables invariably reinforced sex-role stereotypes of male prowess and female vulnerability. They set out to instill conservative standards of behavior in society by projecting nightmare emanations of shameful libidinal passions: big bad wolves, man-eating tigers, and most of all, duplicitous husbands who would capitally punish curious or disobedient wives.[1]

Angela Carter has rewritten these narratives in a startling, bold, provocative feminist register offering "the beginnings of new stories" inspired by her "quarreling furiously with Bettelheim" (Haffenden, 83–84). Throughout *The Bloody Chamber*, Carter deliberately defeats the reader's expectations by emancipating women's bodies from attributions of cultural shame, empowering women characters with independence and agency, and bitterly denouncing the arrogant cruelty of human predators. As Cristina Bacchilega reminds us, Carter's emancipatory fabulations "hold mirrors to the magic mirror of the fairy tale" and make the shame-laden category of female gender the "privileged place for articulating these de-naturalizing strategies" (23–24). Carter self-consciously refracts conventional categories of shameful corporeality associated with the female body's vulnerability to sexual penetration, parasitic colonization, and erotic humiliation. As J. Brooks Bouson notes, "to be made of female flesh is to be well-schooled in the abjections and humiliations of embodiment" (*Embodied Shame*, 1). Subject to the cultural shame of abjection through the implicit contamination of menstrual blood, as well as through embryonic life bleeding beyond the legal boundaries of patriarchy, the shameless body of pornographic pleasure both eludes and defies the law and the word of the Father.

Carter sets the stage for her emancipated hussies when she describes, in *The Sadeian Woman,* her vision of the oxymoronic "moral pornographer" who "might use pornography as a critique of current relations between the sexes" and focus on the "total demystification of the flesh and the subsequent revelation . . . of the real relations of man and his kind. Such a pornographer would not be the enemy of women . . . [and] might begin to penetrate to the heart of the contempt for women that distorts our culture" (19–20). A "male-dominated culture," Carter argues, "produces a pornography of universal female acquiescence. Or, most delicious titillation, of compensatory but spurious female dominance" (20). Carter's Sadeian strategies suggest a scathing critique of the shaming ideologies that tend to shape female identities in Western culture and to validate the contemptuous scopophilic gaze turned inward, by women, against the developing self. As Susan Bordo explains, binary constructions of Cartesian dualism invariably confine woman to the essentialist role of anatomical body—brute, savage, animal, and infantile, "dominated by appetite" (5) and carnally contaminated. Carter's heroines defiantly reject such mortifications and refuse to be defined intrapsychically by the judgmental gaze of an antagonistic other. Through laughter and disavowal, they shamelessly eschew the endopsychic interiorization of a hostile interpersonal regard intended to evince guilt, diminishment, humiliation, or self-loathing.

In this chapter, I have tried to reclaim the word "shameless" to connote, in the tradition of Mary Daly's *Wickedary,* woman's bold assertion of emancipatory strategies of autonomy and self-esteem. Merja Makinen argues that Carter's textual uses of violence succeed "in exploding the stereotypes of women as passive, demure ciphers" (9). According to Bacchilega, *The Bloody Chamber* achieves "a woman-centered reciprocal dynamics of storytelling" that "complicates any either/or, inside/outside construction of gendered identity" (70). Carter's provocative fabulations disgorge female life narratives that expose the corrosive "phallacy" of Oedipal enthrallment. Her work cannily implies that if heteronormative culture sanctions the tacit prostitution of women on the market, then all erotic discourse involves "pornography"—i.e., "writing about whores."[2]

In *The Bloody Chamber,* Carter deliberately sets out to dismantle the Western cultural imbrication of the complicitous female body into the "triad of weakness, defectiveness, and dirtiness" that Léon Wurmser identifies with the masks of sexual shame (*Mask of Shame,* 98). Carter performs the function of a "moral pornographer" determined to endow women with agency and self-esteem in a society whose behavioral paradigms are predicated on sadomasochistic debasement in the service of rape and so-called "romantic" seduction. What if such sex-role stereotypes were challenged by a feminist program that renounced the shaming function of cultural mores and insisted on woman's empowerment through a carnivalesque riot of bestial *jouissance?* Embracing animal appetites and the savage integrity of "shameless" beasts, Carter's unconventional heroines transfer the intrapsychic repercussions of the diminishing, judgmental, and withering gaze of the other to the amoral world of pornographic delight. They refuse to internalize negative evaluations imposed by a hostile judge and, rejecting mortification or self-punishment, turn the incriminating regard back toward its source in critical indictment of the (real or imagined) contemptuous other. Carter's women challenge the fetishistic dictates of ideological state apparatuses, along with male deprecations of female sexuality as "defective or deficient" (Bouson, *Embodied Shame*, 2). Her heroines defiantly reject the "inspecting" gaze of individual self-surveillance that alienates the subject by psychologically interiorizing a derogatory body of shame (Bordo, 27).

Clearly, *The Bloody Chamber* suggests the "weeping womb" of female menstruation, as well as the chamber of horrors encountered by the narcissistic bride in this eponymous story. The entire book is a compendium of poignant pubescent tales that urge the reader to deconstruct thickly woven feminist fabulations of trauma, shame, mortification, self-punishment, and transformation. Like the anthropologist Claude Lévi-Strauss, Carter is always preoccupied with the commodity exchange of women's bodies in a capitalist culture where every woman believes that the hymeneal membrane of virginity is her "sole capital," either to be auctioned to the highest bidder, or to be forfeited in rape or premarital sex (56). *The Bloody Chamber* is a book about female vulnerability, seduction, marriage, or misalliance—and woman's subsequent overturning of the ideologies of shame that would lock her in a socially constructed prison of self-contempt and abjection. In Carter's parables, death is reserved for salacious Bluebeards, impotent ogres, hapless vampires, threatening werewolves, and Bible-thumping grannies. Fair maidens survive, willy-nilly, to collaborate in emancipatory eroticism or reform and regenerate purported animal enemies.

In the titular story "The Bloody Chamber," the infrangible bond of pre-Oedipal attachment eventually triumphs over the kind of Oedipal displacement demanded by the Western economy of exogamous marriage. Carter's indomitable mother figure, who once prevailed against Chinese pirates and a (wo)man-eating tiger, had "defiantly beggared herself for love" (Carter, *Bloody Chamber*, 8). Her rebellious daughter is determined to re-script the future by choosing the kind of upward social mobility promised by a wealthy marriage to an aristocratic suitor. The seventeen-year-old virgin, on a timorous journey into conjugal exile, offers her body, like a stripped artichoke or a naked lamb chop, for the salacious degustation of an "old, monocled lecher" (15).

Garnered for sacrifice, this narcissistic young girl is tantalized by the implicit arousal of her burgeoning sexual power, "aghast to feel [her]self stirring" (15) with the thrill of lascivious desire. Draped in a carapace of funereal lilies and fragmented by the multiple mirrors that tauntingly reflect her shame, the blushing bride is forced to acknowledge the excitement of reciprocal passion. Carter refuses to offer a schematic, monologic tale of male lechery and female victimization, as the ingénue feels thrilled by the exhilaration of libidinous exchange. Her budding sexual drives are curiously amalgamated with the hedonistic pleasures of scurrilous yellow novels and "sticky liqueur chocolates" (16). This dream of sensuous satisfaction entails masturbatory self-pleasuring induced by popular potboilers and a vaguely transgressive feast of alcohol-laced candies. Although her husband devours the decadent texts of Joris-Karl Huysmans and an opulent cornucopia of oriental pornography, the adolescent girl can only imagine incorporating her own figure into this salacious tapestry by ingesting forbidden chocolates as she awaits defloration. She is perplexed, but titillated, by the volumes in her spouse's libertine library. The iconographic illustration "Reproof of Curiosity" strikes her as bizarre in its lascivious representation of a "girl with tears hanging on her cheeks like stuck pearls, her cunt a split fig below the great globes of her buttocks on which the knotted tails of the cat were about to descend" (16–17). The Turkish text that replicates whip, scimitar, and ithyphallic member evokes shameful sadomasochistic associations: the perverse practices of Sacher-Masoch, the seductive philosophy of the Marquis de Sade, and the ubiquity of masked predators in Pauline Réage's *The Story of O*. Intrigued but terrified, the young woman curiously fingers a text whose engraving warns of capital dangers: "Immolation of the Wives of the Sultan" (17).

The honeymooning couple's sole conjugal embrace unfolds as a many-mirrored tableau of virginal sacrifice and masculine aggression: "A dozen husbands impaled a dozen brides while the mewing gulls swung on invisible trapezes in the empty air outside" (17). The Marquise, bedecked in a choker of rubies reminiscent of aristocratic rebellion or of a dog bound by a collar of jewels, feels "infinitely dishevelled by the loss of [her] virginity" (18). She is shamefully scattered and unkempt, her sense of virginal integrity penetrated and her genital flower left wounded and bleeding. Paradoxically, however, the price of her maidenhead has yielded a momentary realization of sexual power over a groom who collapses in satiation, "felled like an oak, breathing stertorously" (17). For a few brief moments, the Marquis's façade of male authority yields to the physiological stress of erection and orgasm. The powerful patriarch lies helpless, exposed in postcoital impotence to the imagined threat of a withering female gaze. The woman who envisages the limp member of her post-orgasmic mate is guilty of secret, unspeakable knowledge. "I had seen his deathly composure shatter like a porcelain vase," admits the stunned bride. "I had heard him shriek and blaspheme at the orgasm" (18). Left with only the sign of his successful act of breaking the hymeneal membrane and entering the bloodied chamber of his consort's vaginal orifice, the husband must cope with a humiliating display of unruly passion. He cannot forgive his wife for arousing sexual desires that threaten the bulwark of male mastery and self-control. Because she has witnessed the spectacle of a deflated penis, the purported temptress must be cruelly tested, then decapitated. Since, according to Wurmser, the scopophilic eye is the principal organ of shame, eyes that have seen a husband's phallic collapse must be rendered sightless; genitals that have temporarily devoured his penis must be petrified in a macabre museum to the memory of partners past. "[S]hame anxiety" proves implicitly "akin . . . to paranoid ideas," as the Marquis imagines himself from his partner's point of view and fears the contemptuous eruption of "taunts and mockery" at the sight of his shrunken manhood (Wurmser, *Mask of Shame*, 53). In this dialogic game of power and loss, unbearable shame and paranoid self-loathing spark psychopathic violence, with arbitrary attributions of "female manipulation" perversely ascribed to the woman caricatured as a seductive siren (Bordo, 6).

Carter cannily reveals how each sexual subject projects his/her emotional vulnerability onto an/other, whose body is degraded as the abject instrument of forfeited mastery and compromised control. Yielding to irrational drives, the beleaguered lover shamefully attributes personal need and torrential desire to the object of his/her erotic fantasies. The old love song accusing one's consort of devious machinations in games of love and war, "You Made Me Love You," opens worlds of amorous recrimination subtly suggested in Carter's provocative prose. Not wanting to love and refusing to be mastered, the sexual subject tends to desire an alienated other, the Lacanian *objet petit a*, whose sensual allure is metonymically associated with corporeal abjection. In Carter's cauldron of contaminated erotic drives, both male and female subjects objectify their partners as perpetrators of ineffable crimes against the autonomy of the desexed, narcissistic ideal of an isolated, independent identity. The loss of sexual control at the moment of orgasm constructs a haunting memory of delirious pleasure laced with peril—a traumatic scene that implicates both partners in a spiral of shame and defilement. The embarrassed lovers feel mortified by the "triad of weakness, defectiveness, and dirtiness" generated by the masks of sexual shame (Wurmser, *Mask of Shame*, 98), and phantasmic mortification sparks homicidal obsession.

The Marquise admits, in the wake of her defloration: "No. I was not afraid of him; but of myself" (Carter, *Bloody Chamber*, 20). Had the Marquis descried a "beastly truth" in his own fantasies of sexual debasement—the truth that, in his bride's "innocence, he sensed a rare talent for corruption" (20)? Tormented by a "queasy craving" for perverse, sadomasochistic pleasures, the bride feels appalled by her own "desirous dread" (22). In a fortuitous rescue magically choreographed by a semiotic bond between mother and daughter, Carter's penitent protagonist witnesses the slaying of Bluebeard by a markswoman's single bullet from an antique firearm turned against the perpetrator in a parody of phallic power. A dauntless maternal heroine proves the omnipotent "selfobject" that enables her daughter to move from infantile narcissism to healthy self-esteem. A red, heart-shaped mark from a magical key is annealed on the young girl's forehead as a perduring sign of the sins of venality that brokered an injudicious union. Fortuitously, her next consort, a blind piano-tuner, can envisage a rejuvenated heart but cannot see the mark of turpitude signifying his beloved's shame. The heroine triumphs by virtue of pre-Oedipal identification with a fearless mother who defeats the villain with a dead husband's deadly firearm, in paradoxical assertion of androgynous maternal triumph. The magical key that sears the girl's skin with corporeal ignominy testifies to the shame of youthful indiscretion in a tattoo of defilement reminiscent of Nathaniel Hawthorne's *Scarlet Letter*.[3]

Mercantile motives behind marital choices are even more apparent in "The Tiger's Bride," a story in which a venal patriarch addicted to gambling squanders his daughter's fortune and sells this pearl of great price to a masked tiger who cannily masters her heart. Lévi-Strauss haunts this parable of avarice and greed, as the tiger's bride self-consciously reiterates her plight in terms of illicit barter: "For now my own skin was my sole capital in the world and today I'd make my first investment" (56). She complains that her "father abandoned [her] to the wild beasts by his human carelessness" (63). Refusing to suffer the shame of a male scopophilic gaze, Carter's spirited protagonist elicits an unexpected epiphany or "showing forth" on the part of the masked, gloved, and booted beast who serves as both implacable captor and surprisingly gracious host. Replicating the epiphany of a radiant god to a mortal woman in Greek myth, the tiger voluntarily removes his mask and accoutrements in a ferocious exhibition of bestial glory: "A great, feline, tawny shape whose pelt was barred with a savage geometry" captivates the protagonist (64).

In this remarkable Blakean tableau, the bartered bride, mesmerized by her predator's self-exposure, summons the courage of reciprocal passion by freely baring her breast to the tiger-king whose eyes glow "like twin suns" burning in a bright, luminescent scopophilic gaze (64). Liberated by the power of her own uninhibited agency, she is licked into a furry, atavistic, and edenic happiness by the tender tongue of her tiger-lover. No longer a simulacrum of her father's treacherous demands, the protagonist is freed into an egalitarian relationship with the bestial suitor who welcomes her into the noble community of a tiger's pride. "Carter's magic," claims Bacchilega, "can only be the product of a differently framed *look*, a new *order* that privileges the 'naked,' neither as pornographic objectification nor as 'natural' state, but simply because it is unmasked" (99–100). "Looked at again," says Makinen, "this is not read as woman re-enacting pornography for the male gaze, but as woman reappropriating libido" (12). Aidan Day celebrates the audacious fable for establishing "animal equality between the sexes" (144). And Margaret Atwood praises Carter's portrait of a woman who forfeits "her status as object, and discovers herself as animal, as beast-as-appetite, as energy" ("Running," 126).

Boldly rewriting the story of "Beauty and the Beast," Carter offers two different versions of the traditional fairy tale. If Beauty is able to save the hapless Beast in "The Courtship of Mr. Lyon" and transform him into a radiant human subject through magical ministrations of tenderness and care, "The Tiger's Bride" takes an opposite turn when the heroine chooses, like a sacrificial lamb, to lie down with her feline companion and revive a primitive ethical nobility annihilated by capitalist culture. Carter's stories startle her readers with anachronistic allusions to telephones and motor cars, and to a twentieth-century society incapable of profiting from medieval legends inherited from sages and foremothers. In "The Tiger's Bride," nature triumphs over a decadent society whose values have degenerated into mechanical ciphers of ruthless exploitation. The Oedipal bond between father and daughter has been corrupted by shameful greed, while the traditional exogamy demanding female economic exchange is reduced to a savage barter ironically contrasted to the noble, enchanting courtship proffered by a tiger-prince.

Carter's postmodern feminist text blurs the boundaries between fabulative fiction and the traditional fairy tale. With a soupçon of magical realism, she makes a tiger talk and a feline beast reveal the skeletal outline of his princely demeanor. Recalling Aristotelian and Thomistic debates about the souls of women and the human exploitation of animals, the tiger's bride acknowledges a cultural liminality engendered by gender through a tacit bond with an unorthodox suitor: "I was a young girl, a virgin, and therefore men denied me rationality just as they denied it to all those who were not exactly like themselves, in all their unreason" (63). Consigned to demeaning categories of alienation and contempt that rob both women and beasts of personal dignity, Carter's newly awakened protagonist angrily rebels against the role of simulacrum assigned her by a ruthless patriarch. Like the "clockwork girl" who mechanically powders her cheeks, she has "been bought and sold" like a piece of valuable china, with little more than the "imitative life amongst men that the doll-maker had given" (63). Shamelessly sending a mechanized doll back to Daddy in her stead, she implicitly shames an ignoble progenitor by exposing his outrageous avarice and seeks conjugal solace in powerful paws that anoint her body with the gift of magical transformation.

The female protagonist in the story "The Erl-King" is trapped in a different kind of illusion, "because everything in the wood is exactly as it seems" (85). In this invaginated habitation of dark interiority, the "woods enclose and then enclose again, like a system of Chinese boxes"—a recursive image of narrative embedding paradigmatic of the textual palimpsest constructing the convoluted story as it trickily unfolds. The erl-king is a mysterious, enigmatic lover—as androgynous as an excellent housewife, and as barbaric as a "tender butcher who showed me how the price of flesh is love" (87). As a solitary figure of male authority, the erl-king seduces his beloved in a vernal idyllic—or vampiric—setting. A shape-shifting projection of female sexual desire, this mythic male rapes his virginal consort into a confusion of vertiginous dis-ease, a dizzying sense of capitulation that entails a fall into desire, madness, subservience, and sexual *jouissance*. "I fall down for him," confesses the narrator, and only by virtue of her lover's ostensible tenderness is she saved from emotional perdition (88). Their amorous union reeks of pain and violence, as the vampiric lover bites her throat, binding her tenderly with a "magic lasso of inhuman music" (89). According to Lewallen, the erl-king is both the "product of nature" and the "created child of desire in an Oedipal configuration" (154). In sexual union, the heroine seeks a womb of embryonic security, a spiritual twinship that effaces the boundaries of individual embodiment. Courting fantasies of cannibalism and incorporation, she imagines a physical diminution that would make her the erl-king's eucharist in a perverse erotic communion. "Eat me, drink me," she passionately pleads, fantasizing oceanic engulfment in the watery garment of a lover's embrace (Carter, *Bloody Chamber*, 89). As object of the erl-king's mesmerizing gaze, "sucked into the black vortex of his eye," the virgin is seduced into a Charybdian whirlpool of sacrificial delight—a vertigo that bodes both ecstasy and obliteration in the potentially traumatic amalgamation of autonomous subjects (89).

Carter has envisioned the lyrical embodiment of a female desire so intense that it constructs the mastery of the lover/beloved in the image of powerful but destructive cannibalistic drives. Longing to be engulfed by her mysterious lover, Carter's protagonist discerns the humiliating irrationality of her own libido in the figure of a demonized erl-king. Helpless to liberate herself from the seductive vortex of amorous attraction, she projects shameful lascivious obsession onto the lover who enthralls her, then determines to slay the cause of her frenzied sexual desire. Hypnotized by a wily seducer, whose eyes of "green liquid amber" exude "incomparable luminosity," the fallen woman feels humiliated by a male scopophilic gaze (90). She is caged like a bird in the osier-woven web of masterful seduction and locked in a prison of erotic compulsion. From their initial meeting, she senses the threat of "grievous harm"; but, like a parodic figure from a popular self-help psychology text, she endures the fate of a woman who loves too much and cannot break free of *l'amour fou*, with its obsessive cycles of repetition. The only way to liberate herself from sadomasochistic addiction is, in seductive maternal guise, to murder her demonic lover, either literally or figuratively, and to string an Aeolian harp with tendrils of his "languorous hair" (90).

Has Carter betrayed her feminist mission in this stark representation of homicidal Eros? Harriet Linkin, tracing the romantic resonance of this lyrical tale, concludes that the protagonist can envision no alternative to male sexual idealization and the shameful objectification of woman than to turn the tables on her seducer. One might suspect, however, that Carter's fabulative tableau engenders a different (post)feminist moral for both male and female readers. Like the Marquis's homicidal terror in "The Bloody Chamber," the narrator has (re)fashioned her demon-lover as an imaginary projection of libidinous compulsion. Sexual drives reduce her to a position of impotence that evinces its own peculiar mark of emotional defilement. Carter seems to imply that popular notions of enthrallment, inherited from medieval romances and a chivalric tradition of self-abasement, are as fruitless and unproductive as this watery tale of erotic obsession. The story functions as a mirror image of Bluebeard's performance anxiety in "The Bloody Chamber." If either sex continues imaginatively to construct the other in the shadow of its own lascivious fantasies, then Carter sees little hope for men and women suffering from the self-inflicted torments of "crazy love." If women find themselves trapped like songbirds in cages they connive in fabricating, then everyone in this age-old story—erl-king and songbird alike—will be hopelessly immured in a tangled web of shame-laden stereotypes and soul-destroying erotic compulsions.

In "The Lady of the House of Love," Carter shows how an outmoded feudal culture based on patriarchal privilege and vampiric need traps its dramatis personae in unregenerate repetition. According to Robert R. Wilson, the virginal vampire at the center of the story "is subordinated, within her decaying castle, . . . to a tradition established, and maintained, by men" (112)—a tradition of inexorable shame and debasement. The vampire's antique wedding dress functions as a "symbol of women's voicelessness, subordination and narrowly limited expectations, their unelected social roles handed down in a patriarchal society" (112). The protagonist is clearly doomed to sacrificial expiration, even as her naïve soldier-suitor survives to face almost certain death in the trenches of World War I.

For Angela Carter, the alternative to such antiquated sex/gender systems might be a figurative collusion with everything in nature that has been "othered" by contemporary society—a self-conscious and redemptive return to the savage libidinal company of wolves. Just as feline figures dominate several stories in the volume, canine imagery is titular in its three culminating tales. Carter is determined to re-script age-old misogynist analogies between women and animals and to deconstruct metonymic structures that subtly inscribe many of the fabulative tropes she devises. Through postmodern play with genre and gender, Carter rewrites the conventional tale of "Little Red Riding Hood" in a "shameless" register whereby a brash adolescent protagonist defies and successfully transmutes shame-based cultural judgments.

In "The Company of Wolves," the author configures her heroine's virginity as both enigmatic and empowering. The undaunted ingénue, fearless in pubescent pride, is wrapped in the cloak of a protective hymeneal membrane that gives her a narcissistic conviction of virginal invincibility: "She is an unbroken egg; she is a sealed vessel" (Carter, *Bloody Chamber*, 114). Even when nuzzled by the snout of a (wo)man-eating wolf, the girl thrusts aside fear, laughs with bravado, and proceeds with the confidence of a woman who knows that she is "nobody's meat" (118) and that her corporeal self is not a helpless embodiment of female abjection. This brash adolescent connives with her lupine or lycanthropic suitor in a bold alliance of psychological equals. Offering her pubescent body, without shame, to an unorthodox savage mate in a tender conjugal embrace, she tames, humanizes, and domesticates the predator. As Margaret Atwood notes, "each participant appears to retain his or her own nature," and Carter's "'wise child' wins the herbivore-carnivore contest" (1994, 130).

The female protagonist of "Wolf-Alice" is perceived, in contrast, as a wild and untamed figure of feral shame by a bigoted and brutal society. In this crossover tale of blurred boundaries and bestial nobility, Wolf-Alice is nurtured, like Romulus and Remus, by a lupine dam tragically slain at the hands of a murderous huntsman. Carter sardonically implies that the most dangerous beast on the planet might well be the human animal—one of the very few predators that takes pleasure in hunting for sport. An ingenuous Wolf-Alice, perplexed by the onset of her menarche, initially believes that she has been nuzzled and bitten by the wolf in the moon. Gradually, her menses introduce her to cyclical temporality and to a chronological sense of time distinct from the instantaneous, moment-by-moment consciousness ascribed by humans to nonhuman animals. As Alice struggles to fathom the mystery of her monthly bleeding, she begins to sense the first glimmerings of logical deduction: "there took root a kind of wild reasoning, as it might have from a seed dropped in her brain off the foot of a flying bird" (122). The volatile image of germination is fleeting but provocative. Out of the seeds of rational curiosity, human self-consciousness takes root and transitions from infantile narcissism to mature self-esteem.

Marginalized by an obtuse provincial populace, Wolf-Alice is thrust into the care and company of the lycanthropic Duke, who is described as a somatophage or corpse-eating carnivore. United in their liminal status as ostracized exiles and figures of shame, the two cohabit in mutual isolation, as Alice learns to play with the ludic littermate who emerges from the Duke's mirror to imitate her every movement. Mimicking Lacanian notions of the mirror stage of maturation, Carter delineates a magical moment of human evolution in a fantasized representation of the beast turning human at the instant of *Spaltung,* or splitting, when a homogeneous sense of self indistinguishable from the surrounding environment gives way, in personal consciousness, to a dim awareness of subject distinguished from object. The *je* identified with fragmented human subjectivity, along with the *moi* of objective integrity and wholeness, is revealed in the mirror image of a maternal gaze or in the form reflected by a silver-backed glass. That image, like a shadow, is not an/other but the self—not enemy or playmate, but a projection of the subject as an identifiable object squeezed into an intractable persona wielding power and agency in the symbolic register of the Father. For Alice, temporality is allied with the motion of clocks and cosmic worlds, growth and maturity with the first pubic "hairs tufting between her thighs," and mirror-play with the revelation that "her companion was, in fact, no more than a particularly ingenious variety of [her] shadow" (124).

With the dawn of human reason, Alice (having moved back through the looking-glass) begins to acquire self-consciousness and personal agency. She realizes that her subjective identity gives form and meaning to the landscape she traverses, which "assembles itself about her" (125). Resembling the intertextual image of Crusoe's Man Friday, the newly awakened subject leaves beautiful and menacing footprints on the damp earth encircling the castle. Like Lewis Carroll's Alice, she has leapt through the looking-glass of civilization to learn the tender, nurturant practices of an empathic selfobject, the beast who nourished and weaned her. Now she steps back into the world of so-called "civilized" culture with all the mysterious powers gifted by Mother Nature to an orphan wolf-child socialized in a lupine pack. Her shame-free sentience and olfactory perspicacity mimic Freud's sexual theories about the evolution of human sexuality, from its origins in the olfactory instincts of animals who sniff and smell, to the scopophilic propensities of a visually oriented desire susceptible to the demands of anthropomorphic bipedalism. Women, Freud argued, are more primitively attuned to olfactory stimuli and more subservient to the bodily shame of genital insufficiency; whereas men, having mastered baser animal instincts, supposedly respond more readily to oculocentric sexual cues.

Carter's beleaguered Duke is lost in a traumatic haze of pathos and helplessness. A lonely somatophage, this bathetic lycanthrope does little more than rob graves and ingest the decomposing bodies of dead, i.e., no-longer-human, beings. He never threatens or kills his prey, as do the hunters and religious fanatics who lay a vicious trap for him in the local church. Armed with bells, books, and candles, as well as a "ten-gallon tub of holy water . . . to drown the Duke" (125), a young widower mourning the untimely death and subsequent ingestion of his hapless bride is determined to avenge the Duke's imagined desecration of her corpse. In memory of his deceased lover, he attempts to kill an unarmed creature who has inadvertently challenged the groom's phantasmic idealization of his deceased consort. The tormented Duke is wounded and "must rise up like any common forked biped and limp distressfully on" (125). Howling and bleeding, this bewildered creature, shot at the moment of metamorphosis, limps forward in the guise of an "aborted transformation, an incomplete mystery," screaming hysterically, like a wounded animal (126).

The fates of Carter's alienated exiles ultimately come together in a marriage of pain and sympathetic communion. A compassionate Alice, emulating her lupine dam, maternally ministers to the Duke's laceration and, free of inhibition, generously suckles the putrescent blood from his open wound. With the tenderness and cunning of a vampire bird, she instinctively licks her lover into manhood. His humanized subjectivity emerges from the loving ministrations of an altruistic and solicitous nurse. Clad in the castoff wedding dress of the Duke's erstwhile victim, Alice becomes mother and lover, physician and wife to the Christlike scapegoat whose blood she voluntary ingests without a sense of corporeal disgust or fear of contamination. She tenderly woos the savage beast, as she herself emerges from unselfconscious bestiality and triumphantly refuses to internalize the mortifying judgments of a bigoted community.

Alice's solicitude for the Duke is framed in a lingual kiss of bestial cunning, an act of nurture learned from her foster mother and redemptive in its power to release the lycanthropic mate she compassionately resurrects. In this shameless gesture of love and generosity, Alice elicits the Duke's human reflection and revivifies her wounded housemate by restoring his atrophied humanity. In Carter's postmodern world of magical realism, the blood of menstruation and of sacrifice releases the power of repressed agency and heals the wounds of both physical and psychological trauma. The magical mirror of the Duke's habitation gradually yields "to the reflexive strength of its own material construction" and, in its "formless web of tracery," reveals the anthropomorphic face of the Duke, nudged into being by Alice's "soft, moist, gentle tongue" (126) through an act of parodic fellatio that functions as the salvific amatory matrix of a "different kind of love: instinctual, merciful, maternal" (Atwood, "Running," 132). For Kimberly Lau, "Wolf-Alice's licking is . . . an erotically charged literary tumescence" suggesting that the "tongues of Carter's women and wolves move us away from language, speech, articulation and into a more sensory realm" (Lau, 91–92). According to Bacchilega, Carter is "redefining what 'human' is, as these differently wounded beings inaugurate new reflections and songs" (65). The "rational humanness" that both protagonists achieve at the end of this tale reveals, for Aidan Day, a "genuine humanity that is to be contrasted with . . . the incomplete humanity of the people who have shunned and persecuted them" (166)—and that shuns, in turn, the judgments of societal shame and mortification implicit in a so-called "civilized" order.

If Carter celebrates the feral disorder of our first, edenic habitation, she nonetheless portrays magical transformations that imbue traumatized human beings with the proverbial wisdom of innocent beasts free of the humiliating constructions of societal shame. Such fantastic metamorphoses re-humanize a violent community of citizens who justify murder in the name of vengeance and exploit one another in the interest of capitalist greed. Carter's fables in *The Bloody Chamber* suggest parables of love and genuine compassion that obliterate obsessive-compulsive power games played by both sexes. Her intriguing tales offer revolutionary strategies of erotic bonding, bestial rationality, heroic self-sacrifice, connubial reciprocity, and intersubjective healing. What more inspiring humanist message could a reader demand of magical millennial stories than the bold defiance of cultural attributions of shame and corporeal abjection in a new era of re-scripted, egalitarian gender relations?[4] In *The Bloody Chamber,* Carter's "shameless" protagonists successfully free themselves and those whom they love from the stultifying mortifications imposed by the arbitrary and humiliating judgments of a shame-based society.

Notes

1. In *Scenes of Shame,* Adamson and Clark address the "question of shame and gender, illustrating how shame is used coercively in a male-dominated society—by both men and women—to enforce socially approved gender roles" (3). In the following essay, I try to redefine and reclaim the word "shameless" in a feminist register, in the tradition of Mary Daly's *Wickedary.* As Daly explains, the "work of the *Wickedary* is a process of freeing words from the cages and prisons of patriarchal patterns" (3). "Wicked Grammarians breaking fatherland's rules are committing the Sin of Creative Dis-ordering, effecting Metamorphosis. Grammar-Hammering Hags, releasing words from male-ordered boxes and cages, enable these to Spin about freely . . . in New Directions" (30).

2. In *The Pornography of Representation,* Susanne Kappeler acknowledges that the definition of pornography has always been highly contested and argues that Western modes of artistic representation have historically been configured according to the "cultural archeplot" of male domination and are thus inescapably complicit with female shame and debasement. "Where," she asks, "do you draw the line between . . . pornography and erotica?" (39). Robert Clark wonders "to what extent [Carter's] fictions . . . offer their readers a knowledge of patriarchy—and therefore offer some possibilities of liberating consciousness—and to what extent they fall back into reinscribing patriarchal attitudes" (147). Avis Lewallen admires the ideas and style of this "high priestess of post-graduate porn" and acknowledges that Carter is "attempting to promote an active sexuality for women within a Sadeian framework," but complains that "sexual choice for the heroines is circumscribed by Sadeian boundaries" (144–146). For Patricia Duncker, Carter's postmodern shape-shifting "merely explains, amplifies and reproduces rather than alters the original, deeply, rigidly sexist psychology of the erotic" (6).

3. Avis Lewallen is troubled by "The Bloody Chamber" for its implicit manipulation of a com-plicitous audience to "sympathise with masochism" and imaginatively identify with "masochistic victims in a pornographic scenario" that envinces ambivalent feelings (151).

4. For perspicacious studies of Carter's feminist fairy tales, see Bacchilega, *Postmodern Fairy Tales*, as well as collections by Roemer and Bacchilega, Lorna Sage, and Lindsey Tucker.

4 "Ecrire pour ne plus avoir honte"

Christine Angot's and Annie Ernaux's Shameless Bodies

Natalie Edwards

Sᴇʟꜰ-ᴇxᴘᴏꜱᴜʀᴇ ʜᴀꜱ ʙᴇᴄᴏᴍᴇ curiously prevalent in recent French literature. In addition to canonical writers like the Marquis de Sade, Georges Bataille, and Jean Genet, more recent writers such as Michel Houellebecq, Marie Darrieussecq, Violette Leduc, Monique Wittig, Virginie Despentes, Catherine Breillat, Hervé Guibert, and Pierre Guyotat have pushed the boundaries of what it means to shock one's reader through self-exposure. By representing in narrative what is deemed by society to be shameful, these writers raise important questions regarding cultural values, the social reception of their works and the limits of the representation of intimacy. Surprisingly, perhaps, for the literary tradition that produced so many *poètes maudits,* and for a nation with strong Catholic traditions that involve sin, guilt and confession, very little work exists on the representation of shame by critics of French literature. Maybe this is due to the intricacies of the French language, which has several different words for the notion: *la pudeur,* insinuating modesty, decency, or propriety; *le dommage,* referring to something regrettable as in "*c'est dommage*" (it's a shame); and *la honte,* which is closer to the English shame, embarrassment, or disgrace. Or maybe in the French literary tradition there is so much sex, sexuality, and desire that studying its representation of shame would seem an unnecessarily prudish act. Certain French philosophers have paid attention to shame, such as Jean-Paul Sartre, Jacques Lacan, Maurice Merleau-Ponty, and Emmanuel Levinas, but this has not crossed over into French literary criticism. Overall, there exist very few scholarly examinations of shame in any field and hardly any in literary studies, despite the recent developments in autobiography, testimonial narrative, and trauma studies.

The reason for this void may be the difficulty of expressing shame in words since, as Stephen Pattison writes, "shame presents as a visual or imagistic experience rather than one that can easily be verbally articulated. Indeed, the experience of shame often reduces the shamed person to speechlessness" (41). Suzanne Henke has argued that the expression of traumatic events in narrative is a cathartic experience that she has termed "scriptotherapy," but the writing of shame presents difficulties to the author that the writing of trauma may preclude. On one level, shame is a necessarily individual experience; although we may feel ashamed of another's actions, we feel shame completely alone. One may experience trauma alone, but a key difference between the two concepts is the element of responsibility; one feels that one is entirely to blame for the shameful thought/action/feeling. Shame is also more of a complete experience: "a sense of personal collapse that implies the loss of self-esteem or self efficacy . . . [the] whole self is bad" (Pattison, 44). And crucially for the writing process, shame is spectatorial, in the sense that one's shame is normally associated with being looked at by an other; as Jenny Chamarette and Jenny Higgins summarize, "I am shamed by the look of an other upon me, and consequently I am shamed by the judging and the judgment of that look upon myself as shameful" (2). The writing of shame is thus particularly difficult since one is writing of one's lack of self-esteem, one's whole bad self, and owning up to that in published writing is an especially fraught and courageous move.

This chapter examines two contemporary French female writers whose work consciously plays with the expression of shame and self-exposure in narrative. Annie Ernaux, whose representation of shame has been the subject of several articles and one book-length study, began publishing in 1974 with her semi-autobiographical text that included the depiction of a backstreet abortion, *Les Armoires vides* (*Cleaned Out*). She has produced a series of works that revolve around her own experience of coming of age in an impoverished socioeconomic situation, and which chart her development from this to a respected writer and teacher. She has achieved recognition not just for her experimentation with genre, her depiction of poverty and her simple narrative style, but for her treatment of female sexuality and desire, and the shame that may accompany these. Christine Angot is a more recent name in French literature, having begun to publish in 1990, and she has achieved fame for her series of works that all revolve around her. The subject of almost all of her works, which have appeared in quick succession at nearly one a year, is "Christine Angot"; her works are narrated by this character and the reader is constantly invited to ponder the relationship between author and narrator. Angot has also become notorious for her deliberately outrageous media persona; she is known for her caustic comments on national television, her vitriolic responses to her critics, and her abrasive personality. In her literary output, this author plays very deliberately with socially codified ideas of shame, as many of her texts display the character of "Christine Angot" recounting her sexuality and her heterosexual, homosexual, and incestuous sex acts in detail. Both authors have produced a series of short works that often do not have any discernible plot and that revolve around one incident or set of incidents—many of which may be deemed shameful— that are seemingly important to the narrator's developing identity. Both engage in a formal experimentation that confronts the genres of autobiography and confession, and that simultaneously questions the limits of propriety in narrative.

The similarities between *L'Inceste* (1999) by Angot, the younger writer, and *Passion simple* (1991) by Ernaux, the more established, begin on the level of content, since both texts begin with the narrators representing their (at times) shameful feeling of having fallen obsessively in love. Both narrators depict their experiences of intimacy and desire in highly confessional ways, all the while playing with the reader as to who is narrating what about whom. In one of Angot's longest books to date, her text recounts her obsessive love for another woman; her lengthy descriptions of her feelings meander from one traumatic memory to another, and the text includes voicemail messages, notes, quotations from other books, and snippets of conversations. Angot's text is structured similarly to a stream of consciousness, with no divisions or chapters; the only thing that ties together the disparate memories of the affair is herself at the center of all of them. Ernaux's text is much shorter but also jumps from one memory to another in a seemingly directionless movement. The separations on the pages and gaps in the text create a nonlinear structure as the narrator recounts isolated episodes of her obsessive love affair with a married man. Ernaux's text has more of a reflective tone as she situates her narrator in the present of the text, in the writing process, and playing with verb tenses to situate herself in relation to the events that she is writing.[1] Simon Kemp reads Ernaux's writing project as "one of writing time" as she moves between the narrating self and the narrated self, repeatedly revisiting past events and recounting them with the perspective of added experience (48). Like Angot, Ernaux includes snippets of remembered conversations, isolated events, and commentary about the writing process among sections that discuss her thoughts and feelings of the affair from the perspective of the narrative present. Unlike Angot, however, her narrator is never named.

This chapter examines how Angot and Ernaux each navigate the spectrum of shameful to shameless, displaying in narrative the emotion that we all recognize as wanting to hide, disappear, run away, or die. It first looks at the catalogue of shameful behaviors that the narrators convey, then examines the role of the "others" in the narrator's shameful tales. It finally analyzes the reader as the recipient of the narrative of shame, and the writing process as the mechanism for both divulging and concealing shame.

Shaming the Self

The source of the shame in these two texts is centered upon sexual desire and the conflicting feelings that such strong desires arouse, and these conflicting emotions are rendered more startling since they are recounted from within first-person narrative. The openings of these two texts are strikingly similar; a first-person narrator describes herself as being obsessively in love with an other, and this obsession is represented as shocking and puzzling to the narrator herself. Both narrators are at a loss to understand their feelings and, amid the description of their sexual acts, is the idea that they are baffled by what they feel. There are indeed plenty of things in these texts to be ashamed of, in the sense that shame is a socially codified value that designates certain behaviors or attitudes as shameful. Angot's narrator begins with "[J]'ai été homosexuelle pendant trois mois. Plus exactement, trois mois, j'ai cru que j'y étais condamnée" (11) (I was homosexual for three months. More precisely, for three months, I thought I was condemned to it),[2] in an opening that is provocative on many levels; first, readers who know Angot's work will be aware of the heterosexual desire normally expressed by her narrator of the same name; second, the confession of homosexuality may still be deemed shocking to some; and third, the indication is that one's sexuality may be abruptly shifted and transformed before returning to "normal."[3] The idea of being "condemned" to homosexuality also implies a judgment of such a sexual orientation, in the eyes of the writer or of society. Although Ernaux's narrator experiences heterosexual desire, her emotions are no less surprising to a reader familiar with her previous works. As Sylvie Romanowski writes, *Passion simple* denotes a change of direction in Ernaux's writing, as it is the first to discuss a narrator's passionate affair with a man, and not coincidentally the first to appear after the death of her mother (99). Her text begins:

> Cet été, j'ai regardé pour la première fois un film classé X à la télévision, sur Canal+ ... Il y a eu un gros plan, le sexe de la femme est apparu, bien visible dans les scintillements de l'écran, puis le sexe de l'homme, en érection, qui s'est glissé dans celui de la femme ... On s'habitue certainement à cette vision, la première fois est bouleversante. (Ernaux, *Passion simple*, 12–13)
>
> (This summer, for the first time, I watched an X-rated film on Canal+ ... There was a close-up of the woman's genitals, clearly visible among the shimmerings of the screen, then of the man's penis, fully erect, sliding into the woman's vagina ... No doubt one gets used to such a sight; the first time is shattering. [Ernaux, *Simple Passion*, 1–2])

The narrator is both intrigued and uncomfortable, as she admits as she calls the experience "bouleversante"; sexuality and desire fascinate and please her, she hints, yet also disturb her. Only after mentioning the pornographic film does she arrive at her confession and begin to recount her affair: "A partir du mois de septembre l'année dernière, je n'ai plus rien fait d'autre qu'attendre un homme: qu'il me téléphone et qu'il vienne chez moi" (*Passion simple*, 13) ("From September last year, I did nothing else but wait for a man: for him to call me and come round to my place" [*Simple Passion*, 3]). Both authors are thus intent on playing with shame, presenting the reader with stark, intimate images of female sexuality and desire from the outset.

Following these provocative openings, both narrators stack up a list of shameful behaviors, actions, and desires, and their texts may at times feel like an assault on the reader's sensibilities. Ernaux moves from watching pornography, to committing adultery, to performing oral sex, to claiming that her children are less important than her sexual desire, for example. She also writes of the backstreet abortion that she had as a student and which she first recounted in *Les Armoires vides;* in *Passion simple* she writes of how she went back to the site of her abortion to find that the old woman who performed the procedure had disappeared and the apartment building was now occupied by high-income families. This author is well known for her treatment of shameful events, and Loraine Day links this to the shame of the writer's lower-class upbringing that she felt acutely upon entering the educated classes; for Day, Ernaux's texts "illustrate the crucial importance of embodied social history in her narrator's sexual choices, and she acknowledges that she herself struggled long and hard to overcome the sexual shame that was a legacy of an upbringing that equated the pursuit of sexual pleasure with social disgrace" (223). Yet, the acuteness of Ernaux's representation of shame in *Passion simple* comes from the matter-of-fact way that she renders it in narrative. Warren Motte has described Ernaux's style as minimalist, claiming that it is "antiliterature," and the way that Ernaux recounts her obsession in this text is strikingly stark, brief, and matter-of-fact. Ernaux writes in passing of sexual acts that she and her lover perform together, refusing any hyperbole or sentimentality and eschewing any avowal of shame; rather, this way of recounting such intimacy creates a sense that the narrator feels comfortable and untouched by such conventionally shocking material; she quotes the man saying "caresse-moi le sexe avec ta bouche" (*Passion simple,* 21) ("stroke my penis with your mouth" [*Simple Passion,* 10]), for example, and claims starkly that "la seule vérité incontestable était visible en regardant son sexe" (*Passion simple,* 35) ("the only undeniable truth could be glimpsed by looking at his penis" [*Simple Passion,* 24]). The narrator writes about masturbation too, recounting how "une fois, à plat ventre, je me suis fait jouir, il m'a semblé que c'était sa jouissance à lui" (*Passion simple,* 52) ("one day, lying on my stomach, I gave myself an orgasm; somehow I felt that it was his orgasm" [*Simple Passion,*41]). Hélène Cixous in her 1975 "Le rire de la méduse" ("The Laugh of the Medusa") writes of how women felt shame when they masturbated, and despite the progress in sexual attitudes and awareness since that time, one may question whether this shame has evaporated. Ernaux's narrator also writes of how her behavior changes and she develops habits such as reading the horoscopes in women's magazines, listening to sentimental music, and focusing excessively upon the romantic episodes in books, in a way that renders her a stereotype; as opposed to a teacher of literature and one of the country's most successful writers, the narrator constructs herself as a silly, naïve, and irrational woman waiting obsessively for her knight in shining armor. Ernaux thus extends the shame of her socioeconomic background, about which she has previously written, to an extensive list of supposedly shameful sexual activities and behaviors, and her stark narration of this creates a tension between the shameful material and the shameless manner of telling it.

In a similar vein, Angot's *L'Inceste* also stacks up a list of so-called shameful actions, playing with what are deemed to be sources of shame in society and inviting the reader to ponder these and, crucially, to compare them. The homosexual affair itself is recounted in detail, with vivid descriptions of sexual acts and in particular of oral sex: "[C]'était la Patagonie pour moi au début, lécher une femme . . . On étouffe dans cette forêt" (24) ("It was uncharted territory for me at the beginning, licking a woman . . . You suffocate in that forest"). Moreover, the obsessive nature of her feelings toward this woman seem to provoke some sort of shame in her, since she is aware that others see her behavior; she repeatedly calls her lover's office, so often that the secretaries know her, and quotes herself speaking like a nonsensical, hysterical female on the telephone. She mentions that she drinks to overcome her obsession, and recounts dreams that evidence her self-obsession, and her sexual fantasies. She confesses that she has a psychoanalyst, that she has had gone through psychoanalysis previously, and describes herself as mad, as having become unhinged by events in her life: "[J]e ne suis pas en train de devenir folle, je suis devenue folle, je le suis, folle" (90) ("I'm not going mad, I've become mad, I am just that, mad"). She quotes descriptions of illnesses from the *Dictionnaire de la psychanalyse* in an open, seemingly shameless depiction of her mental instability. Lastly, of course, is the incest that forms the title of the book and that is only recounted in the final thirty pages of the text. The narrator recounts with a startling frankness acts such as eating clementines placed on her father's penis and the sodomy that he performs on her, burying the actions in short, non-descriptive sentences that play down the trauma, but are an obvious source of shame. Ruth Cruickshank has written of how the incest has been obfuscated by critics of Angot's work, possibly due to the scandal surrounding the author, and obviously due to the taboo of discussing incest. It is clear also that the curtailed description, written in such a stark, brief way and buried among a list of other shameful things, is another reason why the incest was not the focus of critics' attention.

In a similar way to Ernaux, therefore, Angot plays very deliberately with behaviors, feelings, and impulses designated as shameful by society, listing a range of shameful acts—both sexual and non-sexual—that almost form an assault on the reader. Moreover, the stark, brief prose in which the most provocative sequences are narrated create a nonchalance that cannot be a realistic reflection of a shamed self. I do not mean to suggest that these writers' styles are identical; while Ernaux and Angot both write in stark, minimalist prose, the style of the latter is noticeably more varied, including descriptive, poetic language and vitriolic ranting. What is most interesting in these texts is that they comprise a barrage of shameful actions and are recounted in first-person narration through a style that consistently downplays any sense of shame.

Shaming Others

These lists of shames recounted by "Christine Angot" and an unnamed narrator invite the reader to question her/his impressions of the authors, and to wonder about their personal lives. In particular, one is invited to ponder the relationship between the authors and the others whom they include in the text. Both of these writers play consciously with the involvement of others in their shame, and this is one of the most interesting points of convergence and dissimilarity between the two works. One often cannot display one's own intimate sources of shame without dragging other people into the story; although shame is something that we experience alone, one's shameful actions will rarely have no bearing on others, by guilty association or by outright blame, and the telling of one's own intimacy will often involve the telling of others' also. Should one implicate others and write fully about the responsibility they share, or decide that one has taken the decision to write one's shame oneself and spare others the embarrassment?

The first other to whom Ernaux refers, and the one who has the most to lose from her published revelation, is clearly her married lover. The narrator is very conscious of the need to protect this man and does so by refusing to name him by anything further than "A."[4] She divulges very little information about him; the reader knows that he is a diplomat from Eastern Europe, that he drinks heavily, and that he is married, but knows no further details of his life. On the one occasion in which the narrator mentions the man's wife, she is more concerned with her own feelings than with this other woman's trauma: "[A]utant que le désir de lui éviter toute scène avec sa femme, il y avait celui de ne pas encourir de sa part une rancune qui l'aurait conduit à me quitter" (*Passion simple*, 37) ("Naturally I wanted to spare him a scene with his wife but I also feared arousing resentment on his behalf, which might have led him to stop seeing me" [*Simple Passion*, 25]). The reader infers that her anonymity was self-serving during the affair, and her refusal to name the man in the narrative may very well underscore that the book is not about him at all, but is rather about the recording of a passion in writing, and characters, particularly that of the lover, are incidental. Justifying her choice in the present, the narrator writes that "cet homme continue de vivre quelque part dans le monde. Je ne peux pas le décrire davantage, fournir des signes susceptibles de l'identifier . . . Qu'il en aille autrement pour moi ne m'autorise pas à dévoiler sa personne. Il n'a pas choisi de figurer dans mon livre mais seulement dans mon existence" (*Passion simple*, 33) ("This man continues to live somewhere in the world. I cannot describe him in greater detail, or supply information that might lead to his identification . . . The fact that I have different priorities does not give me the right to reveal his identity. He did not choose to play a part in this book, only in my life" [*Simple Passion*, 22]). Interestingly, Ernaux has been very open in her texts about her lovers, going so far as to co-author a book with one of them: *L'Usage de la photo*, with Marc Marie. In *Passion simple*, however, the narrator attempts to write the other out of her story as far as possible, and claims to be aware that she would be shaming him otherwise.

Likewise, the narrator refers to other people, like her children and her former husband, in a way that acknowledges their presence in her life but that does not give any details about them. She mentions, for example, how when the lover called, she had to ask her sons to leave her apartment while they were home during university vacations, claiming of children and mothers in general that "ils ne comptent pas plus pour elle à certains moments que pour une chatte impatiente de courir de vieux chatons" (*Passion simple,* 26) ("at times they mean nothing to her, in the same way that grown-up kittens can mean nothing to a mother cat longing to go on the prowl" [*Simple Passion,* 15]). The reference to the sons reminds the reader that Ernaux is a real person, and she has written that she wants to keep her sons out of her writing. In this instance, the narrator distances these "real" people from her narrative, using them not as characters but as vehicles to push the list of shameful activity yet further; surely the parallel between human and feline maternal behavior would be shocking to many a reader. Moreover, the fact that this narrator writes of her sensitivity to the problem of shaming "real" people invites the reader to read the text as factual, and to retreat from the general practice of distinguishing author from narrator. Indeed, the narrative of a long list of shameful things that includes discussion of how the narrator's "others" should not be shamed serves as a constant tempter; just as Ernaux is stylizing herself as the illicit temptress toward her married lover, so is she with her reader, tempting her/him to read "her" as the narrating "I" and forcing us to face the naïve, childlike temptation to read an author's literary text as though it were a reality TV show. The reader, even the most practiced, is invited to believe that s/he "knows" Ernaux in some measure and is curious about her private life, as Roland Barthes knew very well when he wrote as a tantalizing preface to his partially autobiographical text, "[T]out ceci doit être considéré comme dit par un personnage de roman" (5) ("All this must be considered as having been spoken by a character in a novel").

Angot, however, takes quite a different approach from Ernaux to her fictional/real others. Angot's lesbian lover is referred to by her full name. This lover does nothing to be ashamed of, compared to A's adultery for example, but one might imagine that this woman may not relish being represented and "outed" in text. Angot spares nobody's privacy, and takes special care—both here and elsewhere in her corpus—to answer her critics, mentioning them by name in vitriolic tirades that could be interpreted as an attempt to shame them personally. The narrator targets both professional critics and friends, many of whom are named, quoted, and rebutted in the text. Turning to the published critics, she answers them directly, stating, "Moi je réponds, je vous le dis bien en face, je vais vous répondre quelque chose: Soyez poli" (156) ("Me, I'll answer you, I'll say it to your face, I'm going to say something back to you: Be polite"), and explains how shaming them gives her a certain violent pleasure: "faire honte aux journalistes, les petites piques, comme on lance des fléchettes à la foire, c'est l'éthique, c'est la détente aussi" (59) ("to shame the journalists, with cutting little remarks, like how you throw darts at a fairground, that's the ethic, and it's relaxing too"). Family members are similarly brought into the narrative, and the narrator both divulges intimate details about them and publicly criticizes them. In one episode, she writes of a discussion between her and her long-term (male) partner concerning his opinion of her work: "Claude m'a dit autre chose, quand j'ai rappelé pour lui lire ces deux pages: '[E]n plus c'est coquin et impertinent.' Non, pas du tout. Ce n'est pas du tout coquin et impertinent. Ce n'est pas du tout un jeu" (59) ("Claude said something else to me, when I called to read these two pages to him: '[I]t's mischievous and impertinent.' No, not at all. It's not at all mischievous and impertinent. It's not at all a game"). Claude, the long-term partner and father of her daughter—Léonore in real life and in Angot's texts—is a constant presence in Angot's corpus, and her texts recount intimate details of "their" relationship. In *Sujet Angot*, the author goes so far as to narrate the text from Claude's point of view, rendering herself the object, the "tu" of his speech, and having him record his thoughts upon reading a manuscript that she has written all the while pining for her after their relationship has ended. At the time of writing, Angot is embroiled in a court case over exactly this issue of shaming others: an acquaintance has accused Angot of basing the 2011 novel *Les Petits* on her and her children, and Angot's trial is awaiting.

In *L'Inceste*, the person whom she shames most is the perpetrator of the incest itself, her father. "Did he really do it?" the reader will obviously ask, and "How could she write such a thing if he did not?" The author invites the reader to read this as a trauma narrative, as if she had to narrate such harrowing experiences in order to cope with her memory of them. Moreover, the narrator mentions that her father is suffering from Alzheimer's disease, which may be an added incentive for the reader to assume that the author wants to answer her father in published writing while he can still (barely) remember his crime. Yet the reader knows from the experience of reading not to conflate narrator and author, and knows from reading this particular author not to take her at face value; her daughter, Léonore, dies at the end of *Léonore, toujours,* for example, only to be resurrected with no further explanation in subsequent texts. The reader is tempted at all points to think "But how she can write that of her lover/friend/father/daughter?" and herein lies the playful genius of Angot's work. Readers may even feel that they have some sense of ownership of this author, that they know intimate details about her and her family and that her identity is thus containable, yet Angot seems intent on periodically exposing this as fallacious.

Ernaux's and Angot's treatment of shame thus implicates others in their writing in opposite ways. Ernaux's reluctance to name others puts the emphasis more squarely on herself, heightening the narcissistic element of the text yet also playing with the reader's sensibilities; she invites us to read the narrator as her, to interpret the shameful acts as a confession of real-life trauma, and refers so sparingly to others in order to support this invitation. Angot pushes this yet further, showing the reader how s/he wants to believe that s/he knows her and pushing the narcissism to its limit; she writes "her" own shame and anybody else's she wants to, thus creating a narrator with whom the reader sympathizes but whom s/he may also doubt and even resent.

Shaming the Reader?

These lists of shame, and the process of shaming one's self and one's others, begs the question: Why put this out there to be read? Why try to shock, embarrass or disturb one's reader, repeatedly and relentlessly? The shame becomes the negotiation between reader and writer, and the authors' awareness that they are writing very clearly for a reader is a central motor in both texts. Each implicates the reader as an other in their story of shame, as the reader is the other who makes the shame exist: the spectator who enables the shaming mechanism. Both authors try from the beginning to shock the reader as s/he reads their socially unacceptable behaviors in such stark, seemingly shameless prose. Furthermore, they lay themselves bare to the reader as a stereotype that many women would want to resist; they write themselves as stereotypically hysterical women who have fallen obsessively in love—"obsession" is a word that Ernaux in particular uses repeatedly throughout the text—and whose thoughts and actions are altered by the force of their obsessive yearning. Ernaux's narrator refers to her reader on several occasions throughout the text, in an avowal of the author's consciousness of the possible effects of publication. In a reference to what would seem to be Ernaux's entire corpus, the narrator writes, "[J]e me demande si je n'écris pas pour savoir si les autres n'ont pas fait ou ressenti des choses identiques, sinon, pour qu'ils trouvent normal de les ressentir" (*Passion simple*, 65) ("Sometimes I wonder if the purpose of my writing is to find out whether other people have done or felt the same things or, if not, for them to consider experiencing such things as normal" [*Simple Passion*, 50–51]). Ernaux thus acknowledges her engagement with her reader openly and hints that she is always very aware as she is writing that her work will be read and may have certain effects upon those who read it. Moreover, this invites the reader to view the narrator as the author and to conflate the two as s/he reads; the "I" clearly belongs to the unnamed narrator, but the reference to her other works suggests a wider interpretation. In addition, the confessional tone of the text itself, with its seeming closeness to the reader, invites us to believe that Ernaux is telling us her personal secrets, and showing that she is really like us. For example, she writes: "[J]'étais sûre qu'il n'y avait jamais rien eu de plus important dans ma vie, ni avoir des enfants, ni réussir des concours, ni voyager loin, que cela, être au lit avec cet homme au milieu de l'après-midi" (*Passion simple*, 19) ("I knew that nothing in my life [having children, passing exams, traveling to faraway countries] had ever meant as much to me as lying in bed with that man in the middle of the afternoon" [*Simple Passion*, 8]). Although this is potentially shocking—and shameful—Ernaux seems to be playing with the intimacy of confession to enable us to think that we know her, that we have something in common with her, that there is a selfishness in all of us that corresponds to her emotion. This is also in evidence as the narrator discusses the writing process itself, commenting upon the effects of writing the story and her desire to record something in writing to capture her passion. Tellingly, she writes, "Je ne ressens naturellement aucune honte à noter ces choses, à cause du délai qui sépare le moment où elles s'écrivent, où je suis seule à les voir, de celui où elles seront lues par les gens et qui, j'ai l'impression, n'arrivera jamais" (*Passion simple*, 42) ("Naturally I feel no shame in writing these things because of the time which separates the moment when they are written—when only I can see them—from the moment when they will be read by other people, a moment which I feel will never come" [*Simple*

Passion, 29]). Here, the narrator claims to be distanced from the reader—aware of the reader's presence but existing in a different reality—and to be absolved of any shame due to the different temporalities of writing and reading. Yet by attempting to distance herself from the reader in this way, she draws her/him in all the more, emphasizing the connections between the "I" of the narrator and the phantom "I" of Ernaux herself, and inviting us to read them as one, indissociable entity.

Angot plays upon the reader's sensibilities in very similar ways. The barrage of shameful behaviors is longer and more acute in Angot's text, as this author seems intent on forcing the shame upon the reader, and even to be provoking shame in her/him; the reader may well react when reading, for example, of how she imagines her child, Léonore, having graphic sex with men in adulthood, or when she recounts the scenes of incest. Such intimate confessions both repel and attract the reader as we are drawn into the text and may be tempted to read it with our hands partially covering our eyes as though watching a disturbing film. As Alex Hughes writes, Angot's "game . . . is enacted before a reader who is interpellated by the Angotian narrative voice of the texts under scrutiny, whose reactions Angot's writing anticipates and who, critics concur, cannot fail to be discomfited by that writing" (66). Just as in Ernaux's text, Angot invites the reader to interpret narrator and author as one and the same, and pushes this as far as possible by the name of her narrator, in an orchestrated game that plays upon our readerly desires. The "I" of the narrator is so intimate, so confessional, and so obsessive that the text is at times almost vertiginous; the reader knows "her" so well that s/he is almost uncomfortable, as she reels off random memories associated with the depths of her personality or her search for her pathology in the summaries of mental illness that she quotes from a psychology handbook. In addition to simultaneously pulling the reader in and repelling her/him, inviting her/him to read the text as though it were her personal journal, Angot also refers directly to the reader regularly throughout the work. Amid the narrative of incest, for instance, the narrator breaks off to comment, "Je suis désolée de vous parler de tout ça, j'aimerais tellement pouvoir vous parler d'autre chose" (148) ("I'm sorry to tell you about all of this. I'd really like to be able to talk to you about something else"). Continuing in this vein, and remembering talking to her lesbian lover about the incest, she claims, "Je ne devrais pas écrire ça. Et je ne devrais pas lui en parler. Ce que ça va provoquer, à elle, et à vous, ce sera la même chose, ce sera de la pitié, vous ne pourrez plus m'aimer, ni elle ni vous . . . Vous ne voudrez plus me lire" (148–149; suspension points in original) ("I shouldn't write that. And I shouldn't talk to her about it. What it will provoke, in her, in you, will be the same thing, it will be pity. You'll no longer be able to love me, neither her nor you . . . You won't want to read me anymore"). She is clearly concerned about the effect of her prose upon the reader, and claims to be concerned in particular with the reader's impression of *her.* Yet this will to please the reader, or to find solace or understanding on the reader's part, is presented as tenuous, as she simultaneously rejects the reader's opinions: "Si je parle ça va être pire qu'avant: ça fait du bien d'en parler on va me dire.

Je déteste avoir à écrire ça. Je vous déteste. Je vous hais. Je voudrais ne pas savoir ce que vous pensez. Je sais ce que vous pensez" (149) ("If I talk it will be worse than before: it's good to talk about it, people will say. I hate having to write it. I detest you. I hate you. I don't want to know what you think. I know what you think"). She challenges us directly, forcing us to be absolutely implicated in the text, yet wrong-foots us, changing our position in relation to her constantly; as Isabelle Cata and Eliane DalMolin state regarding Angot's work in general, "[L]ecteur/lectrice, il/elle est alternativement dans le rôle de l'agressé(e) ou dans celui de l'agresseur(e)" (86) ("The reader is in the role of either the aggressed or the aggressor"). As is the case for most of this author's books, a photograph of Angot is on the front cover. She is looking directly at the reader with only the faint beginning of a smile in an open, aggressive challenge, and this challenge is what the book is predicated upon; she challenges the reader to read "her" and know "her." And yet, as is the case with Ernaux, we clearly cannot; the text is thus a deliberate play with the reader, a manipulative game that orchestrates a reading practice that invites her/him to suspend both her/his disbelief and her/his awareness of the distinction between writer, character, and narrator, and all along we are being duped.

* * *

Passion Simple and *L'Inceste* therefore call into question our understanding of shame and its representation in narrative first by confronting the reader with a multitude of shameful thoughts, feelings, and actions. By presenting the reader with a gamut of shame, from sexual acts recounted in stark prose to narratives of incest to stereotypically hysterical behavior, these texts confront the reader with sources of shame as it is socially codified. Moreover, the fact that these are *women* authors who narrate traditionally shameful things, specifically concerning sexuality and desire, through the voices of *female* narrators, pushes the boundaries of propriety still further. There is certainly an empowerment in these women's ability to narrate and publish tales of female sexuality, and their work thus furthers a movement toward free expression of sex and desire. Nevertheless, taken together, these texts move beyond a (very necessary and potentially liberating) representation of shame to comment more broadly upon the parameters of confession and autobiography. By playing with the representation of shame, these authors draw the reader into the texts, inviting her/him to read in a way that blurs the boundary between author and narrator. These texts confront us with our own desires as we read, laying bare our curiosity surrounding the authors themselves and encouraging us to think "Did Ernaux really do that?" or "Did Angot really suffer that?" Ernaux's work has been interrogated by many critics in terms of its representation of shame, but a comparison with Angot's text points up the generic play in which both writers are engaged. Although the writing of shame is very important in both of these texts, it is possible to read the shame as a trope that makes a wry comment upon current practices of writing and reading life writing; whether one is told that a first-person narrative is autobiographical or not, one is often tempted to read it as so, and to build up a developing picture of an author based upon her growing corpus. Although Ernaux confronts us with the reality of passion and Angot with the reality of incest, among other things, they simultaneously expose us as readers who are so fascinated by the everyday lives of our literary superstars. These works show how we are tempted to engage with certain texts in the same way as we watch reality TV, assuming that the participants are "real" and suspending our belief in what we—and the authors—have always known: no matter how grounded these narratives are in lived reality, they are always ultimately fallacious.

Notes

1. For more on this, see Claire Marrone's analysis of the past tenses employed in this text.

2. All translations are my own, except for those from *Passion simple,* which come from Tanya Leslie's published translation.

3. Laurent Demoulin has highlighted the similarities between Angot's work and that of Hervé Guibert, another writer who played with the literary representation of shame. Demoulin notes that this phrase seems to be borrowed from Guibert's *A l'ami qui ne m'a pas sauvé la vie,* which begins "[J]'ai eu le sida pendant trois mois. Plus exactement, j'ai cru pendant trois mois que j'étais condamné par cette maladie mortelle qu'on appelle le sida" (9). ("I had AIDS for three months. More precisely, for three months, I thought I was condemned by that deadly illness called AIDS")

4. Elizabeth Richardson Viti points out that even the choice of "A" is a further concealment, since the lover's real first initial was "S."

5 Interactions of Disability Pride and Shame

Eliza Chandler

IN THIS CHAPTER, I write about the interrelatedness of disability pride and shame. I suggest that when an unwavering satisfaction with our embodiment is understood as a prerequisite for embodying disability pride, we constitute disabled people with wavering relations to their embodiment as "excludable types" (Titchkosky, 149–150).

This chapter explicates my supposition that popular ways of imagining disability pride, as existing in complete abandonment of shame, excludes those of us who relate to our embodiment with a wavering pride. Thus, this chapter presents a configuration of pride and shame in which these two embodied relations can exist together. To begin, I discuss how disability pride appears in popular "discourse," using websites and life narratives (Foucault, *Archaeology of Knowledge*). In my interpretive textual analyses, I am particularly attentive to how these texts articulate that embracing disability with pride requires a turn away from shame. I reveal how this popular structure for telling the story of disability pride excludes those of us whose satisfaction with our disabled bodies wavers—a wavering bodily relation that my experiences of cerebral palsy tell me is often a reality. I then turn my attention to shame. In this section I engage Ahmed's articulation of "stickiness" to explore how shame can swell up under our skin and "stick" us to the world and its common, everyday understandings and interpretations of disability (*Cultural Politics*). Here I use Ahmed's work along with the cultural theorist Sally Munt's 2007 writing on shame in order to think through how an epithet called out to us has the potential to lurch us out of our sense of "being-in-the-world" with pride, by causing us to swell with shame (Sartre). I suggest that because this shame can "stop things moving," we need pride to keep from being shamefully held back (Ahmed, *Cultural Politics*, 27).

This chapter's conclusion suggests that when we constitute a normative standard for how one should come into disability with pride, as always and only articulating the requisite move of turning away from shame, we foreclose the opportunity to tell the other stories of bodily relations. I articulate how the move of turning away from shame—required by us in order to come into disability with pride—requires us to also turn away from possible stories of disability pride that may live beneath our bones in countless ways. This chapter closes with a story that describes how living with disability pride is necessary for me to take care of myself in moments of public humiliation wherein I inevitably feel ashamed.

According to disability studies[1] cultural theorists David Mitchell and Sharon Snyder, "nearly every culture regards disability as a 'problem' in need of solution" (47). The understanding that disability is located in individual problematic minds, bodies, senses, and emotions informs our current Westernized cultural understanding of disabled embodiments (Michalko, *Difference*, 1–8; Titchkosky). The cultural imagination of disability as a problem that "needs" to be solved tells disabled people that shame is one of the most appropriate emotions through which to orient to our embodiment. Shame[2] is appropriate insofar as we, disabled people, are ashamed of "our problem" and this shame drives us to seek a solution through, for example, medicalization, rehabilitation, or simply ignoring our embodiment at all costs. In the midst of the cultural requirement to be ashamed of disability—our own and those of others—the possibility of being proud of disability may seem to be contradictory when one first comes across the idea of disability pride. And yet, from my experience I know that the more time one spends with the conceptual possibility of disability pride, the more likely it is to transform from an unthinkable concept into a desirable way of "being-in-the-world" (Sartre).

Through disability pride, understood as an orientation to disability and not as a solution to it, we can recognize disability as an identity that binds us to others and to the world rather than as an individual problem experienced in isolation. Disability pride can enable us to come together in communities, develop cultures, work out subversive and reclamation languages, and establish a personhood of "disabled people" as an alternative to a disconnected population of "people with disabilities." In other words, disability pride can allow us to "be at home" in our disabled embodiments and live comfortably in the world in disability rather than being estranged from it (Ahmed, *Phenomenology*, 9). "Be[ing] at home" in our disabilities and being honest about the nuances of our embodied experiences also requires us to be open to and engage with the "trouble" our corporeality might cause us sometimes, or all the time, and the resulting shame we may experience (Michalko, "Double Trouble," 401–416). Because of the nuanced character of disability, and indeed the nuanced character of all embodiments and our relationships to them, we may not necessarily always experience pride in the abandonment of shame. Thus, I use this chapter to think through the concept of disability pride as it is currently understood in the disability rights movement in order to make a new pride "materialize" which does not elide those of us who may orient to our disabilities with shame, frustration, or embarrassment (J. Butler). Instead, I conceive of a pride in disability that is accessible to all disabled people regardless of their current and ever-shifting relationship to their embodiment. In this chapter, I offer a configuration of pride and shame that suggests that these bodily relations do not live in isolation within the others' exclusion but instead arise together and cannot be untangled for individual consideration. More than this, I suggest that some disabled people are constituted as "excludable types" when unwavering satisfaction with our embodiment is constituted as a prerequisite for relating to disability with pride (Titchkosky, 149–150).

This chapter begins with a discussion of how disability pride appears in popular texts, such as life narratives and websites. In my analyses of these texts, I am particularly attentive to how they articulate that orienting to disability with pride requires us to turn away from shame. I reveal how this popular structure for telling the story of disability pride potentially excludes those of us whose satisfaction with our disabled bodies wavers. The second part of this chapter interrogates shame in order to argue that the experience of feeling ashamed does not necessarily elide the possibility of feeling proud. Using Sara Ahmed's articulation of "stickiness," I explore how shame can swell up under our skin and "stick" us to the world (*Cultural Politics*). Ahmed's work also helps me think through how an epithet called out to us on the street holds the potential to lurch us out of our sense of "being in the world." I also draw upon Frantz Fanon's writing on the experience of being apprehended by the epithet "Negro," whose interpretation of his black subjectivity is incongruent with his self-definition. This chapter closes with a story that describes how living with disability pride is necessary for me to take care of myself in moments of public humiliation wherein I inevitably feel ashamed.

Disability Pride

When crafting a new disability pride that does not constitute some of us as "excludable types," I do not propose that we do away with the popular conception of disability pride altogether. Not only is the idea that disability can be an identity to take pride in rather than a "problem in need of solution," an idea that may initially disorient us (and may in fact continue to be disorienting for some), disability pride can also be key to inspiring collective human rights action, community, culture, and arts practice. Instead, I am suggesting that we must build upon the version of pride that has emerged in conjunction with the disability rights movement.[3] In this section I analyze three texts that I believe to be representative of how disability pride is currently imagined. The first text, "Why Disability Pride?" (Triano), offers a current definition of disability pride as it is popularly imagined in the disability rights movement. The second text is from the seminal book in disability studies, *Pride against Prejudice*, by the disability activist Jenny Morris. This text articulates how disability pride can be used to mobilize community action. In the third text, "Escape from Shame," Tammy S. Thompson offers a personal account of how she turned away from a life of shame in order to live with disability pride. In my textual analyses, I refer to Tanya Titchkosky, who posits: "Texts never just get it right or wrong insofar as they are also a 'doing'—right or wrong, texts are always *oriented social actions* producing meaning" (21; emphasis in original).

Following Titchkosky, I understand that it is necessary for me to engage these texts in which meanings of disability pride have already appeared, not to judge them as "good" or "bad," "right" or "wrong," but rather to understand how meanings of pride have already materialized in the "doings" of these texts. Titchkosky also writes, following the feminist sociologist Dorothy Smith:[4] "Text gives us a starting place where we can organize an encounter between our embodied selves reading in time and space, and the time of the text with the space it delineates, as all of this orders our consciousness" (15). Starting with texts, I inquire into the meaning of pride as it has already materialized through others' work to discover how my developing work relates to, and finds a place in, this "discourse," which, according to Michel Foucault, establishes "the grounds of possibilities and impossibilities of what can be said" (*Archaeology*, 130).

According to "Why Disability Pride?":

> Fundamentally, Disability Pride represents a rejection of the notion that our difference from the non-disabled community is wrong or bad in any way and is a statement of our self-acceptance, dignity and pride. It signifies that we are coming out of the closet and are claiming our legitimate identity. It's a public expression of our belief that our disability and identity are normal, healthy and right for us and is a validation of our experience. (Triano)[5]

This description of disability pride is powerful and promising. Disability is an embodied experience that appears in our popular imagination as regrettable, problematic, and shameful. And because of this cultural expectation and requirement to be ashamed of disability, disability pride discourses are an investment in rejecting shame altogether. Therefore, resisting the idea that the "difference the disability makes" is simply wrong or bad is a necessary starting point, which this declaration of disability pride provides (Michalko, *Difference*). The claim of "self-acceptance" and the belief that "disability and identity are normal," however, do not necessarily reflect the myriad of goals of an entire disabled personhood. People like me (and possibly you) who do not necessarily want to gain social valorization by suggesting that disabled people simply do "normal" differently, or who do not necessarily reject "the notion that [their] difference is wrong or bad in any way," are excluded from disability pride when the proud disabled person is only imagined in this way. Sometimes disability does give us "trouble" in a way that may seem or feel "wrong or bad" and we may not necessarily want to "accept" this "trouble" with "dignity" all of the time.

This above description of disability pride tells us that we must definitively turn away from shame, and the possibility that we may ever again feel ashamed of our disability, in order to experience our disabled embodiment with pride. In such an articulation, the journey from shame to pride follows a one-way, disappearing path; the arrival at orienting to disability with pride is marked by one's turn away from shame—never to return. This story of finding pride may be useful; certainly turning away from self-hatred and hatred of other disabled people is an essential part of regarding disability as an identity rather than a problem to be solved. Yet, when we constitute a normative standard for achieving disability pride, one that requires us to definitively turn away from shame, we also turn away from the possibility that stories of disability pride can live beneath our bones in countless ways. In adopting such a standard, we foreclose possibilities of both telling and listening to stories that articulate messy experiences of pride—ones that are not constrained to a structure of departure and arrival. To begin to think about how disability pride could be imagined otherwise, I turn to two texts that describe the experience of identifying as disabled with pride as requiring a definitive turn away from shame.

In her book Jenny Morris writes about the experience of becoming disabled later in life, as a result of an accident causing a spinal cord injury that paralyzed her lower body (2). Upon being diagnosed and thus recognized as disabled, Morris was confronted with the assumption by doctors and others around her that her new corporeality was "tragic" (3). "In subtle and not so subtle ways," Morris tells us, "a number of people conveyed to me that they felt my life was no longer worth living" (3). Morris writes that she felt "outraged" by the assumption that her life had taken a tragic turn (3). While it seemed unfair that all she had worked so hard to achieve—personally and professionally—might have been jeopardized by her accident, she did not think of her disability as tragic (3). She quickly resolved that the structure of her life would remain largely "unchanged" and decided that all that would have to change was that she would now be doing things from a "sitting position" from her wheelchair (3).

Soon after her accident, however, Morris realized that things could not continue "unchanged" from "a sitting position" since being disabled, she discovered, made her fundamentally different from, and set apart from, the non-disabled world (3). Moreover, coming together with other disabled people "bound" in community by their disability was perceived by non-disabled people as pitiable rather than something to be celebrated (170). Of this discovery Morris writes:

> Many of us find that joining together with other disabled people brings a feeling of strength. However, when we take collective action together, or organize our own cultural event, we have to fight against the negative connotations of just being together in a group of disabled people. To overcome [the attitude that a group of disabled people are a subject of pity, fascinated repulsion, and, sometimes, fear], however, is to feel empowered by joining together. (170–171)

Throughout her book, Morris articulates that her pride materializes in the politicized act of joining together in disabled communities. By recognizing disability as an identity through which to organize friendships and political actions, Morris and her disability community combat social and systemic discrimination upheld by the assumption that disability is "personal tragedy" (2).

Near the end of her book, Morris tells the story of the day that she and other disabled people came together at their local BBC television station to protest the charitable event "Children in Need," which raises money for "disadvantaged children" (190). Organized by the Campaign to Stop Patronage, disabled people rallied together to protest "the way that the charity system uses negative images of disabled people to raise money for things we should receive as a right, instead of having to beg, conform with or show gratitude to patronizing organizations over which we have no control" (190). Morris writes that the people attending the "Children in Need" event were surprised to see disabled people protesting a charitable organization that was meant to "benefit" them and that in fact initially they treated the disabled protesters as though they had come to express thanks, even though they were positioned behind picket placards (191). But "thanks" was not what they had come to offer. Instead, this group of disabled people had shown up to trouble their normative construction as pitiful by the "Children in Need" campaign and similar charities (190).

Morris's pride is defined in opposition to, and as a rejection of, the assumption that "we feel ugly, inadequate and ashamed of our disability" (18). As such, her pride is constituted by what it is not—shame—and therefore, it seems, dwelling in shame is an impossibility for a proud disabled person. In other words, Morris's proclamation of pride requires us to become *other than* the ashamed subject culture expects her/us to be.

Together, through pride and in the abandonment of shame, Morris and her "crip community" (I prefer this term to "disability community") organize politically and advocate for necessary change. I do not mean to dismiss the gravity of these political actions, which almost definitely changed the way that some of the people who witnessed their presence at the charity event understood and experienced disability.

I have stories, though they are not definitive, in which I was completely proud of my disability, and my shame was (momentarily) eliminated in all of its traces. Through my "crip community" and dwelling in cripped[6] spaces, together we can "do disability differently" and provoke new imaginings of disability in congruence with how we experience our embodiments (Titchkosky). "Being-at-home" in my crip community inspires me to relate to disability *other than* as a "difference which should not make a difference" (Michalko, *Difference*, 94). And within my disability community, sometimes my pride overcomes shame. Sometimes, but not all the time, my pride is steady even when I am wielded as a shameful subject by another's look. Here is one of those stories:

> There I was, moving down the sidewalk, College Street in Toronto. I was walking toward a meeting with my supervisors, Rod and Tanya, to discuss mounting a disability arts exhibit at the Ontario Institute for Studies in Education (OISE), where I go to school. This walk was motivated by my destination for I was excited to get there and worried that I was late. I was hardly dwelling in the in-between, my mind was already there. I moved swiftly down the sidewalk, weaving carefully between and around pedestrians. This walk was different than most. I usually carry a purse on my left shoulder so that the bag hangs down by my right hand. Such positioning disguises the disabled character of this hand, as it appears that its stiffness is caused by its proximity to the bag. But on this morning I carried my bag on my right shoulder—my left one was sore, probably from overuse. My right arm was unattached to do what it may. I passed a woman, my right hand curled up into my stomach, comfortably. I heard her laugh, and then, I heard her say, "Well, well, look at her."

Here, I turned too. Turned away from the robust potential for embarrassment, to be "stuck" back to shame, resisting its temptation, which did not even materialize as a tempt (Ahmed, *Cultural Politics*). I did not think to force my right hand down, hiding it behind my back. Shame did not swell and I sailed on with a steady pride. Still focused on the destination, knowing that at the end of this walk I would land in an unwavering crip community, my pride did not waver either even in the midst of laughter at me. This was a proud walk; the in-betweeness of this walk constituted by the character of the destination.

Although I do not always feel unwaveringly proud of my disability, I recognize that by disregarding the stories in which my pride is steady and shame does not materialize, I neglect the power of crip communities that stay with me, and possibly you too, even when I feel alone on the streets. To treat these stories of unwavering bodily satisfaction as the only stories of pride, however, would be to ignore my stories and those of others.

To continue wondering about being in the in-betweeness of pride and shame, I move to another story with another turn away from pride. This is a story from *Mouth*, a bimonthly magazine dedicated to disability rights and discrimination issues. In this story, "Escape from Shame" by Tammy S. Thompson, pride is again constituted by a "turn" away from shame. Thompson begins her story in the fashion that is often used to articulate pride, namely lingering over the details of the pain and loneliness that she experienced when living in shame of her blindness. Thompson writes: "I've spent many years on a mission to cancel out my disability by frantically stacking up achievements, hoping that someday I would find that final, magic accomplishment which would absolve me of the sin of being disabled" (56). When reading this passage I felt her frenzy of trying to make up for the deficit of her disability by accomplishing more, by doing more. Her description of the isolation and sadness provoked by the "stigma" of her disability reached a memory that lives in my bones; a memory never to be erased by my current, and also shifting, bodily relation (Goffman, *Stigma*). There was a time when I too hated my disabled body; these memories remind me that living in complete shame of my disability before I had any concept of disability pride is, indeed, not a place to which I wish to return.

Halfway through Thompson's description of how she came to identify as disabled with pride, she speaks of a definitive movement in which her shame turned into pride once and for all. After living half of her life ashamed of her blindness, regarding it as a problem in need of a solution, but indeed one that could not be solved, Thompson definitively turned away from shame. Thompson discovered the idea disability pride, which, as it did for me, first appeared an "oxymoron," a strangely unthinkable concept (56). This pride was "sticky," though, and it attached itself to her in a relentless way. Thompson writes, "I had to find out more" (56). She joined the disability rights movement and turned. *Then* Thompson's ways of "being-in-the-world" were "liberated" and the "disability warriors"—her comrades in the movement—taught her "a new way to live" that freed her from her past (56–57). Her strong claim that "[t]oday my friends in the movement are teaching me how to accept my disability and carry myself with pride" provides the emancipatory ending to this narrative of pride which rose up from, and lives in abandonment of, shame (57).

When we choose to tell our stories of pride as living only in the shadow of shame, who are we excluding? Moreover, when the path from pride to shame is imagined as swift and disappearing, which of our experiences are we neglecting to tell or even consider? Are we, the wavering, disqualified from disability pride and all the possibilities it holds? Is this the end of the story? My analysis of this version of pride and of my lived experience prompts me to wonder how I, along with other disability scholars, artists, and activists, might imagine disability pride in new ways. Disability studies offers a critical paradigm that asks us to be unsatisfied with the constitution of a norm and challenges us to rethink the meaning of bodies deemed "abnormal." Might disability studies also invite us to trouble the conceptualization of a "normal" proud disabled person, and come up with more versions of disability pride (Michalko and Titchkosky)? In this project of making a pride "materialize" anew we must hold close the popular imagination of disability pride as we think about how to establish new possibilities for meanings of pride that seek not to normalize disability, but to trouble these popular imaginations of pride, which simultaneously trouble popular imaginations of shame—it is to this later imaginary to which I now turn.

Shame

I now explore the togetherness of pride and shame more specifically as well as continue to engage the in-betweenness that exists in their midst. Here, I pay particular attention to the way that shame can swell up within us when we are in the midst of others.

When describing shame, Sally Munt draws upon Charles Darwin's writings on this emotion. Darwin suggests that shame appears in the moment of our recognition by another, as he writes: "It is not the simple act of reflecting on our appearance, but the thinking what others think of us, which excites a blush" (qtd. in Munt, 6). Munt expands on Darwin articulation, asserting that the noticeable manifestation of shame—Darwin's example, "blushing"—only appears in the midst of others, revealing that shame requires witness. In his description of an encounter between a doctor and a woman "suffering" epilepsy, Darwin suggests that blushing comes to the noticeably disabled body when it meets its (medicalized) gaze. He writes that "the moment that he [the doctor] approached, she blushed deeply over her cheeks and temples; and the blush spread quickly to her ears" (qtd. in Munt, 6). In this description, shame is written upon the noticeably different body with the pen of the blush. Shame comes into being within the subject because of self-attention induced by another; in this case, the other is the doctor.

Shame is not written on the body always and only through a blush, as Darwin suggests. I disagree with Darwin's presupposition that the shame sparked by an interaction is located strictly in the (a)shamed individual—the one with the marked body—

and not shared between the two interacting parties necessary to ignite recognition. Still, I agree with his claim that shame is made manifest in the midst of others. Situations provoked by my disability, for example, that frustrate me or cause me pain when I am alone become shameful when witnessed by another. When I trip on an empty sidewalk, I regard this trip only for the pain it causes me. Shame may swell when I think of how this trip may appear to another. A trip in the midst of others—even helping others or friendly-familiar others—may always be experienced as shameful. Witnessing by others, even when the others may only exist in one's imagination or memory, provokes the significant transmogrification of pain into shame.

Cultural theorist Sara Ahmed also understands shame as that which swells in the midst of others and as well as an emotion that can "stick" us to the world. Ahmed suggests that the transference of emotions is "sticky" (*Cultural Politics*, 89–92) and the "agency of emotions is not to be found in one place, within the self, or within the social" (89). She writes:

> Stickiness . . . is what objects do to other objects—it involves a transference of affect—but it is a relation of "doing" in which there is not a distinction between passive or active, even though the stickiness of one object might come before the stickiness of the other, so that the other seems to cling to it. (91)

Working with Ahmed's words, Munt suggests we consider how much the epithet "queer" is sticky in multiple senses: "A sticky wicket for some to negotiate intellectually or politically, recalling the dual significance of 'tacky' as in gummy and cheap, and even the accusation/appellation 'Queer!' sticks . . ." (12).

Similarly, as a disabled person, ableist epithets "stick" to me. My embodiment of cerebral palsy (CP) does not allow me to endure without becoming noticeably jolted the experience of having the call of an epithet "stick" me back to a time when I exclusively related to my body through shame. When I hear the epithet "retard" called out at me or around me, my head snaps back quickly and my right hand retreats into my stomach, where it is most comfortable. I even make a small noise. These bodily reactions do not indicate that I am ashamed in myself and by myself. My shame only and always swells in the midst of others. By this I do not mean that we necessarily need to physically be in the midst of others in order to feel shame, for we are always with others—in our memories and in our thoughts—even when we are alone. Because of this, we always have the possibility of swelling with shame in solitude. Ahmed tells us: "Insofar as shame is about appearances, shame is about how the subject appears to and for others" (*Cultural Politics*, 105). My shame requires the witness of another, whose normalizing gaze transmogrifies me into the "containment of difference" (Bhabha, 72). Such an apprehension by another provides the difference for me to be different from in order for the other to achieve their subjectivity of sameness (Bhabha, 57–93). In this moment, I am ashamed of the version of my body that materalizes for others: nothing more or less than a failure of the normative standard of corporeality. This swelling of shame does not necessarily indicate that I regard my embodied self as failure, for I do not share these normalizing ideals with this "normate"[7]-other (Garland-Thomson, *Staring*, 8).

Epithets can stick to us and lurch us out of our sense of being by the way that such words, such as "queer" or "retard," when called out to us in an antagonistic rather than communal way, can stick us to the hegemonic understandings of our embodiments. And this "doing" can affect our sense of "being-at-home" in our embodiments. Ahmed tells us that "[s]ome forms of stickiness are about holding things together while others are about blockages or stopping things moving" (*Cultural Politics*, 91). Following Ahmed, I suggest that the epithet shouted out by another can excite shame, an uncontrollable swelling of blood underneath our bones. The epithet can stick to us in a way that stops things from moving—stops meaning from moving. Whenever I hear the word "retard," for example, it will always be stuck to teases and taunts that leaked into my body during a time when I was without pride, filling me up with loneliness, self-hatred, and shame. Unlike other words, such as "crip," "retard" can never be communally reclaimed because of its particular stickiness. I can claim "crip" as my own word, or embrace it as a word reclaimed by my community, to which I/we can assign new meaning, for "crip" has never been hurled at me, carelessly, recklessly, even pointedly, the way "retard" has. Because its stickiness does not attach me to haunting memories, "crip" is the word I have chosen to use to name my disabled identity and refer to my community. "Crip" sticks to me, but it "holds me together" to a community and a sense of pride. It is difficult for me—in this body with its attachments to history stuck to memories that will never leave my bones—to hear "retard" as anything other than a "blockage," for this epithet calls me back to a time when I regarded my disability as nothing other than a problem to be solved or be embarrassed about; a time when this word gained its stickiness and stuck me to shame and silence; a time when these binds were not easily unstuck.

To think further about how my recognition as the "containment of difference" by others can cause us to swell up with, or be jolted into, shame, I turn to Fanon's description of an experience of being apprehended by an epithet called out at him on the street. In his book *Black Skin, White Masks*, Fanon tells the reader of an experience of being apprehended wherein through the "liberating gaze" of others, he is taken out of the world and put back into the world (89). For here, in this world, "not only must the black man be black, he must also be black in relation to the white man" (90). Fanon describes an interaction with another in which he is brought into the world through his recognition when the epithet "Negro" is called at him. Fanon writes:

> "Look! A Negro!" It was a passing sting. I attempted a smile.
> "Look! A Negro!" Absolutely. I was beginning to enjoy myself.
> "Look! A Negro!" The circle was gradually getting smaller. I was really enjoying myself.
> "*Maman*, look, a Negro; I'm scared!" Scared! Scared! Scared! Now they were beginning to be scared of me. I wanted to kill myself with laughter, but laughter had become out of the question. (95)

Fanon had become apprehended, jolted out of, or into, his sense of "being-in-the-world" by an epithet. His epithet—"A Negro!"—uttered by a white boy to his mother, recognized Fanon as someone to be scared of, someone to relate to only through the emotion of fright. And with this recognition, Fanon swelled up with the desire to laugh—a laughter which, for him, "had become out of the question." These words calling him into recognition as "Negro" transform Fanon into a trope of dangerous difference, "sticking" him to a blackness defined by cannibalism, backwardness, fetishism, racial stigmas, slave traders (92). These conceptions cannot be disrupted by his lived reality, even if he does not define himself through this (frightening) version of blackness. These words, these conceptions, as they make up part of the world he encounters, will always be a part of Fanon's world and thus affect his "being-in-the-world."

Fanon also describes wanting to "be a man and nothing but a man" (92), which is similar to how I desire to be a woman unstuck from the past hurt that lives in my bones, that swells me into the world with shame by a call, a trip, or a stare. Through his recognition as "Negro," Fanon is also stuck to the past, stuck to his ancestors, "enslaved and lynched" (92). It is through the stickiness of the interaction that Fanon is brought into, and exists, in the world. In his past, a past and ancestry replete with pride and a past with white others replete with shame, Fanon lives.

Pride and Shame

Disability is not mine to hold or another's to claim. Rather, disability is made meaningful in the midst of others. It is neither yours nor mine, but ours. Living with others, as we do, means that there is always the possibility of being apprehended through the interpretive call of another. In the moment wherein I am recognized and called out as "retard" on the streets, the meaning of my CP/disability is taken away from my shaky grasp and changed into another character. In this moment, my CP/disability is stuck to limited imagination. I appear for others as a convenient trope in which I materialize as a living problem, i.e., my disabled body indicating nothing more than its failure. Through this captivating move by another, the meaning of my bodily matter is taken from me. Here, I stand on the street in a shamefully "stolen body" (Clare). Because I will always be with others, even when I am alone, the possibility of swelling with shame will always be with me. Yet, this shame is never definitive of the whole story of my bodily relations—and it certainly is not the end of the story. I may be "stunned into recognition" of otherness by another (Hughes and Patterson, 603). And this shame, as Ahmed reminds us, may stop things—in this case my body—from moving. In this moment of standing still but still standing, pride has not left my body. Through it, I can eventually keep moving down the sidewalk. These interactions between pride and shame and between others and myself remind me of the temporal beat of pride and shame. For these characters move, shift, mix up, and float away; they stick me to the world never one without the other.

To demonstrate how we can dwell in shame with pride, thereby relating to it differently (in a way *other than* being ashamed), I turn to a final story:

A few days ago, I had tripped on a crack and fallen hard . . . hard enough to break bones in my right hand, which typically bears the brunt of my falls. With my right hand now in a cast, the doctor told me to be "extra careful" in my steps. This bit of professional "advice" did little to steady my shaky gait. My right foot still dragged a little when I walked and sometimes I tripped on the cracks that bind together paving stones. We—two friends and I—were walking together, each carrying another's newly purchased secondhand finds. I was also holding my casted right hand with my left hand, nestling it close into my body. And then, I tripped and fell. Though my walk always holds the possibility of tripping, each trip comes to me as a surprise. This trip was no different: I was startled as I crashed down to the ground, painfully. This time, my body turned to protect my broken hand. My head hit the ground first and took most of the impact. As I lay on the ground, men ran out of stores, pulling down my skirt that had flown up around my head, and my friends crouched down to me carefully, shooing the others away. In this fall, shame was undeniable and potentially unbearable. But, curiously, in the midst of my potential apprehension in which shame most certainly materialized, my pride remained with me. I knew that my head needed care. I had bumped it quite hard. I could not get up just yet. I needed to stay here, on the ground, dwelling in the crack. Though I was not feeling particularly proud in the moments that I lay on the sidewalk, through pride I could relate to this shameful situation differently.

Eventually I did get up—and when I did, I noticed that the cast that I had been so carefully carrying was now broken too. This was too much. Embarrassment, frustration, and annoyance swelled—my head throbbed with pain. And again, I needed to take care. I began crying hard, right there on the sidewalk, without hiding my face or muffling my heavy sobs, in the "coolest" part of town. This was a shameful situation, to be sure—and I recognized it as such. I dwelled in this shame, but I did not relate to it from the body of an ashamed subject. Through pride, I was given the possibility to linger on the sidewalk in my shame and take care.

This interaction of pride and shame demonstrates that these two bodily orientations can, and perhaps, ideally, *must,* exist in togetherness. I cannot be with a pride that does not embrace shame because this wavering between pride and shame makes up the reality of my embodiment. Pride needs shame as its taken-for-granted ground from which it can be distinct. And shame needs pride too. Shame needs pride to exist with it in tandem rather than in its abandonment. Through pride, we can pick ourselves up and move on from the sting of shame. Pride and shame also require the relation between others to materialize. "Being-in-the-world" through disability pride gives us the space, the time, and ultimately the alterity to relate differently to the shameful experiences of disability that are provoked by, and occur in, the midst of others. Through pride, we can dwell with comfort in shameful situations that are bound to come to us and bind us to the world.

Notes

1. Disability studies (DS) is the scholarship that arose alongside the disability rights movement. DS holds that disability is not something to be studied; rather, according to disability studies scholars Rod Michalko and Tanya Titchkosky, it "conceives of disability as a socio-political phenomenon, one that marks an occasion to interrogate what we 'normally' think of and experience as 'normal life'" (7).

2. There are certainly other emotional responses to disability; however, in this chapter I am restricting myself to the emotion of shame.

3. Encouraged by examples of other civil rights movements, the disability rights movement aims to provide equity for disabled people through providing access to built environments, implementing policies aimed at equitable rights for disabled people, and confronting negative attitudes about and representations of disabled people. For more information about this movement, see Paul Longmore and Lauri Umansky, *New Disability History: American Perspectives* (New York: New York University Press, 2001), and Jean Paul Shapiro, *No Pity: People with Disabilities Forging a New Civil Rights Movement* (New York: Times Books, 1993).

4. See Dorothy Smith, *Writing the Social* (Toronto: University of Toronto Press, 1999).

5. I recognize that this is only one of many articulations of disability pride that are widely disseminated. However, this chapter is not dedicated to deconstructing all popular articulations of disability pride, and so I've selected this quote as indicative of a sentiment that is widely expressed.

6. I use "cripped" here to describe spaces in which disabled people are welcomed, even desired. These spaces are distinct, for we live in an ableist culture. Simi Linton describes ableism as "discrimination in favour of the able-bodied." Linton adds, "Ableism also includes the idea that a person's abilities or characteristics are determined by disability or that people with disabilities are inferior to non-disabled people" (*Claiming Disability* [New York: New York University Press, 1998], 9).

7. Disability studies cultural theorist Rosemarie Garland-Thomson defines "normate" as "[u]sefully designating the social figure through which people can represent themselves as definitive human beings. Normate, then, is the constructed identity of those who, by way of the bodily configurations and cultural capital they assume, can step into a position of authority and wield the power it grants them" (8).

PART 2

FAMILIES OF SHAME

6 Colonial Shame in Michelle Cliff's *Abeng*

Erica L. Johnson

The daughters' lives were bound, as are the lives of most children, by the personalities of their parents . . . Which of course is nothing new—only something which makes resistance very difficult, and may even make a child believe that resistance is impossible or unnecessary.

Michelle Cliff, *Abeng*

She felt split into two parts—white and not white, town and country, scholarship and privilege, Boy and Kitty.

Michelle Cliff, *Abeng*

Shame in Postcolonial Theory

In a searing passage of *Black Skin, White Masks*, Frantz Fanon analyzes the intersubjective play of colonial race relations as they coalesce in the shameful and painful cry of a white child: "Look, a Negro!" Fanon describes the violence done to himself in this moment, the way in which the gaze of the Other is distilled in the child's utterance and transforms his entire being from having a comprehensive "corporeal schema" to being stripped down to an "epidermal schema": this "peeling, stripping my skin cause[s] a hemorrhage" (92). He follows through on this imagery in his analysis of how his body is routed through the child's remark to be "returned to me spread-eagled, disjointed, redone, draped in mourning on this white winter's day" (93). The flayed body is subject to the Other's projection of primitivism and wickedness onto blackness, and Fanon describes how the palpable violence of the racist gaze makes him feel "imprisoned" and divided internally, ultimately forcing him to "g[i]ve myself up as an object" (92). There are few descriptions of the workings of shame that exceed Fanon's stark description of an interpersonal dynamic that provokes in him the desperate thought so common to shame experiences, of wanting to disappear from the face of the earth, to erase one's subjectivity—"Where should I hide?" (93). Yet what is remarkable about Fanon's portrait of colonial shame is his use of the intersubjective nature of shame as a mechanism for understanding an important affective *axis* of colonial relations. As an axis, shame flows back and forth across colonial binaries; it works through what Liz Constable refers to as a "relational grammar," and thus as a conduit between two subjects rather than as a structured relationship. Indeed, Fanon's first use of the term "*la honte*" (shame) in this passage refers not to his shame, but to the shame felt by the white woman when the object of her child's gaze says, "'Fuck you, madame.' Her face colored with shame." Although later in the passage he refers to the coercive sense of "shame, shame and self-contempt. Nausea" that he is made to feel, Fanon documents how colonialism operates as a shaming ideology as well as the way in which shame is a non-dialectical flow that can be rerouted across colonial binaries as a powerful tool of critique.[1]

The study of shame has flourished recently in the areas of literary studies and political theory, yet much remains to be done on the ways in which colonialism operates as a shaming ideology. The relevance of shame theory to postcolonial thought is evident in the very language of shame studies, which runs parallel to analyses of colonial relations in its emphasis on the self/Other dynamic. What is more, shame is mediated in this relationship differently than other more strictly hierarchical intersubjective dynamics: whereas shame can work to differentiate subjects, as in the case of a shaming ideology such as colonialism, racism, or sexism, it can also forge deep interconnectivity between self and Other by exposing a shared (if painfully violated) value system. Eve Kosofsky Sedgwick and Adam Frank describe the shame affect as "sublimely alien . . . to any project of narrating the emergence of a core self" (6) and as "the alchemy of the contingent" (6), poetic expressions that reflect shame's transcendence of dialectics. Shame thus restructures relations of the self and Other by bringing them into "cartographic distance, not . . . dialectical struggle" (7) with one another. In essence, shame is predicated on the Other's estimation of one's self—or the incorporation of the Other into one's self—and as such it can orchestrate shared values or strike at one's most vulnerable sense of identity. As an important forerunner of shame studies, Fanon identifies both properties of shame and shows how shame is also central to colonial critique. He demonstrates the role of what Constable refers to as "coercive" shame as a mechanism of colonial ideology, while at the same time taking the larger view of the shameful nature of colonial relations in the first place. While his focus in *Black Skin, White Masks* is the damage done to Afro-Caribbean identity by colonial racism, he consistently points out that white identities are also neurotic in this scenario, thus indicating that whatever approach one may take to understanding colonial relations, shame is an essential quality of them.

Fanon observes both the intrapsychic and the interpersonal properties of shame and adds to them that of colonial critique. He rarely uses the language of shame per se; rather, he explores the theme of shame through his analysis of the ways in which people are made to feel "inferior" or "superior" on the basis of their ability to shame or their subjection to shaming. Using the vocabulary of hierarchy to convey the sources of shame in a colonial context, Fanon parses the intersubjective nature of shame in his assessment that "inferiorization is the native correlative to the European's feeling of superiority. Let us have the courage to say: *It is the racist who creates the inferiorized*" (73; emphasis in original). Placing the humiliating feeling of inferiority squarely in the relational space between the colonizer and the colonized, Fanon deterritorializes the self/Other dynamic so that multiple positions are brought into a valenced orbit around what he shows to be a porous if insidious colonial power structure. His critique of colonial ideology achieves the "cartographic distance" Sedgwick and Frank attribute to the shame affect.

Literary expressions of colonial shame have a significant predecessor, if not originator, of the trope: Aimé Césaire's *Cahier d'un retour au pays natal* (*Notebook of a Return to My Native Land*). Fanon refers to Césaire's poem throughout *Black Skin, White Masks*, for it voices the discovery of colonial shame and its legacy of destruction. In sorting out the ways in which the particular colonial iteration of shame interrogates philosophical treatments of ontological shame, Nick Nesbitt also privileges Césaire as a primary thinker whose portrait of shame differentiates colonial from ontological shame, thus critiquing much of continental philosophy. He credits Césaire's 1939 poem with "a kind of de-ontologizing of shame in the same moment that Heidegger was just being read in France" (Nesbitt, 238).[2] What is more, it is Césaire's repudiation of the idea of ontological shame and his illustration of the phenomenal basis of shame that makes his a keystone text in the process of decolonization; Césaire "initiates and invents the process of decolonization in the symbolic order . . . and in so doing, locates the fundamental role played by shame" (Nesbitt, 243). The painful confrontation with colonial shame and the scathing critique of colonialism as a shameful institution were published to the world by Césaire's imagery of rotten homelands and exilic metropoles.

Families of Shame in *Abeng*

Césaire's portrait of colonial shame has its postcolonial counterpart in the work of another Caribbean writer, Michelle Cliff, who presents intricate, powerful portrayals of colonial shame. Cliff is the Jamaican-born author of numerous autobiographical works including a poem with the telling title *Claiming an Identity They Taught Me to Despise*, which condenses the themes found in her autobiographical novel, *Abeng* (1984). As the child of a class- and color-conscious Jamaican family whose ancestors included enslaved Africans and slave-owning colonial authorities alike, Cliff works out in *Abeng* what it means to live at the axis of colonial shame. That is, she demonstrates vicarious shame for victims of Jamaican slavery and inherits the guilt of colonial privilege.[3] Because her protagonist, Clare Savage, is encouraged by her father to pass as white, and thus to deny as shameful the history she and members of her family share with Jamaican blacks, the colonial battlefield is situated squarely in Clare's conscience. As a result, Cliff's portrait exposes the workings of colonial shame and is an exemplary work of postcolonial shaming.

Cliff's tone in *Abeng* is clinically enraged as she recounts, in what she terms "double voiced discourse" (Raiskin), the ignorance of the colonial child and the travesties of Jamaican history as they converge upon Clare in 1958 (four years before Jamaica became nominally independent from Great Britain). The anger of the meticulously researched narrator rubs up against her uneducated protagonist to produce a queasy, unsettled feeling that underlies the entire novel and rises to the foreground in the most fraught of relationships, such as that between her own parents. Within the family, Cliff registers the violence of her country's history in such personal, intimate form that it haunts even the most loving relationships: the proximity of violence to love is a pervasive theme. For example, "the fighting between her parents frightened Clare. She did not think of their battles as violent—because she thought that violence meant someone had to strike a blow, and this they did not do" (Cliff, *Abeng*, 51), yet the narrator's ironic tone conveys the underlying presence of emotional violence. Susan Miller notes the vulnerability of what can be construed as the self in such intimate relationships, pointing out that "[t]he concept of self and also the concept of boundaries are important to the study of shame and other emotions because the individual's articulation of self-boundaries is crucial in determining the specific quality of feeling experience that will result from insults, personal failures, or contacts with others who are perceived as especially powerful or degraded" (168), and "[a] person may also feel shame if he or she defines the self in a fluid manner that designates contact itself to be the criterion of what belongs to the self" (169). Indeed, the child's first reference point in the world is his/her parent and, as most psychologists agree, the child does not even differentiate between self and mother until he/she reaches certain stages of psychological development. This intimacy between mother and child—which in families such as Clare's extends to an intimacy between parents and child—leads Clare to identify so closely with her parents, Boy and Kitty, that to criticize them would amount to auto-criticism; to judge them would be to judge herself. The categorical fluidity the child feels with his or her parents instills within Clare the painful conflicts between her parents as a feeling of shame when, for instance, Boy degrades Kitty and her family, or when Kitty demonstrates spite for Boy. Clare's fluidity with each of her parents ensures that the flow of degradation or spite will wash through her as well.

In one disturbing illustration of the emotional anarchy that results from Boy's implicit contempt for his wife, Boy calls his daughter "an Aztec princess, golden in the sun. 'Clare, you would have certainly been a choice for sacrifice—you know the Aztecs slaughtered their most beautiful virgins and drank their blood.' It did not occur to Clare to question her father's reading of history—a worldview in which she would have been chosen for divine slaughter" (10). Here we see the untenable overlap of love and violence in a father's suggestion that his biracial daughter's beauty lies in her light skin and that this value system rests on a homicidal myth to which he subscribes. In praising his daughter, Boy simultaneously undermines the beauty and worth of Clare's mother. Moreover, to have one's father condone one's suitability for "divine slaughter" introduces violence into what Clare regards as a nurturing bond between Boy and herself, and insinuates that the racial and class conflicts among members of the Savage family stem from deeply buried secrets that throughout the novel are exposed in comments such as this one. J. Brooks Bouson has written at length about the workings of racial shaming and has argued that for many black characters, "white standards of beauty and lovability form, through identification with the oppressor, part of an inner superego between the demand that one conform to the models of the shaming other—white society—and the conflicting demand that one remain loyal to the reality of one's self," resulting in "self-contempt and self-hatred" (Bouson, "Quiet As It's Kept," 10). This characterization reveals the complexity of Clare's position, for she lives in a predominantly black family and community, yet is told to think of herself as white; therefore, she is exposed to the paradox described by Bouson as one who risks identifying not only with, but *as,* the "oppressor"—but of whom? Is she the oppressor of her darker-skinned mother, sister, and grandmother? Is she the oppressor of those elements of herself that her father suggests are unworthy? This is the underlying question with which she must grapple, and the narrative reflects her struggle in multiple iterations of her sense of doubleness: "She felt split into two parts—white and not white, town and country, scholarship and privilege, Boy and Kitty" (Cliff, *Abeng,* 119); "The Black or the white? A choice would be expected of her, she thought" (37); and various episodes trigger "the confusion she felt—part of the split within herself" (96). The intersubjective implications of Clare's intrapsychic sense of racial shame are that she feels separated from the women in her family, while the intrapsychic consequences of Boy's attempts to instill in his daughter a privileging of white beauty are that his daughter will internalize her own oppression. She is caught in the entrails of a shameful past and in a network of shaming relationships, and the fact that they play out in the intimacy of the family blinds Clare to the painful truths the narrator successfully imparts to the reader.

As Cliff remarks here and in other passages, Clare is unable to see the terrible implications of her father's espousal of racist colonial values because they underlie her family dynamics and figure as a fault line in her own identity. Indeed, Clare is aware that race lies at the heart of her family's dysfunction, for—in yet another expression of her doubleness—she thinks of herself as "both dark and light. Pale and deeply colored. To whom would she turn if she needed assistance? From whom would she expect it? Her mother or her father—it came down to that sometimes" (36). The narrator comments on the ramifications of Clare's position with typical precision: "to reckon with her father's culpability would also mean reckoning with her mother's silences—and to see how silence can become complicity. She felt *that* from time to time even now" (76). The affective impact of Boy's guilt enables Clare to *feel* her way toward an understanding of forbidden knowledge about race relations and their origins in the island's colonial history as they are manifest in her divided family and in her own divided identity. Yet the question of identity is recast by its immersion in shame, for "whereas some view the concept of affect as a means to focus on the agency of the subject, others use it to displace the concept of the subject and to radically rephrase the notion of agency itself" (Koivunen, 9). Cliff accomplishes the latter, and in so doing she develops the important idea that shame is "experienced at the threshold of self and not-self, of object and abject" (Pajaczkowska and Ward, 3); it exists "in this double register of self-consciousness-with-others" (1). Both of these definitions draw on Julia Kristeva's idea that the child experiences abjection before the mother, and they help to explain why twelve-year old Clare can only feel but not think through the guilt she inherits from her father or the silences that keep her mother's shame buried, for the child cannot recognize her parents as Others to her self but rather as shifting elements in the alchemy of who she is. In this coming-of-age story, the child tries to sort out the points at which she merges with or distinguishes herself from her parents, yet Boy and Kitty converge and conflict at so many different point that the familial context for Clare's shame experience renders her unable to discern or, more importantly, to accept the boundaries between herself and her parents-as-Others.

These family dynamics rend her subjectivity into what Miller identifies as "a state of *non-coherence* or *dis-integration* because the self is moving in two directions—outward and into view and inward out of anxiety about the outward motion" (38). This double motion is evident in Clare's shrinking from the praise and privilege granted to her "wavy chestnut hair" and the green eyes she inherited from her father—"which all agreed were her 'finest feature'" (Cliff, *Abeng*, 61), for "[s]he didn't want this. To have to answer questions and have her hair stroked while the women wondered at her" (61). She is the embodiment of her parents' differences, "the family's *crowning achievement,* combining the best of both sides, and favoring one rather than the other" (61; emphasis mine). The narrator's subtle evocation of imperialism and performance of racist discourse in this description serves to convey just how fraught Clare's existence is in her experience of duplicity as she is seen by others in a partial light, and one that condemns elements of her self. Moreover, her sense of shame is utterly inaccessible to Clare as such, for why should she be ashamed of beauty? Why should others' flattering perceptions of her be cause for such uneasiness? Even the narrator leaves Clare's discomfort unremarked upon, yet she squirms because, as Miller explains, "the ashamed person feels that he or she cannot escape from the significant self-image even though longing to do so" (*Shame Experience,* 32). That the image Clare wishes to escape is one of "beauty" makes her desire to do so all the less comprehensible to her and all the more encoded in feelings and emotions.

Fanon, Cliff, and Historicizing Colonial Shame

Cliff thus demonstrates the drama of self and Other that Fanon describes as it plays out within one daughter's inheritance and identity. Cliff makes another important Fanonian move by historicizing Clare's confused feelings of inadequacy and incoherency. Just as Fanon explains the sources of neurosis in the pathologies of colonial relations, Cliff shows how her characters' relationships are steeped in the violence of Jamaican history. This theme crystallizes in a scene in which Cliff addresses the fundamental question of how race and class have been used historically not only to distinguish between people, but to designate humanity—in much the same way that Fanon reveals this to be the underlying function of colonial shame. He points out that, at its most insidious, colonial discourse broadens the hierarchy of superiority and inferiority to the point that it equates "whiteness" with "human." To feel the erasure of one's subjectivity, to feel one's humanity challenged: this is the ultimate power of shame. With roots in the feeling that one is "inferior, unpleasantly exposed, humiliated, or deprived of personal worth" (Seidler, 24), or in feeling that one is not even "'real' . . . or not feeling that one belongs, that one's home is 'real'" (Dalziell, 12), shame's apotheosis is one that Fanon identifies as boldly as any contemporary theorist. The passage in question begins with the narrator's observation that Clare "lived in a world where the worst thing to be—especially if you were a girl—was to be dark. The only thing worse than that was to be dead . . . An unease seemed to live in a tiny space in her soul" (Cliff, *Abeng*, 77). This unease lives in the heart of the novel as well, and it is one that Cliff carefully historicizes in the scene where Clare tells two girls in her class that they are "inhuman" for their rude treatment of an elderly black woman at a bus stop. While Clare magnanimously answers the woman's questions and provides her with fare money, Cliff points out the many social cues underlying the other girls' refusal to engage with the woman, along with Clare's obliviousness to such cues. Clare does not perceive the privilege she bears over her poorer, darker peers, nor does she wonder why the old woman initially approaches them rather than her, and she certainly cannot account for "why the word 'inhuman' was the word which came so swiftly into her mind" (77). As the narrator elaborates, Clare's peers are trapped in the same racial hierarchy that enables Clare's blithe ignorance and "train[s] them to pass beyond the suffering and the expectation of their oneness with this state of being [of the old woman] and to make a separation for themselves" (78) from her. The structure of their relations is predicated on the production of the Other: the girls reject the woman in order to establish their own identities as they play out against hers, thus mimicking the long historical pattern of European thought that Fanon identifies in his observation of whiteness masquerading as humanity.

Cliff goes on to present a Fanonian explication of the scene. In answer to the question of why Clare fastens upon the term "inhuman" for the girls' shaming and shameful behavior, Cliff builds up to the scene with Clare's attempts to comprehend the Holocaust, and her conclusion that "just as Jews were expected to suffer in a Christian world, so were dark people expected to suffer in a white one" (77), and that all suffering is predicated on the expectation that "the sufferer was not expected to be human" (78). Here, Cliff gets to the core of colonial shame in her argument that within it lies the charge that one is not only inferior or seen in a negative light, but that one holds no value whatsoever in the estimation of the Other. In the face of this painful characterization, Cliff swiftly makes the same maneuver that Fanon does by tracing the well-worn path of colonial shame back to its origins in Europeans' productions of "monsters. All inhuman" (78). The narrator-historian refers to such figments of the European imagination as the antipodal creatures of Columbus's time, and cites as the source of such ideas "*that* heart of darkness which has imagined them [non-Europeans] less than human" (79; emphasis in original). She goes on to make the long-anticipated link in the novel between the Holocaust, slavery, and Clare's epithet in her observation that all are products of "the fantasies of *this heart* . . . these are but a few of the heart's excesses" (79; emphasis mine). Thus, she observes the girls' treatment of the woman within a framework of critique through which she shames the colonial legacy of dehumanization as it plays out in daily life.

Affective Postcolonial Critique

Here, Cliff lays bare just how powerful an affective tool shame can be, and how it flows from centuries-old colonial ideology into modern identities. Her elucidation of the shame affect is twofold in that she identifies shame as a mechanism by which colonialism moderates the self/Other relation and she demonstrates how, because it is a flow and not a fixed relationship, shame can be used as an important mode of critique in the field of postcolonial studies. Cliff accomplishes the latter task by alluding frequently to the ways in which the island's repressed histories assert themselves in characters' interactions. This historian-narrator is a critical voice in the process of exposing these buried histories—and thus demonstrating the shameful nature of hiding such important information in the first place, as well as confronting the affective consequences of what then becomes a haunting, ghostly presence "on this island which did not know its own history" (96). It is the narrator who fills in the details of the triangle trade, the British crown's ending of slavery for commercial rather than humanitarian reasons, the legend of freedom fighter Nanny of the Maroons, the particularly brutal nature of Jamaican slavery, and the schoolteachers' espousal of imperial policy such as apartheid and presentations of Jamaican history only as it relates to England. In a powerful passage, the narrator describes the historical consciousness of the congregation of Kitty's church in pure negative relief:

> The congregation did *not* know that African slaves in Africa had been primarily household servants . . . They did *not* know that the death rate of Africans in Jamaica under slavery exceeded the rate of birth . . . They did *not* know that some slaves worked with their faces locked in masks of tin, so they would not eat the sugar cane as they cut . . . The people in the Tabernacle did *not* know that their ancestors had been paid to inform on one another . . . They did *not* know about the Kingdom of the Ashanti or the Kingdom of Dahomey . . . They did *not* imagine that Black Africans had commanded thousands of warriors. Built universities . . . (18–20; emphasis mine)

Just as Clare can only affectively intuit the nature of class and color injustice of which no one speaks, all of the characters in the novel are haunted by the shameful, willfully forgotten past that, as Cliff and Fanon insist, articulates their relationships and identities nonetheless.

The notion that the shame emanating from a silenced, buried, and yet powerfully haunting history is borne within the body speaks to Cliff's Fanonian emphasis on the body, on the "epidermal schema" produced by colonial ideology. The family is clearly articulated by the island's unknown colonial past, and the novel dwells in its later passages on the ways in which the past is inherited through the generations in the institution of the family, and how it then bleeds into one's relations with others outside the family as well. The final move Cliff makes in the novel is to apply the sharp blade of shame as a mode of critique to her own protagonist—who is in many ways Cliff's own avatar. This strategy of auto-critique invokes the audience, just as Bouson argues that Morrison's *The Bluest Eye* "has provoked feelings of shame and by-stander's guilt in readers" (Bouson, "Quiet As It's Kept," 212). Thus, the shame affect exceeds the text, and this is what makes *Abeng* such a fearless look at the shaming ideologies of colonialism and racism. Moreover, Bouson cautions that critics' reactions to feeling vicarious shame is often to "enact the trauma-specific and antishaming roles of advocate or rescuer, or to become unwitting participants in the shame drama of blaming and attacking the other in their critical responses to the novel" (212). By turning the critical device of shame back upon the protagonist, Cliff forces her readers to face the power of shame. Clare may be described as a "colonized child [who] lived within certain parameters—which clouded her judgment" (Cliff, *Abeng,* 77), but Cliff still holds her responsible for her actions and thus forces the reader to feel the unresolved sting of her shame.

Whereas the narrator spends much of the novel pointing out Clare's and others' ignorance of history and describing Clare's bewilderment and attempts to puzzle out her inner conflicts and uneasy feelings, the novel concludes with her actions. Clare is described in the final chapters of the novel as "a girl of twelve . . . feeling her way into something" (Cliff, *Abeng,* 149), as she seeks out a contorted form of agency in her relations with other children. To start, her status in the third and final section of the novel as a friend or playmate to others places more responsibility on her shoulders than do earlier descriptions of her familial status as a daughter. The narrator condemns even children's innocence in the face of colonial inheritance when she describes Clare's school thus: "Color was diffuse and hard to track at St. Catherine's, entering the classrooms as seating arrangements, disciplinary action, entering the auditorium during the casting of a play. The shadows of color permeated the relationships of the students, one to one" (100). These shadows loom not only in the institutional setting of the school, but as they affect Clare's most important friendship of the novel, with a girl named Zoe. "This was a friendship—a pairing of two girls—kept only on school vacations, and because of their games and make-believe might have seemed to some entirely removed from what was real in the girls' lives. Their lives of light and dark— which was real in the girls' lives. Their lives of light and dark—which was the one overwhelming reality" (95). Zoe's mother cautions her that Clare "can't be wunna true friend, sweetie . . . Wunna is she playmate. No fool wunnaself" (102) because Clare comes from money and has a white father, and indeed the girls encounter the limits of class and color in their interactions with one another.[1] "Their battles usually occurred when the differences-already-there surfaced in such a way that they couldn't be avoided or dismissed" (100). It is in her portrayal of the girls' relationship that Cliff shifts from identifying the sources of the colonial shame felt in the Savage family to using shame as a tool of critique, for she shows how our very protagonist's actions are contaminated by the shameful "differences-already-there."

Zoe, for one, does not let Clare off the hook when these differences assert themselves. For example, when Clare refuses to let Zoe wear her pretty new bathing suit with the excuse that her grandmother would not approve, Zoe retorts, "What you mean 'Grandma say no'—is wunna say no" (101). Placing the responsibility for her actions squarely on Clare's shoulders, Zoe succeeds in making Clare feel chagrined for her superior attitude and sense of entitlement, two qualities that ultimately motivate Clare to commit her own act of violence.

This climactic scene opens with Clare and Zoe lying naked on a rock, soaking up the morning sun, when they are spied by a cane cutter. The earliest accounts of shame, by Darwin and Freud among others, trace shame back to the need to cover one's body and in particular one's genitals. Thus the literal exposure of the girls' bodies sets the scene for the shameful encounter, yet Cliff reroutes shame from the man's gaze to Clare's actions: her response is to point a gun at him and to authoritatively enunciate, "Get away, you hear. This is my grandmother's land" in a voice in which "she had dropped her patois—was speaking *buckra*—and relying on the privilege she said she did not have" (122). The shameful exposure in this scene is not of Clare's body, but of her privilege. What is more, her assertion of her *buckra,* or white, privilege is immediately cast as violent, for in firing the gun above the man's head, she kills her grandmother's prize bull. Even Clare concludes that "she had proven what Zoe accused her of—she was at fault" (124), in her admission to herself that she had exercised power over the very person for whom she feels love, friendship, and even the stirrings of desire. In her attempt to assert her agency, in taking her grandmother's forbidden gun in the first place and then in claiming the power of her privilege, Clare's enmeshment in the very hierarchy that torments her in so many other situations is on display.

We are left with a portrait of tremendous emotional complexity, with an understanding of the radical contingency of agency taken in an affective view, and with a representation of shame as an ideological device, an inheritance felt in the bones, and a relational flow that wends through all of the characters' relationships with one another. The family drama of *Abeng* delves into the point where, to reiterate Pajaczkowska and Ward, "the difference between self and not-self ceases to exist" (3). In discovering her own affective contingencies, and that she holds within her both power and its flip side, vulnerability, Clare feels her way toward womanhood even while the novel leaves her suspended upon its brink, awash in her growing sense of unease. Other feelings—

rage, passion, commitment—develop in Cliff's account of Clare Savage as a political activist in her highly acclaimed second novel, *No Telephone to Heaven,* as she comes to terms with her family's and her country's experiences of shame and shaming practices. In telling Clare's story as one of affective enmeshment, Cliff offers an important take on the workings of postcolonial binaries and shows how shame can be identified, rerouted, and applied as a critical tool to convert notions of the self and the Other into the lived experience at the "threshold of self and not-self, of object and abject" (Pajaczkowska and Ward, 3). The postcolonial moment is not just about independence and agency; it is about restructuring the past itself in such a way that the sufferings of colonial subjugation are made to bear on those who perpetuated them, lest those who suffered be left with the stigma and the shame.

Notes

The two chapter epigraphs are from pages 49 and 119, respectively, of Michelle Cliff's *Abeng.*

1. Not only is this passage from Fanon a paradigmatic illustration of shame, but it is quickly becoming central to shame theory, as we see in J. Brooks Bouson's use of it in *Quiet as It's Kept* and in Eliza Chandler's application of Fanon in her essay in this volume.

2. All translations of Nesbitt are mine.

3. I do not wish to digress into a discussion of shame versus guilt, for much has been written on this distinction. Basically, guilt results from consciousness of damage one does to another, whereas shame is experienced as damage to oneself that can result from either having wronged another or having been wronged by an Other. On the topic of vicarious shame: Tomkins, in his writings collected in *Shame and Its Sisters,* argues that this is an important property of shame. In literary study, it should be pointed out, vicarious shame is something felt by not only the characters, but more importantly by the reader as well.

4. "Wunna" is the patois term for "you."

7 Ancestors and Aliens

Queer Transformations and Affective Estrangement in Octavia Butler's Fiction

Frann Michel

> CORDELIA: I think I should work with Wesley.
>
> XANDER: You have no shame.
>
> CORDELIA: Oh, please. Like shame is something to be proud of?
>
> "Earshot," *Buffy the Vampire Slayer*

IS SHAME SOMETHING to be proud of? The African American science fiction and fantasy writer Octavia Butler seems to have thought that it was not. Butler repeatedly cited the goal of refuting shame as a motivation for her writing, particularly with regard to her best-known novel, *Kindred* (1979). While Butler's works are deeply concerned with questions of power and intimacy, and explore situations redolent of shame, many of her protagonists can be read as distinctive for their insusceptibility or resistance to shame. But, as I will argue, Butler's third novel *Survivor* represents shame as transformative for the central character in ways that entail her accepting of shame's regulatory function within a hegemonic social order, and, perhaps for that reason, the novel registers within the context of Butler's oeuvre a moment of authorial shame. *Survivor* is the only one of her novels that Butler refused to allow to be republished; she referred to the 1978 book as an "embarrassing early work" (Kenan, 500). Unlike the other four novels in her Patternist series, *Survivor* was not reissued in the 1990s, nor was it included with them in the 2007 Patternist compilation *Seed to Harvest*. Whether or not "shame" describes Butler's psychological relation to *Survivor*, the term indicates the social shape of the gesture withholding the book from further publication. Examining Butler's stated motivations for this singular embarrassment, as well as the potential motives suggested by the novel itself and by her other comments on shame and its relation to writing, also entails a reexamination of the position of shame in some recent (often queer) cultural theory. Differences between the representation of shame in *Survivor* and the estrangement of shame from protagonists in Butler's other fictions, even while they are in situations of shame, highlight the need for a more intersectional analysis of shame than has sometimes been provided in recent cultural studies. Thus I am interested here in using recent theory about shame for thinking about the work of Octavia Butler, but also in using Butler's work to interrogate some current celebrations of shame.

Some readers of earlier drafts of this chapter have found my reference to "celebrations of shame" jarring. But, as I will discuss below, work by Eve Kosofsky Sedgwick and other feminist and queer theorists has suggested that shame is a potential ground of progressive identity politics. In this view, if political pride movements (including, in Sedgwick's account, "'Black is Beautiful' and gay pride" [*Touching Feeling*, 62]) turn definitionally on the transformational power of shame, then it is shame that is importantly a "structuring fact of identity" with "powerfully productive and powerfully social metamorphic possibilities" (64, 65). Other writers on shame (among them, as I note below, writers in feminist, queer, African American, and Latino/a traditions) do not share this view. But the idea of shame as shaping and transforming identity does apply to the only novel about which Butler admitted she was "embarrassed" (Kenan, 500). Though much of Butler's other work might be read in relation to shame or to transformation—perhaps most obviously, the Earthseed religion of the Parable books asserts that "God is change"—her fiction tends not to frame the relation between shame and change in such apparently causal and positive terms. Instead, her representations of situations of shame often temporally displace or otherwise distance their representation of the affective pain of such situations. Considering Darko Suvin's classic definition of science fiction in terms of "cognitive estrangement," we might even see this aspect of Butler's work as entailing a kind of affective estrangement, a way of recognizing but escaping the oppressions of shame, of managing shame. In *Survivor*, however, the protagonist internalizes and performs the shame that allows her upward mobility within a preexisting social hierarchy.

There is a danger in analyzing a work that Butler did not want disseminated and presumably did not want scrutinized. I risk engaging in a further act of shaming, uncovering what the author would have veiled. But my aim here is not what Sedgwick describes as a "paranoid reading" that would put its faith in exposure (130). Rather, I hope to position this as a "reparative reading" (128), one that appreciates the complexity of the explanations Butler gave for rejecting this one novel, as well as the insights we can gain from its juxtaposition with her other works. My interest is not in giving a biographical account of authorial shame but in considering the implications of the assertion that there is something different about this novel from Butler's other works, of the historically and culturally specific contexts of that assertion, and of the possibility that the difference can be located in the novel's representation of shame.

Survivor in Brief: Am I Blue?

Before turning to a fuller exploration of these theories and contexts and of the novel itself, I will briefly summarize and describe *Survivor*, since its out-of-print status may make it difficult for readers to find. Earth in the Patternist series comes to be divided among the Patternists, who have extraordinary abilities of mental control and manipulation; the Clayarks, descendants of those infected with an extraterrestrial virus that makes them look rather like kangaroos and consider ordinary humans as food; and ordinary humans. The human protagonist Alanna, we learn, was orphaned at eight years old when her black father and Asian mother were killed by a Clayark mob. After surviving alone as a "wild" human for seven years, she is taken in at fifteen by a group of Missionaries. Their religious mission is to preserve the human form apart from Patternist and Clayark mutations, by founding settler colonies on other planets. Adopted by the white Missionary couple Neila and Jules Verrick, despite the objections of other white Missionaries, Alanna accompanied them when they migrated to the planet where *Survivor* largely takes place, the only one of Butler's novels not set on (or in orbit around) Earth. Aside from the interstellar ship that brings them to their new planet, the book's most fantastic elements are the flora and fauna they find there. The staple food of the valley is the meklah fruit, which turns out to be addictive, apparently trapping the settlers there with the furry, humanoid native Kohn, the local group of whom are the (also addicted) Garkohn. But when Alanna is captured by the other Kohn tribe, the Tehkohn, she survives withdrawal and has a child with Diut, the blue leader of that group. The Kohn species has distinctive fur that allows individuals at will to blend invisibly into their surroundings, that shows emotional response through color changes, and that in its resting state reveals the individual's rank within their explicit biological hierarchy. Though Alanna lacks the natural blue of the highest-ranking Tehkohn, the Hao, her liaison with Diut means she is treated "as though" she has some blue in her coloring. Thus her move from the Missionaries to the Tehkohn is not an escape from racial hierarchy so much as a repositioning near the top rank of a different hierarchy of color. This repositioning is marked by her internalization of Tehkohn values, and particularly her sharing of their shame at addiction to meklah. Unlike Butler's other writings, then, *Survivor* suggests the possible value of shame as a switchpoint in personal transformation, although the transformation comes not from shame itself, but from the availability of the alternate value system that it marks.

But while shame is transformational within the diegesis of *Survivor,* the novel's narrative structure is far more fragmented than in Butler's other fictions, in which narrative content is less directly motivated by shame but the narrative is formally more cohesive. Most of her other works are either in sustained first person (*Kindred, Imago, Parable of the Sower, Fledgling*) or in third person, but *Survivor* uses both first- and third-person narration. The only other such exceptions among Butler's novels are *Parable of the Talents,* in which the various source texts (including diaries, memoirs, and news reports) are organized by the guiding editorship of the narrator Asha Vere, and *Mind of my Mind,* in which most chapters are in third person, focalized though the chapter's title character, but the "Mary" chapters are narrated by Mary in first person. In addition, the chronology of *Survivor* is nonlinear. Like *Clay's Ark,* which alternates between chapters labeled "Past" and "Present," *Survivor* alternates between two sequential stories, though in this case the shift comes within chapters. Each chapter begins in first person, narrated by either Alanna or Diut. These sections provide the story of Alanna's earlier life, including her adoption by the Missionaries, her emigration to the planet they call Canaan, and her time with the Tehkohn. The second part of each chapter is in third person, focalized through Alanna, beginning from her recapture (or, as they see it, her rescue) by the Missionaries and the Garkohn, and ending the novel with her final parting from the Missionaries, who are departing to a Kohn-free area of the planet, while she stays with the Tehkohn.[1]

Shame in Theory: Double Consciousness

At the risk of revisiting the theoretical territory canvassed in the introduction to this volume, I want to outline some of this theory from the particular queer/feminist angle from which I approach it here. The potentially positive valence of shame in *Survivor* might seem to confirm the view of a number of feminist and queer theorists that shame might be, if not something to be proud of, then at least the basis for a positive politics. Drawing on the work of Silvan Tomkins, Eve Kosofsky Sedgwick has influentially described shame as "a near-inexhaustible source of transformational energy" (4; cited in Woodward, "Traumatic Shame," 226), energy that she sees transformed in queer culture to performance, flamboyance, and fabulousness. Tomkins is also the inspiration for Liz Constable's description of "the experience of shame as the catalyst in an infinitely and increasingly complex, response-sensitive, analog and digital structuring process of non-teleological, non-developmental, *becoming*, a kind of Deleuzean *devenir*" (Constable, Introduction, 10).[2] More in line with older moral traditions of shame, Berenice Fisher has suggested that white feminists' shame about race is "a sign of our commitment to act . . . a touchstone for understanding what we expect to achieve and how" (188). Sally Munt sees shame as a multifarious "change agent for the self" (8), while Kathryn Bond Stockton sees it as "valuable" (9). Whether drawing on inevitable psychodynamics of early life or on resistance to social oppressions or to our errors as oppressors, shame has been recognized as fueling positive or open-ended transformations.

Yet as the introduction to this collection also explains, shame has also been recognized as itself a function of oppression, a mode of social control particularly exercised against the oppressed (Bartky, Woodward, Locke). Notably, for women, as in the epigraph above, charges of shamelessness have often attached to expressions of sexuality and desire, though the experience of shame may also be, as Sandra Bartky puts it, "a pervasive affective attunement," a "distressed apprehension of the self as inadequate" (97, 86). This sense of shame as a pervasive judgment on the self is one basis on which is it frequently distinguished from guilt, which is seen in contrast as a response to a particular act one has committed or failed to commit (H. B. Lewis, *Shame and Guilt in Neurosis*). Ruth Benedict famously suggested that "shame cultures" (Eastern) rely on external norms while guilt cultures (Western) rely on internal norms. Not only has this Orientalist cultural analysis been refuted in recent years, however (Geaney), but theorists have frequently noted that distinctions between shame and guilt have tended "to blur in actual experience" (Bartky, 87). Moreover, Tomkins uses shame as the broader term that includes guilt and humiliation, and while he distinguishes shame as an affect from contempt, he also acknowledges that that, too, "is not always or necessarily so absolute a distinction" ("Shame," 140). In this chapter, I treat shame and related terms as designating a cluster of affective and emotional responses that share a family resemblance, yet whose phenomenology and implications vary in particular local contexts.

Even those who see shame as transformational, politically useful, or a tool of personal growth usually acknowledge its unpleasantness (exceptions are Munt and Stockton, who both point to potential pleasures of shame). Elspeth Probyn, for instance, suggests in *Blush* that shame is "positive" (xviii) and "productive" (15), and will "set off a nearly involuntary reevaluation of one's self and one's actions" (55), but it certainly "feels bad" (2); while she herself finds it "interesting" (passim), she also recognizes that responses may be different among those with a "collective history of being shamed" (85). With different emphasis, Sandra Bartky notes that the moral agent for whom philosophers have found shame salutary is one who "has escaped the characteristic sorts of psychological oppression on which modern hierarchies of class, race, and gender rely so heavily," while "under conditions of oppression, the oppressed must struggle not only against the more visible disadvantages but against guilt and shame as well" (97). Perhaps shame can be most "interesting" for those most transparently privileged: that is, for those least subject to shame.[3]

Associated in Western culture with tropes of covering and display, as well as with debasement or displacement downward (the story of the biblical fall providing an example of both), shame has thus also been understood as a regulatory effect in a social or moral order. As Bartky describes it, shame "requires if not an actual audience before whom my deficiencies are paraded, then an internalized audience with the capacity to judge me, hence internalized standards of judgment" (86). These may not be the only standards of judgment internalized, and may not even be conscious (Bartky; Probyn also discusses this in terms of Bourdieu's notion of *habitus*), but can create something like what W. E. B. Du Bois famously described as "double consciousness": the "peculiar sensation" of "measuring one's soul by the tape of a world that looks on in amused contempt and pity" (3). Significantly, while the tape is the world's, one does the measuring oneself. In his reading of Du Boisian double consciousness in terms of shame, Jonathan Flatley stresses that unlike depression (melancholia), shame holds out hope of reciprocity, of change. It is thus a more hopeful as well as a more dynamic affect. As Tomkins notes, "When one . . . expresses contempt for another, the other is more likely to experience shame than self-contempt insofar as the democratic ideal has been internalized" ("Shame," 139). For Tomkins, then, the "democratic ideal" of human equality constitutes an alternative value structure that weighs against the debasement of contempt or refused recognition.

Yet shame can be most acute in the regions farthest from the democratic ideal. Saidiya Hartman, discussing *Incidents in the Life of a Slave Girl,* argues that shame "denotes the affective dimension of the general condition of dishonor constitutive of enslavement" and that "[a]s a structure of feeling, shame expresses the devaluation of chattel status, the dissolution experienced in being absolutely subject to another, and the recognition of one's abjection" (Hartman, 109). Given what many readers have noted as Butler's "particular fascination with relationships of dominance and submission, master and slave, predator and prey" (Fowler), and given Butler's turn to explicit representations of the historical era of American slavery in the two novels following *Survivor, Kindred* (1979) and *Wild Seed* (1980), Hartman's point is particularly salient to Butler's work. Moreover, given the continuities, which Hartman traces, between the subjection of African Americans during and after the legal institution of slavery, we can see this structure of feeling operating through subsequent racism, as well as in colonialism and other forms of oppression.

Heather Love groups work on "racial melancholy, gay shame, and historical trauma" (10) by their shared focus on bringing together affect and the social. All are also linked, as she points out less explicitly, by the problem of grappling with a "history of suffering, stigma, and violence" (1). Within the historiography of slavery, one locus of debate has been around Stanley Elkins's thesis that slaves "internalized" the values of the master (cited in Painter, 20). Rebuttals to Elkins noted his failure to acknowledge the countervailing forces of community and religion that provided slaves with resources for survival and resistance. But as Nell Irvin Painter has observed, some of the work done in reaction against Elkins neglected the psychological complexity of enslaved people, as well as the psychological damage also done to the master class. As Anne Anlin Cheng argues, "The connection between subjectivity and social damage needs to be formulated in terms more complicated than either resigning colored people to the irrevocability of 'self-hatred,' or denying racism's profound, lasting effects" (7). Neither the utter debasement of internalizing only the dominant values, nor the absolute pride of invincible freedom from those values, can account for the complex negotiations entailed in surviving oppression and managing shame.

Shame and Power: Just Say No?

Given the influence of Sedgwick's work in fueling the cultural turn toward shame, it is worth exploring her account further. While there might be obstacles in applying to the work of an African American woman writer a theoretical approach developed largely in relation to (not specifically raced) queer studies, both do involve movements beyond binary thinking. Just as Donna Haraway has pointed to Butler's work as offering a vision of cyborg hybridity (179), Sedgwick has looked to Tomkins's work as useful in moving beyond the dualistic thinking of the repressive hypothesis. But in seeking ways to move beyond the narrow view of power as something that says only *No,* some explorations of shame have risked neglecting the persistence of hierarchical relations that include sedimented and crystallized forms. Sedgwick argues that Foucault's analysis "of the pseudodichotomy between repression and liberation has led, in many cases, to its conceptual reimposition in the even more abstractly reified form of the hegemonic and the subversive," where the "hegemonic" becomes "another name for the status quo" and the "subversive" is defined in "a purely negative relation to that" (12). In Foucault's account in *The History of Sexuality, Volume 1,* the "repressive hypothesis" refers to the set of assumptions that locate power only in terms of what he calls the "juridico-discursive" model; the repressive hypothesis thus ignores the more historically recent and pervasive forms of power as generative and shaping rather than only repressive and negating. Indeed, actions that seem directed toward liberation from repression can generate further subjection to power (e.g., endlessly scrutinizing our sexuality). But Sedgwick's discussion provides no concrete examples of what she sees as the reductive reimpositions of the repressive hypothesis. Moreover, that discussion neglects Foucault's account of the "multiplicity of force relations . . . whose general design or institutional crystallization is embodied in the state apparatus, in the formulation of the law, in the various social hegemonies" (*History,* 92–93). He notes: "Major dominations are the hegemonic effects that are sustained by all these confrontations" of "manifold relations of force" (94; and see, for instance, Lacey's application of Foucault's account of power to Butler's work). That is, however the "hegemonic" may function in adaptations of Foucault's work, it has a real and more complex sense in that work itself, and though Sedgwick disavows "naiveté" or a "reluctance to face reality" (12) as motivating her own critique of the reinscription of the repressive hypothesis, her arguments may sanction a failure to attend to major dominations and various sustained social hegemonies.

Sedgwick notes that reifying the status quo risks reducing responses to it to "accepting or refusing," "dramatizing the extremes of compulsion or voluntarity" although "it is only the middle ranges of agency that offer space for effectual creativity and change" (13). Those middle ranges are the spaces in which Butler's fiction chiefly operates, but the directions of the extremes do matter. If, as Sedgwick and Frank suggest in their essay in *Critical Inquiry,* it is reductive to always end up arguing that literary works are "kinda subversive, kinda hegemonic" (500), it is at least equally problematic to imply that hegemonic patterns are irrelevant. Rhetorically, the repressive/subversive binarism can provide a spine for a discussion that is far more nuanced than the binary might suggest, and conceptually, it can also provide a reminder that such major dominations do not vanish just because they are complex or not universal.

In short, the direction given to discussions of shame by Sedgwick's work on Tomkins has been both particularly productive (especially in queer studies) and also risky in that its eliding of hegemonic relations may allow their re-inscription. An institutional instance of this might be the striking absence of brown bodies (except as disavowed objects of the gaze) at the Gay Shame Conference of 2003 that yielded the anthology *Gay Shame*—and which, in turn, includes Sedgwick's essay on "Shame, Theatricality, and Queer Performativity" as a kind of founding document. As analyzed by Hiram Perez, the institutionalized queer theory of the conference (and elsewhere) "predominantly situates shame as a resistance and in opposition to normalization" (174), and thus "accommodates familiar habits of the university's ideal bourgeois subject, among them, his imperial gaze, his universalism, and his claims to a race-neutral objectivity" (172).[4]

But the attempt to read shame in the productive terms inaugurated by Sedgwick may be racially problematic even in works that attempt explicit racial analysis. In *Beautiful Bottom, Beautiful Shame: Where "Black" Meets "Queer,"* a study avowedly indebted to Sedgwick's work (for instance, Stockton, x), Kathryn Bond Stockton herself asks, "Is the conception of valuable shame something only a queer would consider (a white queer at that)?" (9). Although she argues that her conception of shame is "not homosexual in its inception" (10), others may disagree about the racial specificity of the approach. Thus, in a review of Stockton's work, Amy Abugo Ongiri asks, "What role do cultural politics and an intellectual culture that continue to marginalize people of African descent play in the choice to highlight the question of shame and debasement in relation to these categories? Is it possible for such a study to explore the symbolic economy of shame in relation to the 'switchpoints of "black" and "queer"' without simply replicating the historical and cultural politics that created these switchpoints in the first place?" The unanswered question seems rhetorical. But Ongiri's ultimate, somewhat indirect answer, much later in the review, seems to be that what is missing in "the celebration of debasement" is a "counterpoint" such as a "liberatory politics of social transformation."

Without such a counterpoint, the focus on shame might risk Elkins's essentializing of debasement. Moreover, while the flamboyant performance of queerness may constitute a counterpoint to the shame of the closet for queer white people, the visibility of African American shame may "reinforce the spectacular character of black suffering" (Hartman, 3). In *Survivor,* as I discuss more fully in the last section of this chapter, part of the shame of the work may have been its representation of shame and its insufficiently critical relation to binary gender as well as hierarchical racial politics. Yet in other works by Butler, shame is rejected, displaced, or refuted: estranged.

Butler's Shame: Learn and Run

As I have begun to suggest, Octavia Butler's work engages the asymmetrical power relations and social hierarchies in which shame emerges to, perhaps, enlighten the privileged and debase the oppressed. Given the ways that shame refracts political oppressions differentially for the most oppressed, one can certainly see why Butler's work might engage in estrangements of shame as modes of resistance to extant power relations. As many critics have noted, Butler consistently places the "black female body" at the center of her narratives (see, for instance, Hampton, 77). But the narratives in which those bodies appear tend to refuse what Hartman calls "the spectacular character of black suffering."

Certainly Butler's work registers the ways that shame has historically been exploited by those interested in controlling others, even while displacing the moment of shame's visibility. Slavers and torturers have used nakedness to humiliate those they control. Such treatment recurs in Butler's fictions, but typically distanced through narrative temporality. That is, in a number of Butler's works, the focal character is held captive, and has been deprived of clothing, but these scenes are typically presented in retrospect. For instance, in *Dawn*, Lilith is given clothing by her captors not at her first "Awakening" but at the first one represented in the novel: "She had not been allowed clothing from her first Awakening until now. She had pleaded for it, but her captors had ignored her. Dressed now, she felt more secure than she had at any other time in her captivity" (*Lilith's Brood*, 6). In the short story "Amnesty," Noah is introduced to the reader wearing "only shorts and a halter top. The Communities would have preferred her to be naked, and for the long years of her captivity, she had had no choice. She had been naked. Now she was no longer a captive, and she insisted on wearing at least the basics" (598). Placing the shame of nakedness in the narrative past distances it from the reader's vicarious empathy or identification with the character, making it manageable.

For all that Butler's characters find themselves in situations of shame, then, her protagonists tend not to display the affect of shame or the marks of being shame-prone, the internalization of oppression. This is, I take it, part of what readers and critics mean when they describe these characters as "strong." In an early study of Butler's works, Ruth Salvaggio observes of the protagonist of *Survivor*, "As a strong-minded black woman, Alanna submits to a surprising number of constraints" (80). I take this to imply that one would not expect a strong or strong-minded figure to submit to constraints, that the truly strong cannot be constrained, that constraint is thus itself a debasement.

Even the most basic gesture of shame, the lowering of the eyes or hiding of the face in reaction to what is stranger than expected, may be deferred or displaced in Butler's work. The strangest strangers in science fiction are generally, as one might expect, the non-human aliens. In *Dawn*, one of the Oankali asks Lilith to look at him when she is, we're told, already looking at him (*Lilith's Brood*, 12). The Oankali's explanation for his question is that the lights have been kept low in deference to her unreadiness to look at him. But when the lights do come up, her reaction is that "[r]evolted, she turned her face to the wall" (14). For this one of Butler's "strong-minded" characters, then, the look away is described as motivated not by shame but by revulsion, disgust.

Where shame does appear in Butler's narratives, it is usually ascribed to secondary characters rather than to the protagonists. Among the Patternists, shame is experienced by those subordinated, but presented from the perspective of those controlling the Pattern. In *Mind of My Mind*, Mary becomes the first to form and dominate the

Pattern. None of the others in the Pattern can shield their thoughts from her, or see into her thoughts against her will. When she defeats Rachel's attempt to resist her control, the latter "hid her face in her hands. She was shielded to the others. But to me she radiated shame and defeat. Humiliation" (129). But Mary's empathy prompts her to help Rachel move away from the others: "I knew she wanted to be away from us. Tears, especially tears of defeat, were private things" (130). The reader sees this shame not through the experience of the shamed, but through the sympathetic observer with the power not only to cause but also to help hide it.

Although a character's experiences of shame need not be designated as such, it seems nonetheless suggestive that the words "shame" or "shamed" occur only five times in *Kindred*. Moreover, in two of those instances, shame is associated explicitly with externally framed (and clearly troubling) social values: for the slaveholder Rufus, "there was no shame in raping a black woman, but there could be shame in loving one" (124). A third use also refers to Rufus, when the narrator, Dana, attempts to "shame him into letting us go" (187). But when she refers to the shame of another character being whipped by patrollers, the sentence frames the affect in negative and temporally distanced terms: "I had seen people beaten on television and the movies . . . But I hadn't lain nearby and smelled their sweat, or heard them pleading and praying, shamed before their families and themselves" (36). The effect of this sentence for the reader is to highlight the experience Dana is undergoing at the moment—to make us aware of the smell of sweat and the feeling of vicarious shame—but also to highlight, as Marisa Parham notes, the inadequacy of Dana's education to prepare her for the past (Parham, 1323). Constructing the immediacy of the experience in relation to a past absence helps structure the passage so as to help, Parham notes of the neo-slave-narrative genre more broadly, "make readerly identification possible by making manageable the shame of one's encounter with the past" (1321). Moreover, the only instance of Dana referring directly to her own shame suggests that what is particularly shaming in the whipping scene may be the "pleading and praying," the acceptance of the terms set by the patrollers in even "pleading" with them. On one occasion when Rufus has had Dana beaten and is continuing to demand her compliance, she keeps her expression neutral because "I still had some pride left"; but a few moments later, "To my shame, I realized I was almost crying" (215). The moment of shame hinges on what Rufus might see, on the possibility of shame's visible performance.

Thus it is not so much shame as the refutation of shame that occupies a pivotal place in Butler's career. Speaking of *Kindred*, published the year after *Survivor*, she explains:

> My mother did domestic work and I was around sometimes when people talked about her as if she were not there, and I got to watch her going in back doors and generally being treated in a way that made me . . . I spent a lot of my childhood being ashamed of what she did, and I think one of the reasons I wrote *Kindred* was to resolve my feelings, because after all, I ate because of what she did . . . a kind of reaction to some of the things going on during the sixties when people were feeling

ashamed of, or more strongly, angry with their parents for not having improved things faster, and I wanted to take a person from today and send that person back to slavery. (Kenan, 496; ellipses in original)

Insofar as shame provides impetus for literary creation, one could certainly argue that its role in Butler's oeuvre is productive. Yet as Kathleen Woodward notes, disputing Sedgwick's account of shame in a reading of Toni Morrison's *Bluest Eye,* "not all shame can be 'transformational,'" and indeed it is "misleading" to suggest that the affect of shame is itself transformational: "It is not the affect itself—or by itself—that carries the potential for transformation, although it may serve as the catalyst for it" ("Traumatic Shame," 226–227). The shame Butler describes is both a catalyst for writing and a negative feeling to be resolved or reacted to. It is a catalyst only to the extent that it evokes a need for resolution or reaction. Similarly, although, as Sedgwick states, "The forms taken by shame are not distinct 'toxic' parts of a group or individual identity that can be excised" (63), neither are they necessarily benign or beneficial. If, as she notes, "[t]hey are available for the work of metamorphosis, reframing, refiguration, transfiguration, affective and symbolic loading and deformation" (63), such transfiguration or deformation may be necessitated precisely by the pervading toxicity of some forms of shame.

If Butler's reference to sending someone "back to slavery" (Kenan, 496) sounds potentially punitive, it can be read as a redirecting of anger back toward its proper objects by way of a reeducation of the writer's self, cohort, and reader. In another interview, Butler commented:

When I got into college, Pasadena City College, the black nationalist movement, the Black Power Movement, was really underway with the young people, and I heard some remarks from a young man who was the same age I was but who had apparently never made the connection with what his parents did to keep him alive. He was still blaming them for their humility and their acceptance of disgusting behavior on the part of employers and other people. He said, "I'd like to kill all these old people who have been holding us back for so long. But I can't because I'd have to start with my own parents." When he said *us* he meant black people, and when he said *old people* he meant older black people. That was actually the germ of the idea for *Kindred* (1979). I've carried that comment with me for thirty years. He felt so strongly ashamed of what the older generation had to do, without really putting it into the context of being necessary for not only their lives but his as well. (Rowell, 51)

Butler suggests that the shame felt by many in the Black Power generation about their forebears rests on a lack of empathy with the oppression those forebears faced and with their strategies for surviving it. As one term for shamed, "mortified," indicates, such shame is potentially annihilating rather than transformative. Indeed, Parham comments, of the murderous violence expressed in this passage, "Shame always hearkens toward death" (1319).

More specific than the "shame at being human" we have learned in the wake of the Nazi camps (Primo Levi, cited in Deleuze, 172), the shame of being the daughter of a domestic worker emerges from particular intersections of class, race, and gender. In other iterations of this genesis of *Kindred,* Butler describes the scene of her mother's work as "humiliating," "indignities," "wrong," "unpleasant," and "bad" (Sanders) and "disgusting" (Rowell, 51). Particularly insofar as shame attaches to gender, class, race, sexuality, or other social identities, it involves placement within a social hierarchy, placement low within a hierarchy, displacement downward, or debasement (Munt, Stockton). By talking about her "as if she were not there," her mother's employers refuse to recognize her humanity. Shame emerges at the point of disappointed connection, from a failure of human equality.

Moreover, the shame that Butler describes as being resolved or reacted to here is vicarious shame. That is, Butler and others are feeling ashamed not of themselves but of their parents and ancestors. Butler's position is doubly vicarious insofar as she responds to the shame that others express about their forebears. Parham astutely notes that Butler's phrase about having "carried" her acquaintance's expression of shame/anger also emerges in describing her own early reaction to her mother's work: "When we say that we carry something with us, we often mean that we have brought into ourselves a burden someone else has given, a shaming" (Parham, 1319). As Tomkins observes, humans are "capable through empathy and identification of living through others and therefore of being shamed by what happens to others. To the extent to which the individual invests . . . affect in other human beings . . . [the individual] is vulnerable to the vicarious experience of shame" ("Shame," 159). Sedgwick describes the "double movement" of shame: "toward painful individuation, toward uncontrollable relationality" (37). Parham reads *Kindred*'s project as "making manageable the shame of one's encounter with the past" (1321).

But if empathy and identification are conditions for this shame, they are also key to its resolution, along with its transformation into pride in recognizing the heroism of these ancestors and progenitors.

> I . . . wanted to convey that people who underwent all this were not cowards, were not people who were just too pathetic to protect themselves, but were heroes because they were using what they had to help their kids get a little further . . . I wanted to . . . not have it look as though these people were deficient because they weren't fighting. They were fighting; they just weren't fighting with fists, which is sometimes easy and pointless. The quick and dirty solution is often the one that's most admired until you have to live with the results. (Sanders)

While Butler has discussed this aim in relation to *Kindred* specifically, it bears on her other writing as well. Characteristic of Butler's work is the situation of survival coming at the cost of what seems to be humiliation, constraint, enslavement. As Patricia Melzer notes, Butler's female protagonists "refuse to accept the terms we conventionally associate with heroic resistance: armored fight, honored death valued over dishonored capture, self-sacrifice, or resistance until death" (55).

The two modes of resistance are closely juxtaposed, for instance, in *Parable of the Talents,* in events at Camp Christian, where prisoners are controlled with electrical stun collars. David (Day) Turner (not so different from Nat Turner as day and night) leads an active but futile rebellion, while Lauren Olamina counsels her followers to drop to the ground when the fighting starts, so as to avoid stray bullets; they survive and eventually take advantage of a landslide that disables the central control source for the electric collars. While some of Butler's protagonists do at points choose, or try to choose, resistance until death, they more commonly adopt the plan of Lilith Oyapo in the Xenogenesis trilogy: "Learn and run" (*Lilith's Brood,* 248), adapt until there is an opportunity for escape, another alternative to captivity or death.

Survivor's Shame: Same Difference

While Butler's central characters, then, are rarely ashamed in the familiar sense, and the ethos of her work tends toward a repudiation or rejection of shame, an overcoming or displacing or estrangement of shame, there is, as I have noted, one striking instance of the apparent enactment of shame in Butler's career. Butler's scattered comments about her dislike of *Survivor* generally seem to trace the nature of her embarrassment about it to issues in the novel having to do with the treatment of sex and race/species. She implies that she is ashamed of the book's acceptance of colonialist or racist attitudes toward the non-human characters:

> When I was young, a lot of people wrote about going to another world and finding either little green men or little brown men, and they were always less in some way. They were a little sly, or a little like "the natives" in a very bad, old movie. And I thought, "No way. Apart from all these human beings populating the galaxy, this is really offensive garbage." People ask me why I don't like *Survivor,* my third novel. And it's because it feels a little bit like that. Some humans go up to another world, and immediately begin mating with the aliens and having children with them. I think of it as my *Star Trek* novel. (Littleton)

Butler's comments on her objections to *Survivor* thus note its resemblance to science fiction she read when young, which was marred by its racist/colonialist view of "little green men or little brown men" as "less in some way." But *Survivor* resembles such works in this presumably only insofar as the novel represents, and the reader sees, the "little green men" (or large blue Kohn) as "less in some way" than the human colonists. Certainly the settler colonialism of the Missionaries alludes to historical instances of such projects, particularly in the resonance between John Winthrop's "City on a Hill" and the Missionaries' Canaan. But as Patricia Melzer notes, the novel "undermines the binary of colonizer-colonized: . . . the dominated one sets out to dominate, and in turn ends up being dominated" (64). Similarly, the Kohn might seem to have a kind of talent for slyness, given their ability to blend invisibly into their surroundings, and the leader of the Garkohn does attempt (successfully, at first) to manipulate the human Missionaries. But other Kohn, and especially the Tehkohn, are presented as honorable, and their deceptions, like Alanna's, are strategies of survival. Thus to see the natives as "less in some way" than the colonizers is to share the perspective of the Missionaries, who see the Kohn as "lower creatures—higher than apes, but lower than true humans" (Butler, *Survivor*, 5).

Alanna explicitly disputes this view, and the novel as a whole seems largely to endorse her skepticism about the views of the Missionaries, and especially her view that the Kohn are "human enough" (6). Indeed, the very possibility of human-Kohn reproduction might confirm that biologically they are not different species, since the most common biological definition of species is a group of creatures that are capable of interbreeding (Queiroz). The Missionaries had initially condemned Alanna in much the same terms as they later judged the Kohn. As a formerly "wild" human (*Survivor*, 29), Alanna was seen as "more animal than human" (29); they taught her that "[h]er habits were 'dirty,' her speech 'obscene'. She must change" (28). So, in exchange for the valuable resources of food and safe, dry shelter, Alanna conformed her behavior to the rules of Missionary life, but disclaimed any internalizing of their values. When she is captured by Tehkohn, she thinks, "It would . . . be the Missionary experience again then. In exchange for food, shelter, and safety, I would learn to say the right words and observe the right customs—change my cultural 'coloring' and fade into Tehkohn society as much as I could. If I could. If I couldn't, at least I would be able to bide my time until I was strong again. Strong enough to try to find my way back to the valley—or at least to take my revenge" (49).

One of the more dramatic instances evidencing that Alanna's adoption of Mission rules was not an acceptance of their beliefs comes when she is attacked by a group of Missionary children. Alanna fights back ferociously, but her foster father defends her to the group on the grounds of her self-restraint, since she could have killed her attackers, but did not. Talking with her about this later, he asks her why she did not kill her attackers, when she could have. She responds:

> "It's a sin among the people here. Your Bible said it was a sin."
> "Thou shalt not kill," quoted Jules.
> "Not that," she said. "It was one of the other verses that came to me. 'He that smiteth a man, so that he die, shall surely be put to death.'" (30)

Jules is momentarily disconcerted by this, as it becomes clear that Alanna has chosen to obey Mission rules because of their material rather than spiritual consequences. For the sake of "[f]ood, shelter, warm clothing, kindness" (32), "[s]he was careful to observe Mission law, even when, as often happened, it seemed foolish to her" (32).

In particular, their sexual rules seem foolish to her, for they condemned her active sexuality just as they later did that of the Kohn, whose "lasciviousness" they saw as "immorality" (15). Alanna reflects that in her "early days among" the Missionaries, she had known no better than to go with [Missionary men] to secret places where we could break Mission law together. I stopped that as soon as I understood that I was risking the comfort and security that I had found with the Verricks—as soon as I understood that the men and I were "behaving like animals" together . . . now they pretended to find me contemptible because I was not "pure." I had shared pleasure with some of them. I was guilty of sin, but somehow, they were all still innocent. Foolishness! It disgusted me to think I would have to spend my life with anyone so foolish. (16)

While the Missionaries' interest in the purity of the human species is narratively motivated by their experience with the mutated children of survivors of the Clayark plague on earth, it also echoes some of the terms of historical human racism. But such racism itself also appears among the Missionaries. Among her first memories among the Missionaries is a conversation she overhears in which one woman, Bea Stamp, pointing out that "the girl isn't white," encourages the Verricks to turn her over to "one of our black families" so as to be "setting a better example for the young people here—not encouraging them to mix" (31). That this incident is how Alanna "learned for the first time how important some Missionaries believed their own coloring to be" (31) suggests that encounters with racism have not previously been part of her experience, and might help explain her character's freedom from the internalization of racist oppression.

Yet Alanna does internalize Tehkohn values, most clearly in the matter of meklah addiction. In her second withdrawal, she "found herself thinking of Diut, feeling glad that he could not see her as she was now . . . When he saw her again, the ordeal would be over . . . She would be clean. . . . addiction was a shameful stigma in his culture" (82). When a Tehkohn friend tells her they have heard about her being forced to become readdicted, "Alanna lifted her head slightly, stifling a rush of humiliation. 'It is undone. And the Garkohn will pay'" (90). Even in other matters, however, she is susceptible to shaming by the Tehkohn. She "did not want to humiliate [herself] before Jeh and Cheah" (95) by admitting to her fear of Diut. Diut also interprets her behavior as reflecting his own values; when he is teaching her to hunt and she fails to see a dangerous animal as soon as she should have, he narrates, "She made no excuse, only stood with her head bowed" (112) and later "worked silently, and did not look at me. Clearly, she was ashamed" (113). His reading of her response here is not contradicted in the text. Her own feelings about this internalizing of Tehkohn values are initially disturbed; she reflects that "[t]hey were absorbing me" and "I felt myself slipping away" (56). While Alanna thus refuses to accept the shaming that the Missionaries would impose on her, she arguably does sufficiently adopt the value system of the Tehkohn to be ashamed of falling short of their values.

Some readers have apparently overlooked or have sought to minimize the racial hierarchy among the Tehkohn. Crystal Anderson contrasts the Missionary devaluing of color with the Kohn "culture predicated upon the value of color. Rather than a marker of inferiority, color, particularly a certain shade of blue, carries enormous value and privilege" (42). But if the green or blue of the Kohn fighter classes is not a marker of inferiority, the green and yellow of the artisan and farmer "race" may be (*Survivor*, 54). Alanna tells Neila that "[s]ome fighters see nonfighters as lesser people—a little like the way Bea Stamp sees me" (40). Further, the "medium brown" of Alanna's skin (27) carries no value or privilege. Diut tells her that as a human she has "no rights, no freedoms that I do not allow. Without the blue, you are like an animal among us" (97).

The shame of being seen as or treated like an animal by the Missionaries (16) or by the Kohn (97) may recall the historical devaluation of non-whites and especially enslaved Africans and African Americans, (including the failure of Butler's mother's employers to recognize her humanity). But Alanna's route to personhood among the Kohn turns out to be an initially coercive liaison that reinscribes a racialized gender difference. When Alanna understands that Diut's desire to have sex with her is "an experiment," she says her "fear was drowned in anger and humiliation" (97). When she asks him, "Why do you humiliate me?" (99), he tells her, "There need be no humiliation in this for you . . . I am the leader of my people" (99). His reaction registers the possibility of humiliation only as an index of his status, not as an index of the overriding of her will. But what really persuades her to tolerate sexual relations with him is the promise that after their relationship "you will be Tehkohn when you leave me. Tehkohn, and your own person, not dependent on others to guide or guard you'" (99). The exchange suggests that insofar as her personhood among the Tehkohn depends on this relation, her identity is transformed, or indeed instantiated, in the space of shame (Sedgwick, 64). Thus she accepts the encounter because he confirms that after their relationship "I will be free? It will be as though I had some blue in my coloring?" (99). Yet defining her personhood and freedom as dependent on her being "as though" blue might recall the kind of conditional approval behind statements like "You seem like a white person" or "I don't think of you as black." That is, she is clearly being installed within the terms of a color-based social hierarchy.

Alanna's relationship with Diut entails his revision of the terms of her shame. In addition to his assertion that their liaison need not entail humiliation (99), he positions her as not "abject" insofar as she resists, like a captive Tehkohn fighter, first physically and then verbally. A turning point in their relationship comes when she apparently confirms his view of her as warrior-like by refusing to be beaten again, expressing a willingness to die rather than to submit (113–114). Diut's view thus implicitly endorses the death-before-dishonor version of resistance that would preclude survival, and that Butler's work elsewhere resists.

Moreover, the relations of body size in play in the novel signal the persistence of a notion of gender difference that is (on our planet) historically and conceptually racialized. Alanna is a relatively large human. Though Butler did not connect this aspect of the novel with her embarrassment about it, she did comment on the potentially shaming experience of the policing of gender:

> My first attempt at being as big as I am was in *Survivor.* Here I have a character who is not necessarily fat, but she's very tall and androgynous-looking. I used to be mistaken for a man a lot, and, occasionally, somebody would try to chase me out of the ladies room, which used to upset the hell out of me. (Mehaffy and Keating, 69)

That men are larger than women is less a statistical fact than a cultural assumption; thus a big, tall woman is likely to be read as androgynous, even as someone who does not belong in a ladies' room. At least since the development of racial and sexual theories in the nineteenth century, as Sally Markowitz has argued, writers have reconciled the apparent contradictions of ostensibly analogous racial and sexual hierarchies by arguing that the superior (Anglo-Saxon) races were more highly differentiated by sex/gender: "While 'lower' races may often be represented as feminine and the men of these races as less than masculine, the femininity of nonwhite women, far from being heightened, is likely to be denied (the better, no doubt to justify their hard physical labor or sexual exploitation)" (Markowitz, 390). Thus even if, as sociologist Robert Park asserted in 1919, "the Negro . . . is the lady amongst the races" (cited in Kim, 310), Octavia Butler might still find herself chased out of the ladies' room. In Butler's subsequent portrayals of large central characters, the protagonist's sexual relations are configured in terms other than size (and in *Lilith's Brood,* in relations other than binary). Other novels by Butler include similar hierarchical sex/gender differences, and have been criticized for a failure to "visualize the full fruition of gender equality" and by the assertion that Butler's female characters "actively compromise themselves by allying with strong males within predominantly patriarchal societies" (DeGraw, 219). But *Survivor* stresses the size of both partners. We hear repeatedly about "Alanna's own unusual height—nearly two meters" (5), and Diut's size is stressed even more. When he first has sex with her, Alanna experiences him as "too large" (100). Diut is first referred to as "the big blue one" (3), and as Hao he is "the personification of Kohn power" (103). By giving her "big" protagonist an even bigger sexual partner, Butler maintains the masculine/feminine difference within the couple. Thus Alanna's position with the Kohn allies her with the historical discourse of the sexually dichotomized, soi-disant master races.

But if the Kohn are not evidently "less in some way," like the "little green men or little brown men" of earlier science fiction, then the novel is not simply replaying the colonial relations of those works. As Butler stated:

> "I did like the idea, in *Survivor* in particular, that if we go to another world, and if it happens to have people on it, we have to come to some kind of an arrangement with them. It may be a very strange arrangement, but it's not going to be cowboys and Indians or Englishmen and Africans." (Govan)

What Butler's alien Kohn share with their literary- or cinematic-historical precursors is, rather, being a kind of projection of human (narrative) needs. Insofar as what many critics have come to value in Butler's work includes her portraits of hybridity, difference, and becoming, then the material failure of the Kohn to be so biologically different that reproduction with humans is impossible marks a limit to the imagination of difference that can be embraced in *Survivor*. Indeed, Butler has suggested that the *Lilith's Brood* series is a revisiting and revising of this problem:

> One of the things that I was most embarrassed about in my novel *Survivor* is my human characters going off to another planet and finding other people they could immediately start having children with. Later I thought, oh well, you can't really erase embarrassing early work, but you don't have to repeat it. So I thought if I were going to bring people together from other worlds again, I was at least going to give them trouble. (Kenan, 500)

In the Xenogenesis/*Lilith's Brood* series, Lilith is encouraged by the Oankali to help other humans accept their mixed-species families: "Let them learn that it isn't shameful to be together with one another and with us" (200). Such overcoming of shame leads Alanna to commit herself to Diut and the Tehkohn, and leads characters in other of Butler's works to relations of "addiction" (*Lilith's Brood*, 679) or symbiosis, challenges to the bounded notion of self. The narrative shifts in *Survivor* from first person to third person also suggest that perhaps, although Alanna tells Jules that in her time with the Tehkohn "I haven't lost myself" (170), she is nonetheless set apart from her former narrating self. By accepting the value system of the Tehkohn, by becoming ashamed of the things that the Tehkohn find shameful, Alanna yields to a change within herself and thus enables her reconstitution as a member of the tribe.

As a member of that tribe, she remains part of a couple embodying a (racialized) sex/gender difference, as well as part of a society that reads status through color. That Butler's fullest presentation of the transformational possibility of shame comes in a work in which the potentially shame-inducing encounter with difference turns out to be itself an embarrassingly in-different portrait of sham otherness may hint at a further reason for Butler's rejection of *Survivor*. In a study of the ways that Foucault's notions of power can illuminate the strategies of Butler's protagonists for challenging and accruing power, Lauren Lacey delineates several of those strategies, including "building communities that offer alternative models to traditional hierarchies" (380). Yet the community Alanna joins is not only not built by her, but is also, as Butler hints, less alternative than the communities formed in her other works. While *Survivor* is hardly the simple replication of the racist or colonialist patterns of mid-twentieth-century science fiction that Butler's "*Star Trek*" comment might seem to imply, it accepts shame as part of a route to inclusion within a preexisting (and all too human) social hierarchy. But the embrace of shame may be a waste of spirit for the oppressed, risking the contagious endorsement of the very structures by which they are devalued.

Notes

1. Further, unlike Butler's other novels, *Survivor* was substantially rewritten (Champion). Butler's papers might reveal whether there is any correlation between the different narrative voices or

timelines and the different stages of revision. Sue Hodson of the Huntington Library estimated they would be available to researchers in 2012: "work has proven to be far more involved and complicated than usual for an author's archive, because of the way Octavia kept her files and organized materials. These factors will make the collection especially more rich for research, but it means that our work moves forward at a slower pace than we might like" (e-mail communication, February 24, 2011). As of September 2012, however, Butler's papers remain unavailable.

2. Several readers of Butler's work have recently stressed the relevance of Deleuze to her writing (A. T. Walker, Vint, Ackerman).

3. In the *Buffy the Vampire Slayer* episode quoted at the beginning of this chapter, Buffy becomes temporarily able to hear others' thoughts, and Cordelia, the "shameless" character, is the only one for whom there is no difference between what she thinks and what she says aloud. She is also portrayed at this point in the series as far more affluent and privileged than the other characters.

4. These academic, professionalized instantiations of "gay shame" run counter to the Gay Shame activism that began in New York in 1998 in response to what Mattilda Bernstein Sycamore calls "Mayor Giuliani's reign of terror known officially as the 'Quality of Life' campaign": that is, it began as a radical queer resistance to neoliberal policing and gentrification. Groups in Toronto, San Francisco, and other cities went on to protest cuts to public services, commercializing of gay pride events, military invasions, and other crimes of the privileged against the oppressed. The term "shame" in such activist uses has the moral valence of chastening the dominant class.

8 Daughters of the House of Shame

Sinead McDermott

IN THIS CHAPTER I discuss a British novel first published in 1992, Michèle Roberts's *Daughters of the House,* in the light of recent feminist theorizations of shame. I argue that shame acts as a central concept in the novel, delineating the boundaries of the proper feminine body and of the nation-state. Shame is especially resonant in Roberts's exploration of the theme of hidden, traumatic memory and its relationship to a female body which is represented as transgressing sexual and national borders and boundaries. In exploring the aftereffects of shame for a second generation, Roberts's novel also suggests intriguing connections between shame and the concept of "post-memory" (Hirsch), a form of belated, second-generation memory of traumatic events and experiences.

Daughters of the House is set in rural France and moves between the contemporary moment and the postwar past, when the two central protagonists, Thérèse and Léonie, are young girls: the "daughters of the house" of the title. Thérèse and Léonie have been brought up as cousins: Thérèse is the daughter of the house's owner, Antoinette Martin, and Léonie is her half-English cousin, the daughter of Madeleine, Antoinette's sister. Roberts's use of a French setting and her inclusion of a character of dual English-French nationality are hallmarks of her fiction, and can be related to her status as an English woman whose mother was French and who spent much of her childhood in France. The novel also explores aspects of French history, as Thérèse and Léonie seek to make sense of the rumors and secrets associated with the Martins' house and its role during the German occupation before they were born.[1] As Roger Luckhurst argues, the house is presented as containing an encrypted and traumatic memory, one which threatens to reemerge and haunt the next generation.

While the focus on the traumatic aftereffects of the Vichy regime links Roberts's novel to other recent cultural responses to France's wartime history, such as Tatiana de Rosnay's *Sarah's Key* (2007), the novel can also be situated within the field of contemporary British fiction in its concern with what Victoria Stewart has described as the "secret histories" of the Second World War. Roberts's interest in themes of encrypted memory, stalled mourning, and the haunting return of a traumatic past, also places her novel within the international field of late twentieth and early twenty-first century trauma fiction, and her work is discussed in these terms in Roger Luckhurst's "Impossible Mourning" and *The Trauma Question*. However, as both Emma Parker and Edith Frampton point out, the exploration of national history and identity in *Daughters of the House* is also shaped by Roberts's abiding preoccupation with questions of gender, sex, and feminism. Indeed, the two concerns intersect: most notably in the story of Antoinette's past, as the text suggests that Antoinette had a liaison with a German soldier during the war, and that Thérèse and, possibly, Léonie are born as a result of this encounter. In exploring the anxieties circulating around Antoinette's hidden past, and the legacy of these secrets for Thérèse and Léonie's sense of themselves as young girls, Roberts reveals the ways in which female bodies and feminine identities intertwine with national and collective histories.

Roberts's dual focus on the (female) body and the nation suggests that shame may be a useful concept for exploring this novel, as this is an affect with repercussions for both. According to Sara Ahmed, shame can be described as "an intense and painful sensation that is bound up with how the self feels about itself, a self-feeling that is felt by and on the body" (*Cultural Politics*, 103). Shame can also be understood as a collective phenomenon: nations can express shame and regret and say sorry for past crimes, and, indeed, this process can become part of national self-definition (100, 108). As a number of feminist critics have argued, shame can also be viewed as an affect with particular resonances for women. According to Sandra Bartky, "women typically are more shame-prone than men" (85); a point also made by Ullaliina Lehtinen when she argues that "women and other socially subordinate groups are more *shame-prone* than men (or otherwise socially privileged people)" (60; emphasis in original). In Bartky's analysis, understanding women's experiences of shame entails rethinking our assumption that shame occurs as a single or salutary moment, and instead recognizing that "shame is not so much a particular feeling or emotion . . . as a pervasive affective attunement to the social environment" (85). In Kathleen Woodward's summary, shame is "the *condition* in which many women live" (*Statistical Panic*, 95; emphasis in original).

My discussion of *Daughters of the House* begins with an examination of the workings of shame in Thérèse and Léonie's construction as "proper *jeunes filles*" (Roberts, 124): as properly feminine and as properly French. I argue that the text utilizes a variety of iconic figures of femininity to comment upon this construction: the Quimper dish lady; the figure of Antoinette, Thérèse's mother; the Virgin Mary, venerated by Thérèse in particular; and her counterpart, the "red lady" seen in a vision by Léonie. In the story of Antoinette, the novel investigates the relationship between personal and national shame and transgression through the narrative of buried secrets from the house's past. The figure of the red lady is offered in the novel as an alternative vision of spirituality, maternity, and femininity, enabling Roberts to move beyond female shame toward a vision of bliss, unity, and transcendence. The sense of visionary transformation connected with this figure is counterpointed in the novel by the difficult but necessary work of postmemory, as Thérèse and Léonie recognize that they must engage with, and bear witness to, a painful past to facilitate personal and national recovery.

Female Shame and Secrecy

In *Embodied Shame*, Bouson argues that the female body has been closely associated with shame in Western culture. She explains:

> Conceived of as defective or deficient from male norms and as potentially diseased, women have long been embodiments of shame in our culture, and, indeed, the female socialization process can be viewed as a prolonged immersion in shame. (2)

She argues that "the female body remains a locus of shame for women, associated as it is with out-of-control passions and appetites and with something dirty and defiling" (3), and she cites Nancy Chodorow's argument that "[s]hame seems central to many women's feelings and fantasies about mother, self, and gender, and shame and disgust often color women's sense of bodily self" (Chodorow, 121, cited in Bouson, *Embodied Shame*, 8–9).

In *Daughters of the House,* we watch the "female socialization process" at work in the lives of Léonie and Thérèse. In Susan Bordo's terms, they adopt the "normalizing disciplines of diet, makeup, and dress" (Bordo, 166, cited in Bouson, 3) to become what Foucault would term "docile bodies," properly composed, self-contained, and private. The novel foregrounds the role of the domestic in the normalization of Thérèse's and Léonie's bodies, as they carry out routine domestic chores and explore various spaces within the house. While many of these experiences are pleasurable (licking the cake tin in the kitchen, for example), these are also the places where a variety of female adults attempt to train their appetites, tastes, and behavior. For Léonie, this is especially a lesson in Frenchness: brought up in England, she has to acquire French sensibilities and her failures in proper behavior are read as "her bad-mannered English side coming out" (Roberts, 72). Léonie's inculcation into femininity and national identity is represented by the Quimper dish, with its portrait of a French countrywoman: "a squat Breton countrywoman in white bonnet and striped blue gown planted her saboted feet on a clump of vivid grass" (91). Antoinette's instructions to Léonie on carrying the dish are also instructions about femininity: "to be careful, not to drop it, to try at least to walk like a lady" (91). Later, when Thérèse lets the Quimper dish fall, the shattered dish becomes a signifier of the fragmentation of the proper French female body: "The Breton lady had been dismembered. Her head lay near a table-leg. Her flower-clasping hands rested at the foot of the stove" (94).

The anxieties in the narrative about maintaining a properly composed, and contained, feminine body reemerge in Léonie's dreams of her aunt, Antoinette. Antoinette dies of cancer midway through the novel, when Léonie and Thérèse are thirteen years old. Before her death, Antoinette is associated with the anxious policing of spaces and behaviors in the novel: she is the one to warn Léonie to be careful when carrying the Quimper dish, for example. However, Antoinette also becomes associated in the text with the failures of proper boundaries. In the opening chapter of the novel, Léonie dreams that her dead aunt is buried in the house's cellar:

> Antoinette was dead, which was why they had buried her in the cellar. She moved under the heap of sand. She clutched her red handbag, which was full of shreds of dead flesh. She was trying to get out, to hang two red petticoats on the washing-line in the orchard. Sooner or later she would batter down the cellar door and burst up through it on her dead and bleeding feet. (1)

Later, Léonie dreams that her aunt is dragging her through a Customs hall. Antoinette carries a suitcase "bound in scarlet cloth" which the Customs men refuse to let through: "Red and dangerous, that suitcase. The Customs men knew it. They'd been tipped off. A bomb inside it, timed to explode and tear them all to shreds. Red shreds of flesh" (52).

In these two dreams, Antoinette is associated with the fragmented, vulnerable body; with female sexuality (the red handbag and the red petticoats) and with the transgression of domestic and national boundaries (bursting out of the cellar; crossing the Customs Hall). Her body is an object of shame, buried in the cellar, but it is also shameless ("she laughed a guttural laugh, a Nazi laugh" [1]) and irrepressible ("she was tunnelling her way out like a mole" [1]). If Antoinette focuses in the novel on ensuring the rules of decorum and proper feminine conduct, and thus keeping bodies and spaces separate and intact, the dream suggests that the flip side of such maintenance work is always the risk of fragmentation. Just as the composed Quimper lady is shattered into pieces, Antoinette in Léonie's dream disintegrates into "shreds of red flesh" and a "mad red grin" (52). As Bouson explains, the docile, normalized body described by Bordo and Foucault is haunted by the fear of the "out-of-control" body: what Kristeva terms the "abject body" (Bouson, 4).[2]

The image of Antoinette buried under a heap of sand in the house's cellar also raises the question of the relationship between shame, secrecy, and concealment. If shame is a response to how the subject is seen by others or imagines him- or herself being seen, then one reaction to feeling shamed "involves an attempt to hide; a hiding that requires that the subject turn away from the other and towards itself" (Ahmed, 103). For Ahmed, this association can be traced back to the word's roots: "the word 'shame' comes from the Indo-European verb for 'to cover,' which associates shame with other words such as 'hide,' 'custody,' 'hut,' and 'house'" (104, citing Schneider, "Mature," 227). But, as Ahmed points out, shame can also be associated with the opposite of covering: with "exposure, vulnerability and wounding" (104, citing Lynd; Wurmser, *Mask of Shame*). She explains: "[T]he desire to take cover and to be covered presupposes the failure of cover; in shame, one desires cover precisely because one has already been exposed to others" (104). The movement between shame, covering up, and exposure is suggested in Roberts's text by the imagery of secrets hidden in, and being exposed upon, the body of the house. At one point, the family housekeeper, Victorine, pulls up the carpet in the salon to reveal marks on the tiles beneath. The marks, made by the Germans' boots, are described as "the memory of the house made visible. Scars that would never fade" (Roberts, 44). The Martins' shameful secrets are covered up but persistently reappear, in the forms of wounds or scars on the house's surface.

The connection between shame and secrecy in the house's past is paralleled by the connections made by the two girls between female shame and secrecy. Notions of concealment and the fear of visibility are connected in the text with ideas of female propriety and modesty. This is made most explicit when Léonie has her first menstrual period and the back of her shorts is stained. Thérèse's horrified reaction ("Do something. Quick. Don't let them see" [124]) suggests the association of menstruation and the female body with shame and the need for concealment. The narrator's description of the two girls' subsequent appearance for dinner is a pointed comment on the relationship between feminine propriety, secrecy, and shame: "They walked into the dining-room together only five minutes late. Clean white half-moons of nails held out for inspection, hands reddened from hot water and soap, hair brushed. Proper *jeunes filles*. Which meant having secrets" (124).

Léonie's dreams of Antoinette in the cellar and the Customs Hall thus suggest her anxieties about national transgressions (the Nazi laugh; the Customs officer) but also about female modesty. Antoinette's visibly bleeding body is shocking not only because it moves between death and life and bears the marks of violence, but also because its "leaky boundaries" suggest the leakiness of female bodies generally (Shildrick); her laughter becomes not only a challenge to ideas of national purity but also to the expectations of female shame.

Shame and Nation

As Roger Luckhurst points out, the traumatic event at the center of *Daughters of the House* remains opaque (*Trauma*, 108). Thérèse and Léonie (and we, as readers) receive snatches of information, but the text suggests that it is not possible to recuperate the truth of what happened to Antoinette during the war. After Antoinette's death, Thérèse is sent the letters which her mother had written to her older sister, a nun in an enclosed order, during the occupation. Her interpretation of their contents leads her to claim that Antoinette had seduced, or been raped by, a German officer; that she had sacrificed herself to keep the secret of the wine hidden in the cellar of the Martins' house. Later, Léonie offers an alternative version: that Antoinette invented the story of the German officer in order to explain the fact that she slept with Louis before marriage and became pregnant. Either way, "the end of Thérèse's story was that Antoinette had been found out. Proof: her stomach had swelled. Shame brought upon the family. Outrage. Disgrace" (Roberts, 152). Antoinette's shame can be viewed as a specifically female shame. Her sexual encounter (whether consensual or not) places her on the wrong side of what Bouson describes as "the binary oppositions associated with femininity and female bodies: those of good/bad, pure/impure, clean and proper/abject, honored/dishonored" (96). The stigmatization of pregnancy outside marriage means that Antoinette must marry Louis in order to "cover up" her shame. The reference in Thérèse's account to the "shame brought upon the family" also suggests the role of families in policing social norms. As Ahmed comments:

> The domesticity of shame is telling. Family love may be conditional upon how one lives one's life in relation to social ideals . . . The difficulty of moving beyond shame is a sign of the power of the normative, and the role of loving others in enforcing social ideals. (107)

The possibility that Antoinette has had a sexual encounter with a German adds another dimension to her transgression. In her discussion of national shame, Ahmed argues that the nation "is reproduced through expressions of shame" (108). This may occur if shame is "'brought onto' the nation by illegitimate others (who fail to reproduce its form, or even its offspring), such as queer others, or asylum seekers" (108). We could argue that women also "bring shame onto" the nation if they fail to reproduce its offspring. For Antoinette, giving birth to a child with a German father can be read as a failure to properly reproduce Frenchness. In this case, shame is potentially passed on to the products of that shame: the daughter(s) born from this encounter.

Antoinette's secret past is linked with another painful wartime history contained in the novel: that of the Jewish family murdered along with a local man, Henri Taillé, by the Germans after they are betrayed by an informer. Their bodies are covered up and uncovered at a variety of points in the novel. After the murder, the bodies are hidden by the Germans to prevent them being given a proper burial. Their shallow grave in the woods is discovered thirteen years later and the bones are re-interred in the village cemetery, under a headstone bearing only the name of the murdered local man. In the contemporary section of the novel, the grave is desecrated: swastikas are daubed on the headstone and the grave is opened. According to Sara Ahmed:

> The nation is reproduced through expressions of shame in at least two ways. First, shame may be "brought onto" the nation by illegitimate others . . . Such others are shaming by proxy: they do not approximate the form of the good citizen . . . Second, the nation may bring shame "on itself" by its treatment of others . . . In this instance, the nation may even express shame about its treatment of others who in the past were read as the origin of shame. (108)

In Roberts's text, the secret burial(s) of the Jews and Henri Taillé invoke this doubled national shame. First, there is the shame that someone in the village has collaborated with the Germans to betray the Jewish family's hiding place. Next, there is the shame incurred by the manner of their burial and reburial. Here, Roberts suggests that shame lies not only in the treatment of the Jews but also (for some of the villagers) in the Jews' status as "illegitimate others." When Baptiste, the son of Rose and Henri Taillé, tells Léonie about the reburial of the bodies, he confesses that "they buried my father and the Jews all together in the same grave in the cemetery, they couldn't tell whose bones were whose" (Roberts, 137). Léonie realizes that "he sounded ashamed" (137). Baptiste is ashamed of the racial mixing suggested by this muddle of bones, one in which his father's body, and perhaps his identity as a Frenchman, is "mixed up" (137) with Jewishness in death. In Baptiste's shamed reaction and, more forcefully, in the desecration of the grave later on, Roberts suggests that the Jews remain "'strangers' in [the] house" of Europe (Luckhurst, "Impossible Mourning," 257). The reopening of the grave suggests both the persistence of fascism in contemporary Europe and the inadequacy of the protagonists' attempts to cover over the disquieting secrets of the past.

While the two traumatic secrets in the novel (Antoinette's encounter with the German officer and the murder and burial of the Jewish family and Henri Taillé) refer to different events during the occupation, the text also suggests connections between the two. These connections are suggested through the figure of the female collaborator, an unnamed woman who runs one of the bakeries in the village, which the Martin family never visits. According to Victorine, this woman used to work in the Martin house during the war and "got very friendly with one of the German officers billeted here. I used to see her creeping up to his room at night . . . Oh, Thérèse said: you mean a *collaborator*" (Roberts, 45). When Rose, Henri's wife, tells Léonie the story of the discovery of her husband and the family he was hiding, she says, "None of us knew for certain who the informer was. Some people swore it must have been someone in the Martin family. Others said it must have been that girl who worked here, the one who was the German officer's mistress" (127). The figure of the ostracized "female collaborator" raises uncomfortable questions about the relationship between shaming, guilt, and betrayal in the novel; especially as the accusations made against the "German officer's mistress" could potentially be leveled at Antoinette too. The connection between the two women is suggested by the key status of the Martins' house as the site where the Jewish family were held on the night before they were murdered. In the repeated references to the Martins' house and instances of female collaboration, the novel raises the uncomfortable possibility that Antoinette herself may have been the informer responsible for the deaths.

The disquieting possibility of Antoinette's larger betrayal, and its implications for the "daughters of the house," Thérèse and Léonie, generates much of the unease in the narrative. While we might expect that this possibility would remain open in the text, especially given that so much of Antoinette's wartime story is left occluded, it is notable that the ending of the novel directs us very clearly to believe that the true informant is actually the local priest. The voices Léonie heard as a child in her bedroom are revealed as the voices of ghosts: the murdered men and women who chanted their names, and the name of the man who betrayed them, the night before their deaths. While this conclusion allows the reader the satisfaction of a narrative ending which holds out the possibility of retrospective justice, we could argue that it also allows Roberts to circumvent some of the more discomforting potential of her story, by displacing the possibility of blame from the figure of Antoinette to the priest—an unpleasant and reactionary figure throughout the novel.

The representation of Antoinette as a figure of sexual and national transgression in the text thus raises as many questions as it answers. The occluded nature of Antoinette's story means that questions of her agency and her victimhood are ambiguous in the novel: it is unclear, for example, whether she has been raped; has seduced a soldier in order to prevent his discovering what is hidden in the cellar; or whether she has engaged in an consensual affair, either with a soldier or with Louis. The repeated references to Antoinette in Léonie's dreams suggest the importance of Antoinette to the house's secret history of shame, but it also suggests the overdetermined nature of shame in this text. Antoinette is a figure of shame as a woman who dies of invasive cancer; as a woman who was possibly a collaborator and an informer; as a woman who got pregnant outside marriage; and even, as Thérèse recognizes much later, simply as a mother who, unlike the Virgin Mary, "hadn't been perfect. She'd had sex" (Roberts, 163). Antoinette thus seems to represent the almost inescapable nature of female shame in the novel.

Postmemory and Shame

As daughters of the house, Léonie and Thérèse have to contend both with their socialization as proper *jeunes filles* (a process that involves the association of the female body with shame) and with their position as postmemorial subjects, inheriting the shame and trauma of their parents' generation. According to Marianne Hirsch, postmemory can be defined as "second-generation memories of cultural or collective traumatic events and experiences" (22). She uses the term "postmemory" to describe the difficult situation of the children of Holocaust survivors, whose lives may be dominated by traumatic events of which they have no personal memory. The relationship of this second generation to the Holocaust occupies a space somewhere between memory and history: less immediate than memory because of "generational distance," but more immediate than history because of what she terms the "deep personal connection" to the events recalled (22). In Léonie and Thérèse's case, they must deal with the burden of Antoinette's secret past, as transmitted by letters, in the gossip of servants, or the half-heard conversations of adult relatives. Like the second generation described by Hirsch, they must contend with a traumatic past which is so overwhelming that in some ways it takes precedence over their own stories; although in this case, it is the possibility of parental guilt as well as suffering which accounts for the troubling persistence of the past. For Thérèse and Léonie, the facts of Antoinette's story also have implications for their own sense of identity, as they seek to discover whether they are actually twin sisters rather than cousins, and if so, whether their father is a German soldier or Antoinette's eventual husband, Louis. In doing so, they must also decide how to respond to the inherited burden of parental suffering and shame.

Thérèse's response to her mother's perceived failings is to repudiate the body and the life of the senses. This repudiation begins when Antoinette is dying, and is associated with Thérèse's reaction against her own body's maturation. Thérèse's body becomes increasingly a source of frustrating and uncontrollable appetites, as she puts on weight and develops a more markedly female form in adolescence:

> Thérèse stared at the breadknife. She wanted to apply it to her newly grown hips and breasts, to pare off, with quick disgusted flicks of the wrist, the fat that clung to her. She was a slim girl inexplicably encased in walls of fat. She was always hungry. And once she admitted hunger it turned into greed, she was nothing but mouth, teeth, stomach, impossible ever to stop—she was starving. (Roberts, 73)

Feminist theory, as Bouson points out, has shown how "negative and shaming bodily attributions, such as fat, ugly, old, disfigured, or disabled, influence female identity and selfhood" (14). For Thérèse, fatness, and the appetite it signals, is a source of shame ("She screwed up her face and whispered: you're so revoltingly fat you disgusting baboon" [Roberts, 78–79]), allied to the shame of being seen as a sexual being: her father comments, "[M]y goodness, don't girls grow up early these days" (73). Her solution is to turn to religious iconography, and the images of a childlike and asexual Virgin Mary that surround her: "The Madonna with a heavenly look, a light veil over her fair hair, blue sash about her girlish waist, hands clasped in ecstasy and a rosary dangling from one arm" (76). Mortifying her body and disciplining the flesh becomes a means of achieving transcendence over her "female" passions and appetites.

An alternative response to personal and familial shame is suggested in Léonie's visions of the "red lady" (87). As a young girl, Léonie sees visions of a "red gold lady" when she visits the shrine in the woods dedicated to a nameless and ancient female saint. The red lady stands in the text as an alternative icon of female spirituality to the Virgin Mary. In contrast to the Catholic Church's view of female sanctity, the red lady is associated with both maternal nurturance (the saint in the woods is credited with curing childhood illnesses and is a figure of fertility, associated with harvest festivals) and with sexual pleasure: when Léonie first sees the vision, we are told that "the deepest pleasure she had ever known possessed her. It started in her toes and across her shoulders and squirmed through her, aching, sweet" (86). The red lady is also connected with a re-vision of religion and ethnicity in her "black hair" and "dark gold skin" (88). Victorine ridicules Léonie's story of her vision: "she was coloured? Victorine roared . . . oh what a story, well that certainly cuts out the Virgin Mary" (89). Her reaction reminds us of the manner in which traditional iconography of the Virgin Mary constructs her in terms of whiteness. With the figure of the red lady, Roberts attempts to imagine an ethnically marked figure of female spirituality, one that moves beyond conventional religious and national boundaries.[3]

For Léonie, the figure of the red lady and the site of the broken shrine offer a means of reclaiming her sexuality and a way out of the personal and postmemorial shame she endures as a daughter of the house. Significantly, it is at the site of the shrine and in conversation with Baptiste that Leonie confronts and revises the story of her origins. Rejecting Thérèse's story of the German officer, Léonie offers her own explanation for Antoinette's pregnancy. According to her, the story of the German officer is a cover-up; Antoinette has slept with Louis and got pregnant:

> For Louis, Antoinette had kicked off her buttoned high-heeled shoes by the wine racks and lain down on gritty sand. Was it better to be raped by a Nazi than seduced by a Frenchman? Would you be forgiven quicker? (152)

In claiming her identity as the French daughter of Antoinette and Louis, Léonie also reclaims her sexual identity:

> Ripping off her Englishness and casting it aside was as easy as unfastening the collar of her dress . . . Shaking off the very idea of a German father was a wriggle of the shoulders, the thin cotton sleeves pushed down. Becoming French was taking Thérèse as her twin sister and then taking the boy she wanted . . . Léonie wanted to be found out . . . She opened her knees, drew Baptiste to her, held him firmly with both hands . . . She waited for the shouts from behind the trees, for the priest and the Bishop and Thérèse to come running, to come upon this sinful worship on the ground. (152–153)

Léonie's response to postmemorial and female shame is one of shamelessness. Whereas shame involves a covering-up, Léonie invites witnesses to her disgrace ("Léonie wanted to be found out"). In the process, she also chooses the parents (and the nationality) she prefers, disrobing herself of a difficult history along with the clothes she wears. In doing so, the presence of the shrine and the figure of the red lady associated with it seem to enable her redrawing of personal, bodily, and national boundaries.

Léonie and Thérèse, whether twin sisters or cousins, take very different routes in reaction to female and postmemorial shame. While the path chosen by Léonie is in many ways presented as preferable in the novel, just as the figure of the red lady is seen as an icon of femininity preferable to the Virgin Mary, the narrative does not suggest that Léonie's choice resolves all of the dilemmas raised by the text. Her decision to "be" French, for example, seems at odds with the red lady's position as a figure that redraws the boundaries of nation and ethnicity; while the adult Léonie's focus on family, possessions, and the care of the body seems equally as rigid as Thérèse's refusal of all of these. We could ask whether Léonie, in moving from shame to shamelessness, is simply engaging in "a reaction formation against shame" (Bouson, 41) which does not necessarily signal the end of shame. As Wurmser comments: "[I]f it is shame that is fought against by shamelessness, it is shame that returns in spectral form" (Wurmser, *Mask of Shame*, 262, cited in Bouson, 41). In addition, Léonie's nonchalant rejection of the past as a source of self-definition, while refreshing, seems at odds with the text's insistence on the return of the repressed, and the particular impact of those returns on Léonie herself (in the form of childhood dreams and nightmares).

The legacy of Léonie and Thérèse's postmemorial shame is addressed most thoroughly in the present-day sections of the novel, when Léonie and Thérèse, now middle-aged, are reunited at the Martin family home. Thérèse's return is prompted by a sense of the past reemerging: the newspaper stories of swastikas daubed on the gravestone in the local cemetery. Léonie, by contrast, has enveloped herself in the role of mistress of the house, surrounding herself with the Martin family possessions and resolutely turning her back on the past. In these sections, Thérèse acts as the voice of conscience, in a departure from her role as conduit for the voice of authority (the Church's view of the shrine and the visions) earlier in the novel.

For Thérèse, the shameful past that must be confronted is that of Antoinette, her mother. In returning to the cellar and rummaging in the heap of sand, Thérèse finds remnants of the statue of the female saint that had been destroyed and removed from the broken shrine in the woods. The discovery of this dismembered female form provides another, perhaps more convincing, explanation for Antoinette's actions during the war. As Thérèse surmises, Antoinette's encounter with the soldier was an attempt to prevent his discovering, not simply a collection of wine, but the much-loved statue of the female saint. The story of the nameless female saint and of Antoinette are joined together here, and putting the pieces of the statue back together becomes a means for Thérèse to re-member her own mother, from a more sympathetic and less judgmental perspective.

Thérèse must also face the difference between her earthly mother and the "mother of God" with whom she has tried to replace her. Describing the statue of the Virgin Mary in the chapel, the narrator tells us: "She was the Virgin Mother of God. She was flat as a boy. She was the perfect mother who'd never had sex. To whom all earthly mothers had to aspire" (164). Thérèse's idolization of this asexual mother figure has implicitly acted as a rejection of Antoinette, the mother who "hadn't been perfect," who had sex (165). In setting fire to the statue of the Virgin at the end of the novel, Thérèse reclaims her own mother, figured here as another "red lady" and described in terms of transformation and energy:

> Then, at last, after all these years, she saw her for the first time, that red and gold lady. The flames sliding up her forced her old clothes off, gave her new ones. With a red coat and slippers she flew. Skimmed into the air quick and bright as a rocket . . . she held out her hands to her daughter, to pull her in, to teach her the steps of the dance. (166)

If Thérèse's engagement with the shame of the past leads to a transformed understanding of religion, sexuality, and the female/maternal body, Léonie's final revelations engage with history and the national past. Here, the shame is a collective one: the betrayal by someone from the village of Henri Taillé and the Jewish family he had hidden during the war, leading to their execution by the Germans and the hiding of their bodies in order to deny them a proper burial. While not responsible for these events, which occurred before her birth, Léonie does have a responsibility of bearing witness to the ghostly voices she heard in her bedroom as a child. Léonie has attempted to shut those voices away; as she tells Thérèse at the start of the novel, "it's no use raking up the past" (23). Thérèse's return, however, coinciding with the desecration of the grave in the cemetery, forces Léonie to confront "what was rising up in her own village," a legacy of anti-Semitism emerging "out of the grave of the war" (170), and to recognize that "history was voices that came alive and shouted" (171). The novel ends with Léonie's determination to tell her story along with Thérèse, to bear witness to the informer's identity: revealed in the final pages as their old enemy, the priest. She ends the novel poised on the threshold of her old room, ready to encounter the voices that "came from somewhere just ahead, the shadowy bit she couldn't see. She stepped forward, into the darkness, to find words" (172).

According to Helen Merrell Lynd, "if shame is faced fully it 'may become not primarily something to be covered, but a positive experience of revelation'" (Lynd, 20, cited in Woodward, 107). The ending of Daughters of the House suggests that shame is not simply a negative affect to be overcome and discarded. Instead, shame acts as a motivating force, compelling Léonie toward her recognition of individual and collective responsibility and the need for witnessing. Here, shame and postmemory operate not simply as burdens inherited from a previous generation, restricting the present generation's capacity for agency, but as instigators of social transformation.

For both Thérèse and Léonie, facing a traumatic history also entails resolving their individual struggles with their bodies, femininity, and sense of personal identity, as fashioned through and against the range of female figures encountered in the text. The figure of Antoinette, the vision of the "red lady" in the woods, and the image of the Virgin Mary are just three of the paradigms of femininity that Léonie and Thérèse must choose to either live up to or reject. Throughout the narrative, Roberts suggests the ways in which shame operates to police bodily and national boundaries. Perhaps for this reason it is not surprising that the most pleasurable moments in the narrative occur when boundaries (between self and other, sexuality and maternity, Jewishness and Frenchness) are temporarily suspended. The vision of the ethnicized red lady and Léonie's memories of infantile experience are described in terms of bliss and unity that operates beyond national or bodily boundaries.[4] Balancing the pain of a fragmented and traumatic past, such moments offer a possibility of healing and redemption to set against the bodily and national shame experienced by Thérèse and Léonie as girls and women.

Notes

1. *Daughters of the House* is one of a number of cultural texts which engage with France's memory of what Stanley Hoffmann calls "the most dramatic and traumatic episode of contemporary French history" (Rousso, vii): the period of the Vichy regime. As Henry Rousso argues in *The Vichy Syndrome*, memories of the period of German occupation between 1940 and 1944 have proved both "enduring and controversial" (5), and Roberts's novel, with its narrative of a wartime atrocity which returns to haunt the Martin family, suggests that the memory of this time constitutes a form of "unfinished mourning" (Rousso, 15). For a fuller discussion of the historical context of Vichy and its representation in recent film and literature, see Rousso.

2. For a fuller discussion of *Daughters of the House* in terms of Kristeva's theory of abjection, including a discussion of Antoinette's body as an example of the abject maternal body, see Emma Parker, "From House to Home."

3. Edith Frampton also points to the novel's contrast between the fair-skinned Virgin Mary and the dark-skinned woman of Léonie's vision, arguing that the latter represents "the dark, earthy robust goddess, who once presided over a spot in the nearby woods. Her statue [is] exemplary of the black madonnas extant throughout France and much of the rest of Europe" (665).

4. As Edith Frampton points out, the description of Léonie's blissful vision of the red lady bears noticeable similarities to two other moments in the novel: her memory of being breastfed, and her experience as a child crossing the Channel between England and France. In each case, the description is one of bliss, of intersubjectivity, and of a language beyond borders. Frampton reads these moments as instances of the Kristevan semiotic, arguing that "Roberts creates a cluster of associations, linking Kristeva's pre-Oedipal semiotic *chora* with the sea, with pagan fertility goddesses, with the earth mother, Rose, and with breastfeeding" (670).

9 "Bound and Gagged with Thread"

Shame, Female Development, and the Künstlerroman Tradition in Cora Sandel's The Alberta Trilogy

Patricia Moran

CORA SANDEL'S ALBERTA trilogy (*Alberta and Jacob* [1926], *Alberta and Freedom* [1931], *Alberta Alone* [1939]) has long been an overlooked masterpiece of women's modernism, despite its having been available in English translation for some decades now.[1] Like other texts firmly established as canonical texts of women's modernism—Virginia Woolf's *The Voyage Out* and *To the Lighthouse*, Dorothy Richardson's *Pilgrimage*, and Jean Rhys's *Voyage in the Dark* and *Good Morning, Midnight,* among others—Sandel's trilogy blurs the boundaries between bildungsroman and künstlerroman, tracing Alberta's development and her "coming to writing" against a backdrop of themes common to many of these novels: the struggle against late Victorian mores that constrain female expressivity in general and female sexuality in particular; the expatriate experience of Paris, here shaped by gender, nationality, and class; the upheaval and permanent social and cultural ruptures generated by the First World War; and the multiple obstacles that impede female artistry, ranging from the gendered division of domestic labor to the active discouragement of women's ambitions to the crippling demands of maternity.[2] Shame theory provides a particularly useful lens through which to read Alberta's odyssey to artistry, for Alberta's experiences as woman and (would-be) writer are resolutely cast as shame-infused: shame is in many ways the biggest impediment Alberta must overcome in order to claim her autonomy and an identity as a writer. Indeed, it would not be an overstatement to say that shame is both an integral element of Alberta's identity *and* an integral aspect of her literary vocation, for Sandel makes clear that interpersonal relations are not only the source of Alberta's abject and abased self-image, but are also the basis of her narrative imagination. In the moment when Alberta first recognizes her vocation, significantly, she does so by articulating a vision of narrative that specifically situates her experiences of "pain . . . vain longing . . . disappointed hope . . . anxiety and privation . . . the sudden numbing blows"—all experiences of self in relation to others—as "knowledge of life. Bitter and difficult, exhausting to live through, but the only way to knowledge of herself and others" (2:226–227); this insight follows her sudden realization that "[f]or some reason she knew more about people and their relationships than before" (2:226). While the exact narrative content of Alberta's novel remains unstated, the biographical component which typically underwrites the bildungsroman/künstlerroman form suggests that the novel-to-be that Alberta envisions in print at the end of the trilogy is the text we hold in our hands: Alberta's journey to artistic and personal autonomy is, in many respects, a journey through shame.

Sandel's depiction of shame as an integral component of her representative female artist (and as an integral component of the story that artist has to tell) has important ramifications for an understanding of female shame in women's modernism and for an understanding of female shame more generally. Sandel focuses the trilogy on three distinct years of Alberta's life: the first volume, *Alberta and Jacob*, foregrounds one year in the teenage Alberta's life in a provincial town in northern Norway in the waning years of the nineteenth century; it highlights the ways in which the interpersonal dynamics of family life, reinforced and informed by social and cultural mores, mold Alberta's understanding and expectations of self-other relationships. The second volume, *Alberta and Freedom*, set in Paris before the First World War, takes up Alberta's story some eight or so years later: now in her twenties and living a marginal life financed by demeaning jobs as an artist's model and by occasional newspaper articles, Alberta finds herself increasingly lonely and hence vulnerable to the seeming imperative that she needs to involve herself with someone romantically; the volume ends with her discovery that she is pregnant by a man for whom she feels repulsion and with whom she has been intimate out of gratitude and loneliness. The third volume, *Alberta Alone*, which opens in a seaside town in France and unfolds mostly in a Paris irrevocably changed by the war, closes in the rural countryside of Norway: here Alberta finally finishes her manuscript and, fueled by her determination to strike out on her own and make her way independently as a writer, she walks toward the bus that will carry her to the city, leaving her six-year-old son behind with his father and grandparents. These three critical years of Alberta's life journey make up a developmental path that differs considerably from the conventional chronology that structures the bildungsroman/künstlerroman: whereas the latter typically locates the movement toward personal and artistic autonomy as coterminous with the movement away from the artist's family of origin—in other words, as a linear movement from childhood/adolescence to adulthood—here Sandel structures Alberta's life as a series of repetitions that Alberta only gradually comes to recognize and work through in her writing. Hence both volumes 1 and 2 of the trilogy circle back to their openings: the first begins and ends with the onset of winter and Alberta's despairing conviction that she "was back again. Back to it all, to all that was warped and desultory, to the lies and evasions and small, hidden irons in the fire, to humiliation and hopeless longing, to the grey road of uniform days"

(1:233; this passage echoes almost verbatim one near the beginning of the volume, 1:71); the second volume stresses Alberta's entrapment in biological immanence, opening with her standing naked and cold in order to earn a pittance as an artist's model and ending with her unwelcome discovery, at the very moment when she begins to see her way forward as a writer, that she is about to bear a child. But while it would be easy to characterize Alberta's inability to develop autonomy until her early thirties as a logical consequence of gender inequities, that is only a partial explanation of her difficulties: in detailing Alberta's relational dynamic with her parents and brother in volume 1, Sandel draws clear parallels between the abasement and humiliations Alberta suffers in her family of origin and those she suffers later in her relationship with her child's father, Sivert Ness. The engendering of shame in girlhood, then, functions as a crucial determinant in Alberta's halfhearted acquiescence to a relationship with the narcissistic and self-absorbed Ness: shaming propels her into an emotionally and economically abusive alliance. And while Alberta does in fact recognize and work through her crippling lack of confidence and eventually finishes her manuscript, her victory over interpersonal difficulties is indeed pyrrhic: walking to the city where she hopes to publish her manuscript and earn a living as a writer, Alberta wishes only to become an "equal guardian" of her child in time; she eschews all other relational possibilities: "She walked along, certain of only one thing. She had finished groping in the fog for warmth and security. The mist had risen now, there was clear visibility and it was cold. No arms round her any more, not even those of a child: naked life, as far ahead as she could see, struggle and an impartial view. She would go under or become so bitterly strong that nothing could hurt her any more. She felt something of the power of the complete solitary" (3:283). Sandel represents Alberta's autonomy in terms of the renunciation of all desire: "Did she have any desires? To go out into the world? To find anyone in particular? One does not desire the impossible. The person who has once taken life in the wrong way must finally accept life as it is" (3:284). This conclusion, forming as it does a clear contrast with Alberta's brother Jacob's setting out with "a face full of undaunted confidence in his own two strong arms" (1:234), darkens a reading of Alberta's journey to artistic and personal autonomy as a completely successful one, implying as it does that, far from overcoming her desire for meaningful intimacy, she has simply given up on its achievement as a realistic possibility. Artistic autonomy for Alberta, then, is equated with the repression of desire for human connection. Among the major women modernists, only Jean Rhys comes close to sharing this bleak view of the costs of female artistry—and, like Sandel, Rhys connects these costs to the interpersonal dynamics which have generated an abased and abject self-image in the woman writer.

This chapter explores the engendering of shame in the female artist in three parts. First, by carefully examining the relational dynamics of Alberta's family and contextualizing those dynamics within the framework developed by shame theory, it establishes the source of Alberta's artistic vision as a response to her pervasive sense of shame. Second, the chapter examines how Alberta's search for artistic and personal autonomy is impeded not only by a seeming social and cultural imperative that she involve herself romantically with a man, but by her own deep-rooted desire to repair the narcissistic wounds of her childhood through such a relationship: key to this quest is Alberta's persistent linking of the warmth of human connection to a half-remembered childhood memory of "strong arms" around her (e.g., 1:232; 2:135, 146; 3:196–197). Derailed by the unexpected death of her Danish lover, Nils Veigaard, and propelled into an alliance with the Swedish painter Sivert Ness, Alberta unwittingly re-creates the wounding dynamics of her childhood, albeit with an added and menacing twist: Alberta's dependence on Sivert, inaugurated by the birth of their son, gradually deepens into domestic abuse of an economic and emotional nature, abuse that confirms Alberta's long-held sense of herself as abject, abased, and deserving of contempt. The final section of the chapter traces the connections between Alberta's hard-won personal and artistic autonomy on the one hand and her embrace of a clear, "cold" world on the other: autonomy here necessitates the relinquishing of Alberta's long-cherished desire for the "strong arms" around her that could compensate for childhood losses. From this perspective, Alberta's concluding concession that the "person who has once taken life in the wrong way must finally accept life as it is" reads as a valediction: to accept "life as it is" is to accept an "outlaw" status which situates Alberta *outside* the realm of "life." Sandel's bleak equation of autonomy with the renunciation of human connection thus situates shaming at the very core of the modernist female bildungsroman/künstlerroman: the chapter concludes by considering how Sandel's vision of female artistry enriches our understanding not only of this modernist form but of female development more generally.

"Numbing, Inner Cold": The Familial Context of Shame

Alberta and Jacob, volume 1 of the trilogy, opens and closes in early winter, a setting that Sandel uses to underscore the emotional chill that pervades Alberta's family life. In the trilogy's opening pages, in fact, Sandel identifies Alberta's longing for warmth as a key motif of her personal and artistic journey: "The red glow from a stove door, the crackle of fire, were they not symbols of life's happiness? Warmth was life, cold was death. Alberta was a fire-worshipper in the full primitive sense of the word" (1:9). Alberta's futile search for warmth in her cold and loveless home dominates the volume: characterizing herself repeatedly as a criminal and a sinner (e.g., 1:41, 64), Alberta furtively steals coal for her bedroom stove and thieves extra coffee when her mother isn't looking. Indeed, so diminished are her expectations in this environment that the coffee urn assumes for her the hyperbolic status of a "revelation . . . warm, steaming, aromatic, giving life and hope, a sun among dead worlds" (1:11). Yet physical warmth to a large extent only externalizes Alberta's psychic distress: her parents, exiled to a provincial northern town as a result of youthful extravagance and imprudent business decisions, are unable to contain their disappointment in each other, their circumstances, and their children, for neither child lives up to the parents' conventionally gendered hopes. As Alberta herself succinctly puts it, "Jacob was impossible at school and sought out acquaintances from lower down the social scale; Alberta was unfortunate in appearance, incompetent in the house and not very presentable" (1:71). In keeping with the family's conventional Victorian middle-class configuration, Magistrate Selmer is a somewhat remote figure, capable of intermittent warmth and understanding but also prone to alcoholic rages and reluctant to challenge his wife's authority in the home. Mrs. Selmer is the true barometer of the family's emotional life, a woman who exacts obedience and outward conformity from the children and her husband through their fear of her anger, which she expresses through icy disapproval and withholding silences.

Alberta, like other family members, is adept at "sounding the terrain" of her mother's moods (1:12, 13), but she is also her mother's most accessible target: forced to leave school because the family's economic resources cannot encompass the frivolity of educating a daughter who is expected to marry, Alberta must assist her mother in a dreary round of seemingly pointless domestic tasks, such as dusting, mending, and polishing silver. Hence she exists in a state of constant trepidation from having to navigate "Mrs. Selmer's storm-laden atmosphere" (1:75). Indeed, even the sight of Alberta seems to provoke her mother's wrath, for Alberta serves as a visible reminder to Mrs. Selmer that her hopes to live vicariously through her daughter—through the reliving of the courtship and marriage plot—are doomed to failure. Alberta is well aware of this unspoken disappointment. In one passage Alberta compares herself to a youthful photograph of her mother: Alberta judges her mother "not beautiful, but unspeakably charming and captivating all the same. Alberta knew it, and she knew that she would never be anything like Mama. It was her biggest and most obvious failing" (1:82). So painful is the sight of Alberta that Mrs. Selmer often speaks to Alberta without looking at her directly; in these instances Alberta registers her mother's disapproval through the latter's tone of voice, which is variously "weary," "curt," "cold," "icy," or "injured." Even more damaging are the exchanges which bring together the disapproving gaze with the disapproving voice:

> Not until the cosy was back in place over the pot once more did they glance up at each other, Mrs. Selmer with a resigned look that crushed Alberta completely. She blushed and stiffened, her hands shook. Disarmed in the first round, she dared not ask for more coffee. (1:11)

> . . . if it was the kind of day—and this was most frequent—when Alberta was a cross and a burden from early morning onwards, Mrs. Selmer would sigh without addressing her. She would sigh many times . . . Alberta would cringe. (1:12)

> "I don't know that anything was amusing," replied Mama wearily and coldly . . . "What on earth are you standing about here for?" she exclaimed with sudden sharpness, inspecting Alberta . . . Alberta's heart sank. She made a cowardly movement. (1:55)

> When she had the opportunity Mrs. Selmer found time to direct a look of aggrieved and complete despair in her direction, even closing her eyes as if to avoid the sight. Alberta was even more hopeless, even further beneath all criticism than ever. (1:81)

[Mrs.] Selmer looked at Alberta resignedly as she handed her a cup of coffee, and according to established tradition Alberta sank conscientiously into the depth, flushed and quivering. Automatically she continued Mrs. Selmer's train of thought: "I have so few pleasures in life. I don't think I should be deprived of seeing my only daughter looking a little attractive. But even that is denied me." (1:207)

As these representative passages demonstrate, Mrs. Selmer's gaze reduces Alberta to a helpless, inarticulate state of shame. Here Sandel captures what Helen Block Lewis has identified as the "doubleness" of the shame experience, which points both to an intrapsychic sense of diminishment and to an intersubjective dimension of being diminished in the eyes of another (Lewis, "Shame and the Narcissistic Personality," 107–108). Shame, Lewis explains, is "the vicarious experience of the other's negative evaluation. In order for shame to occur, there must be a relationship between the self and other in which the self cares about the other's evaluation" (107–108). Similarly, Sandra Lee Bartky describes shame as "the distressed apprehension of the self as inadequate or diminished: it requires if not an actual audience before whom my deficiencies are paraded, then an internalized audience with the capacity to judge me . . . shame requires the recognition that I *am*, in some important sense, as I am seen to be" (86). Given the traditional emphasis accorded the mother's gaze in healthy ego development (e.g., Winnicott, Bollas, Kohut, Benjamin), the fact that Mrs. Selmer's gaze is one of disapproval means that shame is installed at the very core of Alberta's experience and development of both subjectivity and intersubjectivity. Andrew P. Morrison, drawing on the work of Hans Kohut, identifies the "failure of empathic responsiveness" from a mirroring other as constitutive of early states of shame. The relational dynamics between Alberta and Mrs. Selmer exemplify this sort of failure, and Alberta's sense of herself as flawed and defective—she looks at her mirror image "despondently" (1:17), calls herself "ugly, boring, hopeless and impossible" (1:31), feels herself to be "insignificant, impotent, and doomed" (1:72)—grows out of this crucial and chronic experience of feeling herself diminished by her mother's critical and contemptuous gaze.

Sandel thus explicitly ties Alberta's self-loathing to her mother's chronic shaming of her. As the above passages demonstrate, Alberta feels herself cringing before her mother's gaze, feels herself becoming a coward, feels herself blush, feels herself held captive by her mother's contemptuous assessment of her as "an affliction and a disappointment" (1:100). Feelings of shame, Helen Block Lewis observes, work in an automatic way through helpless modes of "bodily awareness" such as blushing, sweating, and a pounding heart, modes that both register and intensify the victim's captivity to the shame affect. Alberta similarly registers the shame affect through modes of helpless bodily reactions, particularly the reaction of blushing; significantly this fear of blushing plays an important role in her desire not to be seen by others. Worrying at one point that she will meet a bill collector, she fears that she will turn "red and hot," but then consoles herself that "it probably could not be seen in the twilight. She blushed easily, it was one of her misfortunes . . . Invariably she blushed because of people . . . If she had the chance she unhesitatingly took any roundabout way to avoid them" (1:18). Indeed, her fear of being reduced to an inarticulate state of shame eventually plays a role in her definition of her artistry as a type of self-other relationship that exists apart from others, for her painful self-consciousness impedes literal self-other interactions: "She had an ingrained fear of the spoken word, an irreparable horror of argument and explanation. She blushed, was prostrated, lost the thread and might well say something quite different from what she had intended. The mere thought of explaining . . . made her go hot and cold" (1:72). Hence, out of the understandable desire to minimize the chance of further exposure to shaming, Alberta develops defensive modes of interaction with others that involve tactics of withdrawal, avoidance, and concealment. Not surprisingly, her mother serves as one of the primary motivators of such reactions. Throughout volume 1 Alberta uses terms to describe her mother that stress her desire to hide from her: Mrs. Selmer is "Argus-eyed" (1:10, 83), Alberta's "enemy" and "Nemesis" (1:73, 39), a "detective" or "Sherlock Holmes" adept at ferreting out Alberta's failings (1:64, 92). The desire to hide from Mrs. Selmer then extends to the desire to hide from the townspeople's inquisitive eyes: "Quickly and quietly she glided down the street, a shadow among other shadows. Alberta always made herself as small as she could, shrinking inside her clothes, as if that would help" (1:18).

It is important to note that Sandel does not simply represent Mrs. Selmer as individually culpable, as a quintessential "bad mother"; rather, Sandel makes clear that Mrs. Selmer acts as she does because she cares tremendously about Alberta's welfare and future (although it is also clear that her mother's disappointment with Alberta derives from a narcissistic inability to recognize her daughter as an autonomous other). Here the particulars of the mother-daughter relationship assume coherence only within the larger contexts of the Selmers' vexed social standing and the conventional gender arrangements prevalent in this provincial late-nineteenth-century Norwegian town. The Selmer family exists in a constant state of shame over their straitened finances and lowered social expectations, and the desire to maintain appearances and conceal their financial difficulties plays into Alberta's painful self-consciousness about meeting bill collectors or needing to pawn her jewelry. At the same time, this potential social shame reinforces Alberta's desire to hide from the shaming gaze of others. In fact, the enormous lengths to which Mrs. Selmer in particular goes to maintain the family's social standing in the face of their straitened means informs Alberta's dislike of the gender norms governing middle-class femininity: she comes to associate the gender constraints her mother imposes on her with exposure to a generalized shaming gaze directed at her femininity.

If social and economic factors form one of the contexts which reinforce and intensify Alberta's chronic state of shame, then, gender norms form another crucial context. Alberta's unprepossessing appearance and general ineptitude for and dislike of domestic tasks make her a poor candidate for marriage, and her painful awareness of

Beoure Productions present

DISTINGUISHED VILLA
by Kate O'Brien

Aficionados of Limerick theatre and literature can look forward to a rare opportunity to see a rehearsed reading of Kate O'Brien's first literary work. *Distinguished Villa*, a play by Limerick's much loved author, will receive a rehearsed reading by some of Limerick's finest actors, for one night only, on September 21st in the Dance Limerick church on Johns Square.

Kick-starting O'Brien's literary career in 1926, *Distinguished Villa* was the result of a bet by the author that she could write a play within a number of weeks. A charming, romantic and poignant play *Distinguished Villa* had its premiere at the Aldwych Theatre in London in 1926 where it was met with wide acclaim.

The rehearsed reading, directed by Joan Sheehy, will feature Limerick actors Ashleigh Dorrell, Nigel Dugdale, Kevin Kiely, Cillian Ó Gairbhí and Georgina Miller. Distinguished Villa is staged as part of *The Limerick Arts Encounter* artistic programme and is produced in conjunction with the Lime Tree Theatre, Limerick

SATURDAY / SEPTEMBER 21ST
DAGHDHA SPACE, JOHNS SQUARE @ 8PM.

BOOKING VIA THE LIME TREE THEATRE ON 061 774774
TICKETS ARE €5 AND INCLUDE A GLASS OF WINE OR SOFT DRINK

LIMERICK CITY COUNCIL
Comhairle Cathrach Luimnigh

the arts council
funding theatre
ealaíon artscouncil.ie

LIME TREE

MAYBE THE NIGHT
by **Kevin Barry**

AS BROADCAST ON   DRAMA ON

Tommy and Dad are after putting down a night of it - again! *Maybe the Night* is a darkly humorous conversation between father and son as they attempt to face the day and deal with the terrors of the night!

IMPAC Award winner Kevin Barry has created a dramatic gem, a world of banjaxed back boilers, fleas the size of wrens, floating duvets and dead lads callin'. Directed by Joan Sheehy and starring John Olohan and Pat Ryan, *Maybe the Night* will run in Friar's Gate Theatre, Kilmallock and in the basement of Dr. John's/The Blind Pig, Limerick City, for one week only.

Maybe the Night is staged as part of *The Limerick Arts Encounter* artistic programme and is produced in conjunction with the Lime Tree Theatre, Limerick City Council and the Arts Council.

Friars Gate Theatre] [Kilmallock
October 22nd at 8pm
Booking 063 98727] [**Tickets €8**

The Blind Pig & Dr. John's] [31 Thomas St] [Limerick
October 23rd at 8pm and 9pm] [October 24th. 8pm ONLY
October 25th, 8pm and 9pm] [October 26th, 8pm and 9pm

Booking for Limerick City shows is via the Lime Tree Theatre 061 774774

TICKETS €7

her "hopelessness" turns the obligatory social round of teas, dinners, and dances into occasions of mortification and humiliation. Here, too, Alberta's shame-infused desire to hide from the eyes of others comes into play: she notes how the middle-class women watch each other and gossip about matters pertaining to female sexuality—possible and acknowledged courtships, weddings and honeymoons, and especially pregnancies.[3] Alberta's stubborn refusal to be drawn into this life—she mutely observes the letter but not the spirit of her mother's law—results in her despairing sense of entrapment in an inexorable plot. Wondering how the charming young woman in her mother's youthful photograph has become the woman Alberta knows, a woman with furrows of anxiety, a small pinched mouth, and suspicious Argus eyes, Alberta realizes how gender norms within the family enforce and are enforced in turn by social and cultural mores: "Was it so, that generation after generation coerced the next, desiring only to fashion and form their lives in accordance with their own?" (1:83).

Perhaps the most damaging consequence of Alberta's estrangement from gender norms is the shame with which she comes to experience her own budding sexual urges: from this point on Alberta will characterize sexual desire as natural, but she will also recoil from it, and her body, already a source of shame because she is not conventionally attractive, comes to seem as if it now harbors an enemy within, an enemy that will further entangle her in shame and humiliation. Hence Alberta finds herself attracted to the sailor Cedolf against her conscious will. At first "something new and strange flowed through Alberta's body. It was like a deep call, a sweet, strong sigh in the blood" (1:114); she notes as well "something in his voice, a dark purring" (1:114). But this current of desire gives rise to fear, "mortification," and "tears of shame and anger": "The tumult [of the dance], Cedolf's body against hers . . . the wantonness about her, were violence and shock, mortifying and degrading" (1:115). Sandel depicts sexual desire as shameful not because Alberta has been taught to deny it, but because sexuality is for her associated with the marriage and domesticity that inevitably stem from it: Alberta feels her sexual urges as "insidious and dangerous," forces "coiling and twisting beyond all reason in hidden places," because they lead to "imitation leather sofas and china dogs. She would die of it. She hid her face . . . aware of her own degradation" (1:201). Here Alberta considers the plight of her carefree friend Beda Buck, the only girl in her circle who openly defied gender norms, now forced into a marriage of convenience with her employer after becoming pregnant by a man who abandoned her: "Now she sits sewing under the Recorder's lamp . . . knowing that the faces are pressed up against her window, tight as a shoal of fish" (1:229). Remembering Beda with her lover at the dance, Alberta recalls "the sweet tender smile, the closed eyes, both as if spun together and entangled with the deep call, the strong, demanding sigh in Alberta's blood, her paralysis under Cedolf's kiss"; this memory comes to an abrupt halt when Alberta concludes, "Life was a trap. Even Beda, frank, courageous Beda, was she not sitting there like a fly on flypaper?" (1:214). Not surprisingly, then, Alberta reacts with horror when an elderly woman confuses her with Beda: she rushes away "as if pursued . . . A horrible notion . . . had suddenly taken shape and become real. Now it was going about freely, haunting the streets and the market place. Was it not grinning at her from all the eyes she met?" (1:218).

Sandel thus connects Alberta's distrust of her response to sexual desire to the shaming gaze of others, as if she now projects her mother's contemptuous gaze into the faces of everyone else; tellingly, she wants to hide her own face from this now universal mockery. Volume 1 of the Alberta trilogy does not present alternatives to the Scylla and Charybdis of marriage and spinsterhood: Alberta "only knew what she did not want . . . She existed like a negative of herself, and this flaw was added to all the others" (1:98). Her version of "freedom" is shaped by a desire for escape from the shaming scrutiny of others: she longs to get "out into the world . . . somewhere open, free, bathed in sunshine. And a throng of people, none of them her relatives, none of whom could criticize her appearance and character, and to whom she was not responsible for being other than herself" (1:98). As the word "throng" indicates, Alberta imagines losing herself in a crowd of strangers; significantly, she does not imagine a world of intimate relations, as if being "herself" is possible only in a context where she is completely unknown. Alberta will eventually extend this sense of an essential unknown self to her parents near the end of volume 1: she seems to catch glimpses of her parents' unknown selves when she sees "[b]ehind Mama's bitter little everyday face, behind her almost convulsive party face, a face which was the real one, and which was deathly tired and corroded by lonely anxiety—Behind Papa's little catchword, 'Cheer up, back we go,' the set features of one without hope" (1:232); Alberta believes she has "been in touch with what lay beneath and behind ordinary experience" (1:232). Although Alberta has not yet defined her desire to write as a vocation, this apprehension of a split between the social gendered face and a singular lonely one forms the core of her artistic vision. This same split, in fact, characterizes Alberta's reaction to her attempt to drown herself: "One thing was hers. Her bare life. It was hers still, hers . . . They had not succeeded in driving her into the sea, and never would. Something had been roused in her down there in the icy cold as it crept up round her body. It had been terror, violent beyond control, but it had also been something bright and hard, a raging refusal. It had been like touching bottom and being carried upwards again" (1:231).

"Freedom—a Life of Perpetual Opposition"

This bright, hard, raging refusal has carried Alberta into Paris by volume 2, and in many ways she has achieved the negative version of freedom she imagines in volume 1: she passes freely among throngs of strangers; she has cut herself off from her critical and censorious relatives; she ekes out a marginal existence by modeling for painters and by writing occasional essays for local journals. This anonymity among strangers has assuaged somewhat her bodily shame: "The aching wounds of Alberta's childhood, the smarting feeling that she annoyed people merely because of her appearance, had almost healed" (2:30). At the same time, Alberta has still not claimed her artistic vocation: she worries that the creative writing she does is only "a form of idling" and, because she has not yet identified writing as her métier, she "did not yet know what she really wanted. She still had only negative instincts, just as when she was at home. They told her clearly what she did not want to do. Her whole being cringed when faced with certain situations and certain people . . . so that she felt it physically . . . she was left free to reject what she did not want and without the slightest idea of what she should do with herself" (2:32). As her Danish lover, Nils Veigaard, tells her, "What sort of freedom do you have? It's a miserable life, that's what it is, and you are far too good for it. You're not free, you're an outlaw . . . You live in perpetual opposition and believe it to be freedom, independence" (2:139).

There are promising signs, however, that Alberta *has* made progress toward claiming her vocation.[4] Alberta's forays in the streets of Paris leave her "strangely satisfied, as if deep and mysterious demands in her had been pacified for a while. Her brain teemed with fragments of the conversations of strangers. Disconnected pictures of the teeming life of the streets succeeded each other, shutting out regret and uncomfortable thoughts" (2:43). And when Alberta attempts to record her observations, she now does so in the medium of fiction, not in the more personal verse she had employed in volume 1:

> Something she had witnessed had clothed itself in words in the secret recesses of her mind. Or remarks she had heard blazed up out of her memory, appearing to her like mysterious knots into which many threads of human life converged, entwined themselves and retreated into the obscurity from which they came. She wrote them down—and before she was aware of it, was engaged in a struggle with the language as if with a plastic material, trying to force life out of it as Eliel did with his clay. Reality lies hidden in outward occurrences, the words one hears are for the most part masked thoughts. But there are glimpses which enlighten, remarks which reveal. (2:44)

Alberta now perceives her writing as narrative directed at the split between the manifest and latent content she had learned from her family life as a teenager; her comparison of the writing process to the sculptor's encounter with clay suggests she is groping her way toward defining herself as a serious artist. But she does doubt her efforts: her writing is a "sore spot on her conscience" because it leaves her "dazed and incapacitated" for the daytime drudgery of earning her living (2:45); further, she has no clear plot structure for this "muddle of scribbled pages," which she worries has the same value as her earlier poetic efforts, "bad echoes of mediocre poets" (2:45). Alberta must make her way without money, without education, and without encouragement, a difficult task given her already crippling lack of self-confidence.

Alberta also continues to struggle with relational issues, and in some ways the messages she receives confirm her shameful sense that she is destined to be alone because she is flawed in some way. In this respect the artists and models Alberta encounters in Montparnasse are no different from the middle-class women from whom Alberta has fled:

Now Alberta was left by the wayside, while the others drove on with everything settled and a final "You should find someone too."

Find someone! Alberta stood up and walked restlessly about the room. Women repeated it in every tone of voice wherever she happened to be. From old Mrs. Weyer in the little town at home, who had patted her on the shoulder and repeated "A good husband, a good husband" . . . to Marushka, who said: ". . . Love gives happiness— what would life be without love" . . . to Alphonsine . . . who stated quietly "*Il vous manque une affection, Mademoiselle.*" (2:71)

Alberta is well aware of how the constant reiteration of this message has the power to convince women to abandon their own artistic ambitions and become muses for men: she has observed this very process in her friend Liesel, who has "changed course and gradually steered towards Eliel" after listening to Alphonsine enough times (2:71). At the same time, Alberta dreads growing to resemble the older women painters she sees all around her, "elderly women perpetually trudging round Montparnasse . . . The thought that it was possible to go on living here like that, and to be nothing more than an elderly, ugly, poverty-stricken dilettante, bred disquiet" (2:19–20).

When Alberta finally succumbs to her desire for intimacy, significantly, she does so because she meets someone who grants her what psychoanalytic theorist Jessica Benjamin terms "mutual recognition," someone who *sees* her and both accepts and promotes her autonomy. Veigaard is someone with whom the normally mute and inarticulate Alberta can share seemingly irrelevant memories, dreams, and thoughts, someone who listens attentively without becoming censorious and critical; he also puts into words her sense of her "freedom" as "perpetual opposition." Alberta's painful self-consciousness, whereby a kind of objective commentator stands at the ready with an unheard private monologue, momentarily relaxes: "Alberta felt her listening to be different, her brief, half-finished comments to be alive, woven into coherence" (2:112). This image of the conversation as a tapestry woven between the two gestures toward the intuitive quality of their exchanges: "Alberta could not say much about her experiences before Veigaard had found a thread to pull. And pull he did, speculating . . . 'Indeed, so you have . . . so you are . . . so you are used to . . .' he insisted. He wound up the threads too, he remembered things . . . he put two and two together and made four out of them without difficulty" (2:117). Veigaard's conversational ploys function as ways of drawing Alberta out of her usual reticence, and she responds by providing information that fills in conspicuous narrative gaps between the close of volume 1 and the opening of volume 2. It is at this point, for example, that the reader learns for the first time of the death of Alberta's parents in an accident, of her relatives' response to their responsibility for her and their pooling of money to send her to Paris, and of the pretext which actually brought Alberta to Paris (she ostensibly came to study French and become a language teacher). This relationship is unique in the Alberta trilogy: with no one else, not even her closest friends, does Alberta experience this level of mutual understanding and exchange. That Veigaard compensates for the intimacy and affection Alberta lacked in her family of origin emerges in Alberta's telling comparison of him to family members: she likens him to her father and brother (2:137); more importantly, she feels herself nurtured in a manner that recalls for her long-buried memories of her mother: "A sweet sigh of recognition went through her, she was taken back to a time long, long ago when someone else had tucked her in. She had been woken by it, had felt safe and happy, and had fallen asleep again" (2:135; see 1:232).

Images drawn from the natural world underscore the intuitive and seemingly inevitable quality of their mutuality:

> She heard herself laugh an entirely new little laugh, sensed something she had never sensed before in gesture and movement. It streamed from within her, forcing its way out, whether she wished it or not. Something soft and gentle. And it was not humiliating or mortifying. It was submission for the first time to a law of life, an unfurling of herself like a leaf in the sun. Perhaps it made her, the ugly duckling, beautiful. At any rate, it made her different, giving her something of the inevitability of a bird or animal . . . (2:137)

> She would go to meet him as light-footed as if she were flying. She laughed her new laughter. In her were gestures she had not known about, as natural as the swaying of branches in the wind, cadences she listened to with astonishment . . . Alberta felt the new element in her being play like a spring of water that has finally found its way out into the sun, bringing liberation and deliverance. (2:143)

In particular, Sandel infuses her descriptions of Alberta's affective responses to Veigaard with the imagery of liquidity: Alberta's feelings stream out, chuckle with a joyous and festive sound like that of wine poured from a decanter (2:140), well up from the depths of her being with the force of a natural spring, pure and fresh. This elemental imagery suggests the fundamental thawing out of Alberta's frozen affect, frozen by years of shaming and contempt and now released by the warmth of Veigaard's attentive "sun." Alberta depicts her subjection to this new emotion as "having someone in the blood . . . She felt a slow cajoling call in her body to submit and give herself, to be humble and serve" (2:143). Hence she conquers what she calls "the innermost, shining fear of anyone coming near me" and consents to consummating their relationship (2:144).

Alberta's subsequent entanglement with Sivert Ness—a man for whom she feels repulsion and with whom she becomes intimate out of gratitude and loneliness—only assumes coherence within the context of this relationship with Veigaard. For Veigaard returns to Denmark with the understanding that he will return to Paris and resume the relationship when he returns; yet his departure is followed by months of silence. Alberta believes that she has been abandoned, and the old, painful thought that "there was something repulsive about her after all" comes back to haunt her: "Mortification and anxiety and regret crept interlaced through her mind like cold snakes" (2:160). The blighting of natural and elemental imagery forcefully depicts the blasting of Alberta's newly awakened relationality: "Something inside her was just as ready . . . to crumple up and wither as to unfurl itself and blossom" (2:167); her "painful, tearless sobs" caricature "the liberating stream that cleanses the mind and from which one rises assuaged, even perhaps born anew" (2:160). Devastated by her loss—a loss that confirms and intensifies Alberta's shamed sense of herself as contemptible—Alberta fiercely claims for herself what now seems like a necessity: "She *would* have warmth and joy and find them for herself" (2:175). Her longing for this lost intimacy possesses the bodily force of primary needs: "In all her veins there beat an urgent, all embracing hunger for warmth. The words forced themselves up towards her lips and insisted on being spoken, she whispered them, dry as if from thirst" (2:160); her longing registers as "a privation, raging as hunger" (2:190). Everywhere around her she sees couples— "Everybody was two" (2:172)—or, worse, the elderly women artists of Montparnasse, who invoke in her "the feeling of being condemned to death, with the mode of death demonstrated to her: to wither, to wither" (2:185). Depression overtakes her: paralyzed and unable to write the articles that bring in her only income, she falls into debt and finally falls ill.

It is at this critical juncture that Sivert Ness appears and rescues Alberta by taking her back to his studio and nursing her through her nearly fatal fever. Hence what might otherwise seem inexplicable—Alberta's taking up with a man whose "glittering" eyes have "forced themselves on her," eyes she "decidedly did not like" (2:97, 98, 99)—functions as a response to an unbearable psychic loss that re-creates the primary psychic wounds of childhood. When Alberta responds to Sivert sexually, she does so out of gratitude and a desire for "obliteration," but Sandel makes clear that her response is decidedly ambivalent: "she felt an instant of tremendous distress, but made no resistance . . . Shoots, that had once put out tendrils to no purpose and been singed off, were kept in check" (2:194). Alberta tries to assure herself that "they were two lonely, frozen people, who crept together beside the fire of life and warmed themselves as well as they could" (2:199). But when she learns that Veigaard has died in an accident, Alberta's desire to "discover her own form of toil and to work at it" quickly reasserts herself: she returns to her own apartment and, in a sequence of flashbacks that suggest Veigaard's death has released in Alberta the ability to mourn her parents, she recalls her parents' deaths and immediately sees her way forward as a creative writer. The solar imagery that pervades this moment of artistic recognition suggests that Alberta has finally located "the fire of life" within her own subjective experience: "The sun reached right in and shone on her . . . the red light still flickered behind her eyelids. New possibilities dawned on her . . . Other forms of writing were possible . . . New, bold ideas stirred in Alberta. Supposing she were to try! To try to find form for a little reality . . . she, as well as so many others" (2:227).

Had Sandel concluded the Alberta trilogy with this moment of recognition, this female künstlerroman would read very differently than it does: Alberta's claiming of her artistic vocation would read as a success story, one in which the protagonist moves forward in confidence, assured of her own inner vitality. But Alberta suffers yet another crippling detour when she learns that she is pregnant with Sivert's child, a child neither really wants. Only her witnessing of Liesel's botched illegal abortion compels Alberta to carry the child to term and, as is so often the case with her, she consoles herself by imaging maternity as submission to a law of nature and life: "She was reminded of the doe that licks its calf, of horses nuzzling each other" (2:240). Volume 3 of the trilogy, then, traces the resumption of Alberta's odyssey after almost six years of writing work that has been interrupted by childcare and other domestic responsibilities. More crucially, it traces Alberta's growing determination to free herself from Sivert at any cost and her eventual identification of writing as a viable form of work that will enable her to secure her economic and emotional independence. For Alberta's relationship with Sivert has deteriorated into one of emotional abuse: Alberta repeatedly states that she is afraid of Sivert and she repeatedly registers her discomfort with his "glittering eyes," "the old glitter that Alberta could not stand at one time . . . Now it was back, forcing itself up from the bottom, confident and watchful" (3:67). Much of volume 3 consists of Alberta's questioning of the origins of her fear: "When had she begun to be afraid of Sivert? Perhaps she had always been afraid, and simply forgotten it in between? Now she was lying there, so afraid that her heart stood still for sudden painful moments at a time" (3:80). Sivert engages in a number of actions that read like textbook examples of emotional domestic abuse: he cuts her off from her only close friend, Liesel, isolates her in their home, and jealously drives off other men even as he forces her to entertain his own lover: "Alberta felt humiliated by the whole situation, by her own state of mind, by the new dress she had put on, the table she had taken such pains over" (3:167). Sivert also quotes to her from books by Freud and Nietzsche—"'When you go to Woman do not forget your whip'" (3:102)—books significantly left behind by Dr. Freytag, the illegal abortionist who destroyed Liesel's body. As "Woman" Alberta has never been fully human to Sivert: she gradually comes to realize that she has only ever been a convenience; after her pregnancy she had been an inconvenience and now that their son is almost six Sivert feels that he can do without her altogether. "Is there anything a man is incapable of doing? He can take the child out of the womb, physically and psychologically, born or unborn. His is the power," Alberta despairingly thinks (3:235).

Like so many victims of domestic abuse, then, Alberta finds herself forced to stay with Sivert because he threatens to take her child away from her. Sandel's use of an image drawn from the Cinderella fairy tale brutally depicts this emotional violation: "She thought: if I have to live in Hell . . . Hack off a heel and cut a toe, the shoe will fit" (3:227). Yet even though her friends warn her—Alphonsine cautions her about how seriously "children's officers" look upon "abandonment of the marital dwelling" (3:220) and Liesel similarly observes that Sivert "intends to drive you out. That's how men do it. So that in desperation we take the first step . . . That's how they free themselves of responsibility. They're terribly cunning" (3:200)—Alberta flees her home for a single night after Sivert's manipulation of her emotions finally wounds her so deeply that she cannot endure his presence. Her flight strengthens Sivert's hand, and he calmly dictates to Alberta what the terms of her life are going to be: "The question is solely the welfare of the boy. He'll have a wise person for a step-mother . . . You will be given the opportunity to see him, in so far as it's possible. I don't intend to leave you without support" (3:232). Alberta, in turn, grasps "why she had been afraid of Sivert" (3:232): Alberta's economic dependence upon him has always strengthened his control over her, and thus he is in a position to deprive her of her child altogether.

It is at this point that Alberta resolves to use her writing as a means of achieving the economic independence that will allow her to fight for custody of her child. Yet her final resolve is notable for her blaming her own needs for intimacy and human connection for her situation. She condemns herself for the "wave of passion which had more to do with the two strong arms round her in the darkness, the mysterious proximity of another living being, than Sivert himself . . . as her antipathy had thawed there had come a blind faith, an unconditional surrender in those strong arms. . . . she had struggled . . . out of tenderness. In order finally to experience a little tenderness" (3:231). Her words echo Liesel's earlier lament that women need tenderness "more than anything. It keeps us alive . . . As long as we're given tenderness we can put up with anything" (3:88). Hence Alberta defines her emotional needs as the source of her problems, her entrapment with Sivert as the result of her own failure to secure her economic independence: "The fault was hers, for not having found herself a livelihood . . . She was the debtor" (3:231). This resolve initiates the final sections of the trilogy, when Alberta finishes her manuscript and, satisfied that her son is content and flourishing with his grandparents, walks away from the strongest emotional bond she has ever experienced. Her final embrace of her artistry, then, carries with it the chill of one who has turned her back on human connection: "there was clear visibility and it was cold. No arms round her any more, not even those of a child: naked life, as far ahead as she could see, struggle and an impartial view" (3:283).

Female Shame and Artistry

Léon Wurmser identifies "soul blindness," the "systematic, chronic disregard for the emotional needs and expressions of the child, a peculiar blindness to its individuality and hostility to its autonomy," as the core of the shame experience (Wurmser, *Inner Judge*, 191). This disregard for the child's autonomy, he argues, "evokes the conviction of great worthlessness: the contempt by the other expressed in disregard for one's own inner life is matched by self-contempt" (194). Particularly in those families that place a high premium on the repression of strong emotion, shame comes to be inextricable from feelings that may not be sexual per se, but are connected to intimacy, such as neediness, longing, tenderness, or being moved or hurt (194). Such a child may grow into an adult who looks for a partner that Wurmser terms an "anti-shame hero," someone who is "emotionally untouchable, impenetrable, invulnerable, a disdainful ruler" (194). Yet while merger with such a figure may remove the shame of feeling too intensely or feeling the wrong sorts of feelings, this type of relationship results in "an almost incorrigible masochistic bondage" (194). Wurmser's findings accord with those of Jessica Benjamin, who similarly locates the roots of masochistic desire in the tendency to experience agency vicariously through submission, through "accepting the other's will and desire as one's own" (Benjamin, 122). The Alberta trilogy traces this trajectory, as Alberta moves from a conviction of her own worthlessness to a relationship in which emotion is contained—Sivert is always imaged as invulnerable and emotionally untouchable—even as she experiences artistic agency vicariously through Sivert's unflagging dedication to his painting.[5]

Where the Alberta trilogy adds to our understanding of the bildungsroman/künstlerroman genre is in its unflinching depiction of the self-contempt and shame that Sandel identifies as a key component of Alberta's development of femininity. Here Andrew P. Morrison's Kohutian framework for understanding shame sheds light on the intrapsychic dimension of Alberta's shame-prone character. The shame-prone character, he suggests, results from "empathic failure" on the part of the child's earliest caretaker ("selfobject"): "a narcissistic, ashamed parent usually produces a narcissistically vulnerable child . . . As such a parent tends to view the child as a narcissistic extension of himself or herself, that parent will be insensitive, inattentive to the developmentally appropriate needs for affirmation" ("The Eye Turned Inward," 283). Eventually the child internalizes the sense that these needs are unacceptable and shameful: unable to modify or transform narcissistic needs through the developmental process, the child walls off and disavows his/her needs for affirmation and approval. They do not disappear, however, but return "as self-disintegration and searing shame under conditions of provocation by internal or external triggers" (284). Alberta's mother functions as such a narcissistic, ashamed parent, someone who views Alberta solely in terms of an abstract femininity that reflects back on her own needs for affirmation: Alberta is a disappointment and embarrassment because she does not confirm her mother's sense of femininity, nor does she compensate for her mother's disappointment that her beauty and charm did not result in a successful marriage and family life. Alberta's father, who does at times function as the "second chance" for affirmation that Kohut identifies as crucial for healthy self-development, too often capitulates to his wife's authority over what Alberta needs to do or be, as when he directs her "to behave a little more in accordance with your Mother's wishes in the new year" (1:91).

Without empathic responsiveness to support her needs for affirmation and assertion of self, Alberta does indeed develop a "searing" sense of shame, and the story she comes to tell in the Alberta trilogy is the story of how this sense of self came to be. The emphasis on Mrs. Selmer's disapproving gaze and Sivert's later "glittering eyes" highlights Alberta's sensitivity to the accusatory, critical eye, which in turn triggers helpless, shame-infused self-condemnation, for what Morrison terms "the eye turned inward" is an inner eye focused on inalterable deficits of self. Artistic self-expression involves, then, not only the renunciation of human connection and the repression of desire for it, but the need to chart a female developmental process that has the shame experience as its core narrative. It is this narrative of female development that Sandel shares with Jean Rhys, whose novels—set during the same time period and often in Paris—similarly trace the plight of the shame-prone woman whose needs for human connection and intimacy result only in further shame and degradation. Pondering her desire for Pierre, her last and renounced love interest, Alberta thinks, "Here I can unfurl into a person," only to condemn herself to a permanent state of blight: "life wipes out its own traces. One day this feeling would have left her as blossom and foliage leave the tree. She would do without it. A plant dies without sustenance" (3:132). A plant does indeed die without sustenance, but Alberta's story poignantly remains as a memorial to the process of that deprivation.

Notes

1. Cora Sandel, *Alberta and Jacob, Alberta and Freedom,* and *Alberta Alone,* trans. Elizabeth Rokkan, with an afterword by Linda Hunt (1962; Athens: Ohio University Press, 1984). All further references are to this edition and will be included parenthetically in the text. References to Hunt's "Afterword" will refer to volume 1. In addition to Hunt's "Afterword," English studies include Hunt, "*The Alberta Trilogy*: Cora Sandel's Norwegian *Künstlerroman* and American Feminist Literary Discourse"; Ruth Essex, *Cora Sandel*; Erica L. Johnson, "Adjacencies: Virginia Woolf, Cora Sandel, and the Künstlerroman"; Nancy Ramsey, "The Alberta Trilogy Revisited: Today's 'Women's Fiction' vs. the Real Thing"; Ellen Rees, *On the Margins: Nordic Women Modernists of the 1930s* and *Figurative Space in the Novels of Cora Sandel*; Tone Selboe, "Jean Rhys and Cora Sandel. Two Views on the Modern Metropolis"; and Virpi Zuck, "Cora Sandel: A Norwegian Feminist."

2. Classic studies of women's modernist künstlerroman include Susan Gubar, "The Birth of the Artist as Heroine: (Re)production, the *Künstlerroman* Tradition, and the Fiction of Katherine Mansfield," in *The Representation of Women in Fiction*, ed. Carolyn G. Heilbrun and Margaret R. Higonnet (Baltimore: Johns Hopkins University Press, 1983), and Rachel Blau DuPlessis, *Writing beyond the Ending: Narrative Strategies of Twentieth-Century Women* (Bloomington: Indiana University Press, 1985). See also Penny Brown, *The Poison at the Source: The Female Novel of Development in the Early Twentieth Century* (New York: Palgrave Macmillan, 1992), for an examination of female development in the fiction of a number of Sandel's British contemporaries.

3. As Linda Hunt perceptively observes, "Alberta despairs at the prospect of a life like that of any of the women in her town. If spinsters, they are objects of pity and, actually, objectively quite 'odd'; if sexually rebellious, pregnancy tames them. Respectably married, their lives are bounded by food and servant worries, gynecological troubles, and envy of their neighbors. This grim destiny is appropriately emblematized for Alberta by the figure of Nurse Jellum the midwife who keeps reappearing throughout the novel (and indeed recurs in memory in the sequels), 'with her terrible bag and her quiescent know-all smile'" (Hunt, 236).

4. Here I differ somewhat from Hunt, who describes Alberta's life in volume 2 as one of "apparent purposelessness": "she does make occasional undisciplined, almost furtive attempts to express herself creatively through writing, but it is almost impossible for her to take herself seriously enough to have genuine literary ambitions" (237).

5. Hunt discusses Alberta's development to artistry as one in which she learns to demystify the "work" of creation. Although I agree with this view, Alberta's "mystification" functions as a form of projective self-identification as well, a process by which she identifies with the productive artist as an ideal self projected onto another.

10 Girl World and Bullying

Intersubjective Shame in
Margaret Atwood's Cat's Eye

Laura Martocci

> Cordelia doesn't do these things or have this power over me because she's my enemy.
> Far from it . . . Cordelia is my friend. She likes me, she wants to help me, they all do.
> They are my friends, my girl friends, my best friends. I never had any before and I'm
> terrified of losing them. I want to please . . .
>
> Margaret Atwood, *Cat's Eye*, 127

Setting the Stage

Margaret Atwood's groundbreaking novel *Cat's Eye* pulls back the veil on the secret
world of (pre)adolescent girls, exposing the treachery, shame, and confusion underlying their friendships. The narrative unflinchingly probes themes of childhood cruelty,
self-worth, and identity through the underbelly of social control: shaming. The novel's
protagonist, Elaine Risley, returns to her hometown of Toronto after many years. As
she rediscovers once-familiar streets, memories of degradation couched in friendship—psychic abuse wrapped in smiles—overtake her, and compel her to revisit the
(pernicious) playgrounds of her youth. Atwood's tale tops the reading lists of those
compelled, by a variety of motivations, to confront issues of bullying—for good reason. Uncannily chronicling the slow, inevitable erosion of self, Elaine's story (sweetly,
smilingly) exposes pathologies of victimizing and victimization alike. Women who
pick up this novel often discover it unearths their own long-buried pain, and prompts
them to revisit humiliations suffered at the hands of childhood companions. Curiously, however, analyses of *Cat's Eye* have overlooked any exploration of the social
dynamics surrounding shame, or the ontological implications linked to it. Instead,
shame, which functions as a catalyst driving the narrative, is bundled into Atwood's
exploration of both self and time in relation to sophisticated feminist themes. Given
its centrality to character development, movement, and plot, a more comprehensive
analysis of its essence, and consequence, is required. Shame not only informs Elaine's

choices in life, it also fuels the ongoing intrapsychic dances between the ghosts of past, present, and future. Elaine's return to Toronto for a retrospective of her art is a return to a gallery of childhood memories, where the images on display evolve around one central question: is there (or can there be) an Elaine who is not defined by her relationship to Cordelia?

Elaine's Narrative

Elaine is turning eight when her unconventional parents purchase a home, settle in Toronto, and enroll her in school for the first time. There, she must learn to negotiate the culture of other children—and of girls in particular. Uncertain yet curious, Elaine begins absorbing the details of how other girls live. Naïvely, she perceives the vast differences between her lifestyle and theirs as existing without connotation—until her new friend Carol visits her house. At this point Elaine begins to see her home (and subsequently her family and her lifestyle) through the eye of the other, and begins to attach significance to the contrast between her home and family, and the lives, possessions, and norms of another girl. Deep in her psyche, dis-ease uncoils, undermining inquisitiveness, seeding insecurity.

As Elaine discovers herself as object in relation to others, she emerges as subject, driven by a growing desire to be a girl herself, to fit in: "I begin to want things I've never wanted before: braids, a dressing gown, a purse of my own. Something is unfolding, being revealed to me . . . I can be a part of it without making any effort at all . . . all I have to do is sit on the floor and cut frying pans out of *Eaton's Catalogue* and say I've done it badly" (Atwood, *Cat's Eye*, 57). As she learns how girls play, becoming proficient in the construction of scrapbooks of "perfect women" (pastiches of body parts, dissected from numerous magazines and paired with "must have" yet equally disconnected household accessories), Elaine learns the attributes integral to femininity. And, through such games, she begins inscribing feminine virtues (self-effacement, conformity, and submission to authority) on her psyche. As artifacts of desire, these scrapbooks memorialize Elaine's yearning to inhabit the space of this other, and become the measure of her inadequacy.[1] In Bourdieu's terms, Elaine desires to embody the norms of this habitus. Her discomfort is the bodily, felt distance between it and the one which currently articulates her.

The gap between the two worlds appears to lessen with each acquiescent act, as Elaine, anxious to be a girl, a *real* girl, scrambles to accommodate every prescription passed down by her new girlfriends. Regrettably, her eager compliance lays the foundation for the dynamic of domination that emerges between herself, Carol, and Grace Smeath. This unquestioning obedience also quietly cultivates a related gender norm: self as victim. Elaine's victimization will, disturbingly, play itself out in terms of admission to "girl world." Girl games seduce her into the sensibilities of femininity, but soon playing "at" them is not enough. *Being* a girl requires far more than knowledge of their rules, which regulate "frontstage" behaviors. It requires that Elaine's very *being* in the world become gendered. Femininity must be ontologized. And it is her growing compliance on an ontological level (e.g., her newfound deference to purveyors of an abusive male gaze) which leaves Elaine susceptible to, and unable to differentiate between, the requirements of femininity and other, malevolent conditionals attached to her new "friendships."

In time, a new girl moves to the neighborhood and attaches herself to this group. Cordelia's family is wealthy, affecting habits and behaviors foreign to all the girls. Her "worldliness" and "sophisticated gaze" hold them all in thrall and entitle her to unquestioned authority. Cordelia's attention soon fastens on Elaine, who is (obligingly) passive, undeniably inadequate, and most in need of "fixing." The subsequent campaign (of humiliation), undertaken to "correct" Elaine's shortcomings, offers chilling insight into tactics employed in the construction of femininity:

> She [Grace] watches everything I do on Sundays, and reports on me, matter-of-factly, to Cordelia.
> "She didn't stand up straight in Sunday school yesterday." Or; "She was a goody-goody." I believe each of these comments: my shoulders sag, my spine crumples, I exude the wrong kind of goodness; I see myself shambling crookedly, I make an effort to stand straighter, my body rigid with anxiety. And it's true that I got ten out of ten, again, and Grace only got nine. Is it wrong to be right? How right should I be, to be perfect? The next week I put five wrong answers, deliberately.
> "She only got five out of ten . . ." (Atwood, *Cat's Eye*, 131)

This abject need to please,[2] to change herself in order to fit in and become worthy of friendship, becomes increasingly desperate:

> I worry about what I've said today, the expression on my face, how I walk, what I wear, because all of these things need improvement. I am not normal, I am not like other girls. Cordelia tells me so, but she will help me. Grace and Carol will help me too. It will take hard work and a long time. (125)

But Elaine continues to disappoint. And, as her humiliation mounts, she herself crumbles and diminishes. Finally, on a cold day in March, the abuse culminates in an incident which, in all but killing Elaine, frees her from bondage to this "friendship." Cordelia, believing Elaine laughed at her for falling in the snow, snatches her hat and flings it into the ravine where, the girls have been told, they are never to go. Although Elaine hesitates, she soon succumbs to Cordelia's wheedling promises of forgiveness, and climbs down into the ravine and onto the ice to retrieve her hat. As she picks it up, the ice cracks, plunging her into the freezing water. As cold pierces her, she looks toward her friends watching from the bridge, only to discover that they have gone. She is alone. The realization that her hands and feet are too raw for her to climb back up—that she may freeze to death in the cold—causes a deep quiet to come over her. At this point the momentum of ridicule which has been driving the plot snaps, and the Elaine who is then "saved" by a vision which beckons her forward is an Elaine who is no longer seduced by Cordelia's passive-aggressive friendship. But who is Elaine, independent of this defining relationship?

The Elaine who emerges from the ravine is a girl now able to withdraw from Cordelia and all her importuning. Withdrawing, however, does not—and cannot—supply the momentum needed to support the subsequent movement of the novel. Instead, the reader must look to an emotional infrastructure, one slightly out of step with this climax, to understand the impetus underpinning Elaine's unfolding story. While her numbing near death in the ravine destroys the power which Cordelia and the other girls have over Elaine, this breaking point does not propel forward movement. Instead, the critical change in Elaine's response pattern occurs shortly before her experience in the ravine, when she becomes aware that adults are privy to her secret unworthiness, and endorse the cruelties of her friends. The trust and secrecy which cushion her humiliations, insulating them from the gaze of outsiders, are ruptured, destroying Elaine into a new set of psychic responses:

> As I come up the cellar stairs I can hear [Grace's] Aunt Mildred and Mrs. Smeath, who are in the kitchen doing dishes.
>
> "She's exactly like a heathen," says Aunt Mildred . . . "Nothing you've done has made a scrap of difference."
>
> "She's learning her bible, Grace tells me," Mrs. Smeath says, and then I know it's me they're discussing . . .
>
> "They'll learn all that," says Aunt Mildred. "Till you're blue in the face. But it's rote learning, it doesn't sink in. The minute your back is turned they'll go right back to the way they were."
>
> The unfairness of this hits me like a kick. How can they say that, when I've won a special mention for my essay on Temperance . . .
>
> "What can you expect, with that family?" says Mrs. Smeath. She doesn't go on to say what's wrong with my family. "The other children sense it. They know."
>
> "You don't think they're being too hard on her?" says Aunt Mildred. Her voice is relishing. She wants to know how hard.
>
> "It's God's punishment," says Mrs. Smeath. "It serves her right."
>
> A hot wave moves through my body. The wave is shame, which I have felt before, but it is also hatred, which I have not, not in this pure form. It's hatred with a particular shape, the shape of Mrs. Smeath's one breast and no waist . . .
>
> I stand there on the top step, frozen with hate. What I hate is not Grace or even Cordelia. I can't go as far as that. I hate Mrs. Smeath, because what I thought was a secret, something going on among girls, among children, is not one. It has been discussed before, and tolerated. Mrs. Smeath has known and approved. She has done nothing to stop it. She thinks it serves me right. (192–193)

Mrs. Smeath exposes (and corroborates) Elaine's inadequacies, removing intersubjective experiences of shame from the protective cocoon of friendship. Further, she dismisses all effort, situating Elaine's failings in an unalterable, unforgivable condition. In rejecting Elaine's bid for acceptance, she does violence to her desperate, fragile hope of fitting in. Her judgments embody the threat contained in the gaze of all others:

the possibility that, despite her efforts, they will discover she is an impostor who will never truly belong.

Elaine's response to this shaming, her hate and rage, creates the possibility for, and the direction of, forward movement in the novel. Everything that occurs prior to this point chronicles her passivity, her abject complicity in her own emotional destruction. The movement that occurs after this point is triggered by, and relates back to, Elaine's emotional response to Mrs. Smeath.[3] At this pivotal moment in the narrative, hate and rage break her from passive acceptance and provide the means of resisting the further degradation and dissolution of self. Her shame is cathected, turned outward, and projected onto the source of humiliating pain—with a force belying the extent to which she lives in the minds of others.

Elaine's rage inaugurates an emotional response pattern that is difficult to interrupt. Helen Block Lewis, in *Shame in Guilt and Neurosis*, identifies it as a "feeling-trap": a set of emotions which circle round themselves until broken. Elaine's re*action* to Mrs. Smeath's malicious gossip ties an emotional knot: shame and hate/rage come to coexist in a symbiotic relationship. They chase each other, one emerging as an emotional reaction to the felt experience of the other. Even as rage silences her shame by overpowering its threats to self, it situates Elaine as captive to her reactivity, precluding the possibility of unpacking and processing the humiliation which (silently) continues to reverberate between body and psyche. Reactivity[4] salvages self, but at a price which prevents Elaine from taking ownership of her past, and of dialoguing with options in her present and future.

Understanding Elaine's Humiliation

Cordelia, Grace, and Carol control Elaine through judgments which harness her desire. They manipulate her behavior, as well as her conceptions of self, by threatening that which she covets: inclusion in their coterie. The group processes which normalize—if not support—their modus operandi are laid bare and dissected by Erving Goffman in *The Presentation of Self in Everyday Life* (1959).[5] This study, which explores the implicit rules governing social dialogues, led Goffman to contend that *all* interactions are ordered by the (often tacit) threat contained in the eye of the other. The individual, who emerges intersubjectively, is molded and constrained by the prevailing social norms established by, and reflected in, the opinions of those around her. These norms derive their coercive power from the individual's fear of seeming inadequate—even fraudulent, and deserving of rebuke, derision, *and exclusion*. Complex social dances are undertaken to avoid such a valuation. In light of such elaborate social maneuvering, Goffman concluded that the linchpin of social order must be the threat of embarrassment: "embarrassment lies at the heart of the social organization of day-to-day conduct. It provides a personal constraint on the behavior of the individual in society and a public response to actions and activities considered problematic or untoward" (Heath, 137).

In this view, Cordelia and the others manifest the social forces contained in the eye of the other—forces which circumscribe the give-and-take of social interaction. Their judgments organize Elaine's day-to-day conduct. Her vigilant hyperawareness is but a caricature of the normative self-monitoring integral to social intercourse. Wanting to sidestep reproach, she carefully imitates the others, struggling to faithfully execute any instructions which Cordelia, Grace, and Carol give her. With no innate sense of how to behave, she lives in "frontstage performances," attentive to details which enhance her ability to *act like* a girl. Elaine is invested in these performances, hoping they will promote her ability to *become* a girl (e.g., ontologize femininity) and someday stand in a meaningfully reciprocal relationship to her friends, especially to Cordelia.

However, her efforts cannot keep pace with the incessant fault-finding of her friends. Daily, capricious censure begins eroding any coherent sense of self grounding Elaine, deepening her dependence on Cordelia. Repeated social missteps coalesce as character flaws, inadequacies which sharpen and intensify her embarrassment, transforming it into shame.

Shame is anchored in sociation and references social power. It underpins the shadow of embarrassment looming over all interaction, and threatens more than a temporary loss of face: "an experience of shame . . . is not an isolated act that can be detached from the self . . . but revelation of the whole self. The thing that has been exposed is what I am" (Lynd, 50–51). Shame indicts. It dissolves the hived self, correlating what one has done with who one is. Inadequacies and flaws, once sequestered in the context of behaviors (or hidden in Goffman's "backstage"), come to frame identity, betraying essence and impeaching character. Challenges to credibility, competency, or moral integrity compromise relationships, weakening, or altogether severing, social bonds.[6] In this, shame denies the individual full access to the potentialities contained within community. Claims to reciprocity are restricted, ignored, or rejected, reducing the individual to the status of social pariah. (This status may be reinforced by an intrapsychic split, pitting the social self which has internalized group norms against the individual self, engaging the individual's complicity in her own denunciation.)

This power potential, contained within all shaming, signals the strength and import of social bonds. Sociologists since Durkheim have known that an individual's relation to her community has a direct bearing on psychic health.[7] In *Shame in Guilt and Neurosis*, Helen Block Lewis suggested that its significance reflects a biopsychosocial need, and that shame is a social instinct that signals a threat to the social bond. Individuals are carefully attuned to nuances of inclusion, which indicate degrees of connectedness to the other/group. Roy Baumeister and Mark Leary develop Lewis's argument, contending that "belongingness" is a social need on a par with biological needs for food and water. They assert that a majority of behaviors classified as neurotic, maladaptive, or destructive reflect "desperate attempts to establish or maintain relationships with other people or sheer frustration and purposelessness when one's need to belong goes unmet" (521). In their view, "belongingness" is a requirement of psychic coherence—a *need*, which "takes precedence over esteem and self-actualization" (497). And, they argue, the majority of the social dances which constitute daily interactions are undertaken in the service of belongingness. In other words, much of human motivation is derived from a need to avoid being left (or cast) out, or, in Erving Goffman's construction, to avoid embarrassment and shame.[8] Baumeister and Leary believe this is true to such a great extent that "aversive reactions to a loss of belongingness should go beyond negative affect to include some types of pathology" (500).[9]

Elaine is a poster child for their theorizing. Repeated reminders of her peripheral, tenuous status within her friendship group create white noise within her body, eliciting behavior that is neurotic, destructive, and even pathological. Alone in her bed at night, she peels the skin off her feet in narrow strips, "down to the blood." In the morning she pulls her socks over ravaged feet: "It was painful to walk, but not impossible. The pain gave me something definite to think about, something immediate. It was something to hold on to" (Atwood, *Cat's Eye,* 120).

And Elaine desperately needs a way to attach herself to daily life. Her assiduous attempts to become a girl have failed—inevitably. For, the demands being placed on her reach beyond surface knowledge, beyond a deeper knowledge of the habitus, beyond even *being* in the world, and seek to undermine her ability to inhabit her body itself. Gradually, the relationship between Elaine and her friends has slipped from one in which the girls provide information and model behavioral responses in order to correct her frontstage performances, to one which aspires to ownership of her backstage in the name of femininity, to one which aspires to ground her very being in the dictates of another. Her deeply felt desire to belong, to inscribe the rules of a feminized social space on her body, have left her vulnerable to wholesale co-optation and incorporation.

The increasing inconsistencies in the demands placed on her signal the transmutation of this original objective,[10] and lend Elaine's attempts to perform correctly an eerie incoherence. Is she to study and get all answers correct, or is that somehow incorrect? If answering everything correctly is incorrect, *how* correct is correct? As Elaine's intuitive grasp of the world deteriorates, meaning breaks down. Coherence dissolves. Mounting inconsistency challenges her experiences of both self and other, eroding ontological security. At this point Elaine is all but beyond shame, no longer in possession of a coherent sense of self capable of cringing at its own inadequacies. She lives in the mind of her friends, clinging to their image of her, dizzying herself making "corrections," struggling to be worthy of the redemption they hold out. Yet her gestures of self-sacrifice (self-annihilation) are opening a space of nothingness—a void—which seductively draws any shadow of substance left to her:

> I think about becoming invisible. I think about eating the deadly nightshade berries from the bushes beside the path. I think about drinking the Javex out of the skull and crossbones bottle in the laundry room, about jumping off the bridge . . .

> I don't want to do these things, I'm afraid of them. But I think about Cordelia telling me to do them, not in her scornful voice, in her kind one.
>
> I hear her kind voice inside my head. *Do it. Come on.* I would be doing these things to please her. (166)

The social bonds which have forged Elaine are destroying her, yet without them she may cease to exist. Intent on, and in thrall to, the vicious dynamics of this friendship, she is blindsided by Mrs. Smeath's judgments, which endorse the brutalities of the other girls. They inflict a shame that is raw and uncomplicated. Elaine has no embodied attachment to Mrs. Smeath, and is thus able to respond in an equally uncomplicated way, with hate and rage. And it is her ability to respond, to feel this hate, which will allow her to resist further grinding down, even eradication, of her (very idea of) self.

Shortly after her encounter with Mrs. Smeath, Elaine falls through the ice. Significantly, however, she does not sink to the depths, but finds footing beneath the needle-sharp water. In parallel fashion, Elaine unexpectedly hits the solid ground of her rage. This intrapsychic footing (albeit a false bottom) carries her through high school, where the "mean mouth" she develops allows her to effectively control interpersonal relations. Her biting sarcasm precludes genuine connection with others, and forestalls the possibility of shaming—especially by Cordelia, over whom she now holds power.[11]

Her post-high-school intrigue with Josef, which involves explorations of sexuality, cannot be managed in this fashion. Consequently, it is fraught with potential threats to self. Elaine cedes him, her "teacher," the authority to form her as an artist, and acquiesces to *his* desire to "complete her" as a woman.[12] Her willing subordination (allowing him to dress her, accommodating his ongoing relationship with Susie) does not, however, go far enough to further compromise her self. It is not until she becomes pregnant, and marries Jon, that Elaine once again engages *her* desire to inhabit the habitus of white, middle-class femininity—as mother and wife. When her marriage begins to fail, it becomes another humiliating indictment, a rejection of her bids for ownership of this space. Falling short in the ultimate test of womanhood exposes Elaine: she is a fraud, incapable (still) of *being* female correctly. As she clings more desperately to the roles of mother and wife, redoubling her efforts at homemaking, Elaine once again abandons self, disappearing into culturally scripted submissions, attempting to salvage her claims to this world. Not surprisingly, at about this time images of Mrs. Smeath begin demanding space on her canvases:

> Mrs. Smeath sitting, standing, lying down with her holy rubber plant, flying, with Mr. Smeath stuck to her back, being screwed like a beetle. Mrs. Smeath in the dark blue bloomers of Miss Lumley, who somehow combines with her in a frightening symbiosis. Mrs. Smeath unwrapped from white tissue paper, layer by layer. Mrs. Smeath bigger than life, bigger than ever she was. Blotting out God, I put a lot of work into that imagined body, white as a burdock root, flabby as pork fat. Hairy as the inside of an ear. (426–427)

Or again:

> I paint Mrs. Smeath. She floats up without warning, like a dead fish, materializing on a sofa I am drawing: first her white sparsely haired legs without ankles, then her thick waist and potato face, her eyes in their steel rims. The afghan is draped across her thighs, the rubber plant rises behind her like a fan. On her head is the felt hat like a badly done-up package that she used to wear on Sundays.
>
> She looks out at me from the flat surface of paint, three dimensional now, smiling her closed half-smile, smug and accusing. Whatever has happened to me is my own fault, the fault of what is wrong with me.
>
> Mrs. Smeath knows what it is. She isn't telling. . . .
>
> One picture of Mrs. Smeath leads to another. She multiplies on the walls like bacteria, standing, sitting, flying, with clothes, without clothes, following me around with her many eyes like those 3-D postcards of Jesus you can get in the cheesier corner stores.
>
> Sometimes I turn her faces to the wall. (358)

Elaine's preoccupation with Mrs. Smeath illuminates the shame/rage spiral in which she remains trapped. Unable to resist the indictment of self occurring with the disintegration of her marriage, unable, once again, to please and thereby safeguard against humiliating failure, Elaine paints Mrs. Smeath. This forgotten ogress of her childhood emerges onto her canvases with an urgency. Elaine is baffled by her appearance, unable to recognize in Mrs. Smeath the gaze of the other, calling forth a resistance to her own abdication of self. Mrs. Smeath symbolizes Elaine's shame even as she calls up her rage, functioning as an emotional shield, warding against her own complicity in self-annihilation. Elaine cannot control her emergence onto canvases, but she can cover and manage this shame with vengeance, depicting Mrs. Smeath from innumerable humiliating angles, struggling for weeks at a time to get the color of cruelty right.

But Mrs. Smeath is not the object of her rage; Jon is. Mrs. Smeath's materialization merely signifies and enables Elaine's rage, prompting her to hurl ashtrays, shoes, and all manner of objects at Jon.[13] Reactivity does not, however, negotiate Elaine's failure. As the marriage slips further, Elaine is drawn deeper into her own inadequacies, and can no longer cover her humiliation and assuage her pain with these responses. Finally, she ceases to paint, and ceasing to paint signals an inability to (re)actively resist the precipitous edges of her failure:

> I lie in the bedroom with the curtains drawn and nothingness washing over me like a sluggish wave. Whatever is happening to me is my own fault. I have done something wrong, something so huge I can't even see it, something that's drowning me. I am inadequate and stupid, without worth. I might as well be dead. (394)

In the next paragraph Elaine once again lets go, succumbing to the welcoming blackness offered by an "Exacto knife" meeting her wrists.

Cordelia's Shame

Cat's Eye is Elaine Risley's story, and it is her shaming which drives the plot. Nonetheless, Elaine's antagonist, Cordelia, is carrying her own burden of shame—one less visible, yet just as integral to the story which unfolds. Elaine and Cordelia are the other upon whom each depends for the creation of self. As mirror to the other, both are victim and victimizer; subject and object.

Cordelia's subjectivity, however, differs from Elaine's in that her insecurities are rooted in her family. Her name, referencing Shakespeare's *King Lear,* situates her as the one who will be rejected.[14] Cordelia's inadequacies initially appear through contrast to her older sisters, Perdita (Perdie) and Miranda (Mirrie). Both are beautiful and gifted, one taking ballet, and the other studying the viola. When Elaine, not understanding the designation "gifted," asks Cordelia if she is gifted, Cordelia turns away. She is not, in fact, special in any way.

Rather, within her family, Cordelia "disappoints." In who she is, and quite probably who she has always been, Cordelia fails to "measure up":

> She's frightened of not pleasing him [her father]. And yet he is not pleased. I've seen it many times, her dithering, fumble-footed efforts to appease him. But nothing she can do or say will ever be enough, because *she is somehow the wrong person.* (268; italics added)

In other words, she is a girl. This is the underlying inadequacy for which Cordelia cannot, ultimately, compensate. Within her family Cordelia represents failure (or, as R. D. Lane argues, Cordelia represents "nothing").

The shame accompanying this failure is not privileged in the novel. It is, as Michael Lewis has noted in "The Role of Self in Shame," akin to a subatomic particle, known only by the trace it leaves—in this case its displacement onto Elaine. Cordelia's unspeakable inadequacy, her lack, becomes apparent in her need of Elaine. Her cruel criticisms of her friend come to have less and less to do with teaching Elaine, and everything to do with her own desire for control and power. And what Cordelia ultimately wants—needs—is for Elaine to *be for her,* not to be in and of herself. Elaine fills the gaping hole incapable of anchoring self,[15] and occupies the hollowness at her core. This inexpressible emptiness, integral to Cordelia's being (or who she is unable to be), is an ongoing threat to her ability to exist in the world.[16] And, as the outlines of her counternarrative unfold, this lack slowly swallows her.

Swedish authors Stattin and Klackenberg-Larsson have explored failure in relation to parental preference for a child of the opposite gender. Their findings reveal a statistically significant correlation between prenatal gender preference and delinquency. Cordelia is the poster child for their theorizing. She becomes delinquent and begins failing in high school, and continues this pattern of delinquency and failure throughout what we know of her life. Years later, when Elaine visits her at a private mental hospital, Cordelia is barely recognizable. Elaine does not know how to respond to this defeated adult Cordelia, who tonelessly explains that her attempted suicide was merely a response to being "tired." She realizes that "Cordelia has placed herself beyond me, out of my reach, where I can't get at her. She has let go of her ideal of herself.

She is lost" (379). Yet she once again wants to be, and be found, through Elaine; she looks to Elaine to spring her from the asylum, to rescue her from her own inadequacies. "'I can't Cordelia,' I say gently. But I don't feel gentle toward her. I am seething, with a fury I can neither explain nor express. *How dare you ask me?* I want to twist her arm, rub her face in the snow" (380–381). Inexplicable rage rears in response to Cordelia's unanticipated threat: her repeated bid to save herself through Elaine.

Cordelia's need (i.e., her lack), arguably rooted in her father's desire for a male child, places her shame at the feet of the patriarchy itself. Her gender-incorrectness, ascribed by the (male) other looking to reproduce its power, situates inadequacy at her core. This is the failing which cannot be overcome; the source of underlying desperation fueling her attempts to co-opt Elaine. Elaine glimpses this lack once she is able to turn away from Cordelia's demands, and hears, for the first time, the absence in her voice:

> "You get back here right now!"
> I can hear this for what it is . . .
> It's an impersonation of someone much older. (207)

This impersonation is, as Molly Hite points out, "Cordelia's attempt to appropriate [patriarchal power] for herself by applying to Elaine her own father's expressions" (192).

Additional instances ("Wipe that smile off your face" and "What do you have to say for yourself?") reveal further attempts to transcribe this subtext of shame (which colonizes the habitus of white middle-class femininity) onto Elaine's psyche. Cordelia's gendered self is not privileged in this culture, nor can Elaine's be. Cordelia, Carol, and Grace, as well as Mrs. Smeath, turn a male gaze on Elaine, and it is the gaze of the masculine other (in addition to Cordelia's needs—themselves the result of nullification by this gaze) that finds her inadequate. And it is Elaine's experience with an alternate male gaze, not only that of her own father, but that of her brother, Stephen (represented by the cat's eye marble, which is, among other things, his signifier), that is integral to her ability to salvage fragments of self in the face of both Cordelia's and Mrs. Smeath's shamings.

Cordelia is unable to confront her father-qua-patriarchy for reasons similar to those which prevent Elaine from turning and confronting her—namely, because she has constructed herself in interaction with him. In introjecting the other, she (like Elaine) is unable to fully reject her (tor)mentor. Instead, Cordelia attempts to resist her shame and inadequacy, her nothingness, by using Elaine, just as Elaine uses Mrs. Smeath to resist Cordelia's attempts at annihilation. But it is here that the parallel stops. Elaine uses reactivity to resist annihilation, while Cordelia is hollow at the core, and grasps at *being* through Elaine in a manner similar to the patriarchy's *being* through her.

Resolution: Negotiating the Relationship between Shame and Anger

As Elaine emerges in flashback, we discover a woman who came to layer a safe, detached life over the dangerous edges of her inadequacies. This life (simulation of life?)

is one even she has "trouble believing in, because it doesn't seem the kind of life I could ever get away with, or deserve. This goes along with another belief of mine: that everyone else my age is an adult whereas I am merely in disguise" (Atwood, *Cat's Eye*, 14). Elaine's relationship to her life, and her roles within it (e.g., "disguises") reveal a single underlying conviction: that she is not yet good enough to *be* (a mother, a remarried woman, or even an artist). Instead, she continues to *play at* life. However, her performances—assorted, carefully calculated, roles—are no longer enacted with the intent of owning the character. Instead, they are social productions which intercept risk to self, ultimately functioning to maintain Elaine's disconnect from desiring. Her return to Toronto cracks the façade she has erected around this desire, exposing insecurity (shame) and hostility (rage), the cornerstones of her intrapsychic functioning. Once-familiar emotions—humiliation, hurt, uncertainty—lie in wait on the streets, stalking her self-deceptions.

Confronting these feelings, and processing the confusion which attends them, will require Elaine to become, and remain, available to herself. She must find and ascribe meaning to—inscribe it *on*—experiences which (although entombed in her psyche) continue to inhabit her body, influencing movement in the world. Elaine must tell *her* story. She must incorporate humiliation, darkness, and internal chaos into a new narrative whole, one which, in integrating ontological upheaval, looks to contain it. This process itself will bear witness to her struggle for coherence: her attempts to achieve sovereignty over her humiliation, as well as her rage.

The unresolved, crippling emotions which have reemerged in Toronto are the thread for this new narrative. Their capacity to link past and present, refashioning time, reveals how everything has changed yet nothing is different:

> There are days when I can hardly make it out of bed. I find it an effort to speak. I measure progress in steps, the next one and the next one, as far as the bathroom. These steps are major accomplishments. I focus on taking the cap off the toothpaste, getting the brush up to my mouth. I have difficulty lifting my arm to do even that. I feel I am without worth, that nothing I can do is of any value, least of all to myself.
> *What do you have to say for yourself?* Cordelia used to ask. *Nothing,* I would say. (43)

"Nothing" is once again a word Elaine connects to herself—to the voiceless woman crouching behind the roles she has been playing—disguises now in shambles on the streets of Toronto. Her ability to assert an appropriate, coherent "presentation of self" has been interrupted by the chaos reclaiming her psyche. Who should she (can she) affect being? If she is an artist, she knows she *should* be clad in black, but black raises too many questions she cannot answer: Is she good enough to wear black? Is she a painter, or an artist? If the latter, must she present herself as an artist—as a cipher only allowed to wear black?

These huddling doubts come to a head during Elaine's visit to the gallery to in-spect the hanging of her show. Clad in a powder-blue jogging suit, her presentation of self (in contrast to that of the young, chic women eating sprout and avocado sand-wiches while uncrating her art) is immediately, humiliatingly, *wrong*. *She* is somehow wrong. Awareness of her failure to meet the expectations of others cannot, however, be shrugged off, as a reporter has been engaged to interview her for the upcoming show. Unprepared for—and unable to withstand—such scrutiny, Elaine's last vestiges of performed self dissolve in the gaze of this young woman, whose (routine) questions become an interrogation of / judgment on her life: "What I hear is what she isn't saying. *Your clothes are stupid. Your art is crap. Sit up straight and don't answer back*" (95). In-adequate, yet again disappointing, Elaine retreats to familiar contours of humiliation and pain: picking and peeling her fingers in an attempt to ground self, casting about for Cordelia.

But Cordelia remains elusive. Instead, it is Mrs. Smeath who again emerges to redirect Elaine's energies—Mrs. Smeath, poised upon the walls, prepared to judge and summon reactivity. But Elaine, stripped of defensive filters and connected to her pain, is incapable of rousing rage against accusations of inadequacy. Defeated, she wanders the gallery, coming face-to-face with a woman who, she is puzzled to realize, is herself on display, gazed at, no longer gazing. And slowly, as she stops to look at Mrs. Smeath, she *sees* her. Sees, for the first time, that her memorializations of this childhood ogress exist *in conjunction with* other Mrs. Smeaths. This realization invites Elaine to decen-ter the hatred and rage positioning Mrs. Smeath; to explore that which exists *in addi-tion to* the reactivity that has composed her interface with the past:

> It's the eyes I look at now. I used to think these were self-righteous eyes, piggy and smug inside their wire frames; and they are. But they are also defeated eyes, uncer-tain and melancholy, heavy with unloved duty. The eyes of someone for whom God was a sadistic old man; the eyes of a small town threadbare decency. Mrs. Smeath was a transplant to the city, from somewhere a lot smaller. A displaced person, as I was. (427)

In *seeing* Mrs. Smeath, Elaine is able to identify with and *respond* to her, as opposed to *reacting* to, with, and through the body-knowledge she calls forth. In becoming aware of other elements speaking within her paintings, Elaine begins to recognize that the images are capable of signifying in unanticipated ways. Mrs. Smeath is, she realizes, capable of existing in alternate narratives. She has other stories to tell—stories which have the potential to redeem her. Elaine's recognition of this involves a realization of her own role in positioning Mrs. Smeath as signifier. In vilifying her, Elaine objecti-fied Mrs. Smeath in the same manner this woman had judged and objectified her as a child. This unexpected insight, emerging in response to her recognition of con-nectivity to Mrs. Smeath, suggests that Elaine herself has other stories to tell. Mrs. Smeath becomes a narrative bridge, inviting movement between past and present, self and other; opening a space between shame and hate/rage. Reactivity, Elaine sees—an eye for an eye—only led to more blindness. Hatred and retribution did not reduce her shame, only her ability to recognize self in other; to maintain connection to self through other.

Disrupting the feeling trap of (recycled) reactivity brings Elaine face-to-face with her own feelings of worthlessness. De-cathecting Mrs. Smeath (re)exposes the shamed self, yet positions Elaine to finally confront feelings of humiliating inadequacy. In order to negotiate both failure and helplessness, she must own (take control of), give shape to, and impose temporal order upon (e.g., contain) debilitating body memories. Elaine must find and claim her voice, and to do so must embrace her lack, her pain, her truth. The new narrative which emerges will establish/maintain an "I," her "eye," as narrator. In reclaiming self as subject, her accounting will beget significances for her pain, transforming the wreckage of shame into a story that connects past, present, and future.

However, her ability to tell *this* story, to begin to process her degradation, humiliation, and confusion, is—and has been—hampered by a cultural lack: an absence of shame-based metanarratives to guide her. Cultural silence around experiences of shame—their nature, meaning, and requirements for resolution—has made it difficult for Elaine to unpack these incidents and attach meaning to her suffering. On what basis could she negotiate the relationship between her self and her shame (are they coeval?), or the relationship in which she now stands to the community—or the community to her? How to meaningfully (re)create her memories when the absence of metanarratives reflects cultural norms which deny shame's significance? Refuse its potentialities? Culture distances itself from shame's spectacle, endorsing absence and disconnect as normative responses to (and on the part of) the shamed, stigmatized individual. This void swallows the interior landscape of shame, allowing only solitary cries of rage to escape.

Culture's silence, its refusal to affirm the wreckage of its own moral condemnations, suggests a refusal to admit of forgiveness, or the moral possibility of redemption. Cordelia's shaming of Elaine invariably contained this possibility: "'Go on then' she [Cordelia] says more gently, as if she's encouraging me, not ordering. 'Then you'll be forgiven'" (200). Her judgments threatened severance of social bonds *if* Elaine did not struggle to correct her failings. (And, when Elaine does fail, there are penances she is able to do, avenues of re-integration open to her.) Mrs. Smeath's refusal to acknowledge Elaine's struggle—*her refusal to admit a possibility of redemption*—informs the turning point of Elaine's story. It denies the possibility that "shame, as the body's reflection on itself, may reorder the composition of the habitus which in turn may allow for quite different choices" (Probyn, *Blush*, 56).

With no potential in her shame, Elaine fled. Unable, however, to outrun the shame/rage cycle patterning her, she hid it in plain sight, in her art. Significantly, the catalogue of her work contains only one painting of Jon and one of Cordelia—both of whom evoked *her* desire, and with it a complex set of emotions. Instead, it is Mrs. Smeath who crowded canvas after canvas. Mrs. Smeath, whose materializations reinforced the feeling trap which prevented resolution—ransoming self at the cost of desiring; of *being*.

However, the paintings of Jon and Cordelia that did escape from Elaine's brush are particularly intriguing—and quite telling. The picture of Cordelia, entitled "Half a Face," teases because her entire face is clearly visible. Elaine struggled with this painting, wanting to capture Cordelia at about thirteen, looking out with that defiant, almost belligerent stare of hers. *So?*

> But the eyes sabotaged me. They aren't strong eyes; the look they give the face is tentative, hesitant, reproachful. Frightened.
> Cordelia is afraid of me in this picture.
> I am afraid of Cordelia.
> I'm not afraid of seeing Cordelia. I'm afraid of being Cordelia. (Atwood, *Cat's Eye*, 243)

Cordelia, too, has other stories to tell—stories Elaine has always "known," for even when the painting was completed (which is unclear in the novel), Elaine was unable to portray Cordelia with the (signifying) power she has, all along, attributed to her. Half of that face (the eyes?) belongs to Elaine. This recognition, coupled with Cordelia's absence—on additional canvases, as well as in Toronto—are integral to the new narrative Elaine must create. She must grasp that it has always been Cordelia's *absence*; her *lack*, which defined her. On the streets of Toronto Elaine is filled by the presence of Cordelia's absence, unable to ask her "Why? What did it all mean?" because the Cordelia able to answer that question *was never there*. She is absent *as she always has been*. It is Elaine who empowered her, Elaine who, throughout the novel, scripted her, Elaine who, in creating Cordelia's presence, absented her own self.

Elaine's difficulty in capturing Cordelia bears witness to an inability—or unwillingness—to acknowledge the mirrored *and mirroring* self (although, significantly, Cordelia's face is seen *reflected in a mirror* in this painting). Only her recognition of the refracting nature of the relational self will permit Elaine to negotiate absence: to *see* self (shame) in other, and to affirm other (rage) in self.

Admittance of the full measure of interrelational connectivity will allow Elaine to become (and to embrace becoming) the gazing other, an other whose voice is informed by a reconnection to her own (subjective) desiring. And it is in becoming the eye, the "I," of the other that Elaine will see, embrace, and *forgive* Cordelia—will redeem her self:

> I know she's looking at me, the lopsided mouth smiling a little, the face closed and defiant. There is the same shame, the sick feeling in my body, the same knowledge of my own wrongness, awkwardness, weakness; the same wish to be loved; the same loneliness; the same fear. But these are not my own emotions any more. They are Cordelia's, as they always were.

I am the older one now, I'm the stronger. If she stays here any longer she will freeze to death; she will be left behind, in the wrong time. It's almost too late.

I reach out my arms to her, bend down, hands open to show I have no weapon. *It's all right,* I say to her. *You can go home now.* (443)

Notes

1. It should be noted that, despite her compliance, Elaine has her own take on this game. She finds it "tiring" (Atwood, *Cat's Eye*, 57) and, as someone who has moved about frequently, understands the accumulation of objects from the perspective of subjugation to them. This suggests that Elaine in fact has, at this point, her own voice. She simply does not yet know how to speak.

2. A core tenet of Silvan Tomkins's work, as repackaged and revitalized by Elspeth Probyn (2005), is the contention that "interest" is crucial to shame. In fact, without interest there can be no shame. Elaine is *invested in* Cordelia's continuing to have *interest* in her, such that each "wrong action" is a break in their connection, one which threatens the dissolution of their relationship.

3. It is extremely significant to note that Elaine's experience at the ravine (which chronologically *follows* her shaming by Mrs. Smeath) includes a hint of resistance. For the first time, it occurs to Elaine that she may not obey Cordelia's order to retrieve her hat: "What will she do then? I can see this idea gathering in Cordelia as well. Maybe she's gone too far, hit, finally, some core of resistance in me. If I refuse to do what she says this time, who knows where my defiance will end?" (200). This potential defiance may be born of fear to go into the strictly off-limits ravine, or it may witness a newfound potential to respond to/resist shaming—if only toward Cordelia in this limited fashion.

4. Reactivity often presents as spectacle, which in turn is shame-producing, thus completing the cycle.

5. Goffman's theorizing is grounded in the work of Charles H. Cooley (looking-glass self), as well as that of George Herbert Mead (interactionism).

6. Cf. Thomas Scheff, "Shame in Self and Society."

7. Emile Durkheim, *Suicide*, 1897. This classic treatise, which "scientifically" studied, and turned up, a relationship between a lack of belonging—anomie—and suicide, offered the first "proof" of the significance of social bonds.

8. Recent findings in neuroscience appear to support the verity of this claim (MacDonald and Leary). DeWall argues that "social exclusion represents such a basic and severe threat to human well-being that the body encodes the experience of social exclusion in a manner that is similar to physical pain." Arguably, this is a result of evolutionary adaptation. Social exclusion, like physical injury, threatened survival.

9. Research has found that memories of rejection are tainted with anxiety. In fact, even imagining social rejection increases physiological arousal (Craighead, Kimball, and Rehak).

10. This is not to imply that the demands of femininity are themselves entirely coherent and consistent. However, the nature of the mandates issued to Elaine begin to suggest that some other agenda is in play.

11. Elaine's mean mouth also masks the (shameful) knowledge that she still does not fit in: she has no patience for fad diets, does not think of boys as "dreamy," and balks at the thought of gushing over the latest hit recording or celebrity romance. Her mouth keeps her ongoing inadequacy in mastering feminine roles from being exposed, keeps Elaine from being found wanting yet again.

12. It may be countered that in this relationship, Elaine engages *her* desire to become an artist. This, to me, is debatable. Elaine's art, up to this point, is technical. It is full of detail, not desire; mastery, not abandon.

13. Yet she does not—cannot—hate Jon, as she cannot hate Cordelia.

14. See "Cordelia's 'Nothing': The Character of Cordelia and Margaret Atwood's Cat's Eye," by R. D. Lane for a fuller discussion and comparison of Atwood's and Shakespeare's Cordelias.

15. This is literally depicted in a bit of play-acting in the novel, when Cordelia, Grace, and Carol lower Elaine (aka Mary, Queen of Scots) into a large hole which Cordelia has dug in her backyard. "Then they arrange boards over the top. The daylight air disappears, and there's the sound of dirt hitting the boards . . . When I was put into the hole I knew it was a game; now I know it is not one" (112).

16. Elaine's brother, Stephen, says of Cordelia that she "has a tendency to exist" (261).

11 Affliction in Jean Rhys and Simone Weil

Tamar Heller

IN THIS CHAPTER I read Jean Rhys's searing portrayal of an alienated, alcoholic heroine in her novel *Good Morning, Midnight* (1939) through the lens of the philosophy of Simone Weil (1909–1943). Weil, a Frenchwoman who died in exile in London during the Second World War, shared with her contemporary Rhys an intense interest in deracination; much of her work, like her last book, *L'enracinement* (in English *The Need for Roots*), addresses, as do Rhys's novels with their uprooted, drifting heroines, the dispossession of the socially marginal. Unlike Rhys, however, whose critical stock has risen in recent years, Weil is less visible in our day than in the 1950s and '60s, when her work influenced such major thinkers as Albert Camus, who called her "the only great spirit of our time" (qtd. in Panichas, xvii). One reason for the decline in Weil's popularity might be that her life and work, unlike Rhys's, does not obviously invite feminist interpretation. In contrast to her Sorbonne classmate Simone de Beauvoir, Weil never explicitly addressed gender issues, and the trajectory of her short life—a Jewish Marxist increasingly attracted to Catholicism, she became so ascetic that she died at thirty-four of self-starvation—has seemed to some feminists, such as the theologian Ann Loades, an example of how religion can be hazardous to women's health.[1] At the same time, however, during the last few decades Weil has been rediscovered by such feminist scholars as the philosopher Andrea Nye and the political scientist Mary Dietz.[2] Here, by applying Weil's insights into the psychological effects of oppression to the situation of Sasha Jansen, the protagonist of *Good Morning, Midnight*, I demonstrate the relevance of Weil's thought to two important and related fields in contemporary feminist thought: the study of trauma and the study of the emotion which is its common corollary, shame.

Feminist discussions of trauma—an area I will call feminist trauma theory—explores women's psychological and somatic response to gender-related violence, powerlessness, and inequality. Though exploring such personal and familial traumas as sexual abuse, feminist trauma theory necessarily has a macrocosmic dimension, examining the link between women's health and what Ann Folwell Stanford calls "social pathologies" linked not only to gender but to race and class. While there has been groundbreaking work among feminist social scientists on such pathologies—I would single out as exemplary Becky Thompson's study of minority and working-class women and eating disorders, *A Hunger So Wide and So Deep*—increasingly feminist literary critics such as Suzette Henke and Patricia Moran have also examined the representation of trauma in women's fiction and its connection to disabling cultural messages about femininity, messages which are often further complicated by social prejudices relating to racial, class, and national identity.[3] Moran's study of the "aesthetics of trauma" is particularly relevant to this discussion, as it specifically reads Rhys's work as the transformation of the raw material of personal trauma—including, in Rhys's case, her seduction as a teenager by a family friend—into narratives punctuated by unexorcised pain and culturally inflected anxieties about female sexuality.

Moreover, in noting that Rhys's protagonists are typically in "the grip of a disabling and dehumanizing sense of shame" (116), Moran suggests the link between feminist trauma theory and a theorization of the sense of worthlessness and self-hatred that scars women who are victims of emotional, physical, and sexual violence. An example of feminist literary criticism that further explores the link between trauma and shame is the work of J. Brooks Bouson, whose most recent book, *Embodied Shame: Uncovering Female Shame in Contemporary Women's Writing* (2009), defines "embodied female shame" as the "shame about the self and body that arises from the trauma of defective or abusive parenting or relationships and from various forms of sexual, racial, or social denigration of females in our culture" (2).[4] It is my contention in this essay that Weil's theorization of shame, though it does not explicitly address gender, nonetheless offers us a vocabulary through which to understand the transformation of what Bouson calls "various forms of sexual, racial, or social denigration of females" into a deadening sense of shame that causes its female victims to accede to and reproduce their own devaluation. Proclaiming "I have no pride—no name, no face, no country. I don't belong anywhere," Sasha Jansen, the protagonist of *Good Morning, Midnight*, is arguably Rhys's most classic embodiment of the modern condition that Weil, in *L'enracinement*, calls "the disease of uprootedness" (Weil, *Need for Roots*, 47), and its accompanying loss of identity and self-esteem. In Sasha's case, the trauma of uprootedness is exacerbated by such gender-related experiences as pregnancy loss, abandonment by her husband, and the humiliating reliance on the uncertain sexual patronage of wealthy men for her very survival.

A term of Weil's central to my discussion is "affliction," in French *malheur*, which she uses to describe not so much bereavement or bodily trauma as the psychological response to what she calls "social degradation." Affliction, as Weil puts it, is "an uprooting of life, a more or less attenuated equivalent of death" ("Love of God and Affliction," 440), which responds to "humiliation" through a "violent condition of the whole physical being, which wants to rise up against the outrage but is forced, by impotence or fear, to hold itself in check" (440). Thus, though Weil links affliction to physical trauma (440), and is interested elsewhere in her work in what Elaine Scarry calls "the body in pain," her theory of affliction focuses on the most difficult thing to verbalize about the human response to mental pain felt by the individual powerless to contest injustice: the resemblance between such anguish and an all-engrossing physical shock. According to Weil, the trauma of injustice "deprives its victims of their personality, and turns them into things" (445), a negation of the self which she, as a Marxist, saw emblematized by the condition of the worker under industrial capitalism. In her essay "Factory Work," based on her own experience working in the 1930s as an unskilled female laborer in French auto plants, Weil describes how the worker becomes a "thing" or reified commodity, a dehumanization which he or she cannot protest:

> [The worker] is an alien given admittance only in his capacity as intermediary be-
> tween machines and the things to be machined, all this eats into body and soul . . .
> It is as if someone were repeating in his ear at every passing moment and with all
> possibility of reply excluded: "Here, you are nothing. You simply do not count. You
> are here to obey, to accept, to keep your mouth shut." (56)

The workers' response to these negative messages explains why, as Weil noted following her own degrading factory experience, the oppressed do not rebel but instead submit to domination; as she says elsewhere, "In anyone who has suffered affliction for
a long enough time there is a complicity with regard to his own affliction" ("Love of
God and Affliction," 443). Treated as things rather than as human beings, the workers
come to agree they are nothing, and so silence themselves; as Weil's powerful images
of orality suggest, depriving themselves of voice—keeping their mouths shut—means
that they are consumed by self-hatred as their suppressed anger *eats into* their own
bodies and souls.

Thus two types of "censorship silences," to use Tillie Olsen's term (9), are the consequence of affliction: silence imposed by the powerful on the powerless, through fear
and coercion, but, even more importantly, silence that the powerless in turn impose on
themselves, and which robs them of both personhood and the voice that signifies its
presence. As Weil says:

> Affliction is by its nature inarticulate. The afflicted silently beseech to be given the
> words to express themselves . . . the afflicted are not listened to. They are like some-
> one whose tongue has been cut out and who occasionally forgets the fact. When they
> move their lips no ear perceives any sound. ("Human Personality," 327, 332)

In her embodiment of affliction, Sasha Jansen of *Good Morning, Midnight* recalls
Weil's factory workers, while also demonstrating how sexual objectification makes
women particularly prone to humiliation in a capitalist culture. Listing degrading jobs
she has held, for instance, Sasha recalls her brief stint working as a vendeuse in a Paris
dress shop, a position for which she had been hired only because her boss thought her
sexually available; this context makes her bitterly aware how the shop's plastic manne-

quins—"those damned dolls" (Rhys, 18)—are images of women's sexual commodification and loss of voice as speaking subjects:

> I would feel as if I were drugged, sitting there, watching those damned dolls, thinking what a success they would have made of their lives if they had been women. Satin skin, silk hair, velvet eyes, sawdust heart—all complete. (18)

It is no coincidence that before taking this job Sasha herself had worked "as a mannequin" (20), an employee who modeled clothes for customers. What keeps Sasha from being a "complete" mannequin like the "damned dolls," however, is her capacity to feel the pain of rejection, injustice, and traumatic memory—types of pain she tries to numb by becoming, as she says at the beginning of the novel, "a bit of an automaton" (10). Already inanimate, the "damned dolls" cannot feel the pain of being objectified—the fate Sasha experiences both as a kept woman and as an underpaid female worker.

The pain of affliction, then, is the pain of a human being treated as if he or she were inhuman, a pain we see Sasha experience in the exceptionally harrowing episode in which she loses her job at the dress shop. Ironically, she is fired by the visiting boss of the London firm—whom she calls "Mr. Blank"—for not knowing French well enough when in fact she, a fluent speaker, cannot understand the word he himself mispronounces. Called "half-witted" by the boss (27), Sasha is robbed of language like the afflicted who, as Weil says, lack "words with which to express" themselves; indeed, she can only echo Mr. Blank's demeaning assessment, responding to the taunt "[y]ou're a hopeless, helpless little fool, aren't you?" by murmuring "yes, yes, yes" and bursting into tears (28). In this sense, then, Sasha sees herself through the contempt with which Mr. Blank sees her, a distorted perspective typical of women in Rhys's novels, who constantly describe themselves as objects not just of cruelty but of derision. As Sasha says bitterly of her alcoholic free fall at the beginning of the novel, "when you sink you sink to the accompaniment of loud laughter" (10). This image of the self as a grotesque buffoon, somehow deserving of scorn, is reminiscent of Weil's claim that a distinguishing feature of affliction is that it is "ridiculous" in the eyes of others ("Love of God and Affliction," 445).

Calling herself a "fool" and "stupid" when she is fired, Sasha thus directs against herself the anger she is unable to articulate to the boss but to which, in her reminiscent narrative, she finally gives voice:

> Well, let's argue this out, Mr. Blank. You, who represent Society, have the right to pay me four hundred francs a month. That's my market value, for I am an inefficient member of Society, slow in the uptake, uncertain, slightly damaged in the fray, there's no denying it. So you have the right to pay me four hundred francs a month, to lodge me in a small, dark room, to clothe me shabbily, to harass me with worry and monotony and unsatisfied longings till you get me to the point when I blush at a look, cry at a word . . . Let's say that you have this mystical right to cut my legs off. But the right to ridicule me afterwards because I am a cripple—no, that I think you haven't got. And that's the right you hold most dearly, isn't it? You must be able to

despise the people you exploit. But I wish you a lot of trouble, Mr. Blank, and just to start off with, your damned shop's going bust. Alleluia! Did I say all this? Of course I didn't. I didn't even think it. (Rhys, 29)

This passage is remarkable both for its analysis and its acceptance of self-hatred. Furious at Mr. Blank for making her feel ridiculous—in fact contesting his right to make her feel that way—Sasha nonetheless mocks herself for being unable, at the time, to resist *his* mockery: "Did I say all this? Of course I didn't. I didn't even think it" (29). Powerless to evade shame and self-hatred even though she understands precisely how these emotions silence her, Sasha proves how, as Weil says, "Affliction hardens and discourages because, like a red-hot iron, it stamps the soul to its very depths with the contempt, the disgust, and even the self-hatred and sense of guilt and defilement which crime logically should produce but actually does not" ("Human Personality," 442).

Yet if Weil and Rhys both recognize how affliction destroys the self and, with it, the possibility of human communication and community, they also share a strategy for leveling the hierarchy that separates the afflicted from those who are more privileged. For Weil, the privileged can only be brought to renounce the illusion that they are not "of the same species" as the afflicted ("*Iliad*," 163) through the practice of *attente*, the ability to see from the vantage point of the Other; as she defines it, through *attente* the self "empties itself of all its own contents in order to receive into itself the being it is looking at, just as he is, in all his truth" (51). As she elaborates in her essay "The Love of God and Affliction":

> Those whom Christ recognized as his benefactors are those whose compassion rested upon the knowledge of affliction . . . The benefactor of Christ, when he meets an afflicted man, does not feel any distance between himself and the other. He projects all his own being into him. It follows that the impulse to give him food is as instinctive and immediate as it is for oneself to eat when one is hungry. (459)

Weil thus attempts to heal the trauma of affliction by encouraging the reader of her work to "project" him- or herself into the consciousness of the despised and abjected Other. In her study of the "politics of empathy," Judith Kegan Gardiner ascribes a similar narrative strategy to Rhys. Because of the tradition of female nurturance in domestic ideology, Gardiner argues, empathy has been a trait cultivated more by women than by men; thus, she claims, women writers are more likely than men to seek "empathic attunement" with their readers (166), an empathy that the readers are in turn encouraged to feel in regards to the characters. Using the short fiction as an example, Gardiner argues that Rhys uses empathic attunement to break down the barriers of inclusion and exclusion that structure the world inhabited by her heroines (24), an insight that can be applied to the way *Good Morning, Midnight* positions the reader within Sasha's embittered, self-lacerating consciousness.

Still, while recalling Weil's ideal of *attente*, Rhys's narrative strategy also demonstrates the point about *attente* that Weil constantly makes, and that is how rare it is for a human being to achieve genuine empathy with the afflicted. It is, I think, the very power of the empathic attunement that Rhys fosters between reader and character that can make her such an uncomfortable writer to read, especially in an age where rampant individualism has made us impatient with anyone who isn't an obvious success story. When I taught *Good Morning, Midnight* some years ago, several students confessed that they felt uncomfortable and frustrated reading the novel, resentful at being sucked into a cycle of self-hatred in the company of the sort of protagonist our culture labels a "loser." I find myself feeling this way when I read Rhys, and certainly the critics who have called her heroines masochistic seem to have felt, like myself and my students, the urge to buy Sasha a self-help book. I think what is threatening about the way Rhys situates us in the consciousness of an afflicted mind is the potential threat this poses to our own sense of self. As Weil says in "Human Personality," to "acknowledge the reality of affliction . . . is to experience non-being":

> To listen to someone is to put oneself in his place while he is speaking. To put oneself in the place of someone whose soul is corroded by affliction, or in near danger of it, is to annihilate oneself. It is more difficult than suicide would be for a happy child. (332)

According to Weil, it is a "miracle" that anyone who is not afflicted would admit that he or she could become that way.[5]

One episode in *Good Morning, Midnight,* indeed, dramatizes the difficulty of entering empathically into the worldview of an afflicted being. When Sasha visits a friend, Serge, a Jewish artist, he tells her that one night, while he was living in London, he found a woman weeping in the hall outside his room—a mulatto woman originally from Martinique who had moved to England from Paris with her wealthy white lover. When Serge invites her in for a drink, she tells him that even worse than the scorn directed at her as a fallen woman is the pervasive racial prejudice that makes her yearn for invisibility: "She told me she hadn't been out, except after dark, for two years" (96). Struck by how the "Martiniquaise" seemed not so much a living being as "something that had been turned into stone," Serge tells Sasha that upon hearing her story

> "I had an extraordinary sensation, as if I were looking down into a pit. It was the expression in her eyes . . . I said to her 'Don't let yourself get hysterical, because if you do it's the end.' But it was difficult to speak to her reasonably, because I had all the time the feeling that I was talking to something that was no longer quite human, no longer quite alive." (96)

Sensing that the woman wants him to make love to her because such intimacy is "the only thing that would do her any good," Serge is, however, unable to do so (97). Even though, following this incident, he witnesses other tenants in the building, including a child, being cruel to her, he does not intervene and she does not confide in him again.

Sympathetic as he is to the woman's plight, then, Serge is unable to empathize with her, admitting, when Sasha assumes he was "kind to her," that "I wasn't" (97). Rather than feeling with her, he reasons with her. Still, though telling the Martiniquaise not to become hysterical was a "reasonabl[e]" argument, it was not one the woman could absorb as she was beyond reason, still devastated by the insult she had received that very afternoon from the building's already-bigoted child: "I hate you and I wish you were dead" (97). It is significant that Serge feels he is "looking down into a pit" when he gazes into the woman's eyes; presumably to empathize with her—to enter her tortured consciousness—would mean that he would topple into that pit himself and thus, at least temporarily, lose his own identity. As Weil claimed in the passage I quoted above, to "put oneself in the place of someone whose soul is corroded by affliction" is "to annihilate oneself" (Weil, "Human Personality," 332).

Ironically, as a Jew Serge himself is presumably subject to prejudice which denies his humanity—especially in the period in which this episode occurs, 1937, only a few years before the German occupation of Paris and the Holocaust. Indeed, donning an African-inspired mask he has made in the scene when he tells Sasha about the Martiniquaise, Serge becomes eerily faceless, recalling the subhuman status to which fascists reduced despised populations. Interestingly, however, Serge's mask reminds Sasha not of the afflicted themselves but rather of those who look upon them without empathy: "I know the face very well; I've seen lots like it, complete with legs and body. That's the way they look when they are saying: 'Why don't you drown yourself in the Seine?' That's the way they look when they are saying 'Qu'est-ce qu'elle fout ici, la vieille?'" (92). For Sasha, then, the mask becomes an image not so much for the Other as for the process of Othering—a process in which the oppressed may eventually participate when their humanity is denied; in this sense, the mask figures the stony faces of those who, dehumanized themselves, can no longer acknowledge the humanity of others. Struggling to turn herself into an "automaton" free of traumatic memory, Sasha herself strives to create the illusion of such dehumanization, at one point describing her face as a "tortured and tormented mask" which she can "take off whenever I like and hang it up on a nail" (43). That Sasha's mask is "tortured and tormented," however, is a sign that she has not yet succeeded in becoming an inanimate being like the mannequins whose "sawdust heart[s]" she once envied: as I noted earlier in comparing her with the "damned dolls," Sasha is still too pain-filled to become completely inhuman. And, in not being wholly dehumanized herself, Sasha cannot dehumanize others. She feels not only her own pain but the pain of the afflicted she sees everywhere around her: the old woman with the bald head trying on hats in a store while her daughter hisses she's made a "perfect fool" of herself (22), the pitiful girl Sasha once met in a brothel (who "wasn't beautiful, not a star at all") whom she yearned to embrace: "I wanted to put my arms round her, kiss her eyes and comfort her" (161).

Given the rising tide of fascism, to feel empathy with the afflicted is a political as well as personal choice, a resistance to a society increasingly marked, as Weil says in her essay on *The Iliad*, by the ruthlessness with which it "admire[s] might" and "despise[s] sufferers" (183). We are reminded of the encroaching tide of totalitarianism when, at the beginning of the novel, Sasha dreams about a man with a "hand . . . made of steel" who points to a placard saying "This Way to the Exhibition" (13)—a reference, as Mary Lou Emery points out, to the Paris Exhibition of 1937 and its domination by the pavilions of Nazi Germany and Stalinist Russia. Although Rhys has often been seen as a apolitical writer, Emery argues, by carefully positioning her heroine's story in this historical context Rhys "confronts head-on social violence against women and connects it to the persecution of Jews and other racial minorities" (145). Recalling the scene in which Serge's mask reminds Sasha of faces without empathy, her dream about the man with the steel hand envisions fascist society as a collection of steel-cold, heartless robots. In a world increasingly inhabited by such robots, the Martiniquaise, Serge, Sasha herself—a sexually active, unmarried woman of the type deemed decadent by fascists—are all in danger of annihilation by the inexorable tide of inhuman might.

Faced with the manifold afflictions of this historical moment, Weil responded by losing all hope of redressing them through revolution or political change. So antagonistic did she become to forms of power, and so doubtful that we can ever relate to others so as not to make them Other, that she died aspiring to a state of passive non-being that was, as she saw it, the ultimate expression of *attente*. Influenced by Gnosticism and Eastern philosophies in these efforts to empty the self of the self, Weil finally distrusted every act of human agency, or the assertion of being over matter, as an act of aggression that cannibalized the weak;[6] according to Judith Van Herik, Weil's lifelong anorexia, which culminated in her untimely death by self-starvation, reflected her rejection of an orality and appetite she associated with those who, like the factory owners in "Factory Work," consume the souls they dominate.[7] In closing I would like to argue that at the end of *Good Morning, Midnight* Sasha chooses a strategy for dealing with affliction that is strikingly similar to Weil's.

The conclusion of *Good Morning, Midnight* has puzzled critics because it is both ominous and ambiguous. Relaxing her wariness of human contact, Sasha allows herself to respond to the advances of René, a "gigolo" in search of wealthy women (Sasha is convinced he only introduced himself because she was still wearing the expensive fur coat given her by a former lover). When Sasha—daring to hope that her chances of "love, youth, spring, happiness" have not vanished altogether (177)—invites René into her room, however, the scene quickly turns ugly: trying to rape her, the gigolo sneers that "in Morocco it's much easier. You get four comrades to help you . . . They each take their turn" (182). Persuading him to go by offering him money, Sasha, now curled in fetal position on the bed, weeps in an agony of shame and rejection ("I cry in the way that hurts right down" [184]). Yet, disturbingly, she not only fantasizes about the gigolo's return, but welcomes into her bed as a substitute the *commis voyageur*, or traveling salesman, the cadaverous occupant of a neighboring room who at this juncture appears at her door:

He doesn't say anything. Thank God, he doesn't say anything. I look straight into his eyes and despise another poor devil of a human being for the last time. For the last time . . .

Then I put my arms around him and pull him down onto the bed, saying: "Yes—yes—yes . . ." (190)

Unsurprisingly, given Sasha's reference in these final lines of the novel to "the last time," a number of critics have read her "yes" as consent to her own destruction, a prelude quite possibly to her murder at the hands of a skeletal man who evokes the standard personification of death. Patricia Moran, in fact, notes that the scene stages the traditional tableau of Death and the Maiden (146), an allegory which in art typically depicts a naked woman in the embrace of a fleshless Grim Reaper. Yet, in a discussion particularly relevant to mine because of its focus on empathy, Veronica Marie Gregg sees the ending more positively, as a political gesture in which Sasha chooses to stop looking at human beings as inferiors or Others: "Sasha's final embrace of the man in the dressing gown can be read as her accepting her responsibility to the reviled Other" (157). Gregg argues that Sasha's embrace of the repulsive *commis voyageur*—an act which marks her refusal ever again to despise "another poor devil of a human being"—differentiates her response to Otherness from Serge's when he finds it impossible to be truly "kind" to the Martiniquaise. In this sense, Gregg's reading—which sees Sasha attaining a new level of empathy and capacity for unconditional love—would seem to accord more with the interpretations of those critics who have seen the ending as a rebirth than with those who, like Moran, read it as premonitory of Sasha's death.[8]

I would argue, however, that these two interpretations of the conclusion of *Good Morning, Midnight*—the reading which sees Sasha assenting to death and the reading which sees her attaining a new, more empathic understanding of life—are not incompatible; if we read the novel's ending through the theory of Simone Weil, and against the backdrop of the rise of fascism, we can see how Sasha's "rebirth" is predicated upon her death. We can, indeed, identify Sasha's death as an act of what Weil would call "decreation"—and thus analogous to Weil's own end.

"Decreation"—which Weil defined as "mak[ing] something created pass into the uncreated" ("Decreation," 350)—is that complete abdication of selfhood to which she aspired by the end of her life. Imitating Christ's assent to a sacrificial death, decreation purges the will of its inherent lust for power by replacing it with purely disinterested love. In transforming the "created" into the "uncreated," decreation is, as Thomas Nevin points out in his study of Weil, inevitably a "gospel of death." Yet Nevin also claims that, "[h]owever somber these accents, decreation would seem to be, finally, the most positive of acts. It is a reverse imitation of God's *kenosis,* that divine self-emptying that lets creation be" (290–291).

Like the end of *Good Morning, Midnight*, then, decreation is an act open to differing interpretations. As an abdication of the human will to power, decreation, as Nevin argues in his analysis of Weil's political thought, reflects her principled resistance to the Vichy regime's complicity with fascism.[9] As a negation of the self, however, de-creation's "gospel of death" might also seem to be a gospel of self-hatred. Certainly, it is easy enough to dismiss Weil as neurotic, particularly after reading the "terrible prayer," as her biographer Simone Pétrement calls it (486), that she wrote toward the end of her life—a prayer in which she begs God to make her "like a paralytic—blind, deaf, witless" so as to transform her vital substance into food for the afflicted.[10] Even Nevin, who sees decreation as the "most positive of acts," links the doctrine to the "morbid self-disparagement" (291) which made Weil doubt that God could ever truly love her.

And yet this is precisely the point I wish to make about both Weil and Sasha, that their final choices cannot be understood other than as a response to *both* personal shame and historical trauma. After all, Weil wrote so eloquently about affliction because she knew all about it as a multiply abjected being herself—a female intellectual in a male-dominated academy, a Jew (however ambivalent about her faith) in an anti-Semitic society, and a leftist forced to witness the rise of fascism. Similarly, Sasha's acceptance in her bed of the *commis voyageur*—a man who earlier degraded her by calling her a "sale vache," or dirty cow, and who sees her as a sexually exploitable body—is at once the culmination of the crushing shame she has felt throughout her life *and* a response to a world she envisions, shortly before the *commis* arrives, as nothing but "an enormous machine, made of white steel" (187). And yet in her surrender to the *commis*'s advances Sasha rehumanizes this machine-world; choosing to "despise another poor devil of a human being for the last time," she also makes the significant choice of seeing the despised Other as human. It is telling that Rhys has Sasha "look straight into" the *commis*'s eyes; for Weil, the act of looking is a path to *attente*, enabling the self to truly see the Other "it is looking at, just as he is, in all his truth": "it is indispensable, to know how to look at him in a certain way" ("Reflections on the Right Use of School Studies," 51). After looking "straight" into the *commis*'s eyes, Sasha says, "I put my arms round him," as she pulls him onto the bed—a phrase that echoes the words she used to describe the desire she once felt to "put my arms round" the girl in the brothel. In wishing to embrace the girl, Sasha had dreamed of comforting a soul as afflicted as herself in a pure gesture of *attente*: "I wanted to put my arms round her, kiss her eyes and comfort her—and if that's not love, what is?" (161). The sinister *commis* is not nearly so sympathetic a figure as the girl, but Sasha still acknowledges he is "another poor devil of a human being" (190).

Do I see, then, nothing disturbing about Sasha's embrace of a man who will almost certainly degrade, if he does not actually kill, her? Of course not—any more than I applaud Weil's application of the concept of decreation to her own life. I would not recommend either Sasha's or Weil's extreme, and ultimately self-destructive, solutions for responding to personal affliction and the social abuse of power, a solution which, in Sasha's case, entails a troubling assent to sexual abuse and misogyny. Yet I think that Rhys ends *Good Morning, Midnight* as she does—with her afflicted heroine only achieving empathy through these means—because she, like Weil at the same historical moment, could not see any other way of escaping the colonization of the Other than by abolishing the self (which, after all, one has come to hate anyway). Although Rhys herself did not die, as Weil did, as a result of such pessimism, we could possibly see her long hiatus from publication after *Good Morning, Midnight,* and her descent into the trauma of her own depression and alcoholism, as a self-silencing similar to Weil's. Whatever their own misgivings about history and the self, however, in their compassion for affliction these two women writers offer us a potent antidote to despair. Daring to share the shame of the afflicted—as we are invited to do when we read the work of both Rhys and Weil—we can, however temporarily, break down the barriers which condemn the oppressed to suffer in isolation with their own self-hatred.

Notes

1. Loades articulates her most explicitly feminist critique of Weil's theology in "Christ Also Suffered: Why Certain Forms of Holiness Are Bad for You." She also criticizes Weil in "Eucharistic Sacrifice: Simone Weil's Use of a Liturgical Metaphor" and "Simone Weil—Sacrifice: A Problem for Theology."

2. See Andrea Nye, *Philosophia,* and Mary Anne Dietz, *Between the Human and the Divine.* Michelle Cliff also provides a useful feminist perspective on Weil in "Sister/Outsider."

3. See Suzette Henke, *Shattered Subjects: Trauma and Testimony in Women's Life-Writing,* and Patricia Moran, *Virginia Woolf, Jean Rhys, and the Aesthetics of Trauma.* Henke (xiii–xix) provides a useful overview of scholarship on trauma, as does Moran (3–5).

4. Bouson gives a useful overview of shame studies and feminist contributions to this field in her introduction (2–9). For more on women and shame, see also Bouson's *Quiet As It's Kept: Shame, Trauma, and the Novels of Toni Morrison.*

5. Weil's thoughts on the difficulty of attaining *attente* recalls the title of her contemporary Edith Stein's doctoral dissertation, "The Problem of Empathy." Stein shares much with Weil: both were brilliant philosophers in a period when few women achieved such education and distinction, and both were also Jews attracted to Catholicism. (Unlike Weil, however, Stein actually converted and became a Carmelite nun before she died at Auschwitz; in 1998 she was canonized by the Catholic Church.) Stein's theory of empathy—which invites comparison with Weil's views on this subject—receives a useful overview in Alasdair MacIntyre, *Edith Stein: A Philosophical Prologue, 1913–1922,* 75–88.

6. Michele Murray, "Simone Weil: Last Things," provides an excellent discussion of the philosophical underpinnings of Weil's thought in the last years of her life.

7. See both Van Herik essays in the bibliography—"Looking, Eating, and Waiting in Simone Weil" and "Simone Weil's Religious Imagery"—for an in-depth, and highly insightful, discussion of Weil and eating.

8. Moran usefully discusses the imbrication of death and rebirth in the ending of *Good Morning, Midnight* (115–116, 145–147), pointing out that, in this as in her other novels, Rhys "problematizes the possibility of rebirth or redemption" (147).

9. Nevin's tenth chapter, "Waiting, with Vichy, for God" (260–307) offers a historical context for Weil's later thought.

10. For Ann Loades, this prayer is proof that Weil's theology did her "irreparable harm" ("Eucharistic Sacrifice," 43).

PART 3

NATIONS OF SHAME

12 Coping with National Shame through Chinese Women's Bodies

Glorified or Mortified?

Peiling Zhao

SHAME OCCURS WHEN there is a discrepancy between how we are seen by others and how we want others to see us (Kilborne, "Fields of Shame," 231). As this discrepancy presents as a "global attack on the self" (M. Lewis, *Shame,* 75) and typically evokes feelings of disgrace, failure, and weakness about our body, we tend to hide or reshape our body to dissolve the feelings associated with the embodied shame. A nation, treated as a living soul (Abdel-Nour, 698), also feels shame—disgrace, dishonor, and humiliation—when there is a discrepancy between its imposed international image and its national pride, and consequently it changes the bodies of its subjects to dissolve the national shame, typically through, in a Foucauldian sense, historical and cultural forces, discourse, and disciplinary practices.

Although shame is considered as the "master emotion" (Scheff, *Bloody Revenge,* 54), whose powerful functions have been studied by Silvan Tomkins, Helen Block Lewis, and others, few have acknowledged the shame-pride axis as "a yardstick along which we measure our every activity" (Nathanson, *Shame and Pride,* 86) and recognized pride as the basic, constant, universal, and primary emotion that drives our every activity: a bond that binds individuals with others, a high-power emotional energy that motivates people to action. In the words of William Blake, "shame is pride's cloak": this is a clear argument that pride is both the origin of our shame and the emotional energy we use to cope with shame—to shake off the cloak of shame. Although "pride, like shame, involves more than an evaluation of the self, and is reflected in a manner of interacting with others" (Britt and Heise, 255), pride is more public and moves people to interact with others, as prideful behaviors, unlike the shameful behaviors of hiding, withdrawing, and feeling shrunken, typically demonstrate a "tendency to broadcast one's success to the object world" (Nathanson, "Shame/Pride Axis," 184) and make us feel in our bodies "taller, stronger, bigger, and expansive"(Davitz, 77). Therefore, it is important for us, on the one hand, to further investigate the fundamental role of pride as a universal emotion, as Jessica Tracy has done, and on the other hand not to treat shame and pride as binaries.

In studying national shame, I find it important to stress that it is national pride that binds individuals to the nation and motivates individuals to share national responsibility and undo national shame. In "National Responsibility," Abdel-Nour illustrates the importance of national pride to individuals: national pride "allows modern individuals to be something in the world, to have a certain standing in it" (700). Such a bond is strong especially in a culture of connections, such as the Chinese culture, where an individual's sense of the self is directly and openly related to his or her nation's place in the world and consistently correlated with national shame and glory. In combating a century-long "national humiliation" (Callahan, 199), the twentieth-century Chinese nation and governments have successfully evoked national pride through various national movements, campaigns, revolutions, trainings, disciplines, policies, and discourses that helped mobilize individuals to take on national responsibility and dissolve national shame.

As scholars like Helen Block Lewis, Claire Pajacskowska, Ivan Ward, and J. Brooks Bouson have helped us understand how the Western construction of gender and sexuality has determined that women, women's bodies, and female sexuality are often associated with shame, few have investigated whether women, women's bodies, and female sexuality can also be associated with pride. While the universal link between shame and female sexuality/femininity/body does exist for Chinese women, the particular bodies of Chinese women in twentieth-century China are constructed dissimilarly and establish a different relationship between women's bodies and the emotions of shame and pride. Within a culture that relies more on the deployment of alliance—reproduction of connections through marriage—and less on the deployment of sexuality (in Foucault's terms), a dominant technique in Western cultures, Chinese women's bodies in the twentieth century have been associated with both shame and pride and have become paradoxically centralized as symbols and vehicles of nationalism—both national pride and national shame.

In delineating how Chinese women's bodies have been utilized, disciplined, transformed, and enhanced to cope with national shame and regain national pride, this chapter hopes to demonstrate how both shame and pride could be inscribed on the bodies of women. Specifically, it will examine how the liberated—unbound and public—female bodies were promoted as a source of national pride in the revolutionary era in order to cast off the national shame as the "Sick Man of East Asia"; how women's bodies in the new Chinese state were proudly masculinized to shake off the shamed traditional femininity and to symbolize an egalitarian communist state different from both the feudal and capitalist states; and finally how the award-winning women athletes' bodies in the post-Mao era were rigorously trained and publicly glorified and how the fertile bodies of women were closely monitored to reverse Chinese economic backwardness through the one-child policy. While scholars tend to agree that the content of both shame and pride is the self, which is often looked at and objectified, the examples of the bodies of Chinese women illustrate how the confluence of shame and pride has allowed Chinese females to shuttle between object and subject positions and develop a subjectivity both mortified and glorified through close affiliation with national shame and pride, a subjectivity marking the difference between Chinese feminisms and Western feminisms.

Chinese Women's Bodies as Symbols and Vehicles of National Shame and Pride

Twentieth-century China inherited the traumatic humiliation of the one-hundred-year Opium War (1840–1949) that subjugated China to Western powers as a semi-independent, semi-colonial state, a humiliation that haunts China many decades after it declared independence in 1949. As a result, a feeling of unprecedented shame penetrated pervasively into China's dominant discourse in the twentieth century—literature, politics, media, and education, for example. As David Scott notes in *China and the International System, 1840–1949: Power, Presence, Perceptions in a Century of Humiliation*, the Chinese victimization narrative generated during the "century of humiliation" was still a major theme in a 1994 Youth League poster, which vividly captures humiliations from the Opium War to the Unequal Treaties, from the crushing of the Boxer Rebellion to the Nanjing Massacre (xi).

Although Chinese culture is known by Western scholars as a shame culture with more awareness of and emphasis on shame experiences than Western cultures (Ha, 1114), William Callahan was fascinated by the persistent nationalization of shame and humiliation in the dominant discourse in China, for example, in special publications such as *The Atlas of the Century of Humiliation of Modern China*, in textbooks, songs, museums, and parks (199). The celebration of national humiliations, shame, and insecurities, unique to the Chinese communist and socialist historiography, Callahan argues, is so forcefully deployed as "an integral part of the construction of Chinese nationalism" (200) that the "master narrative of the modern Chinese history is the discourse of the century of national humiliation" (204).

Then the question is, how does the nationalization of humiliation and shame construct nationalism and mobilize individuals to participate in fixing the wrongs that other people have done to the nation? Although it is safe to say that the collectivism in China encourages stronger bonds between individuals and the state, such a statement does not explain the specific ways with which individuals incur national responsibility and are motivated to shoulder responsibility for the things other people have done to the nation. As Abdel-Nour reminds us: "National pride is a sign of a very specific way in which participants in national belonging connect themselves to select actions performed by others" (702); the primary emotion that bonds individuals with a nation is not national shame but national pride, from which individuals derive larger meaning, with which individuals imagine themselves as agents who have brought about national achievements. It is only via national pride that individuals render themselves as responsible for the horrors and shame that other people have brought to the nation (713). In this sense, national pride is both the cause and the effect of individuals' identification with national shame.

What, then, constitutes national pride? National identity is commonly constructed as the negotiation between national pride—national consciousness or the image its citizens have of their country—and a nation's perceived or actual international image in world opinion (Rusciano, 361). When China was subjugated to the Western powers during the Opium War, Chinese national identity was in crisis: Chinese citizens' perception of their own country—their government and state affairs—and their international image as Sick Man of East Asia were extremely negative and generated little national pride that could motivate individuals. When the "New China" was established in 1949, both the international image of China and individuals' perception of the old feudal state were hostile. Where did the national pride come from? As Frank Louis Rusciano further argues, national pride also derives from cultural values such as allegiance to the nation as an ethnic or religious entity or allegiance to the state as a set of institutions and laws (361–366).

Drawing heavily upon allegiance to Chinese cultural values, historical forces and political powers in each stage of the twentieth century were able to generate national pride that mobilized individual citizens to cope with their national shame. While both bodies of men and bodies of women went through tremendous changes in a national effort to change their national status and international image, the bodies of the Chinese women were centralized as the major vehicles for change and symbols of national pride. For example, while the men were mandated to cut off their pigtails because they were seen as a symbol of backwardness, the bound feet of women signified the subjugation of China to Western powers. Women's bodies were later mobilized into public arenas—schools, streets, battlefields—to symbolize a liberated and independent nation; women's bodies were masculinized in the New China to wear men's clothes and do everything men did; women's menstruation was closely monitored to ensure the one-child policy, and female athletes' bodies were rigorously trained for glorious international sports prizes.

In many ways women's bodies were centralized as the symbols of national pride and the vehicles of national shame. Such centralization of women's bodies is not a coincidence but an effect of convergence of cultural, historical, and ideological forces as well as discourses on the body. Along with the different historical, political, and ideological forces as well as national discourses, cultural forces and Chinese dominant discourses on the body are constant techniques that facilitated the inscription of national pride and national shame on Chinese women's bodies. While historical forces and state power participated in inscribing nationalism on the bodies of Chinese women, the inscription is deeply rooted in some constant Chinese cultural elements that have been able to provide a stable channel for the invasion of historical and political power on bodies. Stable elements such as the Chinese emphasis on alliance have constructed gender and sexuality differently and created different gendering of shame and pride.

Foucault's notions about alliance and sexuality are very useful in helping us understand the persistent Chinese cultural emphasis on reproduction in the twentieth century. In *The History of Sexuality*, Foucault defines the deployment of alliance as a "system of marriage, of fixation, and development of kinship ties, of transmission of names and possessions," and the deployment of sexuality as a modern invention imposed upon the deployment of alliance (106). On the one hand, the deployment of alliance is built around a system of rules and focuses on the social body of reproducing the interplay of relations and maintaining rules; on the other hand, the deployment of sexuality focuses on the body, a body that produces and consumes (106–107). As Foucault further explains, the deployment of sexuality is constructed around the deployment of alliance and has become a modern device of power that is effective in creating and controlling modern Western bodies in immensely detailed ways. However, in modern China such a deployment of sexuality has not been effectively built around the deployment of alliance, and the deployment of alliance still remains the dominant technology of controlling the body.

As a result of this cultural emphasis on alliance, Chinese women's role in reproduction—reproduction of relationships, reproduction of children, reproduction of rules and laws—allows women's bodies to be utilized as a primary and useful site for the inscription of nationalism. For example, the traditional cultural notion of reproduction and marriage motivated men and women in the early twentieth century to enhance women's bodies as a way to enhance the body of the Chinese population. As Li Li insightfully points out in her review of the Chinese revolutionary literature in this period, it is through "female bodies as imaginary signifiers" that generations of reform-minded Chinese intellectuals were motivated to pursue social changes (93).

While nationalism has apparently "subsumed the woman question to anti-colonial struggle" (Jianmei Liu, 73), the historical, political, and discursive forces, however, cannot inscribe national shame and pride on the bodies of Chinese women if these women do not act as subjects that internalize or interiorize national shame and pride. Even when Foucault emphasizes that "bodies, both in their materiality and in our conceptions of them, are shaped by historical and cultural forces" (McLaren, 82), as well as by discourse and disciplinary practices, we should not assume that these external factors can produce effects on the body automatically. As the feminist scholar Margaret McLaren summarizes for us, Foucault not only believes that there are three modes of body—inscription, internalization, and interpretation—but he also distinguishes between the useful body and the intelligible body (106–108). While the intelligible body, the body as an object of knowledge interpreted through disciplinary discourses, seems to correspond to the mode of interpretation, the mode of inscription seems to explain how the docile, useful body is produced. The internalization mode seems to me to deal with the overlapping between the useful body and the intelligible body, because in order for the inscription mode and the interpretation mode to produce any real effect on the body, the body must act as a subject and internalize the social and cultural values and disciplinary knowledge about body. Only through the process of internalization can power—historical, cultural, political, ideological, and discursive forces—create an interiority to act on the body. This interiority is subjectivity, which is conditioned by the body and meanwhile embodied by the body. While the bodies of Chinese women in the twentieth century were constantly objectified, the following narratives demonstrate to us how Chinese women more often than not have been in constant shuttle between shame and pride, between object and subject positions, mortifying yet enhancing their subjectivity.

Liberated Women's Bodies as a Symbol of National Independence (1900–1949)

In the late nineteenth and early twentieth centuries, Chinese people realized that while they were oppressed under "three mountains"—feudalism, capitalism, and colonialism—Chinese women were oppressed by a fourth "mountain": patriarchy. In the reformist discourse of both the Nationalist and the Communist parties, the subjugation of Chinese women to Chinese men came to symbolize the subjugation of China in the world of nations. Such subjugation is embodied especially in Chinese women's foot-binding and long hair, and in the exclusion of women's bodies from public spheres such as schools, workplaces, and battlefields. Reformers and revolutionaries felt humiliated especially by foot-binding and argued that their women's bound feet and lack of education "made the female population ignorant and weak and were conditions that must be removed" (Ip, 332). They saw Chinese women's bound feet as the most unbearable trait that rendered China as the "feminine, weak counterpart to the masculine strengths of heroic western nationhood," so the language of gender equality "became central to the way people in China have defined their modernity" (Rofel, 236). The May Fourth Movement in 1919 widely promoted the idea that feudal, victimized woman represents the "backwardness and dependency of China itself and the oppression of women shows the worst failures of China's past"; it proposed "nationalism and the strengthening of the state" as a way to cope with the national shame (Raphals, 2). These historical reasons and political movements have made the bound, weak, and submissive Chinese women's body the symbol of national shame and helped inscribe national shame onto women's bodies. Consequently, it seemed a national mandate that women's bodies must be liberated and enhanced so that China could regain its national pride in the Middle Kingdom as a prosperous and strong country, in its sovereignty as an independent nation, and in its rich and unique culture of several thousand years. To transform women's bodies as symbols of national shame into vehicles and symbols of national pride, various political, social, and cultural forces at that time converged.

The cultural emphasis on women's role in reproduction, the discourse of revolution, and social organizations have mobilized women to cut their hair, free their feet, go to schools, join revolutionary organizations, and establish women's newspapers.

As the deployment of alliance is the main technique used to inscribe values and reproduce relationships in China, as the modern Chinese society evolved from a matriarchal and matrilineal society (Kristeva, *About Chinese Women,* 35), women as mothers have always been at the center of Chinese culture and society. This cultural emphasis on motherhood was removed when Chinese male intellectuals and activists endeavored to reform China's image in the early twentieth century. For example, Liang Qichao promoted education for women because the weak, illiterate, and subjugated Chinese women produced weak, illiterate, and subjugated Chinese; therefore Chinese women's schools mushroomed to cultivate "female national citizens" (*nu guoren*), or "the mothers of national citizens" (*guomin zhimu*) (Jianmei Liu, 71). Through the centralized position of motherhood, the new liberated and educated women became the vehicle through which Chinese intellectuals, such as Jin Tianhe, hoped to rejuvenate their preeminent subjectivity:

> Women are the mothers of the nation. If we want to rejuvenate China, we need to first rejuvenate women; if we want to fortify China, we need to first fortify women; if we want to civilize China, we need to first civilize women; if we want to save China, we need to first save women. (Jianmei Liu, 71–72)

The importance of reconstructing Chinese women to regain national pride was also promoted at that time by female writers and activists such as Lin Zhongsu, who recognized that the "weakness of China under Western invasion was due to the lack of female national citizens," and Xiao Xiaohong, who argued that "the name of the mother of the nation" was bestowed upon Chinese women as a "supreme power and a responsibility for handling the nation-state's matters" (Jianmei Liu, 72).

Meanwhile, the cultural emphasis on marriage and relationships further motivated Chinese men to promote the New Woman image as a signifier of the birth of their new subjectivity and a symbol of their national pride. In "Female Bodies as Imaginary Signifiers in Chinese Revolutionary Literature," Li Li carefully examines the short stories by male revolutionary writers such as Lu Xun, Mao Dun, and Zhang Tianyi and points out that women's bodies are reduced to signs and tropes and function as "the imaginary signifiers with which the male-intellectuals figure their social agendas, as well as their own identity crises in a long and difficult process to emerge as the representative of the new cultural discourse in modern China" (93). Strong, powerful, rebellious, and educated modern women are often presented to write off the deformed feudal women and traditional wives or the selfish, pessimistic, and fragile bourgeois women; only through their severance from the shamed female bodies and their relations—romantic, marital, and symbolic relationships—with the modern women did Chinese intellectuals hope to achieve their collective modern subjectivity.

Such an interdependence of women's liberation and national revolution made it mandatory that women's liberation be at the center of both the nationalist revolution and the communist discourse. The nationalist revolution of 1924–1927 encouraged thousands of young women who yearned for freedom from familial restrictions to throw themselves into the revolutionary camp (Lianfen Yang, 119). Unlike Ibsen's Nora, who left home without social support and had to go back home for shelter and survival, a great mass of young female students in the mid-1920s were called upon by male intellectuals and activists, revolutionary organizations and newspapers, and women's schools and magazines to "throw themselves into the grand and spectacular arena of revolution in Shanghai, Wuhan, and Jiujiang" (120). Since its inception in the 1920s, the Chinese Communist Party had developed its politics to link women's liberation to national liberation: emancipating women could strengthen the nation and help transform the nation from a semi-colonial, semi-feudal past into a modern, powerful nation able to reclaim its rightful place in the world. Motivated by this powerful rhetoric of emancipation, millions of women were mobilized to fight for their rights to their feet, their hair, and the ultimate freedom of their bodies to appear in all spheres of their counterparts. Famous women reformists such as Qiu Jin, Xiang Jinyu, Liu Hulan, Yang Kaihui, and many more are their models in challenging the four mountains of oppression through going to school, writing articles for newspapers and magazines, organizing revolutionary associations and clubs, and joining and mobilizing people for protests, as well as in supporting the national revolution by cooking and sewing, and even in fighting on the frontier during the war. Of course, in this massive mobilization, such freedom for their bodies was not won without the breaking up of relationships or shedding of blood or even the sacrificing of their lives.

While all the discourses were demonizing traditional women as symbols of national shame and valorizing liberated women's bodies as vehicles for national pride, the interdependency between women and state has never been at equilibrium. On the one hand, without national liberation Chinese women's oppression would be continually ignored by the state; without women's liberation, the national revolution is incomplete and has no significant marker to distinguish the new state from the old one. On the other hand, some scholars notice that even though women's bodies were at the center, male intellectuals presented female characters simply as "symbols and tropes, paying little attention to women's true bodily dynamics, desires, and pleasures"; such representations, for example, those of Xianglin's wife in the influential fiction of Lu Xun, "were inherently 'castrated' at the hands of their male creators" (Li Li, 94).

While it is important to urge that women have more agency in the revolutionary cause, it is equally important that women's subjectivity be positioned not as binary to men's subjectivity or to nationalism. Without internalizing the revolutionary message, the bodies of women could not be mobilized to change, to participate in the revolution. The development and growth of women's subjectivity took place at the same time when nationalism, revolutionary discourses, and the communist ideology were exercising their power on the bodies of Chinese women. For example, as Jianmei Liu notices, the discourse of revolution at that time allowed female writers access to the real rather than the representative or symbolic power because more than "fifty kinds of women's newspapers and magazines emerged between 1889 and 1918," which not only "participate[d] in the national affairs but also paid special attention to women's education, including topics such as family politics, biology, medicine, science, and art design" (78). Such an example suggests that women's interests in developing themselves and representing their voices were furthered while they were serving the national interests. Such an interlocking, dialogic, and mutually beneficial relationship continued into Mao's time, when women's bodies were further shaped by the new historical and ideological discourses.

Masculinized Women's Bodies as a Symbol of New (Communist) China (1949–1976)

The republican era in the first half of the twentieth century realized and explored the importance of coping with national shame by transforming women's bodies. The Chinese state during Mao's regime completed the transformation and created a classless, genderless, selfless, capable, powerful, and strong communist female image as national pride to signify the superiority of a communist state over capitalist states. Mao's declaration that Chinese women "hold up half the sky" started Chinese women's new life after liberation and fulfilled most of the promises made during the revolutionary years. To ensure the socialist notion of gender equality, the state has further provided rhetorical, legal, and social support to women, allowing women remarkably improved access to politics, work, sports, and education.

In Mao's time (approximately from 1949 to 1976), the state's emphasis on women's equality with men in politics, in education, and in the workforce (in the example of an Iron Girl model) have rhetorically erased gender discrimination and successfully mobilized women, both rural and urban, into the workforce, helping create a relative gender equality that is highly contingent on the massive support of the all-mighty state. To reinforce this women-holding-up-half-the-sky rhetoric, the national discourse, through popular songs and operas, propaganda, and community study groups, facilitated in mobilizing Chinese women to work at factories and fields, join in the armies, wear the same clothes as men did, and behave in the same manners as men. For example, the women warriors in the model operas (*yangbanxi*), such as Tie Mei, Xi'er, Changbo, Ke Xiang, Wu Qinhua, Jian Shuiying, and Fang Haizhen, were created and popularized as communist women models, who are not only different from their historical predecessors such as Mulan and Mu Guiying but also variably "pushed at the boundaries that restricted the role of the woman warrior in the traditional culture" (R. Roberts, 142).

Though the terms "male" and "female" were still used, the state discourse created a term, *funu,* to refer to women's social gender, hiding women's biological sex in the closet; the state also discouraged any discourse that showed women's biological difference from men, because women's biological difference would be taken as women's weakness and would hinder women's liberation. The term *funu,* compared to the traditional term *nuren* or the Western concept of woman, was created with the communist belief that the bodies of men and the bodies of women are the same; thus, the term *funu* helped establish a different female image as the national pride of the communist China.

Under the influence of dominant communist discourses as such, there emerged a unisex dress code: short hair, olive-green army clothes, blue or gray clothes like men's; anything that showed women's sex, from long hair to high heels to revealing blouses, was banned as bourgeois (*zichan jieji*) (L. Yang, 41). The defeminization and desexualization by the state was visible everywhere from magazines such as *Chinese Women* to such state-funded model operas as *Red Detachment of Women* (*hongse niangzijun*) and *White-Haired Woman* (*baimao nu*). Their unisex dress code struck a group of Western intellectuals, Simone de Beauvoir, Julia Kristeva, Alberto Moravia, and Nancy Milton, who visited China in the 1970s, as unfeminine or androgynous, simple or ugly, and "came to symbolize China" (Finnane, 100). In the article "What Should Chinese Women Wear? A National Problem," Antonia Finnane argues that "woman, in whatever clothes, has always been a relatively subdued presence among the symbols of nationalism" (101). For example, the traditional Chinese fashion *qipao,* known in Cantonese as *cheongsam,* was prohibited, as the communist discourse tended to associate it with feudal women or prostitutes or corrupted women (105). As a matter of fact, any attention to feminine beauty in the pre-1966 era was mainly criticized as petit bourgeois or bourgeois and as an unwelcome outcome of gender oppression (Ip, 330).

Communist women participated in every aspect of the workforce, not just to produce food and steel for the nation but also to produce a working woman image different from the traditional housewife or the "parasite" bourgeois woman. As Lisa Rofel points out, participation in "work" symbolizes Chinese women's emancipation from their traditional bondage and enslavement to domestic chores (237). The Iron Girls, twenty-three teenage schoolgirls who wanted to do as well as the "Man of Iron" (a national model worker named Wang Jinxi), in 1963 "formed a shock troop" and planted under very difficult situations "new saplings one by one on the tens of acres of fields" (Kristeva, "On the Women of China," 70). These girls later inspired 5,200 Iron Girls to imitate their physical endurance and perseverance. As Susan Perry argues, "Chinese women's labor power was needed to contribute to rural farming and urban industrialization," as a return "for their work outside the home, women were to be rewarded with considerably improved access to education and political life" (282).

As Yang Mayfair Mei-Hui and many other scholars notice, both in the Chinese constitution (1954) and the marriage law (1950), women's equal rights in the political, economic, cultural, educational, social, and familial realms are explicitly upheld; the state promised women a status that was even higher than in the West. The marriage law did away with polygamy, arranged marriages, child-adoption marriage, prostitution, the buying and selling of women, and other overt abuses from the past against women, and guaranteed women's right to paid maternity leave and equal pay (M. Yang, 37). Women's equal rights are further enforced through the Women's Federation, a state bureaucracy at the national level which plays a double role. It serves as a mouthpiece for the state and disseminates party policies to its constituency, the entirety of China's female population, from its headquarters in Beijing (*Quanguo fulian*). It also represents women in policy decisions and programs at all levels of administration (*fulian*): provincial Women's Federations (*sheng fulian*), to local Women's Federations (*difang fulian* and *funuhui*). The work of the Women's Federation is mostly carried out by women: it "mediates family conflicts and divorce procedures, sees to women's health and birth needs, rewards model families, intervenes to protect women in case of unfair work demands by work units, inheritance disputes, domestic violence" (38).

Historically, it also played an important role in implementing the government's population policy, which aimed to help women further their liberation from domestic work burdens and reproduction burdens so that they could get an education and go out to work. In the revolutionary decades of the 1950s, 1960s, and 1970s, the state's population policy both improved the health of mothers and children and liberated women to participate in education and work, thereby lifting their social status and enhancing their contribution to socialist development (Greenhalgh, 890).

As Yang and others argue, the Chinese state feminism in this period has collapsed the "boundary between public and domestic spheres, brought women out into the world of work, and socialized reproduction"; it also "diminished patriarchal family power to a certain extent through replacing family units with collective units as the basic unit of production and accounting" (M. Yang, 38). In a large sense, however, women's entrance into the world of men has not brought about the full equality predicted by Engels. Women's relative equality was achieved at the cost of the erasure of "gender and sexuality (*xingbie muosha*) in the public sphere" (41).

The Controlled Women's Bodies as the Key to China's Economic Modernization (1979–)

In the late 1970s when the Chinese government decided to reform and open to the outside world, it was stunned and shamed again when it realized that its economy had been one hundred years behind developed countries, such as the United States. The state declared such economic backwardness an urgent national crisis, identified excessive population growth as the cause of the crisis, and decided that the most effective solution to that crisis was to control its population growth. The one-child policy adopted by the Chinese government in 1979 mainly targeted urban people (25 percent of the national population), and the government allowed rural people to have two children, even granting local administrations some flexibility to bend the national population policy to their local needs. Strict birth planning was designated a "base state policy" (*jiben guoce*) in 1982, making it a top priority of the state. Although the number of two-child exceptions to the one-child rule was expanded in the mid-1980s, the policy continued to limit virtually all couples of the Han Chinese ethnic majority (91 percent of the population) to one or at most two children. It also allowed ethnic minority or parents having a disabled child to have two children. Overall, the government encourages single-child families.

Once again, women's liberation and women's bodies are closely tied to this national development strategy. On the one hand, the state announced that birth planning would rescue the whole nation from lagging behind in the world, sacrificing one generation's freedom to choose family size for the benefit of the whole nation and of the coming generations. Women's reproductive rights were thus "naturally" subordinated to the interests of the nation-state, turning women's bodies into "mere object[s] of state contraceptive control, vehicles for the achievement of urgent demographic targets" (Greenhalgh, 851). On the other hand, the state promoted the rhetoric that birth planning would improve women's health and further their liberation: birth planning could reduce the burden of reproduction on women, enhance their health, allow them more opportunities to participate more fully in education and social production, and ensure them more time for leisure and self-development. In responding to Greenhalgh's interview on the one-child policy, Chinese feminist Li Xiaojiang argued that the state's sharp restrictions on fertility have brought about a huge liberation for Chinese women. To understand this emancipatory effect, one needs to jettison the "Western myth" that if the government did not control women's childbearing, women themselves would have ownership rights to their bodies and reproductivity. In fact, as she pointed out, those rights would belong to their husbands' families (X. Li, 365). Before the state intervened in reproduction, women were subjected to intense demands from their communities, families, and husbands to have many children and many sons. Women with professional ambitions were not able to fulfill their career desires because they had no choice but to bear and raise children, tasks that ate up the best years of their lives. When a woman has only one child, she continued, not only does she have more time for work and study but conflicts with her husband (presumably over childcare and housework) are generally reduced. The government's promotion of the one-child family has given women a way to talk back to their husbands, limit their fertility, and develop their intellectual potential (Greenhalgh, 859).

Undoubtedly, Greenhalgh is right when she points out that Li Xiaojiang, a prominent Chinese feminist, is speaking on behalf of a "select group of relatively privileged Chinese women," the educated urban women (859). Nonetheless, while women's bodies were controlled and monitored, the policy has greatly reduced rural women's reproductive burden, facilitated their personal development, enabled them to acquire skills and education, and allowed them to devote themselves to work and income acquisition as never before; consequently, it has enhanced both their social and economic status and their personal autonomy and self-respect.

Strong Women's Bodies as Symbols for a Strong Nation: Training Women for China

The persistent female dominance in China's sports field has perplexed Westerners in the last four decades no less than the foot-binding practice did in earlier decades. On the one hand, we can see that the image of vigorous and victorious bodies of Chinese women athletes not only totally reverses the confined image of foot-bound Chinese women, but it also stands in ironic contrast with the male dominance in Western sports arenas, consequently defining a modern, socialist Chinese womanhood that is different from both feudal womanhood and capitalist womanhood. Chinese women athletes have many times embarrassed their male counterparts with their many world titles and broken records in numerous fields, including middle- and long-distance running, swimming, diving, weightlifting, chess, volleyball, basketball, shooting, archery, wrestling, rowing, badminton, gymnastics, softball, soccer, and table tennis. On the other hand, while the bodies of Chinese women athletes are enthusiastically watched by billions of transnational Chinese people, while their rigorously trained bodies are rewarded by the state with political positions, while their successful bodies are cheered as national heroes and imitated as exemplars, their bodies no longer belong to the women themselves; instead, their bodies belong to the nation, the state, and the public. Reviewing the history of the twentieth century in China, we cannot fail to see that Chinese women's journey from foot-binding to rigorous physical training for the state has shown how dominant discourse has created historical conditions, inscribed cultural values, and exerted sociopolitical forces on women's bodies and on Chinese perceptions about Chinese women's bodies, and how Chinese women's bodies have changed along with cultural values, historical conditions, and national interests.

Western sports from their beginning have been firmly tied to the rise of modern nationalism in China. In *Training the Body for China,* Susan Brownell clearly points out that this link should be viewed historically as well as internationally:

> The development of physical education in Europe was inseparable from the rise of modern nationalism after the French Revolution. Physical education as a way of linking individual bodies to the welfare of the nation is a historically recent phenomenon and must be viewed as one of the disciplinary techniques that developed with the rise of the nation-state. (46)

Sports, imported into China from the West in the late nineteenth and early twentieth centuries, have been utilized as a technique to promote nationalism.

From pioneering modern reformers to socialist leaders, physical education of the body has been tightly linked with moral education and intellectual education, and ultimately with the welfare of the nation. Greatly influenced by Western thoughts on nationalism and meanwhile deeply upset by China's humiliating image as the "Sick Man of East Asia" in front of Westerners, a number of early modern reformers such as Yan Fu, Liang Qichao, and Kang Youwei enthusiastically advocated for training strong and healthy Chinese bodies, especially the bodies of Chinese women, for the health of future Chinese bodies. They strongly believed that strong women were the promise of a strong nation. Under these historical forces, Chinese women were liberated from foot-binding. Meanwhile, the liberation of women's feet has symbolically brought the first dawn of Chinese modernity. From the very beginning of Chinese modern history, the strengthening and liberation of women's bodies has been tied to modernity and nationalism.

In the republican period from 1912 to 1948, the Chinese Communist Party used sports as a technique to recruit young people for the revolutionary cause and to build a strong revolutionary nation-state. The presence and participation of women at national games holds the same revolutionary and symbolic meaning as their active participation in the Long March. While participation in national games as well as in politics and the military has dramatized the immense emancipation of women's bodies, one can never fail to notice that the emancipation of women's bodies is one of the many elements of nationalism that the budding nation-state tries to build, for its way of treating women's bodies is one of the significant dividing lines that distinguish the revolutionary body from the Qing body and from the Western body.

Mao's oathlike slogan, "Develop physical culture and sports, strengthen the people's physiques," repeated by billions of Chinese who exercised their bodies every day, unmistakably expresses the link between the bodies of the people and the welfare of the nation, but in a different way. The historical task that Mao's state faced was to erase differences—class difference, urban and rural difference, social difference, economic difference, and gender difference—so that the newly born socialist nation would be essentially different from a feudal nation and a capitalist nation. Again, women's bodies became the site where the signs of a new nation could be inscribed. In order to promote gender equality, Mao's China promoted an image of women's bodies that was the same as that of men's bodies. To erase class difference, which was believed to be the source of evil both in feudal society and in capitalist society, the state allowed all women equal access to sports training and physical education. To ensure that Chinese women's bodies would be different from the prone-to-faint bourgeois female bodies, from the feudal upper-class female bodies that are portrayed as parasites dependent on men, Chinese women were asked to exercise their bodies and to do the same jobs as men did in such physical fields of labor as farming and factory work.

The inscription of historical forces on Chinese women's bodies came to its apex in the last four decades as the newly open-to-the-outside China became ready to meet any challenge in order to transform the nation from a weak and poor nation to a strong and powerful nation, from a closed society to an open society. Under the influence of the Olympic Games and other international games, the post-Mao China continues its promotion of mass physical education and trains top athletes to win glory for the nation. Women from all over the country are recruited to compete for the nation. The ties between women's bodies and nationalism are strongest at these important international games, which are watched by the majority of the Chinese population, regardless of sex, class, age, ethnicity, or profession. Brownell has made very interesting observations on this spectacle in "Strong Women and Impotent Men: Sports, Gender, and Nationalism in Chinese Public Culture." She writes that even though she trained with Chinese women athletes, she was still overwhelmed by the magnitude of the viewing audience for the 1981 World Cup in women's volleyball, by the dramatic scene of millions and billions of Chinese people converging around television sets in public spaces like courtyards and alleys in spite of the November cold, by their spontaneous outpouring of emotions, by their festive celebrations for the victories of the Chinese women's volleyball team, and mostly by their worshipping of Chinese women volleyball players as national heroes (210).

The body image promoted by these sports, as well as by the widespread media coverage devoted to them and the athletes, is a new image of the Chinese female body: a body that is strong and healthy, a body that has the same physical prowess as a male body (if not more), a body that is different from the feudal body, a body that is different from the Western body, and ultimately a new image of the nation that is strong, that is ready to meet any challenge and competition, that treats its women as equal to if not better than its men. These images are promoted through many state-sponsored ceremonies and rituals as the right way for every Chinese to train his or her body. Stories of the numerous bitternesses that these women athletes have "eaten" (*chiku*) during their training have been repeatedly told and popularized as life texts for cultivating moral as well as patriotic sentiment. Tons of letters have been sent to women athletes who have won glories for the nation. Even the spirit of the Chinese women's volleyball team has been inscribed into the core of China's national movement of "spiritual civilization," which intends to transform Chinese people's spirit through a balanced combination of physical education, moral education, ethical education, intellectual education, and aesthetic education.

On one hand, the success of Chinese women athletes is the result of the unquestionably strong support of the state; on the other, it is used by the state to strengthen unity and nationalism. The nationalism that these women's bodies demonstrate has multiple implications. First, it represents a strong, powerful, and proud nation to the world; second, it represents to the world a strong socialist ideology that liberates women and promotes equality between men and women. In addition, the state has rewarded successful women athletes by according them seats in the National People's Congress, the People's Political Consultative Conference, and other political organizations. In this sense, Chinese women athletes' bodies are also representing the mass to the state and the state to the mass, serving as an indispensable link between individual bodies and the body of the state. Essentially, the bodies of Chinese women have become a site for historical, cultural, political, national, and international forces, and these forces in turn have constructed a new or modern body that is historically, culturally, and ideologically different from other bodies.

Along with historical, political, and ideological forces as well as national discourses, cultural forces and Chinese dominant discourses on the body facilitated the inscription of national shame on Chinese women's bodies. Historical forces and state power have been inscribing their agenda on the bodies of Chinese women, but this inscription has not happened in a vacuum: it is deeply rooted in Chinese culture. It is through the inscription of cultural values that the inscription of nationalism on the bodies of Chinese women has been so successful because these cultural values are constant and are able to provide a stable channel for historical and political power to work on bodies. Two important elements in Chinese culture have aided the inscription of nationalism: reproduction and relationships that are emphasized through deployment of alliance. While training with some successful Chinese women athletes in Beijing, Brownell, like many other Westerners, was shocked by the total lack of sexuality in Chinese women's training. In contrast to the popular display of and concern about sexuality in American women athletes, Chinese women athletes are required to live in training camps, separated from their boyfriends or husbands; they are forbidden to wear long hair, makeup, and sexy clothes within the training camps, for the coaches as well as other Chinese people believe the display of sexuality would distract the athletes' attention from training. After the long deemphasis of sexuality, and especially after the radical blurring of masculinity and femininity in Mao's China, the male coaches and the women athletes themselves have come to believe that sexuality is the least important thing in their training. The emphasis on alliance and deemphasis on sexuality is also evident both in women athletes' refusal to train during their menstruation and in their delaying marriage until their competitive careers are over. Like most young Chinese women, athletes in training would refuse to practice when they were menstruating, for fear that hard physical exercise at this time would harm their reproductive ability. This shocked Brownell as much as her teammates' obsessive concern with marriage. As she observed, instead of prioritizing sexuality in choosing a mate, the majority of women athletes think social status is the primary criterion. Instead of being at a disadvantage as Brownell expected, most of the women athletes have married men of higher status.

The cultural emphasis on relationships has supplied more support and energy for the deployment of alliance to survive in modern China, and this emphasis on alliance has in turn affected the techniques on the modern body of the Chinese women and on the construction of gender identity around their bodies. In the case of Chinese women athletes, the emphasis on alliance, rather than sexuality, has helped Westerners understand the "Chinese first, women second" nationalism expressed in women athletes' training and competition, and the national celebration of their victories. "Chinese first, women second" expresses both China's prioritizing of a social body over an individual body and a cultural emphasis on social identity, rather than gender identity. In the overriding state priorities and among the public, in the patriotic zeal and social integration, produced by the victories of Chinese women swimmers, runners, volleyball players, and others, their Chinese identity is seen as more important than their gender identity. As James Riordan observes, any polarization of males versus females is therefore overwhelmed by feelings of "China versus the world": . . . "this is a phenomenon starkly at variance with the historical 'male versus female' dichotomy common in Western sporting nations" (95).

From a cultural point of view, the subordination of gender identity to national identity is rooted in the Chinese conception of the person as holistic or relational, as opposed to the Western conception of individualism. As many scholars agree, a Chinese person's identity is the totality of his or her social roles, and the gender role is only one of the many social roles that a Chinese woman might have.

The historical, political, and cultural inscriptions on the body have also been affected by disciplinary discourse on the intelligible body. For Foucault, disciplinary discourse interprets how the body functions, and this knowledge validates cultural, historical, and political forces' inscription on the body. Though modern sports are a Western thing, they produce a female dominance in China but preserve male dominance in the West. In addition to the cultural, historical, and political differences between China and the West, dominant disciplinary discourse is another important cause of the sharp contrast. On the one hand, Chinese dominant disciplinary discourse in the twentieth century, especially in the second half of the century, believes that women have the same physical prowess as men, and they are able to do any job that men do. In particular, the scientific discourse in the last four decades argues that the only physical differences between men and women are women's menstruation and pregnancy, but women have better physical prowess when they have their menstruation and pregnancy. In the West, on the other hand, sports are traditionally geared toward males, and the dominant discourse still believes that there is a biological difference between males and females.

During her training with other women athletes in Beijing, Brownell was surprised more than once by the Chinese, especially the Chinese male coaches' unbiased notion about the female athletes' physical prowess. As Brownell recalls in *Training the Body for China*, the Chinese coaches did not think like Westerners that sports is a primarily male preserve, and that sports mean masculinity. Drawing on her historical knowledge as well as her personal experience in sports training in America, Brownell agrees that Western modern sports are a major vehicle for defining and reinforcing gender differences, at least among the middle and upper classes, and a vehicle for constructing masculinity (222).

Chinese Women's Subjectivity: Glorified or Mortified?

While Chinese women's bodies in the twentieth century have served as an interesting central site, symbol, and vehicle for national pride, and while women's interests have always submitted to the national interests, Chinese women's subjectivity has undoubtedly been improved and enhanced, and has complicated Chinese modernism and nationalism. Chinese women's equality, following a path different from Western women's movements, was achieved not only through promotion from the state but also with "blood and sweat" of both men and women (M. Yang, 56).

That the bodies of Chinese women have been conditioned and constructed by so many forces does not lead to the conclusion that bodies are only passive receptacles. As McLaren summarizes for Michel Foucault, the body is not only the site of inscription but also the site of resistance: without an active subject, it is impossible for cultural, historical, and political forces to exert power on the body; without an active subject; it is also impossible for the body to internalize the values inscribed. Even though Chinese women's bodies have been transformed by the massive combination of multiple forces, Chinese women have achieved their agency and increased their subjectivity by internalizing values that lead to the liberation of their bodies. In a culture of relationships and connections, it is only through symbolizing national pride that women assume agency. Linking the bodies of women with national shame and national pride has not totally consumed women's subjectivity; as Lydia Liu points out in "Female Body and Nationalist Discourse," "it has opened up the possibility for women to assume historical agency and challenged the very authority of discourse" (44).

It is not a coincidence that the liberation of women's bodies is conflated with national shame and pride and establishes an interdependent relationship between women's bodies and the emotions of shame and pride. What it means to Chinese feminists is that even though Chinese women's interests still need to serve the interests of the state, to be tied even more firmly to nationalism, the liberated bodies of Chinese women symbolize their liberated subjectivity. To Western feminists and scholars of emotions, it is important to note how the specific conditions and construction of women's bodies in different cultures may help construct different links between women's bodies and emotions.

13 Shamed Bodies

Partition Violence and Women

Namrata Mitra

S PEAKING TO ETHNOGRAPHIC researchers about fifty years after the partition of British India in 1947, Durga Rani says that during partition violence several Hindu families in the villages of Head Junu had anticipated attacks against their kinswomen by Muslim men. Accordingly, they took a series of measures: many killed their daughters by burying them alive while others encouraged them to electrocute themselves. Soon after, the villages were attacked and many young girls were abducted, gang-raped, and then abandoned. When these girls tried to return home, they found that their families rejected them; some parents encouraged their daughters to kill themselves, while others mourned "their fate" (Menon and Bhasin, 33). Durga Rani's testimonial reveals how women were not only vulnerable to men of other communities but also to men and women of their own families and community. During partition, sexual violence against women of "other" communities (aimed to humiliate them), and preemptive attacks against one's kinswomen (to safeguard family and community honor) became one of the predominant forms of violence. The ideal of honor conflated with the ideal of one's kinswomen's sexual purity was clearly valued more highly than the lives of women (and men) themselves.

Veena Das, Sangeeta Ray, and Jill Didur have shown how the nationalistic investment in the images and conduct of upper-class Hindu and Muslim women framed the ways in which violence against women was represented in partition literature. Drawing on the implications of those arguments, this chapter explores how literary representations of widespread sexual violence and bodily mutilation of women during partition are frequently constructed through concepts of honor, shame, and national identity. In novels such as Khushwant Singh's *Train to Pakistan* and short story collections such as *An Epic Unwritten* by Muhammad Umar Menon, which are set during partition, the perpetrators of violence frequently justify their actions in terms of "honor" and "shame." Therefore, the aim of this chapter is to address the following questions: First, what is the relation between the rape/mutilation of women's bodies and the "shame" brought to the family, community, and nation? Second, to what extent has it been possible for survivors of sexual violence to resist the "shame" as the necessary consequence of their assault? Finally, in what ways do post-partition narratives of justice or reconciliation efforts reiterate or trouble this particular gender-based concept of shame?

The first section of this chapter sets up a dialogue among contemporary theories on shame and its purported role in regulating individual behavior and social values. The second section is a close reading of Bapsi Sidhwa's *Ice-Candy-Man* (Indian edition), renamed *Cracking India* (U.S. edition), which aims to analyze the link between a perpetrator's attempts to humiliate someone and the shame experienced by the survivor. In this context it is necessary to explore the extent to which a survivor of public humiliation is able to resist the instruments of her public shaming. The third section is a dialogue between two Western feminist proposals on how to end practices in which unprivileged identity groups are routinely shamed by privileged identity groups, which are then examined in the context of violence in South Asia.

Making a Distinction between Shame and Humiliation

Nearly all the contemporary approaches to the study of shame by political philosophers, cultural theorists, and psychologists make a distinction between the experience of shame in infancy (when one's parents define one's social sphere and institute taboos), and the experience of shame in adulthood, which is shaped by social institutions and norms. I will be focusing on the latter. Moreover, since social norms themselves are subject to change, the types of actions, claims, and identities that are considered to trigger shameful responses also change depending on their historical and cultural contexts.

What triggers the feeling of shame? Moreover, what does that reveal about the individual and her social and political context? "If we feel shame, it is because we have failed to approximate 'an ideal' that has been given to us through the practices of love" (Ahmed, *Cultural Politics*, 106). Such ideals are partly shaped collectively, such as when members of a nation share ideals of either plurality or exclusivity of national membership on grounds of race or religious identity. Since one comes to share certain ideals, if one does something contrary to those ideals then one feels shame. In one's shame, one is confirming both those ideals and one's failure to uphold them. Some who take psychological approaches to the emotion of shame, such as Donald Nathanson and Carl Schneider, have argued in favor of giving shame a high social value. According to them, we are living in a society that is rapidly losing its sense of shame, and this loss is not good for two reasons: first, shame is an important emotion that provokes us to reflect upon our moral transgressions, and second, our sense of shame is linked to our need for privacy, which is necessary for our emotional maturity.

The study of the mechanism of shame becomes far more complicated when we read about individual experiences in the context of structural social inequalities. Jennifer Manion illustrates the blind spots in micro-level analyses of the experience of shame, which do not seek to include how social structures shape the formation of individual ideals. Manion complicates Gabriele Taylor's distinction between genuine shame and false shame by illustrating how social ideals are gendered. According to Taylor, in genuine shame one feels shame for betraying a set of standards one has set for oneself (Manion, 176). Meanwhile, false shame refers to feeling shame for violating a principle upheld by others but not by oneself (176). Manion analyzes Taylor's framework through an interview in which Carrie, a woman in her thirties and a mother of three, leaves her job as a lawyer to become a full-time mother; however, she continues to feel shame in not fulfilling the ideal of the "Perfect Mother and Good Wife" (Orenstein, qtd. in Manion, 29). Since Taylor's formulation of genuine shame constitutes falling short of one's own values, and false shame constitutes falling short of the values of another which one does not share, then in this case Carrie's shame is indeed genuine. In distinguishing genuine from false shame, Taylor does not analyze the content of the values themselves; rather, the distinction rests upon the whether the person experiencing shame herself identifies with that set of values or not (34). Manion argues that Taylor's particular structure of shame does not give Carrie the space to doubt and reflect upon how her values have been shaped in the first place since it does not take into account how larger social and cultural forces shape value systems which in turn shape the construction of gender and shame (37).

Several postcolonial writers on pre-partition colonial India, such as Lata Mani, Sumit Sarkar, and Partha Chatterjee, show how nationalistic values and ideals (especially concerning the construction of gender, caste, and religious identity) were not created freely or democratically by everyone; however, everyone was expected to uphold these ideals regardless of whether they wished to endorse it. For instance, in pre-partition British India, the ideal of sexual purity was given the highest value in the construction of Hindu and Muslim womanhood. Within such a framework the sexual purity of women indicated family, communal, and national honor, whereas sexual taint indicated the loss of such honor and subsequent shame. As a result, sexual violence against minority women on the Indian and the Pakistani sides of the newly created borders became a means to humiliate and annihilate the minority community, thereby literally and metaphorically marking the women's bodies as outside of national membership. The survivors of sexual violence experienced humiliation at the hands of the perpetrators and their families whether or not they personally upheld these nationalistic investments in the ideals of women's sexual purity. The extent to which survivors of sexual violence are able to question and resist these modes of public humiliation is the central concern of this chapter.

A particular challenge in the theoretical discussions of shame and its social worth is that the value of shame as an individual or social moral compass has been deeply contested. On the one hand, Michael Morgan argues that shame is a more reliable moral compass than any other emotion, such as guilt. He is concerned about the growing apathy of the United States toward genocides occurring elsewhere, and he finds that a carefully cultivated sense of shame in response to such apathy would be a "moral" resource (1–7). His argument relies on the particularity of the experience of shame; it is the only emotion in which one fails in one's own eyes and in the eyes of those whom one values, and it is an excruciatingly painful experience. Morgan contends that *if* the citizens of the U.S. are able to develop a sense of shame around denials of atrocities and apathy toward genocides, then in the case of such an event the pain involved in the experience of shame will jolt or shock them out of their apathy (45–54). Morgan clearly feels that the only way one can rouse whole populations of people into action is through the painful, self-reflexive emotion of shame, because he fears that in the absence of the experience of shame for apathy toward genocides, it will be easier for people to ignore events of genocide in other parts of the world, which has been the case through the twentieth century. Unfortunately, his argument does not address its possible opposite allegation that the main reason people deny the events of genocide, or dismiss them as exaggerations, is in order to avoid responsibility and the excruciating pain of shame that accompanies the awareness of failing a responsibility, that is, failing in one's own eyes and in the eyes of one's family, community, and nation.

On the other hand, thinkers such as Michael Warner and Cheshire Calhoun are concerned about the hegemonic character of the emotion: therefore they argue against the high value assigned to shame as a moral compass. They worry that those who are most vulnerable to being publicly humiliated (such as gay, lesbian, and transgendered people in the U.S., and in the case of this chapter, survivors of sexual violence during partition) are those who do not conform to social norms that themselves need to be questioned.

What is the difference between the experience of shame and humiliation? According to Martha Nussbaum, one's desire to humiliate another can be traced to one's own fear of suffering shame.[1] Analyzing Andrew Morrison's case studies of patients suffering from acute shame, she concludes, like Ahmed, that the feeling of shame indicates one's failure to attain a desired goal or ideal state. We recognize it in our infancy when we see the distance between our desire to be omnipotent and our actual helplessness. She calls this type of shame experienced in childhood "primitive shame." We can only outgrow this overwhelming sense of shame when we learn to trust others, allow ourselves to become dependent on them, and reconcile ourselves with our own vulnerability. Humiliation, on the contrary, is the "public face of shame" (Nussbaum, 203). The desire to humiliate another stems from an insidious motive: "Behind the parade of moralism and high ideals, there is often likely to be something much more primitive going on to which the precise content of the ideals in question, and their normative value, is basically irrelevant" (220). Nussbaum argues that the motive to humiliate another emerges from one's fear of reconciling with one's vulnerability. The perpetrator attributes his fear of vulnerability and finitude to "deviant" identities, and seeks to humiliate them and exclude them from the community. The desire to humiliate has little to do with the actions of the other or even punishment for those actions; Nussbaum writes, "When the public laughs at someone in the pillory, they are not invited to focus on any particular act: They are invited to scoff at the person's spoiled identity" (230–231).

In the context of partition violence, Menon and Bhasin show that one of the most widespread and common ways for perpetrators to humiliate the "other" community and mark them as the other was by the forced uncovering of women's bodies, such as women being made to parade naked in the marketplace or dance naked in gurud-waras, and being raped before the men of the household (41). Tracing the Indo-European origin of the word "shame," meaning "to cover," Carl Schneider argues in favor of society retaining a sense of shame as a means to recognize human vulnerability and the need to protect it.

> Does a healthy human being need covering? Some think not, and equate "covering" with "hiding," and "hiding" with that which is disgraceful. I propose that there are times and phases in all places of human life where covering is appropriate—"fitting," "proper." Human experience, always vulnerable to violation, needs protection. Thus an element of reticence is always present and appropriate to human relationships, including one's relation to oneself. ("Mature Sense of Shame," 200)

Interestingly, like Schneider, most writers discuss "shame" as "cover" in metaphorical terms. Here, "cover" does not indicate cloth on one's body but rather how one seeks to hide one's vulnerability. While the metaphorical connotation is a crucial dimension in unpacking the structure of shame, the literal connotation of covering one's body with cloth is equally significant in the context of partition violence, which is discussed in the next section of this chapter, in the context of the violence enacted against Ayah and Hamida in Bapsi Sidhwa's novel.

Unpacking specific instances of public humiliation can help us identify the social norms that are being enforced when someone is being humiliated. Accordingly, resistance to certain forms of humiliation can also be read as a concurrent resistance to specific social norms and power relations in force. Therefore, a study of literary representations of humiliation and shame and possible resistance to them in partition literature is at the same time a discussion of resistance to specific social norms and cultural ideals.

Shame Shaped by Gender, Class, and Religious Identity in Sidhwa's *Ice-Candy-Man*

In Bapsi Sidhwa's *Ice-Candy-Man/Cracking India* we encounter two very different types of shame: in one, a young girl called Lenny lies and so experiences shame since she accepts the principles of honesty which she fails to uphold, while in the other, two "fallen" women, Ayah and Hamida, are raped and humiliated in the eyes of the perpetrators and their communities, and they experience shame even though they may not uphold these ideals of female sexuality and its role in the construction of the nation.

The novel is narrated by Lenny, a seven-year-old girl. She is the older of two children in a middle-class Parsi family living in Lahore (which after partition falls within the borders of Pakistan).[2] As a polio survivor Lenny has to visit the doctor frequently for different casts for her leg. Her mother tries to ensure that she is never in want of anything, so a nursemaid, or ayah, is appointed for her care at all times. Lenny is continuously rewarded for bearing the pain with courage and for always telling the truth, so the first time she breaks a plate and admits to it, her mother does not reprimand her but tells her "I love you. You spoke the truth! What is a broken plate? Break a hundred plates!" (85). While she spends most of the day in her ayah's care, she has a few playmates of her own age, such as her younger brother Adi, her cousin, and the neighbor's children, Rosy and Peter. One day, when playing at Rosy's house, Lenny comes across some small glass jars that catch her fancy. She steals them and looks for a safe hiding place for them at home; unable to find one, she stashes them in her schoolbag. After school the next day she goes to Godmother's house, still carrying her schoolbag and its hidden secret (83–84). She often spends her afternoons at this house, lying on the bed with Godmother, closely nestled against her. Soon these jars are discovered by Slavesister, who lives with Godmother. When she asks Lenny how she came into possession of these jars, Lenny says that Rosy gave them to her. No sooner does she say so than Godmother suspects it is a lie and Lenny, overcome with shame, relates, "I leap back to my original roost, not able to meet [Godmother's] eyes, and hide my face in her sari" (84). When confronted with her lie, she remains buried in Godmother's sari and "vehemently" denies having stolen the jars. She is then told not to lie again, because lying does not "suit" her (84). While the narrator herself does not describe her feeling as that of shame, her act of turning away from Godmother and Slavesister to hide her face indicates her feeling of shame. Silvan Tomkins explains that the affect of shame is painful and characterized by a turning away from the other. "Shame is both an interruption and a further impediment to communication which is itself communicated. When one hangs one's head or drops one's eyelids or averts one's gaze, one has communicated one's shame and both the face and the self unwittingly become more visible, to the self and others" ("Shame," 137). According to Tomkins, shame reveals one's continuing interest in another which has been interrupted or rejected by the other (134). While the affect of shame has a social trigger, it is also a self-reflexive emotion, and the return to oneself generates "the torment of self-consciousness" (136). To read Ahmed through Tomkins: in shame, one experiences an interruption in one's interest in the other whose existence is necessary for the mediation of one's values, and in this interruption or the other's refusal to reciprocate interest, one is made aware of the ideal one has failed to achieve.

Lenny's lie, subsequent shame, and realization that she has violated the principle of honesty is an example that might work in favor of arguments that support the value of shame as a worthy moral compass. However, reading Lenny's experience of shame, in comparison with Ayah's and Hamida's experience of shame, through Manion's argument is helpful in revealing the extent to which people, depending on their class, gender, and minority status, are able to choose certain social ideals, which they fail to uphold. Their failure in turn triggers the experience of shame. According to Taylor's distinction of "genuine shame" and "false shame," if Lenny genuinely believes in truth telling and has fallen short of that standard, then she feels genuine shame. However, if Lenny feels shame because her Godmother will think ill of her but she herself does not uphold a principle of honesty, then her shame for telling the lie will be false shame. In Lenny's case there is at least the possibility of a debate about whether or not she upholds the principle of honesty and why she decides not to lie again. However, as we will soon discover, in the case of Ayah and Hamida the possibility of such a debate is closed from the outset because they are ostracized for failing to uphold the ideal of "sexual purity" because they were raped.

The second form of shame in Sidhwa's novel is radically different from Lenny's experience of shame. It is experienced by Lenny's Hindu ayah, who is called Ayah in the novel, and her Muslim ayah, Hamida, who is introduced in the second half of the novel. They are both survivors of rape, and the shame that is brought upon them is not determined by their actions (as it was in Lenny's case), but rather by their identities as raped women. Acts of rape and mutilation during partition, on both sides of the new borders, were not random acts of violence but rather specifically aimed at shaming communities and thereby excluding them from membership in the nation. My interest in studying the representation of Ayah's and Hamida's humiliation is motivated by two questions: What are the specific differences in the structure of Lenny's shame and the structure of Ayah's and Hamida's humiliation? Unlike in Lenny's case, claims about the moral worth of shame cannot be made in the latter instances. Therefore, the second question is to what extent are Ayah and Hamida able to question their rape-based humiliation?

Nearly every evening Ayah takes Lenny on evening walks and visits to the park. Ayah bears a special gift for bringing together men of Hindu, Muslim, and Sikh faiths in their desire for her. In the evenings, they sit together in the park exchanging anecdotes, jokes, and news of violence among the different political factions. Beneath a veneer of politeness each of the men vies for Ayah's attention, and as news and rumors of partition and violence among Hindu, Sikh, and Muslim men reach them, their jokes come to be based on particularly vicious stereotypes of each other's religious group. As talk of partition draws near, Lenny becomes aware of differences in religious affiliation within the group she meets in the park every evening. "It is sudden. One day everybody is themselves—and the next day they are Hindu, Muslim, Sikh, Christian. People shrink, dwindling into symbols. Ayah is no longer my all-encompassing Ayah—she is a token. A Hindu" (93). Ayah begins buying flowers and joss sticks for her prayers; Imam Din (Lenny's cook, who is Muslim) now begins attending prayer every Friday. The gardener and the sweeper, who belong to the untouchable caste, "become even more untouchable" (93). While to Lenny, a seven-year-old, it seems sudden that on the eve of partition, sharp differences begin dividing a previously undifferentiated group,

partition scholars have pointed out that since 1909, when the British organized different electorates based on differences in religious identity (so that they were represented
by their "own politicians"), there was a gradual paradigm shift in how religious difference came to be conceptualized (Daiya, 33–31; Khan, 19–20). In the early twentieth century, religious differences mostly signaled differences in cultural practices and prayer
rituals; however, after two decades of nationalistic movements divided along religious
lines, religious differences came to signify differences in political claims and party
politics.[3] Of course, to imagine and romanticize a deep friendship among regional
Hindu, Sikh, and Muslim families prior to partition would also be an error, as a Hindu
woman interviewed by Menon and Bhasin said: "Roti-beti ka rishta nahin rakthe, baki
sab theek tha" (We neither broke bread with them [the Muslims], nor intermarried but
the rest was fine) (12).

On June 3, 1947, British viceroy Mountbatten, Congress Party leader Jawaharlal
Nehru, Muslim League leader Muhammad Ali Jinnah, and Sikh representative Baldev
Singh each delivered a speech on All India Radio stating their reasons for agreeing to
the partition of British India. They claimed it would not occur later than June 1948.
However, that date was soon to be changed to August 15, 1947, nearly ten months before the proposed date and two and half months from the date of the radio broadcast
(Khan, 2–3). This announcement was made in a context of growing violence among religious communities in British India, and the worst fact of all was that while August 15
was the date when India and Pakistan declared their independent statehood, the actual
lines of territorial division determined by a committee led by Sir Cyril Radcliffe were
not made known until three days later. Commenting on the dominant constructions
of partition narratives, Gyandendra Pandey laments a misleading separation made
between a political history of partition with a focus on the legislative development of
the nation-states and the memory of partition with a focus on stories of losses and violence suffered by individuals. Such a conceptual division between political history and
memory makes two events out of partition and violence, as though they are separate
and coincident. However, this division is contrary to the experience of the survivors of
partition for whom "Partition *was* violence" (Pandey, 7). Therefore Pandey seeks to recover the memories of violence as a historical narrative, and according to him this latter narrative disrupts the dominant construction of the nation-states narrated in terms
of political decisions made at the federal level. Interestingly, Khan's discussion of partition weaves both narratives continually, because, as she argues, if the story of the high
politics of partition and the recounting of the various violent outbreaks before and
during partition are traced separately, in opposition to each other, then both the narratives overlook how on the one hand, deliberations by political representatives at the
federal level were largely influenced by the "communal violence" on the streets while,
on the other hand, regional political organizations with specific political interests and
goals orchestrated many outbreaks of violence. "The Partition plan itself was brought
about through acts of violence. Partition's elitist politics and everyday experiences are

not as separate as they may seem at first glance because mass demonstrations, street fighting and circulation of rumors all overlapped with the political decision-making process" (Khan, 7).

Lenny's narrative of partition is not a historical overview of events, but rather it takes the form of memory of multiple stories about the people in her life and the kinds of violence, betrayal, and trauma they suffer. To Lenny and her evening companions it soon becomes evident that the governments of India and Pakistan are not equal to the task of controlling the violence. In response to the growing violence the governments agree to organize the transfer of population via trains. The plan was simple-minded if not naïve from the start: Muslims who felt unsafe in India could take the train to Pakistan, and Hindus who worried for their safety in Pakistan could take the train to India. These trains are now bitterly remembered on both sides of the border as they were frequently attacked midway. Whole trainloads of people were burned alive and the women were most often raped and mutilated. One of Ayah's admirers, an enterprising young Muslim youth, plies multiple trades each season. In summer he sells ice-candy. Several of his family members find themselves on the Indian side of the new border, in Gurdaspur, where the majority population is Sikh and Muslims form a minority. One evening as Lenny, Ayah, and her admirers are sitting on her verandah "grouped around a radio," Ice-Candy man comes rushing in to deliver his news: "A train from Gurdaspur has just come in [. . .] Everyone in it is dead. Butchered. They are all Muslim. There are no young women among the dead! Only two gunny bags full of women's breasts! [. . .] I was expecting relatives . . . For three days . . . For twelve hours each day . . . I waited for that train!" (149; bracketed ellipses added). As he speaks, his glance keeps returning to Sher Singh, a Sikh who by virtue of his identity is somehow deemed complicit in the atrocity. The gunny bags full of young women's breasts sent across on the train by the perpetrators is not a random, meaningless act of violence. One way to analyze the perpetrators' aim in such an attack is to read it through Veena Das's argument in which attacks against the women's bodies are recognized as a means to defy the abstract concept of the nation (and honor) since in most cultural productions ideas of honor and nation are represented in images of women. Another way to unpack the symbolism invoked in such attacks is through Menon, Bhasin, who explain that an attack against women's sexual organs is marked by a desire to annihilate the other community, not only through massacres but also by mutilating and tattooing sexual organs that could have actually borne subsequent generations. These types of violence seek to make the culturally produced idea (such as that of a nation or of honor) indistinguishable from an actual human body, so that the humiliation and annihilation of one is simultaneously the humiliation and annihilation of the other. Menon and Bhasin mention that in several attacks women's bodies were mutilated with slogans such as "Hindustan, Zindabad!" (Long live Hindustan!) or "Pakistan, Zindabad!" (Long live Pakistan!) (43). How does this affect our understanding of humiliation and shame in the context of partition?

Schneider's definition of "shame" as "cover" is particularly relevant here. Ayah and Hamida both experience a form of humiliation in which the attackers seek to remove their literal and the metaphorical "cover"/shame and thereby take away their dignity. Ironically, Lenny's compulsive truth telling, which may have provided an instance of Taylor's "genuine"/"good" shame earlier, plays a role in Ayah's abduction later in the novel. When instances of murder, kidnap, and rape rise in Lahore, Lenny's family tries to hide Ayah in the basement. Ice-Candy-Man, rejected by Ayah in love (since she returns the affections of another) and raging against the loss of Muslim lives at the hands of Hindus and Sikhs, directs all his anger against the Hindu Ayah. Accompanied by a large group of young men, he arrives at Lenny's doorstep demanding to know Ayah's whereabouts. Everyone denies any knowledge of her current location. Then Ice-Candy-Man crouches before Lenny and tells her in reassuring whispers that she mustn't be scared, he won't let anything happen to Ayah. Lenny confesses all, telling him that Ayah is either on the roof or in one of the storerooms (Sidhwa, 182). The men search the house till they find her. "[They] drag her in grotesque strides to the cart and their harsh hands, supporting her with careless intimacy, lift her into it. Four men stand pressed against her, propping her body upright, their lips stretched in triumphant grimaces" (183).

Soon Lenny comes to learn of a terrible connection between the rape of a woman and her community's subsequent rejection of her. After Ayah is dragged away from her house, she drops out of the narrative until nearly the end of the novel, when she reappears as the bride of the Ice-Candy-Man. She is then rescued by Godmother and the women of Lenny's family, who send her across the border to India (225). Citing Sidhwa's own reflection on her novel, Ambreen Hai points out that the author's aim was to recount the traumatic history of partition through the traumatized gendered national allegory of which Ayah becomes the chief representative (391). The middle-class women are cast as rescuers of the "fallen women," while the "lower-class" men are the only perpetrators of violence in the novel. Hai's argument can be summed up thus: the protagonist of the first half of the novel is Ayah, but after her abduction her position in the novel is supplanted by the "heroic" middle-class women engaged in rescue operations. The narrative is structured like many unfeminist narratives of rape, where the plot reaches the climax at the moment of rape and entirely omits narratives of possible recovery after the rape (Hai, 403).

When Lenny first hears that Ayah has been relocated, she begs Godmother to take her to Ayah. Godmother tells her that Ayah has refused this request because "she is ashamed to face us," then adds that "she has nothing to be ashamed of" (253). However, Lenny is sure that "Ayah is *irrevocably ashamed*. They have shamed her. Not those men in the carts—they were strangers—but Sharbat Khan and Ice-Candy-Man and Imam Din and Cousin's cook and the butcher and the other men she counted her friends and admirers. [. . .] *I am certain of her humiliation*" (253–254; emphasis and bracketed ellipsis added). In Sidhwa's novel, as in most works of partition literature, a woman's shame is determined by another, not herself. A rapist's intention to humiliate a woman coincides almost exactly, if not exactly, with shame felt and lived by the survivor. As Hai points out, Ayah's absence and continued silence in the novel after her abduction comes at a heavy price since we hear of her "shame" from the middle-class women who are subsequently cast as her rescuers. In order to recognize a gap between the perpetrator's intention to humiliate and the survivor's feeling of shame, since it is in this gap that she might be able to question or reject the humiliation thrust upon her, it is necessary to invoke Nussbaum's distinction between shame and humiliation, where shame refers to one's recognition of having failed to uphold one's ideals (which becomes more complex if read through Manion) and humiliation refers to the stigmatization of people as a way to mark their identities as "the other." The feeling of humiliation is never voluntary or determined freely by the subject; it is always controlled by another and exercised in order to enforce structural inequalities of power. However, in Sidhwa's novel the absence of a distinction between the two emotions erodes Ayah's ability to defy the shame that marks her body, and we shall see that Hamida's case is similar.

Hamida, Lenny's new Muslim woman servant, is another "fallen woman" newly arrived from the Indian side of the border, where Muslims became one of the vulnerable minority groups after partition. When Lenny demands to know what a "fallen woman" is, Godmother explains that "Hamida was kidnapped by Sikhs. Once that happens, sometimes the husband or his family—won't take her back" (215). This reminds Lenny of an evening with Himat Ali, when he stops her from returning a fallen sparrow nestling back into the nest. Himat Ali tells her, "If our hands touch it, the other sparrows will peck it to death [. . .] even its mother" (215; bracketed ellipsis added). To Lenny the sparrow and the raped woman have "fallen" the same way in the eyes of their families; however, Ayah's and Hamida's apparent "fall," unlike that of the sparrow, cannot be read through a law of nature but through the categories of nation, gender, and shame. Moreover, in this narrative, once the victim's cover/cloth is forcibly removed, she is made to experience shame and accept her status as a shamed woman. The perpetrators intend to humiliate Ayah and Hamida, attack and stigmatize their bodies, in order to avenge the shaming of their own communities. After they are raped, Ayah and Hamida fall silent. While Lenny rages against the injustice of the world, these women are not given the opportunity to show their reactions in the narrative. The extent of their perpetrators' intention to humiliate them is made to correspond to the shame they experience.

Resisting Humiliation, Refusing Shame

How is it possible to resist the public humiliation of one's "spoiled identity" by a majority group? The problem is that the act of humiliating another produces an asymmetrical power relation between the perpetrator and the accused or survivor. The survivor has almost no resources to make her oppressors see the injustice of the situation, since as Nussbaum argues it is her identity, not her action, that is supposed to shame her. Michael Warner points out that even President Bill Clinton discovered how public humiliation can make resistance to humiliation nearly impossible: "Sexual shame is such that exposing it taints a person, no matter how moral or immoral the sex might otherwise be. [. . .] How could Clinton and Lewinsky challenge that humiliation? They didn't even try" (19; bracketed ellipsis added). In the case of the subaltern woman who is already denied power and is vulnerable to being humiliated for deviating from social norms that have been determined by the privileged, the question of possible resistance against humiliation becomes even more difficult.

Several contemporary feminists in the United States have explored the social, political, and cultural contexts in which shame is produced. Writing about the U.S., they point out that the people who are most vulnerable to being humiliated are politically, economically, and socially subordinated groups. For instance the socially dominant view of the poor in the U.S. is not based on an analysis of economic privilege and exploitation of labor; rather the poor are stigmatized as lazy and dependent on welfare because of it (Calhoun, 146). Sexual minority groups are stigmatized as so overcome by sexual appetite that they are harmful to society's well-being. Even though the subordinated and stigmatized groups do not endorse the grounds on which they are being humiliated, they are nevertheless routinely humiliated and therefore they are more vulnerable to shame than those in positions of privilege. Before I return to a discussion on partition and post-partition violence, I will briefly address two proposals on resisting such forms of humiliation made by two thinkers in the U.S.

Cheshire Calhoun suggests that the most tempting mode of resistance to such practices of shaming would be if "[w]e—particularly the 'we' who is socially subordinate—might be better off to train ourselves not to feel shame" (144). She argues that while this might appear to be a strategic move that could eradicate the effects of shaming and therefore the practices of humiliation itself (since shame, unlike guilt, relies upon its recognition by another for its existence), this suggestion overlooks the fact that our vulnerability to being shamed or our capacity to humiliate is intrinsically bound to our condition of shared social interaction. She explains that our moral identities are "inescapable": first, our identities are not determined by ourselves as much as by others with whom we share moral practices, and second, we do not get to choose these moral practices—rather, we can choose certain professions and communities in which certain moral practices already exist (155). Calhoun suggests that the human vulnerability to shame and being shamed is a part of our social existence itself (145). Therefore we (feminists and allies) need to change the triggers (the social norms/ cultural and political ideals which the shamed have purportedly failed) of shame. Where do we learn which triggers we should cultivate? According to Calhoun, we should take our cues from the socially, politically, and economically subordinated who are always subject to humiliation from the hypocritical standards of the dominant cultural norms (146).

If the solution is to change the cultural and political frameworks that produce "deviant" identities, which are subsequently humiliated by prejudiced majority populations, then we need to ask how much should we rely on the self-examination and change in privileged groups (which have been or are in positions of power from which they stigmatize "deviant" identities) to be willing to disavow that privilege and become allies with the groups they have stigmatized? The historical persistence of public shaming and its abuses makes Jill Locke cautious about relying on an inward change in the hearts and minds of oppressive groups, such as racists or anti-Semites, as a means for social change. Instead of seeking an overall transformation of the social whole in which we all exist, she recommends that "feminists and democrats might redirect their efforts toward building a world for the shame ridden and shame prone—creating counterpublics and spaces where alternative images of life can emerge" (159).

In the context of partition violence women's resistance to the idea of women's sexuality as a repository of communal honor (when "pure"/unviolated) or communal shame (when "tainted"/violated) has rarely been recognized as resistance. In the discussion of Sidhwa's novel we have only examined those cases in which the perpetrator is a rapist/ torturer belonging to another community. However, it is equally significant that violated women appeared "fallen" to their own communities and were in most cases rejected by them. Menon and Bhasin are deeply troubled by the preemptive violence against women by their own kinsmen and kinswomen who tried to avoid the possible shame brought upon them. Women who refused to kill themselves or refused to allow themselves to be killed by their family members as a way to preempt possible abduction and rape were accused of cowardice and shamed for their lack of courage. One woman who refused the poison given to her and refused to give it to her daughter had to justify it through her gendered role of a caregiver: "someone had to stay back and cook for the men if they survived" (54). The sociologists also analyze the narrative of the men's testimonials in which they discuss their kinswomen's "suicides" (where women were encouraged to jump into wells, take poison, or electrocute or drown themselves). The men narrated these incidents as heroic tales about courageous women who valued their honor over their lives. Their deaths are remembered as willing suicides. The framework of such narratives does not allow any room for the women to question, defy, or protest against these honor-based requirements. Very few testimonials by men see their killing of their kinswomen as something against the will of those women, that is, as murder (Menon and Bhasin, 55).

Silence around the abduction and rape of one's kinswomen during partition was pervasive. In an interview with Isabella Bruschi, Sidhwa discusses how she came to write "Ranna's Story," a section in Ice-Candy-Man, in which Ranna, a young Muslim boy, suffers a series of assaults but finally manages to escape to the Pakistani side of the border. At a party in the U.S., Sidhwa had met a gentleman who told her about the violence he suffered during partition and his eventual escape, which inspired Sidhwa to write about the village of Pir Pindoo, on the Indian side of the border, which is attacked by a militant Sikh group. While Ranna manages to escape, the women are gang-raped (Sidhwa, 200). Sidhwa says that the gentleman, who had not mentioned incidents of sexual attacks in their conversation, was extremely angry with Sidhwa for including such details in the story. "I think he was angry because I had written about the women in his family being kidnapped. That is something nobody talks about, nobody: it is such a dishonor to admit that a woman in one's family was raped" (Sidhwa, "Making Up for Painful History," 144). Urvashi Butalia traces how the construction of the nation through gender, honor, and shame framed not only the abductions and violence against women but also the formulation and execution of the Abducted Persons (Recovery and Restoration) Bill (passed on December 31, 1949) in India. After a large number of "recovered" women were rejected by their families and their own villages, Nehru and Gandhi made extensive speeches asserting the "purity" of these women. Public pamphlets urging the acceptance of the women also claimed the continued "purity" of the rape victims, by drawing parallels from the Ramayana: Sita's abduction to Lanka by Ravan and her subsequent return to Ram later (Butalia, 160). Thousands of women, especially those who were left pregnant after being raped and then either rejected by their families or too ashamed to face them, eventually found their way to ashrams set up by women's organizations in Jalandar, Amritsar, Karnal, and Delhi (162). This does not mean that the women under the threat of attack from the men of other communities or their own kinsmen did not attempt to or were unable to resist the shame, but that even if they did the ideological framework of gender-based communal honor and shame was so pervasive (indicated by the silence surrounding the rape of one's kinswomen) that the dominant narratives did not recognize instances of resistance as resistance but as "cowardice."

From partition through the twenty-first century, there have been several instances of excessively brutal sexual assaults aimed to shame either the family or the community of the women, both in India and in Pakistan.[4] In recent events, the terrible link between sexual violence against women and their humiliation, in which the survivor, not the perpetrator, is made to embody familial, communal, or national shame, has not undergone any major paradigm shifts from the perspective of the perpetrator. However, we have seen a variety of different responses from the survivors, many of whom have come forward with painful narratives of the assaults they suffered, through which they have sought to sever the previously unbroken link between the perpetrator's intention to humiliate and the survivor's shame as its inevitable consequence. In doing so they have repeatedly exposed the failure of the police and the judicial system, who have rarely brought the perpetrators to justice.

Notes

1. In *Hiding from Humanity*, Nussbaum argues against Dan Kahan, who proposes ways for the experience of shame to be transferred into the legal system (i.e., shame-based punishments for offenders of the law) from its current place in the moral sphere (i.e., reassessing oneself or one's situation inwardly). His argument is that a shame-based punishment will gratify the society's demand for moral denunciation. John Deigh, in "The Politics of Disgust and Shame," weighs in on this exchange;

he responds to Nussbaum's claim that practices of public humiliation are invariably carried out by those in privilege as a response to threats to the status quo. Deigh argues that the problem is not with the internal structure of shame or humiliation but rather with the social conditions of privilege. Reading this exchange through feminists responses to shame and humiliation such as those by Jill Locke and Kathleen Woodward show that Deigh's clean separation between shame and social conditions, as though the former were not shaped and experienced through structures of the latter, can be misleading. In "Replies," Martha Nussbaum addresses this charge by illustrating the difference between experiencing shame privately and willingly (which can be a corrective) as opposed to public humiliation, which only aims to stigmatize "deviant" identities and assaults human dignity. It is worth noting that Dan Kahan in 2007 "recants" his previous enthusiasm for humiliation-based punishments (for nonviolent offenses); however, as he argues, it is not for the reasons that Nussbaum points out regarding the stigmatization and assaults upon the dignity of individuals but rather because it is "deeply partisan" and divides society based on whether people subscribe to certain social norms or not and thereby gives a higher place to a communitarian values rather than individuality.

2. Objecting to the frequent representation of the Parsi community, in popular culture, as anglicized, middle-class, and allied with the British administration, Rashna B. Singh points out the need to recognize the ways in which Parsi novelists, such as Sidhwa, show how Parsis had to negotiate their identity especially during partition, when they were excluded from all political decision making, since the main players demanding Pakistan, Khalistan, and India were Hindus, Muslims, and Sikhs.

3. Khan points out that in the 1936 elections, regional Muslim parties gained far more seats than the federal party called the All-India Muslim League, since Muslims in different regions identified with other religious groups in their province rather than with Muslims in other regions in India, which were marked by different languages and different cultural practices. However, in the 1946 elections the All-India Muslim League won every single Muslim seat (38). This was because political campaigns came to be infused with religious rhetoric, political duty, and religious duty. To be a Muslim and not support the demands of Pakistan was tantamount to betraying one's faith. During this period there was a corresponding growth of right-wing Hindu cultural-political groups, which strongly opposed the formation of Pakistan, which although a political claim was frequently cast in religious terms.

4. Some of the stories well covered by the media would include the massacres of Muslim men and women, especially the systematic rape and torture of Muslim women at the hands of supporters of the right-wing Hindu nationalist party (BJP) in Gujarat in 2002. For further details, see Tanika Sarkar's "Semiotics of Terror: Muslim Children and Women in Hindu Rashtra," *Economic and Political Weekly*, June 13, 2002, 2872–2876. In 2002, in Pakistan, a village council decided to punish the family of a twelve-year-old boy whom it accused of having sex with a woman of a high-caste Mastoi tribe. The council ordered Mukhtar Mai, the boy's elder sister, to be gang-raped in public and then paraded naked in order to deliver justice by humiliating/"dishonoring" the family for its alleged role in dishonoring the high-caste tribal community. Since then Mukhtar Mai has spoken of her attack in public, filed cases against her perpetrators in the court of law, and opened schools for girls in order to bring about structural social change. She had accused twelve men of gang-raping her; six of them were nearly automatically released in 2002, and six others were sentenced to death. On April 21, 2011, five of the six men in jail were also acquitted and will return to the same village. "Pakistan: Acquittals in Mukhtar Mai Gang Rape Case," BBC, April 21, 2001; and "Pakistan Top Court Upholds Acquittals in Notorious Rape Case," *New York Times*, April 21, 2011.

14 Interrogating the Place of *Lajja* (Shame) in Contemporary Mauritius

Karen Lindo

Concerned with the whole self, shame involves more bodily awareness, more visual and verbal imaging of the psychic and physical life of the self than guilt, with which it is often confused. As an affect, shame reveals the instinctual life that is innate to all human experiences. The dynamics between shame and the body are such that the most shame-inducing moments are in fact those in which the body appears to have lost control. Controlling the body's relationship with the outside world is polarized around the ability to demonstrate, in large part, a sense of shame so as to remain within the sociocultural edicts that govern its conduct. Shame can then function as a protective layer for bodily experiences to guard physical and psychic boundaries and protect their contours. Conversely, because the body is a source of pleasure, seduction, conquest, and pain, its boundaries are vulnerable in its relations with others. As Elizabeth Grosz explains: "One's psychical life history is written on and worn by the body just as in turn, the psyche bears the history of the lived body, its chance encounters, its punctures, transformations and extensions" ("Psychoanalysis and the Body," 270). Shame, as an emotion, carries a biography of the body that is specific to the individual and the cultural context from which the individual originates.[1] Since these biographies do not necessarily coincide, shame is often scripted into cultural practices so as to organize a coherent and systematic means of having bodies signify specific cultural values. Historically, the female body is given this charge.

In this chapter, I examine the way in which the sociocultural script for shame—*lajja*—attempts to regulate the Indo-Mauritian female body. Taking into account the historical function of shame to police the female body in Hindu traditional practices, I analyze the way in which the Mauritian author Ananda Devi, in her novel *Pagli* (2001), challenges the role that shame plays in determining female subjectivity in contemporary Mauritius. Whereas the historical place of shame within the Indian diaspora reiterates a masculine investment in the domestication of the female body through shame, I will show how Devi takes a counter-position to expose women who remain wedded to cultural practices that encode their bodies as sites for shame. Revealing women's willingness to use shame as a weapon against other women, Devi not only unveils how shame works as the subtext to cultural practices that regulate female conduct but also inaugurates an alternative model of female empowerment which lays claim to a larger sociocultural milieu than that circumscribed by Hindu customs. Through the trajectory of the eponymous heroine, the author unburdens the Indo-Mauritian female body of its historical allegiance to Mother India and brings her into an embodied subjectivity that is enriched by the cultural métissage that characterizes contemporary Mauritius.

Devi is recognized internationally as one of the most prolific Mauritian female authors today. Since her earliest collection of short stories, written at age fifteen, her literary production has yielded ten novels, a recent autobiographical work (*Les hommes qui me parlent* [2011]), three collections of short stories, and two collections of poetry. Concerned with marginalization, Devi's work focuses predominantly on the plights of female characters forced to submit to or rebel against sociocultural practices that muffle or imprison individual yearnings and desires. The female body often figures as the site of resistance and/or subjugation in her narratives, in which women are beaten, violated, or otherwise forced into self-effacement because of their seemingly unruly natures in the face of patriarchal scripts which determine their expression and significance.[2] For Devi: "La honte du corps, et une sorte de culpabilité primaire du corps est ce qui a de tout temps maintenu la femme en état d'asservissement"[3] (Shame of the body and a sort of primary guilt have forever maintained the woman in a subservient position).

In *Pagli* (2001), the author interrogates the place of the female body and the legitimacy of her desires in the Indo-Mauritian context. The novel narrates the story of the forbidden love of a married Hindu woman for a Creole fisherman, Zil. Pagli, the "crazy one," is the Hindi name assigned to the female protagonist when she commits her first infraction and entertains an untouchable female beggar in the family home of her in-laws. Following Hindu custom, Pagli has married her cousin, who, unknown to other family members, had raped her at age thirteen. She agrees to marry him, reasoning that as his wife she will be better positioned to avenge the violation to her body as a young girl. On their wedding night, she reveals her fully blossomed body and forthrightly refuses him its pleasures and the promise of an offspring, her duties as his wife. This first transgressive strike against him in the wedding chamber leads to a progressive unveiling of the suffocating and ossified practices of her social milieu, upheld by the *mofines*, female guardians of Hindu religious and cultural practices in the mother-in-law's home. *Mofine* is the Mauritian Creole term attributed to those who are connected to evil and therefore cause bad luck. While the term is gender-neutral, in Mauritian popular culture, *mofine* is often associated with women who are both healers and "witches" because it is believed that everything they touch is imbued with bad energy. In the novel, Devi designates the mother-in-law and her female consort *mofines* to insist on the way in which these women, who incarnate bad energy, use shame to forestall the female protagonist's will to live her subjectivity corporeally.

Each choice that Pagli makes against the demands on her as a Hindu wife, serving the female beggar in the finest china, attiring this untouchable woman in her wedding veil, befriending the local prostitute Mitsy, falling in love with the Creole fisherman, unravels a collection of narratives of shame of those who are excluded from the privileged Hindu milieu. These narratives unfold in step with the mobility and confinement of Pagli's body, guarded by the Hindu female community to which she is said to belong. The force of Pagli's agency is revealed over time in the character's lived experience of shame, which is juxtaposed to shame used as an instrument of containment by the *mofines*.

In the Indian diaspora, marriage is the context in which women's issues most saliently come to the fore. The critic Uma Narayan remarks that as a young girl growing up in India, the repeated threat made to her childish pranks was "Wait till you get to your mother-in-law's house. Then you will learn how to behave" (Narayan, 9). Narayan's anecdote resonates with Pagli's narrative, in which the figure of the mother-in-law is congealed into the representation of the *mofines*. The role that the *mofines* play in Pagli's narrative in fact harks back to the historical tensions between the Indian nationalist movement and the British during the nineteenth century, in which the female body had a critical political function. In response to the derision and humiliation of what British colonial rulers designated barbaric and primitive cultural practices, Indian nationalists modernized their material life in the public domain, but aimed to preserve their superiority over the West in the spiritual realm, deemed the "inner core of the national culture" (Chatterjee, 121). This inner core was localized in the domestic sphere where women held court.

In the home, women were made responsible for maintaining traditional religious practices. While men adapted to new habits in terms of attire, consumption, and religious practices that reflected the changing political and social conditions of their material world in the public sphere, women were charged with upholding spiritual purity in the home, and therefore with preserving the true essence of the nation. Self-sacrifice, benevolence, devotion, and religious piety were feminine qualities linked to woman's representation as both goddess and/or mother, female figures which, as Partha Chatterjee has argued, "erase[d] her sexuality in the world outside the home" (131). The embattled relationship between Pagli and the *mofines* reflects a continuation of the exigencies for a pure Hindu woman in the home. Ketu Katrak interprets this historical disavowal of the physical yearnings of the female body as indicative of the degree to which female sexuality is connected to the expression of her power and subjectivity (395–420).

Shame beneath the Veil

Female sexuality and power are complicated by the manner in which Pagli gradually unfurls the desires of her body on her wedding night. Under the sign of the wedding ceremony, where a series of religious rituals commit Pagli to her new husband, the female protagonist lives the occasion as the opportune moment to express her buried humiliated rage toward the perpetrator who violated her at age thirteen. Beneath the red and gold veil with which she is adorned for the ceremony, Pagli declares: "J'étais un monstre qui attendait de pouvoir se repaître de l'homme à ses côtés" (74) (I was a beast waiting for the right moment to feast on the flesh of the man beside me [81]).[4] Each ritual that seemingly solidifies the couple's union in the eyes of the Hindu familial community is rearticulated on Pagli's terms, to further distance her from the man to whom she is bound by law. The disparity between how the rituals are performed and how they are interpreted becomes apparent when she breaks her silence at the moment of the pronouncement of the wedding vows. In the place of vows to obey and care for him and bear his offspring, she rewrites the terms according to the inner humiliation with which she struggles: "Le feu qui me demandait mes serments a reçu la promesse de ma vengeance" (74) (The fire asks for my vows. It receives the promise of my vengeance [82]). Tapping into her buried rage, Pagli performs the rites with a force that jolts her husband and the pundit, who oversees the ceremony, into a nervous state. The festivities nevertheless proceed and the union is sealed.

Finally, in the quiet of their conjugal quarters, Pagli performs an unveiling that weds her words to her body. Confounding her husband in a game of seduction, she gradually unravels her red and gold wedding sari, which Françoise Lionnet reads symbolically as "an archive of the unspeakable," and stands before him in the nude (300). Crumpling and disposing of the sari in a far corner, Pagli disentangles and distances herself from the patriarchal fabric that constricts and muzzles the woman that she is. Reinserting the silenced history of the previous violations to her body into the context of their marital rites, she takes command of her body with these words:

> Regarde ce corps que tu ne toucheras plus jamais.
> Regarde ce qui t'est à présent interdit.
> Regarde ces lieux sombres et touffus.
> Regarde ces endroits que tu ne visiteras jamais.
> Regarde ces formes qui ont bien changé depuis le jour lointain où tu les as massacrées.
> Regarde ce dont tu vas rêver pour le restant de tes jours et qui ne t'appartiendra pas.
> Regarde ce ventre qui ne portera pas d'enfant de toi. (77–78)

> Look at this body you will never touch again.
> Look at what's forever forbidden.
> Look at these dark and bushy places with their odorous warmth.
> Look at these folds you will never push apart.
> Look at these shapes that have changed so much since you last punched them to submission.
> Look at the stuff of your dreams for the rest of your life.
> Look at this belly that will never bear your child. (85–86)

The future that the ceremony promises is summarily thwarted. Long-silenced anger has reshaped the body her cousin knew and now reshapes the experience to which he will, as her husband, have access. The gaze that overpowered the discovery of her own body and forced her into silence and self-loathing at age thirteen is now confronted with the rage for which her body has become a repository. Further, by removing the *sindoor* (the red cosmetic powdered dot placed on the forehead of the Hindu woman by her husband to signal that she is married), the garland, the jewelry, and the sari, the female protagonist calls into question the very sanctity of the Hindu marriage ceremony. Vicram Ramharai interprets Pagli's first act of revolt against the Hindu cultural and social norms in the following terms: "Elle renie à la fois son époux et la part d'indianeté qu'elle possède parce que celle-ci tend à opprimer la fille" (She renounces both her husband and her Indian identity as this latter oppresses the daughter that she is [70]). In Pagli's eyes, the familial ease with which, as her cousin, he had entered into her home and claimed her body as a young girl can never be rewritten in official rites.

In response to her husband's perplexed expression, Pagli explodes in laughter. A woman's laughter resonating throughout the new family home is a peculiar, if not unusual, sound emanating from the conjugal quarters of newlyweds. This audible reverberation throughout her body laments, "un petit cri mince" (53) (a brittle cry [60]), that was never heard on the afternoon she was violated. A shameless, immodest ("sans pudeur, sans honte" [78]) laughter, Pagli knows, is sure to cause a stir in the home. It is a misplaced sound that not only dares to make a mockery of her husband, but also forewarns her new family against their perception of a successful union. The innocence promised to her new husband is dismissed in a guffawing laughter that exposes him now as impotent before her as his wife.

Laughter also covers over the humiliation, rage, and shame that have marked Pagli's trajectory. On the one hand, laughter protects the female protagonist as she stands in a physically vulnerable space before her husband and perpetrator. But this laughter betrays, on the other hand, the emotional fragility in which Pagli grapples with her past even in a moment where she appears to most assert her person. Humiliation, a variant of the shame experience, occurs when one finds oneself in an abased position at a particular moment. One is brought to a lowly or degraded position as a result of the more powerful position of the other (S. Miller, 43). Recurring humiliation leads to increasing resentment and an impotent rage toward the other with whom one finds oneself in a power differential. Susan Miller uses the term "impotent rage" to underscore the lapses in time between the experience of humiliating feelings and the moment in which the rage associated with these feelings is finally expressed (44).

Pagli alludes to a power struggle with her cousin when he gazed at her as a young girl in such a manner that her only recourse was to repeatedly cover herself with ever larger shawls so as to deflect the lust that her body seemed to invoke in his eyes. The powerlessness she experienced then and which eventually led to the physical violation of her body is reversed on her wedding night. Reenacting the humiliating experience, this time so that her perpetrator experiences humiliation, Pagli reclaims her body from the objectifying gaze, which has haunted her self-image. However, in redressing her position, Pagli cannot immediately evacuate her self-image, which she experiences as tainted by the actual experience of the violation. The recurring eruptive moments of rage in the character's narrative point to the degree to which she struggles internally in her attempt to recover a favorable perception of the self.

Where Paul Gilbert argues that humiliation can lead to shame, Pagli's plight suggests that humiliation is in fact subsumed by shame (Gilbert, 10). Although shame is also linked to one's relations with others, it differs from humiliation because it becomes an *enduring* experience of the self by the self. Eve Sedgwick describes the visceral experience of shame as "an inner torment, a sickness of the soul" (Sedgwick, 133). Pagli reveals the vacillation between humiliation and shame in her experience of the self in the way she retells the rape scene. Recounting the incident, at first in great detail, the narrative becomes elliptical as she narrows in on an image of herself that betrays an underlying hurt associated with the abandonment and helplessness she experienced as a young girl. The narrative evolves from power struggles between perpetrator and victim to "une voix d'enfant totalement perdue, totalement orpheline" (53) (a child's distant treble, entirely lost [60]). The repetition of the adverb "entirely" ("totalement") betrays an all-encompassing experience of the self abandoned, orphaned and lost. This glimpse into Pagli's intrapsychic world underscores her loss of innocence because of the rape but also points to an anterior loss and abandonment that overshadows how she sees and relates to herself in the present. Voicing the past rape scene leads Pagli to uncover how much feeling shame is also bound to the recurring images of an abandoned Pagli.

"Orpheline" calls attention to another unexpressed dimension of Pagli's shame narrative: the parental absences in Pagli's life as a young girl. The protagonist's emphasis on the term "orpheline" recalls how her birth as a baby girl sealed her fate. Once Pagli's mother learned that she had given birth to a girl, she had turned away, enraged that she had survived the delivery. A guardian was subsequently summoned to take charge of the baby girl. The mother-child bonding experience, in which the child is first recognized in the mother's eyes, is intercepted by the weight of the cultural script that modulates the mother's conduct toward her baby girl. For shame theorist Gershen Kaufman, the internalization of the shame experience is the result of the initial rejection by the parents. Parents who do not want a child or are disappointed at the gender of the child will express these feelings in a manner that the child, in turn, internalizes (*Shame*, 37–78). Léon Wurmser, like Kaufman, places great emphasis on the role of the eyes and the face of the caretaker in expressing lovability. Wurmser further explains that however shame is experienced and expressed, at one's core one struggles with the underlying sense that one is unlovable (*Mask of Shame*, 93).

Pagli's mother's response points to an intergenerational shame that is scripted according to her milieu. Her daughter's gender signifies the prescribed path her life will take. Honor and/or family shame will be determined by each gesture that this young girl's body makes. Daya, pity of the earth, is the name given to Pagli at birth, thus ascribing to the character a determinist vision of her fate. Turning away from her child, Pagli's mother expresses with her silence the unspoken cost of self-sacrifice. She knows what delivering her daughter over to Hindu customs will subject her to and cannot bear the sense of powerlessness with which she, as Pagli's mother, is confronted. Her shame experience is thus muzzled by silence, which in effect amplifies the degree to which she remains subjugated. It is precisely the absence of communication between mother and child in this first home that Devi denounces as part of what facilitates passing Pagli into the hands of her mother-in-law in the new marital home.

Where Pagli's inability to describe her mother is symptomatic of her alienation from her as a young girl, the mother figure becomes nevertheless omnipresent in the depiction she provides of the *mofines* in her husband's home:

> Il y en a qui donnent et il y en a qui prennent. Il y en a qui construisent et il y en a qui détruisent. Les mofines font partie de ceux-ci. Les mofines ne sont pas des femmes ordinaires. Ou plutôt elles ne sont pas des femmes du tout. Elles sont des gardes-chiourme. Leur ventre est un horizon de fertilité et de continuité. Elles sont là pour produire et créer la descendance héroïque qu'elles ont reçu l'ordre de perpétuer . . . Imprégnées de cette charge, elles cessent un jour d'être mères ou femmes pour devenir les soldats de la pureté et promener leurs ailes d'aciers au dessus de chaque ombre menaçant de s'échapper. C'est ainsi qu'à mon premier pas hors du sentier tracé pour moi, elles me sont descendues dessus, avec leur hargne et leurs poings levés. (41)

> There are those who give birth and life and those who trample on every beautiful thing because their eyes are only comfortable with ugliness . . . The *mofines* are like that. They are not women. Or only half-women, transformed by centuries of slow carving into something harmful and vindictive. They have nurtured and produced and procreated, turning their bellies into enormous factories. Not of children but of continuity and permanence. That's what they are there for. To preserve the descent of a once heroic ancestry . . . Soldiers of purity who patrol the night, their wide open steel wings casting shadows over people's hearts . . . At my first step away from the path, they came down on me to bring me back before I strayed too far. (42–43)

The maternal imago remains wedded to the Indian historical time frame evoked by Partha Chatterjee, in which the spiritual realm is protected in the home and spiritual purity is materialized in the expression of female bodies. The shift from reproductive vessels to soldiers of purity is seamless because these women in effect sustain the reproductive practices by the measures they undertake to ensure the reiteration of the woman's role in the domestic sphere. The passive depiction of Pagli's mother is contrasted with the stature of the mother-in-law, who, in the company of her female entourage, is charged with imposing the model of femininity to which the daughter-in-law must adhere. Her legitimate authority to physically afflict or cause affliction to Pagli's body is revealing both of the mother-in-law's culturally sanctioned position and of the unstable code of conduct that she is positioned to enforce. Judith Butler would argue that the reiteration of this expression of femininity is revealing of the anxiety within which it is performed (9). The evocation of the physical violence visited on Pagli by these women, moreover, unravels yet another layer of domestic violence that has been historically lodged in silence and shame. The *mofines'* practices in the novel reflect what Brinda Mehta calls "the pathology of Hindu maternity" (211). Devi shows how these women, allotted the dubious task of policing the "home," continue to transmit a maternal heritage that effectively dis-empowers their daughters. These experienced mothers seek to repress Pagli's desires into a monolithic presentation and (re)presentation of the Hindu woman, who remains fixed in time and space.

The Hindu Woman Attired in Shame

This investment in a monolithic Hindu woman responds to a cultural logic that holds women responsible for cultural integrity. An historical inquiry into the composite discourses that have molded the figure of the Hindu woman unearths, however, a far less spiritual foundation than one imagines. While the claim to a spiritual life was a significant part of the indigenous values of the Indian people as a whole, the division into material and spiritual realms during nineteenth-century British colonial rule solidified and fixed the place and representation of women in ways that surpassed her status in the home. The Indian woman's body became a site of competing discursive practices of reform in which, on the one hand, British missionaries hoped to rescue her from such indigenous practices as sati, child marriage, and harlotry; and on the other hand, the Indian nationalist movement sought to make visible social reforms and signs of progress by means of the female body such that a "civilized" Indian woman would occupy center stage in the public sphere. For the Indian nationalist agenda, the Victorian, Christian, well-educated, middle-class British woman needed to be matched by an equally polished Bengali Hindu woman.

Lajja, the Bengali term that defines a sense of shame and/or modesty, became the female ethic used to construct a brand of femininity in which the Indian woman in the public sphere became the signifier of a translucent morality.[5] Beyond reproach, her adornment consisted of gentleness, politeness, innocence, tranquillity and refinement, which all became markers of her "civilization" and as such brought Indian civilization in line with the dominant proto-rationalist thought. Measures were advocated to enhance her education and cultural activities so that she could become an active participant in the public arena, equal to her male counterpart. The enclosure to which she had been previously confined in the inner space was finally realized in a version of the sari that now covered all but her feet in the public domain. The nationalist investment in reformations to Indian femininity was to yield the *bhadramahila*—a genteel, well-educated, civilized Indian woman who stood in pleasing contrast to the Victorian model of a woman of virtue. After 1870, the majority of these reforms, which had been initiated by men for the benefit of the nationalist movement, were adopted as part of the official discourse of the *bhadramahila* herself. She became the *porte-parole* and overseer of all expressions of Indian femininity. While she in fact originated within the propertied middle-class family, the hegemonic design of the gentlewoman would become a typology to which women of all castes would aspire.

Deploying *lajja* as a moral mechanism to civilize women was, in effect, paradoxical. On the one hand, the conflation of *lajja* with female virtue distanced women from their bodies. On the other hand, the mise-en-scène of *lajja*, that is, the public performance of this virtuous woman, made all the more visible her corporeality. As Himani Bannerji explains, *lajja* "as a concept . . . subsumes all kinds of physical and social needs within a sexual discourse, enclosed in a general imperative of self-censorship" (Bannerji, 83). *Lajja* effectively civilized women, by casting a shadow over the material desires of her body. Motherhood remained a legitimate role for the Indian woman, but her sexuality was forcefully denounced.

Rereading the role shame played during the nineteenth-century Indian anti-colonial struggle underscores the complex relations of power that spawn terms like "tradition," "culture," and "religion." The Indian nationalist agenda indeed campaigned for reforms that gave a more visible stature to the Indian woman, and undoubtedly certain castes and classes did benefit from these changes. Yet in probing the discourses that were constructed in favor of this brand of female subjectivity, visibly aligned with national authenticity, the patriarchal (European as much as Indian) imperatives that fostered these changes become apparent. The way in which *lajja* was manipulated to represent a virtually inherent quality specific to the Indian woman reveals, as Bannerji notes, "a curious blend of indigenous and colonial values regarding women, nature and the body" (81).[6]

In the Mauritian context, *lajja* is doubly potent. As part of the Indian diaspora who crossed large expanses of water to new land, displaced Indians are perceived by those who remain in India as culturally defiled and contaminated. This perception is, in part, due to the castes and classes of people who initially left the mainland. Among these were former convicts, and men and women of lower castes who endured ongoing discrimination within the Hindu classification system in India. In the eyes of the higher castes, these Hindus (including women of higher castes who had braved the waters to escape domestic violence and/or Hindu social strictures) were deemed menacing social pollution. Going on to new lands (among them Mauritius, Reunion, Fiji, South Africa, and the Caribbean islands) as indentured laborers, these Hindus were nevertheless offered social and economic possibilities that were difficult to come by on the mainland.

The traversing of immense bodies of water, designated the *kala pani* crossings, also meant the dissolution of the connection to the class and caste from which one originated—"a loss of the 'purified' Hindu essence" (Mehta, 5). In Hindu diasporic communities and no less so in Mauritius, these castoff Hindus, distanced as they were from Mother India and confronted with new social groups, felt ever more compelled to assert their allegiance to the mainland. Hindu customs were therefore revitalized, and the position of the Hindu woman's body, in particular, was key to demonstrating their sustained loyalty to and affinity for Indianness/Hinduness. Paradoxically, many of the women who left the mainland to be freed of the Hindu cultural exigencies were to find themselves in even more dramatic domestic circumstances than those from which they had originally escaped.

Considering the historical function of *lajja* in Hindu customs originating in India together with the *kala pani* phenomenon illuminates the circumstances with which Pagli is confronted. Once the *mofines* learn of Pagli's alliance with Zil, the Creole fisherman, the result of her friendship with Mitsy, the local prostitute, these women are determined to bring her body back into the Hindu cultural framework by evoking images of generations of self-sacrifice. These images, however, remind Pagli of how much allegiance to a mythical India has stricken these women with myopia and mummification. Fixated on the transgression and shame that Zil and Pagli as a couple represent for Indian national history, the *mofines* fail to see:

> Qu'un tel frappe sa femme tous les soirs en rentrant de la buvette abruti de violence. Qu'un père viole sa fille depuis qu'elle a cinq ans. Qu'un enfant est martyrisé sous les yeux de sa mère. Qu'une femme infecte les gens de sa médisance comme une maladie qu'elle sème dans le vent. (106)

> Someone is hitting his wife when he comes back from the bar. A father is raping his daughter from the age of five. A child tortured under his mother's eyes. A woman injecting her venom into people's minds. (113)

The everyday narratives of shame in which Mauritian families fracture and violate themselves in the domestic sphere remain invisible to these women, whose gaze aims to distill any potential signs of danger from a "pure" representation of the Hindu woman and family.

Performing *lajja* in order to protect family honor firmly disavows the existence and agency of the female body. The beatings and brandings to Pagli's body and her eventual confinement to the henhouse in the rear of the family home all attest to the *mofines*' adherence to the nineteenth-century model of Hindu femininity. Repeatedly reclaiming her body for the domestic sphere, the *mofines* attempt to publicly shame Pagli into assuming her prescribed reproductive role in the family home. The reiteration of the beatings suggests the anxious state in which the performance of Hindu femininity takes place to contain Pagli within Hindu customs. In their hands Pagli's body is an emblem for their cause, a body that must not betray the culture of silence and shame in which it is imprisoned.

The Locus of Abject Female Bodies

Where Pagli's body occupies a liminal space in the narrative, offering simultaneous potentialities for return to the Hindu cultural fold or else explosion into the profane domain of the untouchables, Mitsy's body operates beneath the Hindu cultural radar. As a prostitute, she is the antithesis of the virtuous woman, the figure of the abject.

The very self-division that conceptually estranges the *bhadramahila* from her physical person also separates the *mofines* from women of the street. Yet it is precisely Mitsy's status as an outcast that reveals where disavowed female sexuality is localized and the burden that her body must bear for its physical labor. Where Pagli's body is beaten over and over again so that she may reproduce offspring, by contrast Mitsy's body is discovered sprawled in blood because of her attempt to abort a fetus. Ostracized by the female community whose husbands seek her body for pleasures they do not know at home, Mitsy undertakes a risk to her own life. Her abortion and silent suffering spare these wives the shame of exposing the consequences of their constricted sexuality. At the sight of the blood flowing from Mitsy's body, Pagli, frightened for the life of her friend, initially seeks to call on a midwife or doctor but is soon dissuaded. Mitsy knows intimately the alienation in which she lives and can only turn to Pagli for help: "Je n'appartiens pas. A rien, à aucun lieu" (100) (I don't belong . . . To nothing, to no place [109]). Beyond the purview of the homes of purity, it is through Pagli's eyes that we witness an alternative narrative of self-sacrifice, which never enters into the official pages of history:

> J'ai vu alors tout ce sang qui coulait d'elle, qui s'écoulait en longs flots crus, qui charriait des fragments épais et coagulés . . . J'ai respiré sa sueur et son haleine, j'ai tenu sa main engluée de peur et comprimé son ventre et sa chair, j'ai nettoyé ce qui sortait d'elle comme une boue détachée de ses rives, j'ai recueilli les particules de regret et de vie démembrée, de vie refusée et reniée et je les ai enfouies loin dans mon silence et dans ma promesse du secret et je les ai lavées à l'eau glacée de nos yeux même si longtemps après j'ai ressenti entre mes doigts cette sensation si fragile et si neuve de quelque chose qui commençait et qui aurait peut-être voulu être, mais qui n'avait pas été. (96–97)

> I saw all the blood coming out in huge raw spurts, carrying thick, clotted fragments . . . I smelled her sweat and her bitter breath, I held her hand clotted with fear and then I pressed on her belly, I probed inside her, removed what was still waiting to come out like mud sliding from a hillside, I received on a cloth the particles of regret and dismembered life, life rejected and life refused, I made it all come out, promising to keep her secret even if I was horrified by this sensation of something fragile and unbearably new that had begun, but that would never be. (104–105)

Unveiling the masked indifference with which Mitsy struggles in shame, Pagli brings together in her vision of this scene the mother-whore figure with which all female bodies are taxed. Pertinently, Pagli's first-person account, reiterated with innumerable expressions of "je" (I), is likened to an incantation and accompaniment to the silent and pained voice of Mitsy. Exposing what the inner walls of Mitsy's body have suffered invokes the notion of the "irreducible specificity" of the complex female body of which Elizabeth Grosz speaks (*Volatile Bodies,* 207). Mitsy's bodily experience collapses the false divides between legitimate bodies and abject bodies that discursive practices like *lajja* attempt to organize. The blood in which her body bathes makes manifest the violence in which the binary representation (mother-whore) of female subjectivity is realized. Mitsy's blood, moreover, colors the quest for purity that the *mofines* pursue, exposes the hypocrisy that unifies this community of women.

The procreative power of the woman brings with it an ambivalent and problematic relationship toward the figure of the female body. Julia Kristeva suggests that the underlying fear of pollution in society is haunted by "the uncontrollable generative mother" (*Powers of Horror*, 79). As the carrier of menstrual blood, amniotic fluids, milk, and excrement, the female body oscillates between profane and sacred worlds. Her body is the risky polluting, disorderly body that, because of its potential for uncontrollable flows, personifies abjection.[7] As Kristeva puts it, "At the limit, if someone personifies abjection without assurance of purification, it is a woman, 'any woman,' the 'woman as a whole'" (85). The critic interprets the Hindu cultural praxis of purity versus impurity as but a reconfiguration of the sexual differences that would otherwise point up the underlying anxiety of the haunting abject maternal figure. Devi contests the figure of the abject not only in the depictions of the characters Pagli, Mitsy, and Zil but also in the manner in which the notion of procreation is reformulated through the theme of rebirth in the novel.

Rebirth from a Liminal Space: "Love Is Our Sole Rebellion"

The possibility of new life to which Pagli alludes in the scene with Mitsy highlights a polyvalent notion of rebirthing that is an overarching narrative theme. The sensation of the inexplicably novel and fragile within her grasp indicates the new paths that the expression of her rage and buried shame bring her to know. On a separate occasion, Pagli escapes from the henhouse where the *mofines* have placed her to find refuge in Mitsy's home. At the sight of her frazzled and depraved friend, Mitsy's touch revives Pagli's body and its sensuality, thus engendering what Pagli lives as a rebirthing experience. In Pagli's words:

> Elle a lentement enlevé mes habits usés, déchirés par endroits, et les a jetés par terre comme un tas de chiffons répugnants, car ils gardaient l'odeur de ma détresse. Puis sa main s'est mise à voguer sur mon corps, rugueuse et sans but particulier, seulement très féminine. Elle m'a caressée comme seules les femmes savent le faire, sans heurter parce qu'elles sont habituées à la fragilité des enfants. Elle le faisait sans doute pour que je redevienne moi-même un enfant qui croirait encore dans la sécurité de ces mains de femme, mais au bout d'un moment ce toucher sur ma peau s'est mis à ressembler à celui d'un homme, et mon corps a réagi d'un seul coup, avec tant de violence que je l'ai obligée à me toucher là où elle ne désirait peut-être pas aller. Je l'ai appuyée très fort contre moi, et, les yeux fermés, j'ai repensé à toi [Zil] parce que c'est ainsi. Je n'ai pas d'autre refuge. (21)

> She slowly removes my old, torn clothes. Peels them off my skin and they go willingly, releasing me from their despair. Then her hand begins to move. It is a rough hand, moving aimlessly and yet very feminine. She caresses me like only women know how to, without hurting, as they do with children to smooth their fears. Maybe she wants me to become a child again in the safety of these hands for a short

while, but then, this slow touch on my skin, eyes closed, begins to resemble a man's touch, begins to tremble into memories and vibrate into past sensations and my body reacts with a sudden violence.

I pull her hand where she had no intention of going and press it hard against me with an immediate, overwhelming need because that's the way I want you [Zil]: with the immediacy of coming and the surge of renewed wanting. (16)

The scene unfolds on a continuum that alternates between the sexual arousal of Pagli, the woman, and as a response to a long-lamented original maternal touch for Pagli, the child. The flux of her body experiencing varying sensorial zones calls to mind Kristeva's conception of the female in which she moves beyond the appearance of her identity into an encounter with an unnamable otherness, that gives rise to a truly subjective experience (Kristeva, *Powers of Horror,* 47–48). Pagli hints at a means by which to suspend language and by so doing suspend differences to privilege the body *feeling.* Indeed the sexual pleasure that Pagli comes into in this sequence (as she says, Mitsy's touch "s'est mis à ressembler à celui d'un homme" [begins to resemble a man's touch]) invokes a difference between the touch of a woman and that of a man. Yet the supple formulation ("s'est mis à ressembler" [begins to resemble]) remains approximate rather than categorical. Blurring the boundaries between Mitsy's role in her life and that of her lover Zil, Pagli suggests a complementarity that both characters offer to her that exceeds the heteronormative imperative.

Rebirth is further magnified in Pagli's love relationship with Zil. Framing the forbidden couple in an oneiric sequence, the narrative underscores at once the marginal and contestable status of the couple's fragile existence as much as the author's visible investment in the imaginative space as a first step toward imagining couples like Zil and Pagli. The infraction that a Creole fisherman and a Hindu married woman represent to Hindu customs is countered by the author's revalorization of such terms as "love," "touch," and "darkness/blackness" in the representation of their union. Mauritian history becomes the foundation upon which these terms and this couple are realized; and Zil is notably described as "le miracle issu de l'île dans sa vérité et non dans sa hantise de l'autre" (70) (the miracle of this island in its truth and not in its fear of difference [76]). A Creole fisherman, Zil invokes the history of former slaves, who once freed opted to take to the sea rather than continue to toil on the land. Residing on the outskirts, these fishermen today continue to live at the periphery of mainstream economic development. Distanced from Indian history under colonial rule, Zil and Pagli represent a specifically Mauritian history in which African slaves and Indian indentured laborers came to inhabit the island and today reflect a facet of Mauritian national identity.

The hands that Pagli's mother had used to give her child over to a life of isolation, violation, beatings, and confinement extend this time from Zil toward Pagli to provide a haven in which she finally unburdens herself of the shame in which her mother's rejection initially cast her. Pagli's yearning for rebirth within Zil—"renaître à l'intérieur de toi" (72); (to be born . . . in your arms [96])—magnifies the feeling she experiences with him, which effectively destabilizes the gender prescriptions in place. A privileged site in Devi's imaginary, the banyan tree, which the author evokes to stand in for a maternal space, is notably the site where the couple consummate their union. Léon Wurmser's assertion that love resides in the face and the eyes (*Mask of Shame*, 96) is validated in Zil's eyes, which offer Pagli "une vaste compréhension de moi, comme si d'un seul coup ils m'avaient vue, prise, comprise, aimée" (36) (something so full of understanding that it is as if you have already known me and loved me [36]). Whereas Zil's touch renders Pagli "intouchable" (111) (untouchable) in the Hindu cultural praxis, in *her* story his touch brings her body back from the *no-man's-land* in which the rape experience had lodged her. Zil's touch opens her up to the sensorial pleasures of her body and becomes the symbolical wedding band for their love. Because of the light and love that Zil's touch brings to Pagli, she ably displaces the condemnation of darkness away from epidermal slandering to highlight those experiences that, to her mind, belong under the rubric of what is truly black—experiences that derail paths toward love, and thus the freedom to be, in the present.

Pagli's rebirth in her love relationship with Zil eventually tempers her rage toward the *mofines*. Love, from which she was originally alienated, becomes the antidote to the shame experiences she has known. In the same way that the shame experience disrupted the potential to *see* Pagli as she really is (Pagli's mother, her cousin, the *mofines*), love through the eyes, this time Zil's eyes, restores the reciprocity and emotional attunement that allows for mutual recognition: Zil sees Pagli as she is; Pagli sees Zil as he is in the light of shared feelings. As Jessica Benjamin explains: "[T]o experience recognition in the fullest, most joyful way, entails the paradox that 'you' who are 'mine' are also different, new outside of me . . . The joy I take in your existence must include both my connection to you and your independent existence" (15). Where Wurmser reminds us that shame is at its core about feeling oneself to be unlovable (*Mask of Shame*, 93), love, a near synonym for mutual recognition (Benjamin, 15–16), is precisely the feeling that emboldens Pagli's subjectivity in configuring her relationship with Zil and Mitsy. An equally intersubjective feeling, love brings the eyes back to the experience of the self that the shame experience denied. As Pagli extols: "seul l'amour nous insoumise" (113) (love is our sole rebellion [120]).

More generally, Pagli's alliances with both Mitsy and Zil bring her into a broader framework of knowledge in which sharing multiple narratives of shame forges an alternative community. Where the *mofines* were previously viewed under the sign of rage as closed hearts and rigid bodies, much like figurines covered over in dust and mold, through the eyes of love they become, for Pagli, children "qui ont encore tant à apprendre" (150) (who still have so much to learn [154]). Gayatri Spivak reminds us that "internalized gendering perceived as ethical choice is the hardest roadblock for women the world over" (xxviii). Love, Pagli hopes the *mofines* will discover, is what is really pure and most human. Confined in the henhouse, she offers the narrative of her lived bodily experience as a testament to what love can do. Patrick Sultan, in his examination of the way in which the author displaces the classic Western mythical tale of Tristan and Isolde with the exemplary singularity of Pagli's self-affirmation and re-appropriation of her body in the company of Zil and Mitsy, concludes that in Devi's Weltanschauung "[l]'amour libère en ce qu'il permet d'accéder à son identité singulière, de déjouer la Loi d'un système social qui soumet la femme et la réduit au silence" (love is freeing for it allows one to come into one's unique identity, to elude the Law of a social system that subjugates the woman and reduces her to silence) (Sultan, *Orées*). Through love, Pagli discovers her body, her heart, her sexuality, and the space in which she might enjoy motherhood. In love, she sets aside the names attributed to her within Hindu strictures—Pagli, the crazy one; Daya, pity of the earth—and declares her longing to be called woman ("femme" [115]) on her terms and in accordance with the life experiences that have structured her self-knowledge. It is within the context of love that she imagines a deluge of rain that would carry away all the shame ("l'eau transporte et transvase toutes les hontes" [125]) that separates communities, one from the other.

Indeed the author recognizes that the utopian chant in which Pagli and Zil's love is expressed is the privilege of the poetics of literature: "L'amour est ce qui te porte et t'envole. L'amour est ce qui te construit, ouvre en toi des silences et en même temps t'interdit les paroles qui font mal" (134). (Love is what takes you and lifts you high. Love is what builds you. It opens strange holes of silence inside you and at the same time fills with you noise and forbids you to utter the words that hurt [141].) Yet within this poetic space, Devi gives voice, visibility, and texture to narratives that are covered over in cultural strictures like Hinduism. The deluge Pagli imagines toward the end of her narrative points to a longed-for national cleansing that would unearth those narratives that belong to Mauritian history and people.

The feelings through which the female protagonist expresses rage, humiliated fury, and revenge to give voice to shame and love mark a personal evolution that reflect junctures in a larger historical narrative that is specific to Mauritius. The choices Pagli makes for her body belong to this framework, as does Mitsy's choice to abandon the violence to her body brought on by repeated abortions. These women refuse a culture of silence and shame that cannot recognize the other. Hybridity is not only to be imagined in the child that would be the offspring of Zil and Pagli's love but also in each of the dialogues in which Pagli, Mitsy, and Zil engage, corporeally and linguistically (French and Creole). Reconfiguring the idea of abjection into these narratives of shame, Ananda Devi gestures at a novel way in which to engage with perceived differences. She denounces both in her work and in interviews the myriad permutations of "le culte de la différence" (an obsession with differences), however, and wherever it is practiced to perpetuate human injustices (Mongo-Mboussa, 2; Devi, "Écris hors de sa bulle," 13). In a 2003 interview, when asked to explain the harshness with which she addresses the Indo-Mauritian community in *Pagli*, Devi made clear:

Ce que je dénonce? C'est l'éternelle emprise du "communalisme," c'est-à-dire des divisions d'ordre ethnique, dans cette société, avec son cortège de préjugés, de mépris, d'incompréhension, ou plutôt de refus de comprendre. . . . C'est que les voix que l'on entend ne parlent pas de compassion ni de compréhension, mais de haine et de méfiance. C'est que c'est une pseudo-moralité basée sur des croyances religieuses aveugles et sans questionnement qui prend le dessus.

What do I denounce? The eternal stranglehold of "communalism," the ethnic divisions in this society, that are accompanied by a trail of prejudices, hate, lack of understanding, or rather refusal to understand. . . . It's that the voices that one hears speak neither of compassion nor of understanding but of hate and mistrust. It's that what has taken over is a sort of pseudo-morality based on a blind conviction in religious beliefs that does not dare to question. (Devi, "L'écriture est le monde"; translation mine)

In Pagli's narrative, Devi sheds light on how communalism, anchored in a Manichaean conception of the Mother/Whore principle, underwritten by patriarchal edicts, effectively impairs the specific desires of the individual woman, and alongside her, the potential of a society to transform itself. In this respect, while one can read rebirth materialized through the choices that Pagli makes in favor of an alternative community with Mitsy and Zil, the narrative notably suspends new births of children from contested unions. Mitsy refuses to bring a child into the world that is not born from love, and Pagli experiences only a form of "maternité sublimée" (sublimated maternity) insofar as she can only imagine (and the reader along with her) the child that could be the fruit of her union with Zil (Ravi, "Ananda Devi nous parle," 276). Véronique Bragard argues that the author's depiction of patriarchy in Mauritius suggests that the potential to break away from these forms of constraints can only be realized "at the metaphorical and discursive level" (190). Françoise Lionnet furthers Bragard's argument by pointing out that, in the face of the patriarchal invocation for a view of reality, Devi skillfully navigates the tensions between representation and will by "'hand[ing] over truth' to power" rather than "'speaking truth' to power" (Lionnet, 303). Fragility is therefore the leitmotif that Devi uses to weave together and hand over the narratives of Pagli, Mitsy, and Zil because as she forthrightly declares in the epigraph to the novel: "Tout roman est un acte d'amour" (All novels are acts of love). By representing the transformation of the female protagonist, who over the course of the novel comes into her own identity most powerfully because she practices love, compassion, and understanding, the author then gestures at an alternative prism through which to legitimize the rich tapestry of individual identities that constitute Mauritian society. The narratives of shame exchanged among Pagli, Mitsy, and Zil further hint at how to proceed to collapse illusory categories of difference predicated on purity and impurity. Privileging those differences that invariably interpenetrate, Pagli's, Mitsy's, and Zil's brands of subjectivity moreover recognize the need for the other to forge subjects.

Notes

1. Elspeth Probyn's work on shame has been instrumental in clarifying the distinction between shame as an emotion and shame as an affect. See "Doing Shame" in her *Blush: Faces of Shame*, 1–35.

2. See for example Véronique Bragard's analysis of the female body in "Eaux obscures du souvenir: Femme et Mémoire dans l'oeuvre de Ananda Devi," *Thamyris/Intersecting* N8 (2001): 187–199.

3. Interview with Ananda Devi: "L'écriture est le monde, elle est le chemin et le but," http://www.indereunion.net/actu/ananda/intervad.html, February 2003, accessed 31 May 2010. My translation. All subsequent translations are mine, unless otherwise indicated.

4. All quotations are from the principal literary work *Pagli*. The translations that follow refer to the English version of the novel, translated by the author in 2007.

5. *Lajja* is also the Sanskrit and Hindi term for shame. I choose to emphasize the Bengali usage given the historical context in which the term gained momentum. Much has been produced in contemporary intellectual circles on the topic, including Salman Rushdie's *Shame* (1983) and the novella *Lajja*, first published in 1993 by Taslima Nasreen, for which the author was publicly persecuted and forced into exile in Sweden.

6. This historical background is indebted to a number of works, including Partha Chatterjee's chapters on "The Nation and Its Women" and "Women and the Nation" in *The Nation and Its Fragments: Colonial and Postcolonial Histories;* Himani Bannerji's chapter "Attired in Virtue: The Discourse on Shame (Lajja) and Clothing of the Bhadramahila in Colonial Bengal" in *From the Seams of History;* and "Mapping the Colonial Body: Sexual Economies and the State in Colonial India," by Janet Price and Margrit Shildrick, in *Feminist Theory and the Body: A Reader.*

7. While I have referred to the works of both Elizabeth Grosz and Julia Kristeva to advance my argument here, the reader should note that Grosz does contest Kristeva's thesis on woman's bodily fluids in her chapter "Sexed Bodies" in *Volatile Bodies.*

8. Anjali Prabhu analyzes the historical tensions between the larger Indo-Mauritian community and Mauritians of African ancestry in her study of the significance of hybridity in post-independence Mauritius. See *Hybridity: Limits, Transformations, Prospects* (Albany: State University of New York Press, 2007). In the Anglophone context, Shalini Puri addresses the difficulties of racial mixing between Africans and Indians in "Facing the Music: Gender, Race and Dougla Poetics," in her *The Caribbean Postcolonial: Social Equality, Post-Nationalism and Cultural Hybridity* (New York: Palgrave Macmillan, 2004).

15 Shame and Belonging in Postcolonial Algeria

Anna Rocca

> Man above all other animals insists on walking erect. In lowering his eyes and bowing his head, he is vulnerable in a quite unique way. . . . [T]he nature of the experience of shame guarantees a perpetual sensitivity to any violation of the dignity of man.
>
> Silvan Tomkins

In Assia Djebar's last autobiographical work, *Nulle part dans la maison de mon père*, shame is experienced in several forms and cultural settings. The earliest memory of shame that the author recalls is when she was a baby. Sleeping in the same room as her parents at approximately eighteen months old, she remembers hearing her mother's moaning of pleasure. The "dérangeante" (disturbing) proximity to the parents' bed makes her feel ashamed (97). Once she becomes an adult, the author recaptures the confused sensation that she felt at that time, describing it as a "malaise" (uneasiness), a discomfort that takes the form of a "culpabilité, pour ainsi dire animale. Comme si je ne devais pas entendre!" (culpability, so to speak savage. As if I should not hear!) (96).[1] Her feeling of shame therefore influences both her adolescence and adulthood. This experience echoes Silvan Tomkins's words, when he says that the sensation of shame implies the inevitability of "a perpetual sensitivity to any violation" of dignity (*Affect, Imagery, Consciousness*, 2:132). By searching for the causes of her suicide attempt in *Nulle part dans la maison de mon père*, Assia Djebar meticulously recaptures the overlapping causes of personal and social abuses in order to make sense of the loss of self-respect that she and her people experience.

In this chapter, by using both literary and psychoanalytic theory, I argue that in *Nulle part* the author confronts the daughter's disillusionment with paternal love and progressively reveals its connections and layered perversions with shame. Furthermore, by representing the reality of no return and placelessness for the narrator-author, and by extension for Algerian women, Djebar fights against the oblivion that would condemn her to self-effacement. Additionally, by means of exposing her deeper feelings and emotions, the narrator-author-and-reader-of-herself discovers the origins and dynamics of the shame of being. Eventually, her progressive awareness will allow the re-creation of new forms of belonging, for one can say that she belongs when she starts to face and trust her own feelings. I will first analyze the relationship between shame and belonging and then discuss the problematic association between Assia Djebar and belonging. I will lastly examine the ways in which shame, belonging, and desire interrelate with each other in *Nulle part*.

Shame and Belonging

In 1962 and 1963, the publication of the first two volumes of *Affect, Imagery, Consciousness* marked the beginning of the profound impact that American psychologist Silvan Tomkins had on our understanding of human emotions and motivations. Tomkins used literary works to support his discoveries in the study of shame. Almost forty years later, the essay collection *Scenes of Shame: Psychoanalysis, Shame and Writing* cogently proves the centrality of literature to understanding affects and the potential of collaboration between psychoanalysts and literary scholars in the study of shame. In fact, as co-editors Joseph Adamson and Hilary Clark underscore: "[O]ne of the most important functions of literature has been to provide a privileged place of redress, a sphere of expression where emotional life can be explored and refined in ways that are discouraged elsewhere" (6). Additionally, Donald Nathanson reminds us how this collection "forces new awareness of all affective experience on those who search for the source of meaning in the writers who have moved them" (Foreword, viii).

At the present time, Tomkins's idea that shame originates from the profound experience of being not wanted has taken root in psychology. This feeling of being both cast out and unaccepted undermines one's ability to fit into one's own community. For this reason we can say that shame is at the same time a personal and a social experience engaging, as J. Brooks Bouson reminds us, "not only the individual's feelings of inferiority and inadequacy in comparison to others but also the individual's deep inner sense of being flawed or defective or of having failed to meet the expectations of the 'ideal self'" ("'Quiet As It's Kept,'" 208). *Scenes of Shame* ties shame to disempowerment in a variety of ways, on the basis of gender, sexual orientation, race, physical disability, and subjection in general. It also underlines how shame plays the essential role of "threat to attachment" in the establishment and regulation of social bonds and interactions (Adamson and Clark, 3). Shame and belonging are thus constitutionally related, in the sense that wherever shame manifests, there is also a perception of isolation, of disconnection and a lack of sense of belonging. Concerning this topic, Brené Brown notices how "[s]hame is often associated with the feeling of 'not belonging' or being rejected from a valued group or community" (113).

Shame and belonging share at least three important traits: they cross the boundaries between private and public; they are crucial in the development of identity; and they are linked to desire. Shame and belonging, as we said, are at the threshold between private and public. Among the multiple definitions of shame, Virginia Burrus offers one that defines it as passages from private to public, from personal to common:

> Shame is at the heart of the anguished awareness of human limits at the point where those limits are exceeded, conveying the power as well as the danger of relationality itself . . . Shame underlies and nourishes our complex and differentiated, self-transgressing and self-transcending capacities for intimacy and empathy, creativity and sociality, ethical response and political action. (4)

Belonging too could be personally experienced, as feeling part of something, of being welcomed, accepted, and engaged. It could additionally be described as an understanding of public interconnectedness, or as an experience of values that are common to a larger group and that are influenced by the actions of others.

Because both overlap between private and public spheres, shame and belonging are also critical in the formation of identity and self-image. Tomkins observes:

> In contrast to all other affects, shame is an experience of the self by the self. At the moment when the self feels ashamed, it is felt as a sickness within the self. Shame is the most reflexive of affects in that the phenomenological distinction between the subject and object of shame is lost. Why is shame so close to the experienced self? It is because the self lives in the face, and within the face the self burns brightest in the eyes. Shame turns the attention of the self and others away from other objects to this most visible residence of self, increases its visibility, and thereby generates the torment of self-consciousness. (2:133)

Inspired by Tomkins to analyze the close relationship between shame, performance, and identity, Eve Kosofsky Sedgwick notices how "[i]n the developmental process, shame is now often considered the affect that most defines the space wherein a sense of self will develop . . . it is the place where the *question* of identity arises most originally and most relationally. At the same time, shame both derives from and aims toward sociability" (37). Concerning belonging, social studies have often talked about identity as a complex system that is primarily shaped by where we are and with whom we are. Belonging both enriches and challenges identity, for it can give and deny humans a sense of identity and security in their lives. Belonging is never static; it changes in reaction to the new emotional and geographical spaces that people experience or it conforms to a community's values, needs, and priorities. As Aimee Carrillo Rowe emphasizes, belonging is in constant movement and produces itself through the combined processes of being and becoming. Belonging, she notices, is formed by two words, "Be-longing . . . placed beside each other," that are there to suggest an imperative: "The command is to 'be' 'longing,' not to be still, or be quiet, but to be longing" (16).

Shame and belonging are also intrinsically linked to desire. Shame is related to desire because it implies one's self-awareness in relation to the other. Additionally, shame is also the experience of the way one imagines him- or herself to appear to the other; in this latter case, shame manifests as a suspension of desire. Helen Block Lewis defines this side of shame as the "vivid imagery of the self in the other's eyes" ("Shame and the Narcissistic Personality," 107). Belonging implies at the same time the desire to share, the expectation of being part of and being included, as well as the fear of irrecoverable loss. Elspeth Probyn defines belonging as "a tenacious and fragile desire that is . . . increasingly performed in the knowledge of the impossibility of ever really and truly belonging, along with the fear that the stability of belonging and the sanctity of belonging are forever past" (*Outside Belongings*, 8).

Assia Djebar and Belonging

Belonging, desire for connection, and the visualization of alternative ways to belong are central traits in Djebar's work. Particularly in *Nulle part,* her revisitation of the oppositional societal dynamics in which she grew up in Algeria make her aware of the damaging overlap of shame and lack of belonging, which eventually leads to her attempted suicide. By looking at shame as a social and personal issue, Brené Brown stresses how women in particular *"often experience shame where they are entangled in a web of layered, conflicting and competing social-community expectations"* (30; emphasis in original). These expectations, Brown continues, are coming from rigid social values enforcing who, what, and how women should be and behave. These expectations are frequently contradictory and in opposition to each other. For this reason, one may wonder what level of incongruous anticipatory desires we are going to find when the community has also been subjected to colonization. The latter is intended as a structure that has its functionality and identity embedded in an oppositional system of hostility. For the most part in *Nulle part,* Algeria is defined through the adverse development of two societies, the Algerian and the French, set against each other. Because of multilayered indigenous and imported clashing beliefs, Algerian women carry deeply the consequences of this adversity in that they are isolated in their shame and alienated from themselves.

Among other critics, Valérie Orlando emphasizes the problematic aspects of Djebar's belonging as an Algerian female author. Underscoring Djebar's risks of alienation as public persona and writer, Orlando writes: "All women, whether white or of color, must step into a public space in order to establish agency and voice. This public sphere is often an exiled space—a place of marginalization on the peripheries of traditional feminine roles" (11). A second challenging connection for Djebar is the one between belonging and language. Adlai Murdoch was one of the first to analyze how the author's exile needs to be understood not just as a separation from sites of belonging but from language itself, her maternal language, the language of affection and tenderness. In 1993, by reading *L'Amour, la fantasia* through a Lacanian psychoanalytic discourse, Murdoch emphasizes the inherent risk in the use of the colonizer's language to express desire, and thus comments: "[T]he question [is] whether language will merely mark desire or whether it will mask it as well. In other words, if the colonizer's language is read as the mark of colonial desire, then its appropriation by the colonized may undermine the very goal it sets out to achieve, screening the desire of the colonized subject" (78).

Most recently, in *Literary Disinheritance,* Najat Rahman further explains the awkwardness of the author's paternal heritage, the French language: "[T]his heritage is not proper to the self. It is a heritage not in one's language and not in one's mode of expression. It is an unexpected inheritance of conquest and of violence that is given out lovingly to the female child by the father. It is also the father as symbolic order who is inherited with language" (71). However, Rahman also sees how in Djebar's work "[a] new beginning . . . lies in language, where possibility beyond the violent history can emerge" (110). Years before, Clarisse Zimra arrived at the same conclusion by observing how in *Ces voix qui m'assiègent* Djebar places herself on the side of writers who "invest the only space that is fully theirs: writing" (152). This apparent contradiction between a language that simultaneously expresses her alienation and a writing through which the author is able to recreate a different reality could be explained by analyzing Djebar's poetics.

The author's quest, as Mireille Calle-Gruber elucidates, is not a discovery of identity but the finding of "la singularité dans l'altérité" (the uniqueness in otherness), explained as a "mouvement de ré-union et de deuil," (movement of re-union and mourning) (*Assia Djebar*, 253). In this way, Calle-Gruber defines Djebar's discourse as a place where writing neutralizes a dichotomous view of the world, thus allowing the self to both inhabit the other and also be inhabited by it, in order to re-patch and together mourn shared memories. Furthermore, in Djebar's work one needs to distinguish between the process of writing and its product. The author often associates the act of writing with suffering and struggle. She emphasizes, on the one hand, the impossible task of narrating death and violence, and on the other, the constraint of having to express emotions in the language of Descartes. However, Djebar's reinvention of the French language is a powerful tool that allows her to remold reality as a multifaceted entity in which the Western system of thought is replaced with a conception of place, home, and body as they are all interrelated in a single dimension. It is thanks to this reinvention that she engages with issues of connection, reconstruction, and transformation.

The association between belonging and homeland is particularly problematic. Both in Djebar's fictions and her autobiographical writings, her country and town are depicted as historically marked by colonization, which is to say by separation and opposition, and thus defined through the hostile development of two societies, the Algerian and the French. Algeria is characterized as well as being internally unable to socially embrace changes. Furthermore, several critics also notice a progressive movement of expatriation in her last twenty years of writing, accelerated by the outbreak of the civil war in Algeria and the emergence of Islamic fundamentalism. In 2006, by analyzing Djebar's production from her early novel, *La Soif* to the later *La Disparition de la langue française,* Jane Hiddleston observes how the author "gradually, increasingly, finds that her native land is lost to her" (2). Hiddleston interprets Djebar's trajectory as "a movement out of Algeria . . . a partial expatriation haunted by the apparition of an Algeria she cannot grasp . . . a gradual withdrawal from any possible identification with Algeria as a knowable point of reference" (10, 11).

In *Ces voix,* Djebar gives a name to her process of expatriation: "la falaise du non-retour" (the cliff of no-return), a tangible reality representing a turning point in her life (206). In 1999, at the time she published *Ces voix,* the author was dealing with feelings of forced expatriation and exile. These feelings were the result of her home country collapsing into a civil war between 1992 and 1994. By 1995 other countries' embassies in Algeria were closed, and four years later the country's new president sought a way to end the eight-year-old conflict. Djebar's early decision to study in France gave her a privileged position of distance from and proximity to both Algeria and France. That distance, described at times as a gift but also as a sacrifice and a tribute, in *Ces Voix* had come to an end by showing its other side: the beginning of a rupture (206–207). The link Djebar makes between expatriation and freedom to write underscores the author's moral and political engagement as a female witness. Writing allows her to express agency, to have a voice, and to remain historically alert toward the present and future collective amnesias of both countries. As Djebar says, this responsibility is first of all toward herself, "pour ne pas me perdre de vue" (not to lose touch with myself). This is a statement which emphasizes her undeniable desire for self-connection and her hopes of establishing new places of connection and nourishment (207).

Later on in *Ces voix,* the author's initial feelings of destabilization toward exile turn into a voluntary and fully conscious act of self-expulsion from and opposition to her country. Her task is to reject postcolonial Algeria and to escape its social oppression and moral contamination. The author thus maintains that "dans un monde qui tend à s'installer comme Islam politique, être écrivain . . . c'est évidemment . . . être voué à l'expatriation" (in a world that heads toward political Islam, being a writer . . . is evidently . . . being doomed to expatriation) (216). Writing and geographical mobility are thus crucial to visualizing and constructing alternative spaces and ways of belonging. In *Ces voix,* Djebar's distinction between language and land emphasizes how, while the land is lost, her reinvention of language enables the manufacturing of her own sense of belonging (215).

Shame, Belonging, and Desire in *Nulle part dans la maison de mon père*

Eight years later, in 2007, her last autobiography brings to the extreme both the responsibility toward herself and the desire for belonging. Belonging here exceeds the experience of home as homeland and becomes a process and a desire for historical reconnection with her inner self, set against the multilayered origins and dynamics of the shame of being. The author's self-examination will eventually allow her to envision ways to both emotionally connect with herself and to reconfigure her world. For the author, being "nulle part dans la maison de mon père" means to recognize her lack of belonging first as Algerian and then as an Algerian woman. It then means facing the multiple self-destructive processes, feeding divisions and hatred, which are ingrained in her society of origin.

Strategically placed in isolation to mark a space of difference and consideration, the chapter "*Intermède*" acutely describes the subtle perversion of the colonization process.[2] The latter starts from the colonizer's delusional idea of conquering a place as if it were virgin and uninhabited, in order to project in this space his desire for creation (35). The colonizer's denial of the existence of natives triggers an irreversible rupture between natives and their land, women and men, and finally between compatriots (35). Inhabitants are invisible presences for the conqueror, who then feels no responsibility toward them (35). The colonizer leaves natives with the burden of the consequences of the colony: self-destruction (35). Natives ravage and alienate themselves and their land under the illusion of continuing to claim a virile idea of past glories and heroism (35). In reality, because the link between natives and their past has been broken by the colonizer's denial, the past, which is visible at present in the form of ruins, is now "anonyme" (anonymous), with no name or belonging (35). From this point on, the rupture is permanent because the perception of time has changed: time is no longer indefinite, it now has a beginning and end; history possesses an oppositional meaning for the two parties (35).

From this first French denial of Algerians' existence, which Djebar refers to above, division infiltrates Algerian families and relationships between men and women and appears in the form of hatred and lack of understanding (35). Separation penetrates also as torment and harassment between generations within Algerian society, in the form of alienation and denial (35). The consequences of these processes are devastating, and they impact Algerian women first. This is why, to this complex scenario, the author adds another self-destructive aspect of her society, this time generated by the complicity between patriarchy and religion, and aimed against women. In the second part of *Nulle part,* after approaching and analyzing her past memories, the author decides to stop the narration: "J'interromps ici ce récit" (I interrupt the story here) (207).

This break seems to mark a space of shared reflection with her readers. After it, she rhetorically asks herself where the origin of being "nowhere" starts. Is it from women's segregation, which creates rivalry and divisions among them, or from lack of trust between fathers and daughters, as in the case of the Prophet Muhammad with his last daughter? The lack of trust between fathers and daughters is the answer. As the author emphasizes, the Prophet's last daughter, finding herself "dépossédée de l'héritage paternal, en souffrira au point d'en mourir" (dispossessed of paternal heritage, will suffer to such an extent as to die from it) (207). The painful association between the Prophet and his daughter's death anticipates the description of the author's attempted suicide and links the latter with the daughter's introjection of paternal condemnation. Being "nowhere" means in this case that the narrator is not able to associate home with a place that can nurture, include, support, and respect her as a daughter. Division and hatred feed the relationship between fathers and daughters as well as the interaction between women, who can only share oppression and a lack of freedom (207).

In 1993, Winifred Woodhull pointed out how the association between Algerian land and Algerian women is a fantasy common to both Algerian and French men. In this sense Algerian women incarnate the colony's cultural identity for both groups of men. Within this male collective imagination, Woodhull continues, women are "at once the emblem of the colony's refusal to receive France's 'emancipatory seed' and the gateway to penetration" (19). This argument that women signify at the same time the societal barricade and the entrance recalls Brené Brown's notion of conflicting expectations. Moreover, this paradoxical situation is further exacerbated by the inability of Algerian women to meet the hopes of contradictory desires coming from two societies set against each other. Finally, these clashing imaginations make it unthinkable for women to envision an alternative place of desire that originates from their own needs and preferences.

In *Nulle part*, conflicting male expectations and contradictory desires emerge as a tension between desire for belonging and experiences of shame. The latter is pervasive, affects both genders, and in its manifestations matches Tomkins's definition of shame as "the affect of indignity, of defeat, of transgression and of alienation" (2:118). In particular, body shame is often crucial, causing mixed feelings of transgression, indignity, alienation, disgust, contempt, and self-contempt. All the episodes concerning body shame happen in public spaces or are imagined as happening in a dichotomized public space. The latter is characterized by the presence of the desiring other's gaze as well as by the idea of the self being perceived by the desiring other's gaze. Concerning this "doubleness of experience," Helen Lewis reminds us, "In order for shame to occur, there must be a relationship between the self and the other in which the self cares about the other's evaluation . . . Fascination with the other and sensitivity to the other's treatment of the self renders the self more vulnerable in shame" (107–108). We will see how in the chapter "La bicyclette," both fascination with, and sensitivity to, the other make shame and alienation surface and collide.

"La bicyclette" narrates a particularly intense episode of paternal violence directed against the narrator, at the time she was between four and five years old. At the origin of the father's hostility is the fear that his daughter's legs could be seen in public. In different versions, the same episode is narrated in *Ombre sultane, Vaste est la prison,* and *Nulle part.* This repetition with differences recalls Tomkins's notion of nuclear scenes. According to him, these are described as scenes that "we can never totally or permanently achieve or possess" (3:96). Whereas in *Ombre sultane* and in *Nulle part,* the father is present and his rage against his daughter directly causes her deep sense of shame, and subsequently her alienation, in *Vaste est la prison* the father is physically absent but emotionally internalized by his daughter as limit, judgment, and punishment. The author here remembers herself as a child feeling guilty by only imagining her father's gaze looking at her, while innocently playing with Maurice, the French son of a family friend (265).

Shame, as Tomkins maintains, can be activated even without the physical presence of the other. In this case, though, it is the narrator's sense of guilt that surfaces. Guilt differs from shame because it is more about doing something wrong than feeling internally wrong. In *Vaste est la prison*, the narrator feels paralyzed and unable to move her arm toward Maurice, who is inviting her to climb a tree and reach the branch that he is on. Because she imagines her father judging her and making her feel at fault, she is unable to physically respond. In this imagined scene, the narrator includes her mother too, looking impotently at her daughter when the father arrives and catches her at fault. The mother's powerlessness returns in greater detail in *Nulle part*. For now, it is sufficient to notice how the non-intervention of her mother emphasizes, first, the narrator's inability to feel supported and understood within the family, and subsequently her feelings of deep alienation and isolation.

The episode of "La Balançoire" in *Ombre sultane* mirrors the one of "La bicyclette" in *Nulle part*. At the center of both, there is the paternal condemnation of public exposure of his daughter's legs. Similar aspects characterize both episodes. The dichotomized public space of the courtyard in the teachers' building is the setting for both incidents. While Algerian and French adults seem to be extremely aware of their cultural differences and thus spatially alert, Algerian and French children are playing with each other. In both episodes, the daughter first recalls the unpleasant tone of her father, its lack of humanity; then, she perceives him as an alien, a stranger that she has never met before (*Ombre sultane*, 147; *Nulle part*, 49, 50). In both "La Balançoire" and "La bicyclette," the daughter feels ashamed of both her father's behavior and his language; therefore she experiences contempt. In *Nulle part* her shame turns additionally into pure disgust for him (*Ombre sultane*, 148; *Nulle part*, 50). In both episodes, the disturbing violence marks a rupture for the daughter. It is described as an expulsion and an exile from childhood in *Ombre sultane* (145, 148) and as a disruption and trauma in *Nulle part* (52). Additionally, in *Nulle part*, the narrator's sense of confusion, solitude, and alienation is highlighted by her mother's passivity. This repeated episode takes up a few lines in *Vaste est la prison*, four pages in *Ombre sultane*, and twelve in *Nulle part*.

Furthermore, in "La bicyclette," the scene describing the narrator's attempt to ride a bike with the help of Maurice is remembered twice, as if the narrator desires to finally seize some form of control over it (48–49, 55–56). Multifaceted aspects of the shame of being emerge here along with intertwined dynamics of shame, belonging, and desire. In this episode we witness the father's hostility against the daughter; the father's shame toward his compatriots, about the exposure of his daughter's legs; and the acquiescence of the mother that neither takes her daughter's side nor eases her state of confusion by talking to her. On the side of the narrator, we also witness the emergence of different affects. Shame for her father progressively changes into disgust and rage. Anger at her father originates with his appropriation of the taboo image of her naked legs, which gives the author a fragmented and sinful vision of her body. The feelings of confusion and alienation come as a result of not being understood and then being unfairly punished. Finally, there is the emergence of her unachieved desire to be seen, loved, accepted, and respected for what she is: a five-year-old child wanting to physically explore and experiment in the public space.

Colonial, patriarchal, and religious forces coexist in their contradictory aspects and act here as an invisible presence. At the center of the microcosm of this colonized village, the father stands as a tragic figure caught up in the dynamics of being shamed and feeling shame. He is caught in the desire to represent simultaneously a symbol of modernity that his position as a French teacher implicitly gives him, defend his Algerian belonging and sense of identity, and preserve patriarchal values such as protecting his daughter from being ashamed in the village. It is the violent surfacing of this last desire that will eventually set off the hostility against his daughter. It will also trigger his own sense of alienation from himself for being different from his compatriots. The narrator clearly explains in this chapter the contradictory elements her family lives in. Her parents show acceptance and admiration for French society, honor its educational system, and respect its religion and emulate its lifestyle (51–52). Furthermore, the narrator's parents live in a building reserved for teachers of French and let their daughter play with Maurice, the son of a French widow, whose inclusion in the narrator's family is documented by his presence in a family picture.[3] Besides the conflicting position of the father, the mother too is split between her own personal process of emancipation and integration in French society and her traditional place within the family that never questions her husband's authority. In this fluctuating situation of unstable values, the exposure of her child's legs symbolically stands as an absolute and clear symbol of the paternal patriarchal resistance to colonialism.

"Je ne veux pas . . . devant les autres, au village!" (I do not want . . . in front of the others, in the village!): these two phrases, screamed by the father at his wife in regard to his daughter's shame, can be seen from two directions (56). In the father, they show indignity and transgression; in the daughter, they are alienation and loss. The suspension of paternal love signifies for the daughter the beginning of the fragmentation of her body's image. The narrator underlines how, by submitting her to the figurative ancestral tribunal against women, the father appropriates his daughter's body and reinstates the duty of invisibility (55). In addition, by focusing his attention on her physical self, the father positions himself in the place of the desiring other's gaze, the compatriot, and thus becomes one more desiring male among all the others. The narrator observes: "C'était déclarer que tout garçon, tout adulte, tout vieillard est forcément un voyeur lubrique devant l'image nue de deux jambes de fillette, séparées du reste de son corps et pédalant dans une cour!" (It was like admitting that all young men, adult and elder are inevitably lecherous voyeurs once confronted by the image of a little girl's legs, separated from the rest of her body and pedaling in the courtyard!) (52). Eventually, by dismissing the privileged bond of love between father and daughter and by projecting his fear of the imagined desiring others over her body, the father's rejection makes his daughter feel unwelcome and misrecognized for what she really is (58).

Because the father is in the ambiguous position of being at the same time the progressive spouse with his wife and the unconscious guardian of the gynaeceum with her daughter, the latter will grow up with a harsh responsibility (381). She will have to hide and protect her father's shameful and conservative side initially, in front of her French classmates and teachers, and later, in society: "preserver l'image de mon père devant les 'Autres' m'importait davantage" (to preserve the image of my father in front of the "Others" was what mattered more) (260). But most importantly, after the first episode of paternal violence against her, which symbolizes the beginning of a disconnection between father and daughter, the latter unconsciously starts to protect the only possible relationship of love between him and her. In order to be loved, she cannot betray the father's idealized expectations of her as "la petite princesse de mon père" (my father's little princess) (386). Because of that, she is forced to repress her desires and to make him always feel proud of her by means of intellectual achievements. This inner compromise with herself to safeguard her paternal love explains the narrator's impulse to attempt suicide. It also clarifies her subsequent rage, once she realizes she has obliterated her true self for so many years. The narrator thus tragically reflects upon her life: "Ainsi le plus grave, le plus triste . . . fut d'avoir entretenu mon propre silence: *après*. Je me suis engloutie à force de m'être tue . . . Se taire devant soi-même: ce fut le plus grave" (Thus the most serious, the saddest . . . was to have kept my own silence: *after*. I swallowed myself through silence . . . To hush up in front of myself: this was the most serious) (385).

Shame, belonging, and desire surface in contradictory ways in the chapter "Dans la rue" too. This time it is the narrator that speaks about herself, once she has been exposed to the public spaces of Algiers. On the streets of the city, disguised in European clothing, she feels shame for being taken as a foreigner. The affect of shame appears in all its physical manifestations, including the dropping of eyes and blushing (305). This conscious exposure of her shameful self points to the narrator's own sense of belonging, cornered between the desire to belong and to be recognized by her compatriots and its impossibility: "[J]e me sentais en même temps quêteuse, mendiante—d'un désir de solidarité! . . . —Je suis de chez vous! Je suis comme vous! Ils auraient ricané, m'auraient insultée. C'était pourtant la soif de 'leur' reconnaissance qui me taraudait!" (I felt at the same time in search of and begging—for a desire of solidarity! . . . —I am coming from your same place! I am like you! They would have sniggered, they would have insulted me. And yet, it was the thirst for "their" recognition that tormented me!) (312).

Besides her negative feeling of being rejected, she is also excited about being in public on her own and she is even euphoric about being on her own without being controlled. At that time, as the narrator reminds us, only a few adolescents were allowed to go on the street just for the pleasure of walking (305). To be able to circulate in public space and interact with locals she had to conceal her maternal language and pretend to be French. In this way, she could avoid being recognized as one of them and thus evade being publicly shamed by her compatriots. In fact, what the narrator describes as a "natural respect" that Algerian men show toward European women turns easily into hostility with regard to their own women (305). This relational dynamic echoes Tomkins's position that "shame in interpersonal relationships comes not from the increase in distance between the self and the other, but from the decrease in such distance whenever there is any taboo on intimacy. In any such interpersonal relationship it is the sudden loss of distance or the threat of it which may provoke shame" (2:193). In our case, the cultural and physical distance between Algerian men and European women makes possible a form of respect. Conversely, when confronted with the perceived shamelessness of an emancipated woman of their own clan, the dynamic of feeling shame and making the other/woman feeling ashamed happens.

In this complex relationship between Algerian men on the one side, and European and Algerian women on the other, desire and denial play a paramount role. In remembering the feeling of transgression that was produced by the first exchange of presumed love letters, the narrator gives us an excellent portrayal of the mirroring development of desire and repression between Algerian and French society. The scene is spatially constructed in concentric rings: at the center, under the light of street lamps, during one of the many French celebrations, couples are dancing clutched to each other while enjoying staring into each other's eyes. Around them, outside of the ring of light, in the dark, Algerians look at them dancing, in silence. The French couples feel their presence and seem to be pleased to be seen. From her house, eyes glued to the window glass, the narrator sees the whole scene but looks in particular at the way Algerians stare at French couples and feels ashamed for them. She is also attracted by their dancing, but acknowledges a difference between her vital physical yearning and the Algerian male's eyes; gaze and desire are respectively described as voyeuristic, lecherous, and barbaric (248). She finds herself ashamed for their repressed desires that surface as hypocritical envy. She knows that those Algerian men will never share their pleasures with their women; they will keep them undesirable and under control. By gazing at the French couples as the Algerians are doing, the narrator starts feeling their own libidos penetrating her.

I would like to conclude by underlining how in this homeland that Djebar describes, there are no winners. The tragic emergence of multifaceted forms of shame parallels a profound lack of belonging and of thwarted desire. As we have seen, in the society the author portrays, women are the most vulnerable to shame. In fact, in addition to the dynamic of feeling shame and being ashamed in the public arena that affects both genders, men often project on women their limits, fears, and expectations, the latter born in a confrontational system with a male other. Because of that, women often lack human connection, complicity, support, and a sense of nurturing within their own families. These needs deeply undermine their possibilities for imagining life as exploration of self. The few episodes described are remarkably centered on the principal characters' confusion between local and foreign, trust and hostility, compatriot and enemy, complicity and confrontation, desire and contempt. When the child becomes for the father the object of shame, when the father becomes to the daughter the pure stranger, when the mother must respect her husband even at a cost to her daughter, when silence is a social rule that is enforced in order for women to fit into families and communities, when women are kept silent, when spouses are unable to show their desires to their women, when these last are unable to feel desire and desirable and are pitted against one another, what can we do?

In *Nulle part,* Djebar starts by facing her own denial and personally confronts the disorder by using basic social common values. Through writing, her effective tool of critical awareness, she envisions first a connection with herself and then one with her readers. In fact, as Adamson and Clark suggest,

> writing, precisely because it allows one to hide and reveal oneself at the same time, also allows for an intimacy and trust to be established with another or others, perhaps, in a way that no other situation provides . . . The writer seeks some degree of display, even when she is in hiding, and must be able to trust in an audience, in the willingness of others to see her as she is without undue fear of overexposure or invasion or rejection. (28–29)

During the reading of *Nulle part,* Calle-Gruber observes, one can measure "la peine de l'écriture" (the sorrow of writing), yet the author finds the freedom to become resilient in the face of shame and the energy to consider this work as only the beginning of a much deeper discovery of her own path ("Écrire de main morte," 13).

Notes

The chapter epigraph is from *Affect, Imagery, Consciousness,* 2:132.

1. Starting from here, all translations from French into English are mine.

2. In the table of contents, this chapter title is the only one intentionally placed without a number. It is also the only one in italics.

3. The picture the narrator refers to appears in Mireille Calle-Gruber, *Assia Djebar* (Paris: ADPF, Ministère des Affaires étrangères, 2006), 3.

Bibliography

Abdel-Nour, Farid. "National Responsibility." *Political Theory* 31.5 (Oct. 2003): 593–719.

Abella, Rafael. *La vida cotidiana bajo el régimen de Franco.* 1984; Madrid: Ediciones Tema de Hoy, 1996.

Abós Santabárbara, Ángel Luis. *La historia que nos enseñaron.* Madrid: Foca, 2003.

Ackerman, Erin M. Pryor. "Becoming and Belonging: The Productivity of Pleasures and Desires in Octavia Butler's Xenogenesis Trilogy." *Extrapolation* 49.1 (Spring 2008): 24–44.

Adamson, Joseph, and Hilary Clark. Introduction. *Scenes of Shame: Psychoanalysis, Shame, and Writing.* Ed. Joseph Adamson and Hilary Clark.

———, eds. *Scenes of Shame: Psychoanalysis, Shame, and Writing.* Albany: State University of New York Press, 1999.

Ahmed, Sara. *The Cultural Politics of Emotion.* Edinburgh: Edinburgh University Press, 2004.

———. *Queer Phenomenology: Orientations, Objects, and Others.* Durham, NC: Duke University Press, 2006.

Amara, Fadela, and Sylvia Zappi. *Ni Putes ni Soumises.* Paris: La Découverte, 2003.

Anderson, Crystal S. "'The Girl Isn't White': New Racial Dimensions in Octavia Butler's *Survivor*." *Extrapolation* 47.1 (2006): 35–50.

Angot, Christine. *Léonore, toujours.* Paris: Gallimard, 1994.

———. *L'Inceste.* Paris: Stock, 1999.

Atwood, Margaret. *Cat's Eye.* New York: Bantam, 1989.

———. "Running with the Tigers." *Flesh and the Mirror.* Ed. Lorna Sage. London: Virago Press, 1994. 117–35.

Bacchilega, Cristina. *Postmodern Fairytales: Gender and Narrative Strategies.* Philadelphia: University of Pennsylvania Press, 1992.

Badinter, Elisabeth. *Man/Woman: The One is the Other.* London: Collins Harvill, 1989.

Bannerji, Himani. "Attired in Virtue: The Discourse on Shame (Lajja) and Clothing of the Bhadramahila in Colonial Bengal." *From the Seams of History: Essays on Indian Women.* Ed. Bharati Ray. Delhi: Oxford University Press, 1995. 67–106.

Barthes, Roland. *Roland Barthes par Roland Barthes.* Paris: Seuil, 1975.

Bartky, Sandra. *Femininity and Domination: Studies in the Phenomenology of Oppression.* New York: Routledge, 1990.

Bauer, Alain. *La Criminalité en France. Rapport de l'Observatoire national de la délinquance 2007.* Paris: OND and INHES, CNRS Editions, 2007.

Baumeister, Roy F., and Mark R. Leary. "The Need to Belong: Desire for Interpersonal Attachments as a Fundamental Human Motivation." *Psychological Bulletin* 117.3 (1995): 497–529.

Beauvoir, Simone de. *The Second Sex.* Trans. H. M. Hartley. New York: Vintage, 1989.

Bellil, Samira. *Dans l'enfer des tournantes.* Paris: Denoël, 2003.

Benjamin, Jessica. *The Bonds of Love: Psychoanalysis, Feminism and the Problem of Domination.* New York: Pantheon Books, 1988.

Bennassar, Bartolomé. *El infierno fuimos nosotros: La Guerra Civil Española, 1936–1942.* Madrid: Taurus, 2004.

Bernstein, Richard. "*By the Light of My Father's Smile*: Limp, New-Age Nonsense in Mexico." *New York Times*. 7 Oct. 1998. Web. Accessed 19 Mar. 2010.

Bhabha, Homi K. *The Location of Culture*. London: Routledge, 2004.

Bollas, Christopher. "The Aesthetic Moment and the Search for Transformation." *Transitional Objects and Potential Spaces: Literary Uses of D. W. Winnicott*. Ed. Peter L. Rudnytsky. New York: Columbia University Press, 1993. 40–49.

Boonin, David. *The Problem of Punishment*. Cambridge: Cambridge University Press, 2008.

Bordo, Susan. *Unbearable Weight: Feminism, Western Culture, and the Body*. Berkeley: University of California Press, 1993.

Bourdieu, Pierre. *Distinction: A Social Critique of the Judgment of Taste*. Cambridge, MA: Harvard University Press, 1984.

Bouson, J. Brooks. "'Quiet As It's Kept': Shame and Trauma in Toni Morrison's *The Bluest Eye*." *Scenes of Shame: Psychoanalysis, Shame and Writing*. Ed. Joseph Adamson and Hilary Clark. 207–236.

———. *Quiet As It's Kept: Shame, Trauma, and Race in the Novels of Toni Morrison*. Albany: State University of New York Press, 2000.

———. *Embodied Shame: Uncovering Female Shame in Contemporary Women's Writing*. Albany: State University of New York Press, 2009.

Bragard, Véronique. "Eaux obscures du souvenir: Femme et Mémoire dans l'oeuvre de Ananda Devi." *Thamyris/Intersecting* N8 (2001): 187–199.

Brison, Susan J. "Trauma Narratives and the Remaking of Self." *Acts of Memory: Cultural Recall in the Present*. Ed. Mieke Bal, Jonathan Crewe, and Leo Spitzer. Hanover, NH: University Press of New England, 1999. 39–55.

Britt, Lori, and David Heise. "From Shame to Pride in Identity Politics." *Self, Identity, and Social Movements*. Ed. Sheldon Stryker, Timothy J. Owens, and Robert W. White. Minneapolis: University of Minnesota Press, 2000. 252–268.

Broek, Aart. *Schaamte Lozen*. Leiden: Carilexis, 2010.

Brooke, Patricia. "Lyons and Tigers and Wolves—Oh My! Revisionary Fairy Tales in the Work of Angela Carter." *Critical Survey* 16.1 (2004): 67–88.

Brown, Brené. *Women and Shame: Reaching Out, Speaking Truths and Building Connection*. Austin, TX: 3C Press, 2004.

Brownell, Susan. *Training the Body for China: Sports in the Moral Order of the People's Republic*. Chicago: University of Chicago Press, 1995.

———. "Strong Women and Impotent Men: Sports, Gender, and Nationalism in Chinese Public Culture." *Spaces of Their Own: Women's Public Sphere in Transnational China*. Ed. Mayfair Mei-Hui Yang. Minneapolis: University of Minnesota Press, 1999.

Burrus, Virginia. *Saving Shame: Martyrs, Saints, and Other Abject Subjects*. Philadelphia: University of Pennsylvania Press, 2008.

Butalia, Urvashi. *The Other Side of Silence: Voices from the Partition of India*. New Delhi: Penguin, 1998.

Butler, Judith. *Bodies That Matter: On the Discursive Limits of "Sex."* New York: Routledge, 1993.

Butler, Octavia. *Mind of My Mind*. 1977; New York: Warner Books, 1994.

———. *Kindred*. 1979; Boston: Beacon Press, 1988.

———. *Survivor*. New York: Signet Books, 1979.

———. *Lilith's Brood* (Xenogenesis). New York: Warner Books, 2000.

———. *Parable of the Talents*. New York: Warner Books, 2000.

———. "Amnesty." *Callaloo* 27.3 (Summer 2004): 597–615.

Caine, Barbara. *Victorian Feminists*. Oxford: Oxford University Press, 1992.

Calhoun, Cheshire. "An Apology for Moral Shame." *Journal of Political Philosophy*. 12.2 (2004): 127–146.

Callahan, William A. "National Insecurities: Humiliation, Salvation, and Chinese Nationalism." *Alternatives* 29 (2004): 199–218.

Calle-Gruber, Mireille. *Assia Djebar ou la Résistance de l'écriture: Regards d'un écrivain d'Algérie*. Paris: Maisonneuve et Larose, 2001.

———. "Écrire de main morte ou l'art de la césure chez Assia Djebar." *L'Esprit Créateur* 48.4 (2008): 5–14.

Carrillo Rowe, Aimee. "Be Longing: Toward a Feminist Politics of Relation." *NWSA Journal* 17.2 (Summer 2005): 15–46.

Carter, Angela. *The Bloody Chamber*. London: Victor Gollancz, 1979.

———. *The Sadeian Woman: An Exercise in Cultural History*. London: Virago, 1979.

Caruth, Cathy. *Trauma: Explorations in Memory*. Baltimore: Johns Hopkins University Press, 1995.

Casanova, Julián. "Una dictadura de cuarenta años." *Morir, matar, sobrevivir: La violencia en la dictadura de Franco*. Ed. Julián Casanova. Barcelona: Crítica, 2004. 3–53.

Cata, Isabelle, and Eliane DalMolin. "Ecrire et lire l'inceste: Christine Angot." *Women in French Studies* 12 (2004): 85–101.

Cazorla-Sánchez, Antonio. *Las políticas de la victoria: La consolidación del nuevo estado franquista*. Madrid: Marcial Pons Editorial, 2001.

Cenarro, Ángela. "Memories of Repression and Resistance: Narratives of Children Institutionalized by Auxilio Social in Postwar Spain." *History and Memory* 20.2 (2008): 39–59.

Césaire, Aimé. *Cahier d'un retour au pays natal*. Paris: Presence Africaine, 2000.

Chamarette, Jenny, and Jennifer Higgins, eds. *Guilt and Shame: Essays in French Literature, Thought and Visual Culture*. Bern: Peter Lang, 2010.

Champion, Edward. "Octavia Butler." *The Bat Segundo Show*. 1 Dec. 2005. Podcast. http://www.edrants.com/segundo/the-bat-segundo-show-15/. Accessed 16 Aug. 2009.

Chatterjee, Partha. *The Nation and Its Fragments: Colonial and Postcolonial Histories*. Princeton, NJ: Princeton University Press, 1993.

Cheng, Anne Anlin. *The Melancholy of Race: Psychoanalysis, Assimilation, and Hidden Grief*. Oxford: Oxford University Press, 2001.

Chodorow, Nancy. *The Power of Feelings: Personal Meaning in Psychoanalysis, Gender, and Culture*. New Haven, CT: Yale University Press, 1999.

Clare, Eli. "Stolen Bodies, Reclaimed Bodies: Disability and Queerness." *Public Culture* 13.3 (2001): 359–365.

Clark, Robert. "Angela Carter's Desire Machines." *Women's Studies* 14 (1987): 147–161.

Cliff, Michelle. *Abeng*. New York: Plume, 1984.

———. "Sister/Outsider: Some Thoughts on Simone Weil." *Between Women: Biographers, Novelists, Critics, Teachers and Artists Write about Their Work on Women*. Ed. Carol Ascher, Louise DeSalvo, and Sara Ruddick. Boston: Beacon Press, 1984. 311–325.

Constable, Liz. Introduction. "States of Shame/La honte." Ed. Liz Constable. *L'Esprit Créateur* 39.4 (1999): 3–12.

———, ed. "States of Shame/La honte." *Esprit Créateur* 39.4 (1999). Special issue.

Craighead, W. Edward, William H. Kimball, and Pamela J. Rehak. "Mood Changes, Physiological Responses, and Self-Statements during Social Rejection Imagery." *Journal of Consulting and Clinical Psychology* 47 (1979): 385–396.

Cruickshank, Ruth. *Fin de millénaire French Fiction: The Aesthetics of Crisis*. Oxford: Oxford University Press, 2009.

Cuevas Gutiérrez, Tomasa, 2004. *Testimonios de mujeres en las cárceles franquistas*. Huesca: Instituto de Estudios Altoaragoneses.

Daiya, Kavita. *Violent Belongings: Partition, Gender, and National Culture in Postcolonial India*. Philadelphia: Temple University Press, 2011.

Daly, Mary, and Jane Caputi. *Webster's First New Wickedary of the English Language*. Boston: Beacon Press, 1987.

Dalziell, Rosamund. *Shameful Autobiographies: Shame in Contemporary Australian Autobiographies and Culture*. Victoria: Melbourne University Press, 1993.

Das, Veena. "Language and the Body: Transactions in the Construction of Pain." *Life and Words: Violence and the Descent into the Ordinary*. Berkeley: University of California Press, 2006. 38–59.

Davidson, Arnold E. *Seeing in the Dark: Margaret Atwood's Cat's Eye*. Toronto:: ECW Press, 1997.

Davitz, Joel R. *The Language of Emotion*. New York: Academic Press, 1969.

Day, Aidan. *Angela Carter: The Rational Glass*. Manchester, UK: Manchester University Press, 1998.

Day, Loraine. *Writing Shame and Desire: The Work of Annie Ernaux*. Bern: Peter Lang, 2007.

DeGraw, Sharon. "'The More Things Change, the More They Remain the Same': Gender and Sexuality in Octavia Butler's Oeuvre." FEMSPEC 4.2 (2004): 219–238.

Deigh, John. "The Politics of Disgust and Shame." *Journal of Ethics* 10.4 (2006): 383–418.

Delbo, Charlotte. *Days and Memory*. Evanston, IL: Northwestern University Press, 1995.

Deleuze, Gilles. *Negotiations, 1972–1990*. New York: Columbia University Press, 1995.

Deleuze, Gilles, and Félix Guattari. *Anti-Oedipus. Capitalism and Schizophrenia*. Trans. Robert Hurley, Mark Seem, and Helen R. Lane. London: Athlone Press, 1984.

Demoulin, Laurent. "Angot Salue Guibert." *Critique* 58 (Aug.-Sept. 2002): 638–644.

DeShazer, Mary K. *Fractured Borders: Reading Women's Cancer Literature*. Ann Arbor: University of Michigan Press, 2005.

Devi, Ananda. *Pagli*. Paris: Gallimard, 2001.

———. *Pagli*. New Delhi: Rupa, 2007.

———. "Écrire hors de sa bulle." *Nouvelles Etudes Francophones* 23.1 (2008): 12–18.

———. "L'écriture est le monde, elle est le chemin et le but." Interview. *Indes réunionaises* (2003). http://www.indereunion.net. Accessed 31 May 2010.

DeWall, C. Nathan. "The Pain of Exclusion: Using Insights from Neuroscience to Understand Emotional and Behavioral Responses to Social Exclusion." *Bullying, Rejection, and Peer Victimization: A Social Cognitive Neuroscience Perspective*. Ed. Monica J. Harris. New York: Springer, 2009.

Didur, Jill. "A Heart Divided: Education, Romance, and the Domestic Sphere in Attia Hosain's *Sunlight on a Broken Column*." *Unsettling Partition: Literature, Gender, Memory*. Toronto: University of Toronto Press, 2006. 94–124.

Dietz, Mary G. *Between the Human and the Divine: The Political Thought of Simone Weil*. Totowa, NJ: Rowman and Littlefield, 1988.

Djebar, Assisa. *Ombre sultane*. Paris: J.-C. Lattès, 1987.

———. *Vaste est la prison.* Paris: Albin Michel, 1994.

———. *Ces voix qui m'assiègent . . . en marge de ma francophonie.* Paris: Albin Michel, 1999.

———. *Nulle part dans la maison de mon père.* Paris: Fayard, 2007.

Donawerth, Jane. "Beautiful Alien Monster-Women." *Frankenstein's Daughters: Women Writing Science Fiction.* Syracuse, NY: Syracuse University Press, 1997.

Douglas, Kelly Brown. "Twenty Years a Womanist: An Affirming Challenge." *Deeper Shades of Purple: Womanism in Religion and Society.* Ed. Stacey Floyd-Thomas. New York: New York University Press, 2006. 145–157.

Douglas, Mary. *Purity and Danger.* New York: Routledge, 1966.

Du Bois, W. E. B. *The Souls of Black Folk.* 1903; New York: Bantam Books, 1989.

Duncker, Patricia. "Re-imagining the Fairy Tales: Angela Carter's *Bloody Chamber.*" *Literature and History* 10.1 (Spring 1984): 3–14.

"Earshot." *Buffy the Vampire Slayer.* Writ. Jane Espenson. Dir. Regis Kimble. The WB. 21 Sept. 1999. http://www.imdb.com/video/hulu/vi553911065/. Accessed 16 Aug. 2009.

Egido León, Ángeles. *El perdón de Franco: La represión de las mujeres en el Madrid de la posguerra.* Madrid: Los libros de la catarata, 2009.

Emery, Mary Lou. *Jean Rhys at "World's End": Novels of Colonial and Sexual Exile.* Austin: University of Texas Press, 1990.

Ernaux, Annie. *Les Armoires vides.* Paris: Gallimard, 1974.

———. *Passion simple.* Paris: Gallimard, 1991.

———. *Simple Passion.* Trans. Tanya Leslie. New York: Seven Stories, 2003.

Ernaux, Annie, and Marc Marie. *L'Usage de la photo.* Paris: Gallimard, 2005.

Essex, Ruth. *Cora Sandel.* New York: Peter Lang, 1995.

Fallaize, Elizabeth. *French Women's Writing.* London: Macmillan, 1993.

Fanon, Frantz. *Black Skin, White Masks.* Trans. Richard Philcox. New York: Grove Press, 1967.

Fayard, Nicole, and Yvette Rocheron. "Ni Putes ni Soumises: A Republican Feminism from the *Quartiers Sensibles.*" *Modern and Contemporary France* 17.1 (2003): 1–18.

Felman, Shoshana. "The Return of the Voice: Claude Lanzmann's *Shoah.*" *Testimony: Crises of Witnessing in Literature, Psychoanalysis, and History.* Ed. Shoshana Felman and Dori Laub. London: Routledge, 1992. 204–283.

Fernández García, Antonio. "España, 1939–1975: Líneas de investigación sobre el régimen y la sociedad." *España-Portugal: Estudios de Historia Contemporánea.* Ed. Hipólito de la Torre Gómez and António Pedro Vicente. Madrid: Editorial Complutense, 1998. 89–106.

Finnane, Antonia. "What Should Chinese Women Wear? A National Problem." *Modern China* 22.2 (Apr. 1996): 99–131.

Fisher, Berenice. "Guilt and Shame in the Women's Movement: The Radical Ideal of Action and Its Meaning for Feminist Intellectuals." *Feminist Studies* 10.2 (Summer 1984): 185–212.

Flatley, Jonathan. *Affective Mapping: Melancholia and the Politics of Modernism.* Cambridge, MA: Harvard University Press, 2008.

Foucault, Michel. *The Archaeology of Knowledge.* New York: Pantheon Books, 1972.

———. *Histoire de la Sexualité. La Volonté de Savoir.* Paris: Gallimard, 1976.

———. *The History of Sexuality: An Introduction.* Vol. 1. Trans. Robert Hurley. New York: Vintage Books, 1990.

Fowler, Karen Joy. "Remembering Octavia Butler." *Salon.* Posted 17 Mar. 2006. Web. http://www.salon.com/books/feature/2006/03/17/butler/print.html. Accessed 26 Aug. 2009.

Frampton, Edith. "'This Milky Fullness: Breastfeeding Narratives and Michèle Roberts." *Textual Practice* 20.4 (2006): 655–678.

Frank, Adam. "Some Affective Bases for Guilt: Tomkins, Freud, Object Relations." *ESC* 32.1 (Mar. 2006): 11–25.

Freud, Sigmund. *Civilization and Its Discontents.* Trans. James Strachey. New York: W. W. Norton, 1961.

Gardiner, Judith Kegan. *Rhys, Stead, Lessing, and the Politics of Empathy.* Bloomington: Indiana University Press, 1989.

Garland-Thompson, Rosemarie. *Extraordinary Bodies: Figuring Physical Disability in American Culture and Literature.* New York: Columbia University Press, 1997.

Geaney, Jane. "Guarding Moral Boundaries: Shame in Early Confucianism." *Philosophy East and West* 54.2 (Apr. 2004): 113–142.

George, Rose. "Courageous Writer Who Forced France to Confront the Outrage of Gang Rape." *The Guardian* 11 Oct. 2004.

Gilbert, Paul. "What Is Shame? Some Core Issues and Controversies." *Shame,* Ed. Paul Gilbert and Bernice Andrews. 3–38.

Gilbert, Paul, and Bernice Andrews, eds. *Shame: Interpersonal Behavior, Psychopathology, and Culture.* New York: Oxford University Press, 1998.

Gilbert, Paul, and Jeremy Miles. *Body Shame: Conceptualisation, Research, and Treatment.* Hove, East Sussex: Brunner-Routledge, 2002.

Goffman, Erving. *The Presentation of Self in Everyday Life.* New York: Anchor Books, 1959.

———. *Behavior in Public Places.* New York: The Free Press, 1963.

———. *Stigma: Notes on the Management of Spoiled Identity.* New York: Simon and Schuster, 1963.

Govan, Sandra. "Going to See the Woman: A Visit with Octavia E. Butler." *Obsidian III: Literature in the African Diaspora.* 6.2–7.1 (Fall 2005–Summer 2006): 14–39.

Graham, Helen. "Gender and the State: Women in the 1940s." *Spanish Cultural Studies: An Introduction; The Struggle for Modernity.* Ed. Helen Graham and Jo Labanyi. Oxford: Oxford University Press, 1995. 182–195.

Greenhalgh, Susan. "Fresh Winds in Beijing: Chinese Feminists Speak Out on the One-Child Policy and Women's Lives." *Signs* 26 (Spring 2001): 847–874.

Gregg, Veronica Marie. *Jean Rhys's Historical Imagination: Reading and Writing the Creole.* Chapel Hill: University of North Carolina Press, 1995.

Grosz, Elizabeth. *Volatile Bodies: Toward a Corporeal Feminism.* Bloomington: Indiana University Press, 1994.

———. "Psychoanalysis and the Body." *Feminist Theory and the Body: A Reader.* Ed. Janet Price and Margrit Shildrick. New York: Routledge, 1999. 267–271.

Grunebaum, Heidi, and Yazir Henri. "Re-membering Bodies, Producing Histories: Holocaust Survivor Narrative and Truth and Reconciliation CommissionTestimony." *World Memory: Personal Trajectories in Global Time.* Ed. Jill Bennett and Rosanne Kennedy. London: Macmillan, 2003. 101–119.

Ha, Francis Inci. "Shame in Asian and Western Cultures." *American Behavioral Scientist* 38.8 (Aug. 1995): 1114–1131.

Haffenden, John. Interview with Angela Carter. *Novelists in Interview.* London: Methuen, 1985. 76–96.

Hai, Ambreen. "Border Work, Border Trouble: Postcolonial Feminism and the Ayah in Bapsi Sidhwa's *Cracking India.*" *Modern Fiction Studies.* 46.2 (2002): 379–424.

Halperin, David M., and Valerie Traub. *Gay Shame.* Chicago: University of Chicago Press, 2009.

Hamel, Christelle. "'Faire tourner les meufs'. Les viols collectifs: Discours des médias et des agresseurs." *Gradhiva.* 33 (2003): 85–92.

Hampton, Gregory J. "Vampires and Utopia: Reading Racial and Gender Politics in the Fiction of Octavia Butler." *CLA Journal* 52.1 (2008): 74–91.

Haraway, Donna. "A Cyborg Manifesto: Science, Technology, and Socialist-Feminism in the Late Twentieth Century." *Simians, Cyborgs and Women: The Reinvention of Nature.* New York: Routledge, 1991. 149–181.

Hargreaves, Alec. "Testimony, Co-Authorship and Dispossession among Women of Maghrebi Origin in France." *Research in African Literatures* 31.1 (2006): 42–54.

Hartman, Saidiya. *Scenes of Subjection: Terror, Slavery, and Self-Making in Nineteenth Century America.* New York: Oxford University Press, 1997.

Heath, Christian. "Embarrassment and Interactional Organization." *Erving Goffman: Exploring the Interaction Order.* Ed P. Drew and A. Wooton. Cambridge, UK: Polity, 1988.

Henke, Suzanne. *Shattered Subjects: Trauma and Testimony in Women's Life-Writing.* New York: St. Martin's Press, 2000.

Heyward, Carter. *Touching Our Strength: The Erotic as Power and the Love of God.* San Francisco: Harper, 1989.

Hiddleston, Jane. *Assia Djebar: Out of Algeria.* Liverpool: Liverpool University Press, 2006.

Hirsch, Gordon. "Ardor and Shame in *Middlemarch*." *Scenes of Shame. Psychoanalysis, Shame and Writing.* Ed. Joseph Adamson and Hilary Clark. 83–99.

Hite, Molly. "An Eye for an I: The Disciplinary Society in *Cat's Eye*." *Various Atwoods: Essays on the Later Poems, Short Fiction, and Novels.* Ed. Lorraine York. Concord, ON: House of Anansi Press, 1995.

Hoffmann, Stanley. Foreword. *The Vichy Syndrome: History and Memory in France since 1944.* By Henry Rousso. Trans. Arthur Goldhammer. Cambridge, MA: Harvard University Press, 1991. vii–x.

Hughes, Alex. "'Moi qui ai connu l'inceste, je m'appelle Christine Angot': Writing Subjectivity in Christine Angot's Incest Narratives." *Journal of Romance Studies* 2.1 (2002): 65–77.

Hughes, Bill, and Kevin Patterson. "The Social Model of Disability and the Disappearing Body: Towards a Sociology of Impairment." *Disability and Society* 12.3 (1997): 325–340.

Hunt, Linda. "*The Alberta Trilogy:* Cora Sandel's Norwegian *Künstlerroman* and American Feminist Literary Discourse." *Writing the Woman Artist: Essays on Poetics, Politics, and Portraiture.* Ed. Suzanne W. Jones. Philadelphia: University of Pennsylvania Press, 1991.

Huntington, John. *Rationalizing Genius: Ideological Strategies in the Classic American Science Fiction Short Story.* Piscataway, NJ: Rutgers University Press, 1989.

Hurcombe, Linda. *Sex and God: Some Varieties of Women's Religious Experience.* London: Routledge, 1987.

Ip, Hung-Yok. "Fashioning Appearances: Feminine Beauty in Chinese Communist Revolutionary Culture." *Modern China* 29.3 (July 2003): 329–361.

Jazouli, Adil. *Les Années banlieue.* Paris: Seuil, 1992.

Jin Lee, Scott. "Aged Bodies as Sites of Remembrance: Colonial Memories in Diaspora." *World Memories: Personal Trajectories in Global Time.* Ed. Jill Bennett and Rosanne Kennedy. London: Palgrave Macmillan, 2003. 87–101.

Johnson, Erica L. "Adjacencies: Virginia Woolf, Cora Sandel, and the Künstlerroman." *Woolf Editing/Editing Woolf.* Ed. Eleanor McNees and Sara Veglahn. Clemson, SC: Clemson University Digital Press, 2009. 90–95.

Kahan, Dan M. "What's Really Wrong with Shaming Sanctions." Faculty Scholarship Series. Paper 102. Web. 2006. http://digitalcommons.law.yale.edu/fss_papers/102.

Kaiser, Mary. "Fairy Tale as Sexual Allegory: Intertextuality in Angela Carter's *The Bloody Chamber.*" *Review of Contemporary Fiction* 14.3 (Fall 1994): 30–36.

Kansteiner, Wulf. "Testing the Limits of Trauma: The Long Term Psychological Effects of the Holocaust on Individuals and Collectives." *History of the Human Sciences* 17 (2004): 97–123.

Kaplan, Temma. "Reversing the Shame and Gendering the Memory." *Signs* 28 (2002): 179–199.

Kappeler, Susanne. *The Pornography of Represention.* Minneapolis: University of Minnesota Press, 1986.

Katrak, Ketu H. "Indian Nationalism, Gandhian 'Satyagraha' and Representations of Female Sexuality." *Nationalism and Sexualities.* Ed. Andrew Parker, Mary Russo et al. New York: Routledge, 1992. 395–420.

Kaufman, Gershen.. *Shame: The Power of Caring.* Cambridge, MA: Schenkman, 1980.

———. *The Psychology of Shame: Theory and Treatment of Shame-Based Syndromes.* New York: Springer, 1989.

Kaufman, Gershen, and Lev Raphael, eds. Introduction. *Coming Out of Shame: Transforming Gay and Lesbian Lives.* New York: Doubleday, 1996.

Kemp, Anna. "Marianne d'aujourd'hui? The Figure of the *Beurette* in Contemporary French Feminist Discourses." *Modern and Contemporary France* 17.1 (2003): 19–33.

Kemp, Simon. *French Fiction into the Twenty-First Century: The Return to the Story.* Cardiff: University of Wales Press, 2010.

Kenan, Randall. "An Interview with Octavia E. Butler." *Callaloo* 14.2 (Spring 1991): 495–504.

Khan, Yasmin. *The Great Partition: The Making of India and Pakistan.* New Delhi: Penguin, 2007.

Kilborne, Benjamin. "Fields of Shame: Anthropologists Abroad." *Ethos* 20.2 (June 1992): 230–253.

———. "The Disappearing Who: Kierkegaard, Shame, and the Self." *Scenes of Shame.* Ed. Joseph Adamson and Hilary Clark. 35–51.

Kim, Daniel. "Invisible Desires: Homoerotic Racism and Its Homophobic Critique in Ralph Ellison's *Invisible Man.*" *Novel: A Forum on Fiction* 30.3 (1997): 309–328.

Kingston, Maxine Hong. *The Woman Warrior: Memoirs of a Childhood among Ghosts.* New York: Vintage, 1975.

Kleinman, Arthur, and Joan Kleinman. "How Bodies Remember: Social Memoryand Bodily Experience of Criticism, Resistance and Delegitimation Following China's Cultural Revolution." *New Literary History* 25 (1994): 707–734.

Kohut, Heinz. *The Analysis of the Self: A Systematic Approach to the Psychoanalytic Treatment of Narcissistic Personality Disorders.* Madison, CT: International Universities Press, 1971.

Koivunen, Anu. "An Affective Turn? Reimagining the Subject of Feminist Theory." *Working with Affect in Feminist Readings: Disturbing Differences.* Ed. Marianne Liljeström and Susanna Paasonon. New York: Routledge, 2010.

Kristeva, Julia. "On the Women of China." Trans. Ellen Conroy Kennedy. *Signs* 1.1 (Autumn 1975): 57–81.

———. *About Chinese Women.* London: Boyars, 1977.

———. *Powers of Horror: An Essay on Abjection.* Trans. Leon Roudiez. New York: Columbia University Press, 1982.

———. *Black Sun: Depression and Melancholia.* Trans. Leon Roudiez. New York: Columbia University Press, 1989.

Lacan, Jacques. *Ecrits.* Paris: Editions du Seuil, 1966.

Lacey, Lauren J. "Octavia E. Butler on Coping with Power in *Parable of the Sower, Parable of the Talents,* and *Fledgling.*" *Critique: Studies in Contemporary Fiction* 49.4 (Summer 2008): 379–394.

Lane, R. D. "Cordelia's 'Nothing': The Character of Cordelia and Margaret Atwood's *Cat's Eye.*" *Essays on Canadian Writing* 48 (Winter 1992/93): 73–89.

Lau, Kimberly J. "Erotic Infidelities: Angela Carter's Wolf Trilogy." *Marvels & Tales: Journal of Fairy-Tale Studies* 22.1 (2008): 77–94.

Laub, Dori. "An Event without a Witness: Truth, Testimony and Survival." *Testimony: Crises of Witnessing in Literature, Psychoanalysis, and History.* Ed. Shoshana Felman and Dori Laub. London: Routledge, 1992. 75–92.

Lazreg, Marnia. "Feminism and Difference: Writing as a Woman on Women in Algeria." *Feminist Studies* 14.1 (1998): 81–107.

Lehtinen, Ullaliina. "How Does One Know What Shame Is? Epistemology, Emotions, and Forms of Life in Juxtaposition." *Hypatia* 13.1 (1998): 56–77.

Lejeune, Philippe. *Le Pacte autobiographique.* Paris: Seuil, 1975.

Levi, Primo. *The Drowned and the Saved.* London: Abacus, 1989.

Lewallen, Avis. "Wayward Girls but Wicked Women? Female Sexuality in Angela Carter's 'The Bloody Chamber.'" *Perspectives on Pornography: Sexuality in Film and Literature.* Ed. Gary Day. New York: St. Martin's Press, 1988. 144–158.

Lewis, Helen Block. *Shame in Guilt and Neurosis.* New York: International Universities Press, 1971.

———. Introduction. "Shame—the 'Sleeper' in Psychopathology." *The Role of Shame in Symptom Formation.* Ed. Helen Block Lewis. 87]1–28.

———. Preface. *The Role of Shame in Symptom Formation.* Ed. Helen Block Lewis. 87]xi–xii.

———. "The Role of Shame in Depression over the Life Span." *The Role of Shame in Symptom Formation.* Ed. Helen Block Lewis. 87]29–50.

———. "Shame and the Narcissistic Personality." *The Many Faces of Shame.* Ed. Donald L. Nathanson. 87]93–132.

———, ed. *The Role of Shame in Symptom Formation.* Hillsdale, NJ: Lawrence Erlbaum, 1987.

Lewis, Michael. *Shame: The Exposed Self.* New York: The Free Press, 1995.

———. "The Role of Self in Shame." *Social Research* 70.4 (Winter 2003): 1181–1204.

Li, Li. "Female Bodies as Imaginary Signifiers in Chinese Revolutionary Literature." *Chinese Revolution and Chinese Literature.* Ed. Tao Dongfeng, Yang Xiaobin, Rosemary Roberts, and Yang Ling. Newcastle, UK: Cambridge Scholars Publishing, 2009.

Li, Xiaojiang. "Economic Reform and the Awakening of Chinese Women's Collective Consciousness." *Engendering China.* Ed. Christina K. Gilmartin, Gail Hershatter, Lisa Rofel, and Tyrene White. Cambridge, MA: Harvard University Press, 1994.

Linkin, Harriet Kramer. "Isn't It Romantic?: Angela Carter's Bloody Revision of the Romantic Aesthetic in 'The Erl-King.'" *Contemporary Literature* 35.2 (Summer 1994): 305–324.

Lionnet, Françoise. "Cinq mètres d'ordre et de sagesse, cinq mètres de jungle soyeuse: Ananda Devi's Unfurling Art of Fiction." *Écritures mauriciennes au féminin: Penser l'altérité.* Ed. Véronique Bragard and Srilata Ravi. Paris: L'Harmattan, 2011. 283–314.

Lionnet, Françoise, and Ronnie Scharfman, eds. *Post/Colonial Conditions:Exiles, Migrations, and Nomadisms.* Yale French Studies 83. New Haven, CT: Yale University Press, 1993.

Littleton, Therese. "Octavia E. Butler Plants an Earthseed." Web. http://www.amazon.com/exec/obidos/tg/feature/-/11664/. Accessed 12 Aug. 2009.

Liu, Lydia H. "Female Body and Nationalist Discourse: Manchuria in Xiaohong's *Field of Life and Death.*" *Body, Subject, and Power in China.* Ed. Angela Zito and Tani Barlow. Chicago: University of Chicago Press, 1994.

Liu, Jianmei. "Nation, Women, and Gender in the Late Qing." *Chinese Revolution and Chinese Literature.* Ed. Tao Dongfeng, Yang Xiaobin, Rosemary Roberts, and Yang Ling. Newcastle, UK: Cambridge Scholars Publishing, 2009.

Loades, Ann. "Simone Weil—Sacrifice: a Problem for Theology." *Images of Belief in Literature.* Ed. D. Jasper. London: Macmillan, 1984. 122–137.

———. "Eucharistic Sacrifice: Simone Weil's Use of a Liturgical Metaphor." *Religion and Literature* 17.2 (Summer 1985): 43–54.

———. "Christ Also Suffered: Why Certain Forms of Holiness Are Bad for You." *Searching for Lost Coins: Explorations in Christianity and Feminism.* Ed. Ann Loades. Allison Park, PA: Pickwick Publications, 1988. 39–60.

Locke, Jill. "Shame and the Future of Feminism." *Hypatia* 22.4 (2007): 146–162.

Lorde, Audre. "Uses of the Erotic: The Erotic As Power." *Sister Outsider: Essays and Speeches.* Trumansburg, NY: Crossing Press, 1984.

Love, Heather. *Feeling Backward: Loss and the Politics of Queer History.* Cambridge, MA: Harvard University Press, 2007.

Luckhurst, Roger. "'Impossible Mourning' in Toni Morrison's *Beloved* and Michèle Roberts's *Daughters of the House.*" *Critique: Studies in Contemporary Fiction* 37.4 (1996): 243–260.

———. *The Trauma Question.* London: Routledge, 2008.

Lynd, Helen Merrell. *On Shame and the Search for Identity.* New York: Harcourt, Brace, 1953.

MacDonald, G., and M. R. Leary. "Why Does Social Exclusion Hurt? The Relationship between Social and Physical Pain." *Psychological Bulletin* 131.2 (2005): 202–223.

MacIntyre, Alasdair. *Edith Stein: A Philosophical Prologue, 1913–1922.* Lanham, MD: Rowman and Littlefield, 2006.

Makinen, Merja. "Angela Carter's 'The Bloody Chamber' and the Decolonization of Feminine Sexuality." *Feminist Review* 42 (Autumn 1992): 2–16.

Mani, Lata. "Contentious Traditions: The Debate on *Sati* in Colonial India." *Recasting Women: Essays in Indian Colonial History.* Ed. Kumkum Sangari and Sudesh Vaid. Piscataway, NJ: Rutgers University Press, 1990. 88–127.

Manion, Jennifer C. "Girls Blush, Sometimes: Gender, Moral Agency, and the Problem of Shame." *Hypatia* 18.3 (Fall 2003): 21–41.

Markowitz, Sally. "Pelvic Politics: Sexual Dimorphism and Racial Difference." *Signs: Journal of Women in Culture and Society* 26.2 (Winter 2001): 389–414.

Marrone, Claire. "Past, Present and Passion Tense in Annie Ernaux's *Passion Simple.*" *Women in French Studies* 2 (1994): 78–87.

McDermott, Sinead. "The Double Wound: Shame and Trauma in Joy Kogawa's *Obasan.*" *Sexed Sentiments: Interdisciplinary Perspectives on Gender and Emotion.* Ed. Willemijn Ruberg and Kristine Steenbergh. Amsterdam: Rodopi, 2011.

McLaren, Margaret A. *Feminism, Foucault, and Embodied Subjectivity.* Albany: State University of New York Press, 2002.

McLaughlin, Becky. "Perverse Pleasure and Fetishized Text: The Deathly Erotics of Carter's 'The Bloody Chamber.'" *Style* 29 (Fall 1995): 404–422.

Mehaffy, Marilyn, and AnaLouise Keating. "'Radio Imagination': Octavia Butler on the Poetics of Narrative Embodiment" MELUS 26.1 (Spring 2001): 45–76.

Mehta, Brinda. *Diasporic (Dis)locations: Indo-Caribbean Women Writers Negotiate the Kala Pani.*Kingston, Jamaica: University of the West Indies Press, 2004.

Melzer, Patricia. *Alien Constructions: Science Fiction and Feminist Thought.* Austin: University of Texas Press, 2006.

Memmi, Albert. *Portrait du colonisé precede de Portrait du colonisateur.* Paris: Gallimard, 1997.

Menon, Ritu, and Kamla Bhasin. *Borders and Boundaries: Women in India's Partition.* New Delhi: Kali for Women, 1998.

Merril, Judith. *Homecalling and Other Stories: The Complete Solo Short Science Fiction of Judith Merril.* Ed. Elisabeth Carey. Framingham, MA: NESFA Press, 2005.

Michalko, Rod. *The Difference That Disability Makes.* Philadelphia: Temple University Press, 2002.

——. "Double Trouble." *Disability and the Politics of Education: An International Reader.* Ed. Scott Danforth and Susan Gabel. New York: Peter Lang, 2007. 401–416.

Michalko, Rod, and Tanya Titchkosky. *Re-thinking Normalcy: A Disability Studies Reader.* Toronto: Canadian Scholars' Press, 2009.

Miller, Nancy K. "Memory Stains: Annie Ernaux's *Shame.*" *Extremities: Trauma, Testimony and Community.* Ed. Nancy K. Miller and Jason Tougaw. Chicago: University of Illinois Press, 2002. 197–213.

Miller, Susan. *The Shame Experience.* Hillsdale, NY: Analytic Press, 1985.

Miller, William Ian. *The Anatomy of Disgust.* Cambridge, MA: Harvard University Press, 1997.

Millett, Kate. *Sexual Politics.* London: Hart-Davies, 1971.

Mitchell, David, and Sharon Snyder. *Narrative Prosthesis: Disability and the Dependency of Discourse.* Ann Arbor: University of Michigan Press, 2001.

Mitchell, Stephen A. *Relational Concepts in Psychoanalysis: An Integration.* Cambridge, MA: Harvard University Press, 1988.

Molinero, Carme. "Silencio e invisibilidad: La mujer durante el primer franquismo." *Revista de Occidente* 223 (Dec. 1999): 63–82.

Mongo-Mboussa, Boniface. "Contre le culte de la différence: Entretien avec Ananda Devi." *Africultures* 35 (2001): 40–42.

Monk, Patricia. *Alien Theory: The Alien as Archetype in the Science Fiction Short Story.* Lanham, MD: Scarecrow Press, 2006.

Moran, Patricia. *Virginia Woolf, Jean Rhys, and the Aesthetics of Trauma.* New York: Palgrave, 2007.

Moreno Sardá, Amparo. "La réplica de las mujeres al franquismo." *El feminismo en España: Dos siglos de historia.* Ed. Pilar Folguera. Madrid: Editorial Pablo Iglesias, 1988. 85–110.

Morgan, Michael. *On Shame.* New York: Routledge, 2008.

Morris, Jenny. *Pride against Prejudice: Transforming Attitudes to Disability.* Philadelphia: New Society, 1991.

Morrison, Andrew P. "Shame, the Ideal Self, and Narcissism." *Contemporary Psychoanalysis* 19.2 (1983): 295–318.

——. "The Eye Turned Inward: Shame and the Self." *The Many Faces of Shame.* Ed. Donald Nathanson. 271–291.

——. *Shame: The Underside of Narcissism.* Hillsdale, NJ: Analytic Press, 1989.

———. *The Culture of Shame.* New York: Ballantine, 1996.

Motte, Warren. *Small Worlds: Minimalism in Contemporary French Literature.* Lincoln: University of Nebraska Press, 1999.

Mucchielli, Laurent. *Le Scandale des 'tournantes': Dérives médiatique, contre-enquête sociologique.* Paris: La Découverte, 2005.

Munt, Sally. *Queer Attachments: The Cultural Politics of Shame.* Burlington, VT: Ashgate Publishing, 2007.

Murdoch, Adlai H. "Rewriting Writing: Identity, Exile and Renewal in Assia Djebar's *L'Amour, la fantasia." Post/Colonial Conditions.* Ed. Françoise Lionnet and Ronnie Scharfman. 71–92.

Murray, Michele. "Simone Weil: Last Things." *Simone Weil: Interpretations of a Life.* Ed. George White. Amherst: University of Massachusetts Press, 1981. 47–61.

Narayan, Uma. *Dislocating Cultures: Identities, Traditions, and Third-World Feminism.* New York: Routledge, 1997.

Nash, Mary. "Towards a New Moral Order: National Catholicism, Culture and Gender." *Spanish History since 1808.* Ed. Adrian Schubert. Oxford: Oxford University Press, 2000. 289–300.

Nathanson, Donald. "The Shame/Pride Axis." *The Role of Shame in Symptom Formation.* Ed. Helen Block Lewis. 183–205.

———. "A Timetable for Shame." *The Many Faces of Shame.* Ed. Donald Nathanson. 1–63.

———. *Shame and Pride: Affect, Sex, and the Birth of the Self.* New York: W. W. Norton, 1992.

———. Foreword. *Scenes of Shame: Psychoanalysis, Shame, and Writing.* Ed. Joseph Adamson and Hilary Clark. vii–viii.

———, ed. *The Many Faces of Shame.* New York: Guilford Press, 1987.

Nesbitt, Nick. "Honte, culpabilité, et devenir dans l'expérience coloniale." *Lire, écrire la honte.* Ed. Bruno Chaouat. Lyon: Presses Universitaires de Lyon, 2007.

Nevin, Thomas R. *Simone Weil: Portrait of a Self-Exiled Jew.* Chapel Hill: University of North Carolina Press, 1991.

Nietzsche, Frederick. *On the Advantage and Disadvantages of History for Life.* New York: Hackett, 1980.

Nora, Pierre. "Between Memory and History: *Les Lieux de Mémoire." Representations* 26 (1989): 7–25.

Nussbaum, Martha. *Hiding from Humanity: Disgust, Shame, and the Law.* Princeton, NJ: Princeton University Press, 2004.

———. "Replies." *Journal of Ethics* 10.4 (2006): 463–506.

Nye, Andrea. *Philosophia: The Thought of Rosa Luxembourg, Simone Weil, and Hannah Arendt.* New York: Routledge, 1994.

O'Doherty, Caroline. "The Virgin Mary and the 'Tainted' Teenage Girl Who Came to Her for Sanctuary." *Irish Examiner,* Jan. 26, 2004.

Olsen, Tillie. *Silences.* New York: Delta/Dell, 1978.

Ongiri, Amy Abugo. "The Color of Shame: Reading Kathryn Bond Stockton's *Beautiful Bottom, Beautiful Shame* in Context." *Postmodern Culture* 18.3 (May 2008).

Orenstein, Catherine. *Little Red Riding Hood Uncloaked: Sex, Morality, and the Evolution of a Fairy Tale.* New York: Basic Books, 2002.

Orlando, Valérie. *Nomadic Voices of Exile: Feminine Identity in Francophone Literature.* Athens: Ohio University Press, 1999.

Painter, Nell Irvin. *Southern History across the Color Line.* Chapel Hill: University of North Carolina Press, 2002.

Pajaczkowska, Claire, and Ivan Ward. Introduction. *Shame and Sexuality: Psychoanalysis and Visual Culture*. Ed. Claire Pajaczkowska and Ivan Ward. New York: Routledge, 2008.

Pandey, Gyandendra. *Remembering Partition: Violence, Nationalism and History in India*. Cambridge: Cambridge University Press, 2001.

Panichas, George A. Introduction. *The Simone Weil Reader*. Ed. George A. Panichas. Wakefield, RI: Moyer Bell, 1977. xvii–xxxiii.

Parham, Marisa. "Saying 'Yes' to Textual Traumas in Octavia Butler's *Kindred*." *Callaloo* 32.4 (Winter 2009): 1315–1331.

Park, Robert E., and Ernest W. Burgess. *Introduction to the Science of Sociology*. Chicago: University of Chicago Press, 1921.

Parker, Emma. "From House to Home: A Kristevan Reading of Michèle Roberts's *Daughters of the House*." *Critique: Studies in Contemporary Fiction* 41.2 (2000): 153–173.

Pattison, Stephen. *Shame: Theory, Therapy, Theology*. Cambridge: Cambridge University Press, 2000.

Perez, Hiram. "You Can Have My Brown Body and Eat It, Too!" *Social Text* 23.3–4 84–85 (Fall–Winter 2005): 171–191.

Perry, Susan. Review of *Chinese Feminism Faces Globalization*. *Chinese Review International* 9.1 (Spring 2002): 281–283.

Pétrement, Simone. *Simone Weil: A Life*. Trans. Raymond Rosenthal. New York: Pantheon Books, 1976.

Pohl-Weary, Emily. "Judith Merril's Legacy." In *Homecalling*. By Judith Merril.

Prabhu, Anjali. *Hybridity: Limits, Transformations, Prospects*. Albany: State University of New York Press, 2007.

Price, Janet, and Margrit Shildrick. "Mapping the Colonial Body: Sexual Economies and the State in Colonial India." *Feminist Theory and the Body: A Reader*. Ed. Janet Price and Margrit Shildrick. 388–398.

———, eds. *Feminist Theory and the Body: A Reader*. New York: Routledge, 1999.

Primo de Rivera, Pilar. *Discursos*. Barcelona: Editora Nacional, 1939.

Probyn, Elspeth. *Outside Belongings*. New York: Routledge, 1996.

———. *Blush: Faces of Shame*. Minneapolis: University of Minnesota Press, 2005.

Puri, Shalini. *The Caribbean Postcolonial: Social Equality, Post-Nationalism and Cultural Hybridity*. New York: Palgrave Macmillan, 2004.

Queiroz, Kevin de. (2005). "Ernst Mayr and the Modern Concept of Species." *Proceedings of the National Academy of Sciences* 102, Suppl 1: 6600–6607. Web.

Rahman, Najat. *Literary Disinheritance: The Writing of Home in the Work of Mahmoud Darwish and Assia Djebar*. Lanham, MD: Lexington Books, 2008.

Raiskin, Judith. "The Art of History: An Interview with Michelle Cliff." *Kenyon Review* 15.1 (Winter 1993): 57–71.

Ramharai, Vicram. "Problèmatique de l'Autre et du Même dans l'oeuvre romanesque d'Ananda Devi." *Écritures mauriciennes au féminin: Penser l'altérité*. Ed. Véronique Bragard and Srilata Ravi. Paris: L'Harmattan, 2011. 61–77.

Ramsey, Nancy. "The Alberta Trilogy Revisited: Today's 'Women's Fiction' vs. the Real Thing." *Book Forum: An International Transdisciplinary Quarterly* 7.3 (1985): 12–15.

Raphals, Lisa. *Sharing the Light: Representations of Women and Virtue in Early China*. Albany: State University of New York Press, 1998.

Ravi, Srilata. "Ananda Devi nous parle de ses romans, de ses personnages, de son écriture, de ses lecteurs. Propos recueillis par Srilata Ravi." *Écritures mauriciennes au féminin: Penser l'altérité*. Ed. Véronique Bragard and Srilata Ravi. Paris: L'Harmattan, 2011.

Rawls, John. *A Theory of Justice*. Cambridge, MA: Harvard University Press, 1971.

Ray, Sangeeta. *En-gendering India: Woman and Nation in Colonial and Postcolonial Narratives*. Raleigh, NC: Duke University Press, 2000.

Rees, Ellen. *On the Margins: Nordic Women Modernists of the 1930s*. London: Norvik Press, 2005.

———. *Figurative Space in the Novels of Cora Sandel*. Laksevåg, Norway: Alvheim and Eide, 2010.

Rhys, Jean. *Good Morning, Midnight*. 1939; New York: W. W. Norton, 1986.

Riordan, James. *Sports under Communism: The U.S.S.R., Czechoslovakia, the G.D.R., China, Cuba*. London: C. Hurst and Company, 1978.

Roberts, Michèle. *Daughters of the House*. 1992; London: Virago, 1994.

———. *Food, Sex and God: On Inspiration and Writing*. London: Virago, 1998.

Roberts, Rosemary. "Maoist Women Warriors: Historical Continuities and Cultural Transgressions." *Chinese Revolution and Chinese Literature*. Ed. Tao Dongfeng, Yang Xiaobin, Rosemary Roberts, and Yang Ling. Newcastle, UK: Cambridge Scholars Publishing, 2009.

Roemer, Danielle M., and Cristina Bacchilega. *Angela Carter and the Fairy Tale*. Detroit: Wayne State University Press, 2001.

Rofel, Lisa. "Liberation Nostalgia and a Yearning for Modernity." *Engendering China*. Ed. Christina K. Gilmartin, Gail Hershatter, Lisa Rofel, and Tyrene White. Cambridge, MA: Harvard University Press, 1994.

Romanowski, Sylvie. "Passion simple d'Annie Ernaux: Le trajet d'une féministe." *French Forum* 27.3 (2002): 99–114.

Roura, Assumpta. *Mujeres para después de una Guerra: Informes sobre moralidad y prostitución en la posguerra Española*. Barcelona: Flor del Viento Ediciones, 1998.

Rousso, Henry. *The Vichy Syndrome: History and Memory in France since 1944*. Trans. Arthur Goldhammer. Cambridge, MA: Harvard University Press, 1991.

Rowell, Charles H. "An Interview with Octavia E. Butler." *Callaloo* 20.1 (1997): 47–66.

Rusciano, Frank Louis. "The Construction of National Identity: A 23-Nation Study." *Political Research Quarterly* 56.3 (Sept. 2003): 361–366.

Russ, Joanna. *To Write like a Woman: Essays in Feminism and Science Fiction*. Bloomington: Indiana University Press, 1995.

Russo, Mary. "Female Grotesques: Carnival and Theory." *Feminist Studies/Critical Studies*. Ed. Teresa de Lauretis. Bloomington: Indiana University Press, 1986. 213–229.

Sage, Lorna. *Flesh and the Mirror: Essays on the Art of Angela Carter*. London: Virago, 1994.

Salvaggio, Ruth. "Octavia Butler and the Black Science-Fiction Heroine." *Black American Literature Forum* 18.2 (1984): 78–81.

"Samira Bellil: Elle avait dénoncé 'l'enfer des tournantes,'" *Le Télégramme*, 8 Sept. 2004.

Sandel, Cora. *Alberta and Jacob, Alberta and Freedom,* and *Alberta Alone*. Trans. Elizabeth Rokkan, with an afterword by Linda Hunt. 1962; Athens: Ohio University Press, 1984.

Sanders, Joshunda. "Interview with Octavia Butler." *In Motion Magazine*. Web. Mar. 14, 2004. http://www.inmotionmagazine.com/aco4/obutler.html.

Sarkar, Sumit. *Beyond Nationalist Frames: Postmodernism, Hindu Fundamentalism, History*. Bloomington: Indiana University Press, 2002.

Sartre, Jean-Paul. *Being and Nothingness: An Essay on Phenomenological Ontology*. Trans. Hazel E. Barnes. New York: Washington Square Press, 1966.

Scarry, Elaine. *The Body in Pain: The Making and Unmaking of the World.* New York: Oxford University Press, 1985.

Scheff, Thomas. "The Shame-Rage Spiral: A Case Study of an Interminable Quarrel." *The Role of Shame in Symptom Formation.* Ed. Helen Block Lewis. 109–149.

———. *Microsociology: Discourse, Emotion, and Social Structure.* Chicago: University of Chicago Press, 1990.

———. *Bloody Revenge: Emotions, Nationalism, and War.* Boulder, CO: Westview, 1994.

———. "Shame in Self and Society." *Symbolic Interaction,* 6.2 (2003): 239–262.

Schneider, Carl. *Shame, Exposure, and Privacy.* 1977; New York: W. W. Norton, 1992.

———. "A Mature Sense of Shame." *The Many Faces of Shame.* Ed. Donald L. Nathanson. 194–213.

Scott, David. *China and the International System, 1840–1949: Power, Presence, Perceptions in a Century of Humiliation.* Albany: State University of New York Press, 2008.

Scott, James C. *Domination and the Arts of Resistance.* New Haven, CT: Yale University Press, 1990.

Scott, Linda. "Fresh Lipstick: Rethinking Images of Women in Advertising." *Women in Culture: A Women's Studies Anthology.* Ed. Lucinda Joy Peach. Oxford, UK: Blackwell Publishers, 1998. 131–141.

Sedgwick, Eve Kosofsky. *Touching Feeling: Affect, Pedagogy, Performativity.* Durham, NC: Duke University Press, 2003.

Sedgwick, Eve Kosofsky, and Adam Frank. Introduction. *Shame and Its Sisters: A Silvan Tomkins Reader.* Ed. Eve Kosofsky Sedgwick and Adam Frank. Durham, NC: Duke University Press, 1995.

———. "Shame in the Cybernetic Fold: Reading Silvan Tomkins." *Critical Inquiry* 21.2 (Winter 1995): 496–522.

———, eds. *Shame and Its Sisters: A Silvan Tomkins Reader.* Durham, NC: Duke University Press, 1995.

Seidler, Günter Harry. *In Others' Eyes: An Analysis of Shame.* Trans. Andrew Jenkins. Madison, CT: International Universities Press, 2000.

Selboe, Tone. "Jean Rhys and Cora Sandel. Two Views on the Modern Metropolis." *European and Nordic Modernisms.* Ed. Mats Jansson, Jakob Lothe, and Hannu Riikonen. Norwich, UK: Norvik Press, 2004.

Sellers, Susan. *Myth and Fairy Tale in Contemporary Women's Fiction.* New York: Palgrave, 2001.

Shalit, Wendy. "Daddy's Little Girl." *First Things* (Mar. 1999): 13–14.

Sheets, Robin Ann. "Pornography, Fairy Tales, and Feminism: Angela Carter's 'The Bloody Chamber.'" *Journal of the History of Sexuality* 1.4 (Apr. 1991): 633–657.

Shildrick, Margrit. *Leaky Bodies and Boundaries: Feminism, Postmodernism and (Bio)ethics.* London: Routledge, 1997.

Sidhwa, Bapsi. *Ice-Candy-Man.* New Delhi: Penguin, 1988.

———. "Making Up with Painful History: The Partition of India in Bapsi Sidhwa's Work." Interview by Isabella Bruschi. *Journal of Commonwealth Literature* 43 (2008): 141–149.

Singh, Rashna B. "Traversing Diacritical Space: Negotiating and Narrating Parsi Nationness." *Journal of Commonwealth Literature* 43.2 (2008): 29–47.

Spelman, Elizabeth. "Woman as Body: Ancient and Contemporary Views." *Feminist Studies* 8.1 (1982): 109–31.

Spivak, Gayatri Chakravorty. Translator's Preface. *Imaginary Maps: Three Stories by Mahasweta Devi.* Trans. Gayatri Chakravorty Spivak. New York: Routledge, 1995. ix–xxix.

Stanford, Ann Folwell. "Mechanisms of Disease: African-American Women Writers, Social Pathologies, and the Limits of Medicine." *NWSA Journal* 6.1 (Spring 1994): 28–47.

Stattin, H., and I. Klackenberg-Larsson. "Delinquency as Related to Parents' Preferences for Their Child's Gender: A Research Note." Report No. 696. Stockholm: University of Stockholm, Department of Psychology, 1989.

Stockton, Kathryn Bond. *Beautiful Bottom, Beautiful Shame: Where "Black" Meets "Queer."* Durham, NC: Duke University Press, 2006.

Sultan, Patrick. "L'enfermement, la rupture, l'envol: Lecture de *Pagli* d'Ananda Devi." *Orées* 1.2 (2001). Web. http://orees.concordia.ca/numero2/essai/lecture de PAGLI corrig.html. Accessed 20 Dec. 2011.

Sunder Rajan, Rajeswari. *Real and Imagined Women*. London: Routledge, 1995.

Suvin, Darko. "Radical Rhapsody and Romantic Recoil in the Age of Anticipation: A Chapter in the History of SF." *Science Fiction Studies*. 1.4 (Fall 1974): 255–269.

Sycamore, Mattilda Bernstein. "Gay Shame: From Queer Autonomous Space to Direct Action Extravaganza." Web. http://www.gayshamesf.org/slingshotgayshame.html#4. Accessed 2 Oct. 2012.

Taylor, Charles. "The Politics of Recognition." *Multiculturalism*. Ed. Charles Taylor. Princeton, NJ: Princeton University Press, 1994. 25–75.

Taylor, Gabriele. *Pride, Shame, and Guilt: Emotions of Self-Assessment*. Oxford: Oxford University Press, 1985.

Thatcher, Adrian, and Elizabeth Stuart, eds. *Christian Perspectives on Sexuality and Gender*. Grand Rapids, MI: Eerdmans, 1996.

Thompson, Becky W. *A Hunger So Wide and So Deep: American Women Speak Out on Eating Problems*. Minneapolis: University of Minnesota Press, 1994.

Thompson, Tammy J. "Escape from Shame." *Mouth Magazine* 47 (1993): 56.

Thomson, Rosemarie Garland [Garland-Thomson]. *Extraordinary Bodies: Figuring Physical Disability in American Culture and Literature*. New York: Columbia University Press, 1997.

———. *Staring: How We Look*. New York: Oxford University Press, 2009.

Thrane, Gary. "Shame." *Journal for the Theory of Social Behavior* 9 (1979): 39–166.

Titchkosky, Tanya. *Reading and Writing Disability Differently: The Textured Life of Embodiment*. Toronto: University of Toronto Press, 2007.

Tomkins, Silvan. *Affect, Imagery, Consciousness*. 4 vols. New York: Springer Publishing, 1962–1992.

———. "Shame." *The Many Faces of Shame*. Ed. Donald Nathanson. 133–161.

Torres, Rafael. *El amor en tiempos de Franco*. Madrid: Grupo Anaya, 2002.

Triano, Sarah. "Why Disability Pride?" 2012. Web. http://www.disabilityprideparade.org/whypride.php. Accessed 21 July 2012.

Tucker, Lindsey. *Critical Essays on Angela Carter*. New York: G. K. Hall, 1998.

Van Deusen, Nancy E. "The Faces of Honor: Sex, Shame, and Violence in Colonial Latin America." *The Hispanic American Historical Review*. 80.1 (2000): 169–170.

Van Herik, Judith. "Looking, Eating, and Waiting in Simone Weil." *Mysticism, Nihilism, Feminism: New Critical Essays on the Theology of Simone Weil*. Ed. Thomas A. Idinopulos and Josephine Zadovsky Knopp. Johnson City, TN: Institute of Social Sciences and Arts, 1984. 57–90.

———. "Simone Weil's Religious Imagery: How Looking Becomes Eating." *Immaculate and Powerful: The Female in Sacred Image and Social Reality.* Ed. Clarissa W. Atkinson, Constance H. Buchanan, and Margaret R. Miles. Boston: Beacon Press, 1985. 260–282.

Vint, Sherryl. *Bodies of Tomorrow: Technology, Subjectivity, Science Fiction.* Toronto: University of Toronto Press, 2007.

Viti, Elizabeth Richardson. "P.S.: *Passion simple* as Postscript." *Women in French Studies* 8 (2000): 154–163.

Walker, Alison Tara. "Destabilizing Order, Challenging History: Octavia Butler, Deleuze and Guattari, and Affective Beginnings." *Extrapolation* 46.1 (Spring 2005): 103–119.

Warner, Michael. *The Trouble with Normal: Sex, Politics, and the Ethics of Queer Life.* Cambridge, MA: Harvard University Press, 1999.

Webster, Alison. *Found Wanting: Women, Christianity and Sexuality.* London: Cassell, 1995.

Weil, Simone. "Decreation." *The Simone Weil Reader.* By Simone Weil. 350–356.

———. "Factory Work." *The Simone Weil Reader.* By Simone Weil. 53–72.

———. "Human Personality." *The Simone Weil Reader.* By Simone Weil. 313–339.

———. "The *Iliad*: Poem of Might." *The Simone Weil Reader.* By Simone Weil. 153–83.

———. "The Love of God and Affliction." *The Simone Weil Reader.* By Simone Weil. 439–468.

———. "Reflections on the Right Use of School Studies with a View to the Love of God." *The Simone Weil Reader.* By Simone Weil. 44–52.

———. *The Simone Weil Reader.* Ed. George A. Panichas. Wakefield, RI: Moyer Bell, 1977.

———. "Factory Journal." *Formative Writings, 1929–1941.* Ed. and trans. Dorothy Tuck McFarland and Wilhelmina Van Ness. Amherst: University of Massachusetts Press, 1987. 149–226.

———. *The Need for Roots: Prelude to a Declaration of Duties towards Mankind.* Trans. A. F. Wills. London: Routledge, 1995. Trans. of *L'enracinement.* Paris: Gallimard, 1949.

Wilson, Robert Rawdon. "SLIP PAGE: Angela Carter, In/Out/In the Postmodern Nexus." *Ariel* 20.4 (1989): 96–114.

Winnicott, D. W. *The Maturational Process and the Facilitating Environment.* New York: International Universities Press, 1965.

Wolmark, Jenny. *Aliens and Others: Science Fiction, Feminism and Postmodernism.* Iowa City: University of Iowa Press, 1994.

Woodhull, Winifred. *Transfigurations of the Maghreb: Feminism, Decolonization, and Literatures.* Minneapolis: University of Minnesota Press, 1993.

Woods, Nancy. *Vectors of Memory: Legacies of Trauma in Postwar Europe.* Oxford, UK: Berg, 1999.

Woodward, Kathleen. "Traumatic Shame: Toni Morrison, Television Culture, and the Cultural Politics of the Emotions." *Cultural Critique.* 46 (2000): 210–240.

———. *Statistical Panic: Cultural Politics and Poetics of the Emotions.* Durham, NC: Duke University Press, 2009.

Wurmser, Léon. *The Mask of Shame.* Baltimore: Johns Hopkins University Press, 1981.

———. "Shame: The Veiled Companion of Narcissism." *The Many Faces of Shame.* Ed. Donald L. Nathanson. New York: Guilford Press, 1987.

———. *The Power of the Inner Judge: Psychodynamic Treatment of the Severe Neuroses.* Northvale, NJ: Jason Aronson, 2000.

Yang, Lianfen. "Women and Revolution in the Context of the 1927 Nationalist Revolution and Literature." *Chinese Revolution and Chinese Literature.* Ed. Tao Dongfeng, Yang Xiaobin, Rosemary Roberts, and Yang Ling. Newcastle, UK: Cambridge Scholars Publishing, 2009.

Yang, Mayfair Mei-Hui. *Spaces of Their Own: Women's Public Sphere in Transnational China.* Minneapolis: University of Minnesota Press, 1999.

Zimra, Clarisse. "Hearing Voices, or, Who You Calling Postcolonial? The Evolution of Djebar's Poetics." *Research in African Literatures* 35.2 (Winter 2004): 149–159.

Zuck, Virpi. "Cora Sandel: A Norwegian Feminist." *Edda* 1 (1981): 23–33.

Contributors

ELIZA CHANDLER is a PhD candidate in the Sociology and Equity Studies in Education department at the Ontario Institute for Studies in Education, University of Toronto (OISE/UT), working predominantly in Disability Studies. Chandler holds a doctoral fellowship from the Social Sciences and Humanities Research Council (SSHRC) and is the Equity Studies Senior Doctoral Fellow at New College, University of Toronto. She teaches courses in Disability Studies at New College and at OISE/UT.

NATALIE EDWARDS is Lecturer in French at the University of Adelaide, Australia. She specializes in contemporary women's writing in French and autobiography. Her book *Shifting Subjects: Plural Subjectivity in Contemporary Francophone Women's Autobiography* was published in 2011. She is co-editor with Christopher Hogarth of *This "Self" Which Is Not One: Francophone Women's Autobiography* and *Gender and Displacement: Home in Contemporary Francophone Women's Autobiography*. She also edited, with Amy Hubbell and Ann Miller, *Textual and Visual Selves: Photography, Film, and Comic Art in French Autobiography*.

JOCELYN EIGHAN is a PhD candidate in the Program for Writers at the University of Illinois at Chicago. Her research interests include shame theory, disability, and the female body in literature. She has served on the editorial board for *Another Chicago Magazine* (ACM), and she is the former fiction editor and co-editor in chief of *Packingtown Review*.

NICOLE FAYARD is Director of French Studies at the University of Leicester. Her research focuses on twentieth century and contemporary French theater, in particular Shakespeare in France. She is the author of *The Performance of Shakespeare in France Since the Second World War: Re-imagining Shakespeare* and has also published articles on the work of Georges Lavaudant, Daniel Mesguich, and Stéphane Braunschweig. More recent research has taken her into the fields of contemporary French women writers and gender violence. Her current project investigates sexual violence in France in the twenty-first century. Dr. Fayard has also published on the methodology of language teaching.

TAMAR HELLER is Associate Professor of English and Comparative Literature at the University of Cincinnati. She is the author of *Dead Secrets: Wilkie Collins and the Female Gothic*. She also edited Rhoda Broughton's *Cometh Up as a Flower* and co-edited, with Patricia Moran, *Scenes of the Apple: Food and the Female Body in Nineteenth- and Twentieth-Century Women's Writing*, and, with Diane Hoeveler, *Approaches to Teaching Gothic Fiction: The British and American Traditions*. She is completing an edition of Broughton's *Not Wisely but Too Well* and a study of Broughton, *A Plot of Her Own: Rhoda Broughton and English Fiction*.

SUZETTE A. HENKE is Thruston B. Morton, Sr. Professor of English at the University of Louisville. She is the author of *James Joyce and the Politics of Desire* and has published widely in the fields of modern literature and women's studies. A revised edition of her book *Shattered Subjects: Trauma and Testimony in Women's Life-Writing* was brought out in 2000, and she co-edited, with David Eberly, a collection of essays, *Virginia Woolf and Trauma*. Professor Henke is currently working on a study focused on the fictions of trauma of Woolf, Joyce, and Lawrence.

ERICA L. JOHNSON is an Associate Professor of English at Wagner College in New York. She is the author of *Caribbean Ghostwriting* and *Home, Maison, Casa: The Politics of Location in Works by Jean Rhys, Marguerite Duras, and Erminia Dell'Oro*, as well as articles on a number of postcolonial and modernist writers. Her work has appeared in such journals as *Modern Fiction Studies, Meridians, The Journal of Caribbean Literatures, Biography*, and *The Journal of Narrative Theory*.

KAREN LINDO received her PhD from the University of California, Los Angeles, in 2007. Her dissertation examined shame in the context of women and transnationalisms, and she has published several articles on this topic in such journals as the *International Journal of Francophone Studies*. Formerly at Bowdoin College, where she taught courses in nineteenth- and twentieth-century French literature and film as well as in Francophone literatures and cultures, she is now an independent scholar in Europe.

LAURA MARTOCCI received her PhD in Sociology from the New School for Social Research, and until recently held a dual appointment at Wagner College, where she was an Associate Dean and faculty member in the Department of Sociology. She is the founder and director of the SARA (Students Against Relational Aggression) program, an anti-bullying initiative which sends college students who have been trained in an interactive curriculum into elementary school classrooms. She is the author of the forthcoming *Bullying: The Social Destruction of Self*.

SINEAD MCDERMOTT lectures in English and Women's Studies at the University of Limerick, Ireland. Her teaching includes courses on feminist literary and cultural theory and contemporary women's writing. Her research focuses on questions of gender, cultural memory, and the representation of home in contemporary British and

North American women's fiction, and she has published on these topics in a number of feminist journals, including *Signs, Feminist Theory,* and the *Journal of Gender Studies,* and in literary journals including PMLA, M/MLA, and *Critical Survey.*

FRANN MICHEL is Professor of English at Willamette University in Salem, Oregon, where she co-founded the Women's and Gender Studies program and also contributes to programs in American Ethnic Studies and Film Studies. Her essays on feminist and queer theory and on narrative and film studies have appeared in a number of edited collections as well as in journals including *Rhizomes, GLQ, PostScript,* and *Psychoanalysis, Culture, and Society.*

NAMRATA MITRA is Visiting Assistant Professor of Philosophy at John Carroll University. Her research interests include feminist philosophy, postcolonial literature and theory, and social and political philosophy.

PATRICIA MORAN is the author of *Word of Mouth: Body/Language in Katherine Mansfield and Virginia Woolf* and *Virginia Woolf, Jean Rhys, and the Aesthetics of Trauma,* and editor (with Tamar Heller) of *Scenes of the Apple: Food and the Female Body in Nineteenth- and Twentieth-Century Women's Writing.* Formerly Professor of English at the University of California, Davis, she now teaches at the University of Limerick.

ANNA ROCCA is Assistant Professor of French and Italian at Salem State University, Massachusetts, where she teaches courses in contemporary women writers of North Africa, autobiography, feminism, and transnational feminist movements. She has published articles on Assia Djebar, Nina Bouraoui, and the Moroccan artist Lalla Essaydi, and is the author of *Assia Djebar, le corps invisible: Voir sans être vue.* With Névine El Nossery, she has co-authored a collection of essays on Francophone migrant women writers, *Frictions et devenirs dans les écritures migrantes au féminin: Enracinements et renégociations.*

PEILING ZHAO received her PhD in Rhetoric and Composition from the University of South Florida in 2005. Formerly at Millikin University, Illinois, she is now Professor of English at Central South University, China. She has published a number of articles on feminist rhetoric and pedagogy, writing program development, and emotions.

Index

CPSIA information can be obtained at www.ICGtesting.com
Printed in the USA
LVOW130131220413

330212LV00004B/5/P